TIME AND HUMAN COGNITION
A Life-Span Perspective

ADVANCES IN PSYCHOLOGY

59

Editors:

G. E. STELMACH

P. A. VROON

NORTH-HOLLAND
AMSTERDAM • NEW YORK • OXFORD • TOKYO

TIME AND HUMAN COGNITION
A Life-Span Perspective

Edited by

Iris LEVIN
School of Education
Tel Aviv University
Ramat Aviv, Israel

Dan ZAKAY
Department of Psychology
Tel Aviv University
Ramat Aviv, Israel

1989

NORTH-HOLLAND
AMSTERDAM • NEW YORK • OXFORD • TOKYO

ISBN: 0 444 87379 1

Publishers:

ELSEVIER SCIENCE PUBLISHERS B.V.
P.O. Box 1991
1000 BZ Amsterdam
The Netherlands

Sole distributors for the U.S.A. and Canada:

ELSEVIER SCIENCE PUBLISHING COMPANY, INC.
655 Avenue of the Americas
New York, N.Y. 10010
U.S.A.

PRINTED IN THE NETHERLANDS

To our chidren Dotan and Yotam Gideon and Uri
when young—used up all our time, and now,
as young adults, leave us too much time.

Contents

CHAPTER 2

Time Concepts in Language and Thought: Filling the Piagetian Void from Two to Five Years

Richard M. Weist

CHAPTER 3

Measuring Time via Counting: The Development of Children's Conceptions of Time as a Quantifiable Dimension

Iris Levin
Friedrich Wilkening

CHAPTER 4

Principles Underlying Time Measurement: The Development of Children's Constraints on Counting Time

Iris Levin

CHAPTER 5

Strategy Choices in Children's Time-Telling

Robert S. Siegler
Kate McGilly

CHAPTER 6

Assessing Children's Understanding of Time, Speed and Distance Interrelations

Curt Acredolo

CHAPTER 7

The Representation of Temporal Structure in Children, Adolescents and Adults

William J. Friedman

CHAPTER 8

Judging the Duration of Time Intervals: A Process of Remembering Segments of Experience

Douglas Poynter

CHAPTER 9

Experiencing and Remembering Time: Affordances, Context, and Cognition

Richard A. Block

CHAPTER 10

Subjective Time and Attentional Resource Allocation: An Integrated Model of Time Estimation

Dan Zakay

Preface

This book deals with perception and conception of time from infancy to adulthood. A rich concept such as time sheds light on a wide variety of major topics in psychology. Consequently the book is addressed to psychologists interested in different areas such as development, cognition, perception, psycholinguistics and education.

Many people contributed to this project – primarily, of course, the authors, who were committed to such an extent to the topic of time that they have always met deadlines.

The preparation of this book would not have been possible without the help of the School of Education and the Social Sciences Faculty of Tel-Aviv University.

Thanks are extended to Dr. K. Michielsen, of North-Holland publishing company, for his encouragement and patience.

Thanks are also due to Talia Appelbaum for her secreterial help and for preparing the indices, to Sara Kitai for her editorial support, to Sonia Glickliech for proofreading the maunsucripts and to Tami Gutman for her skillful typing.

Contributors

CURT ACREDOLO, Department of Applied Behavioral Sciences, University of California, Davis, California 95616, U.S.A.

RICHARD A. BLOCK, Department of Psychology, College of Letters & Science, Montana State University, Bozeman, Montana 59717, U.S.A.

WILLIAM J. FRIEDMAN, Department of Psychology, Oberlin College, Oberlin, Ohio 44074, U.S.A.

IRIS LEVIN, School of Education, Tel-Aviv University, Ramat-Aviv 69978, ISRAEL

DAVID J. LEWKOWICZ, Institute for Basic Research, 1050 Forest Hill Road, Staten Island, New York 10314, U.S.A.

KATE McGILLY, Department of Psychology, Carnegie-Melon University, Schenley Park, Pittsburgh, Pennsylvania 15213, U.S.A.

DOUGLAS POYNTER, General Motors Research Laboratories, Warren, Michigan 48090–9055, U.S.A.

ROBERT S. SIEGLER, Department of Psychology, Carnegie-Melon University, Schenley Park, Pittsburgh, Pennsylvania 15213, U.S.A.

RICHARD M. WEIST, State University of New-York, College of Fredonia, Fredonia, New-York 14063, U.S.A.

FRIEDRICH WILKENING, Institute fur Psychologie, Johann Wolfgang Goethe Universitat, Frankfurt am Main, 6000, Frankfurt, WEST GERMANY

DAN ZAKAY, Department of Psychology, Tel-Aviv University, Ramat-Aviv 69978, ISRAEL

TIME AND HUMAN COGNITION
A Life-Span Perspective
I. Levin and D. Zakay (Editors)

IRIS LEVIN
DAN ZAKAY

Introduction

"Either the well was very deep, or she fell very slowly, for she had plenty of time as she went down to look about her, and to wonder what was going to happen next" (Lewis Carroll, 1920). As she fell down the rabbit hole, Alice seems to have fallen into the very heart of the major problems of time: the relation of time to distance and speed; the relation between objective and subjective time; the relativity of time and the relation between the experience of time and the type of information processing which accompanies that experience.

The nature of time has puzzled human beings from the dawn of civilization, and has not ceased to intrigue us (Szamosi, 1986). Saint Augustine (354–430) expressed his bewilderment in his *Confessions*: "What then is time? if no one asks me I know, but if I wish to explain to him who asks I know not." Several centuries later, Maimonides (1135–1204) wrote in his *Guide to the Perplexed*: "The greatest philosophers have confounded the matter of time, and some have failed to comprehend it." In modern times, Whitehead (1861–1947) admitted that the contemplation of time inevitably leads to a sense of the limitations of the human mind. (Mays, 1959).

This unending struggle to understand time stems from its centrality in human life. Michon & Jackson (1985) claim that all behavior is under the control of time, and Navon (1978) argues that time is the most important dimension in our conception of the world.

The complexity and abstraction of the concept of time is apparent in the way it is defined. In a dictionary of psychology (Drever, 1952), time is defined as "a fundamental directional aspect of experience, based on direct experience of the *propensity* (duration) of sensation, and on experience of change from one sensory event, idea, or train of thought to another, and distinguished in experience beginning, middle, and end, as well as past, present, and future." Hence, as this volume clearly illustrates, time can be viewed from quite a number of different angles: on a short scale of seconds (Block, Poynter), or on a long scale of days or months (Friedman) on a "sensory" (Lewkowicz) perceptual (Zakay) conceptual (Acredolo) or linguistic (Weist) level; as a qualitative or quantitative dimension (Levin & Wilkening); and as estimated spontaneously (Levin) or measured by conventional clocks (Siegler & McGilly). Each of the chapters of this book. however, deals with psychological time, namely time as it is processed by the human mind.

The study of psychological time grew in part out of questions raised in other domains, in theology, philosophy, logico-mathematics, and physics. Fraser (1978) posed no less than 300 questions related to time and its passage. Philosophy, for instance, raises the questions of whether time has an independent existence from the objects or events that occupy it, whether it is continuous or discrete, and whether it is unidirectional. In the realm of psychology, William James (1890) posited a relationship between the events which take place within an interval and its subjective duration: "In general a time filled with varied and interesting experiences seems short in passing, but long as we look back. On the other hand, a tract of time empty of experiences seems long in passing, but in retrospect short" (p.408). He did not mean to say that people believe that time accelerates or decelarates on the objective level; rather he was speaking of the subjective estimation of duration. Piaget (1969), however, argued that children do indeed believe in the dependence of time on the events that fill it. Hence, they treat different motions as though they have separate clocks: a fast moving object is viewed as moving for a longer time than its slow moving counterpart, even though they start and stop together. As to time continuity, while Piaget (1969) assumed that with age people come to view time as a continuous dimension, contextualistic models of time perception can be said to treat perceived time as a discrete dimension. Unidirectionality is taken for granted by most psychologists, (See Navon, 1978 for an exception) as the way children and adults perceive and conceive of time.

Nevertheless, as Freud noted, in dreams and the imagination, time's arrow can change its direction.

As is already apparent, the psychological literature on time has grown in different and unrelated directions. The widespread understanding that psychological time is a product of cognitive processes developed only after it was recognized that the experience of time, at least for durations shorter than 1 hour, cannot rest on biological pacemakers or internal clocks (Hoagland, 1933; Aschoff, 1984). Piaget's structuralist-organismic model served as the point of departure for many of the developmental studies of time in childern, while models of storage and attention such as that of Ornstein (1969) served as the basis for cognitive studies of time in adults. Thus, research pertaining to children has till now, focused mainly on general reasoning abilities in application to time, whereas that investigating adults has concentrated on the perception of short durations. Furthermore, the new areas of infants' perception of time and of encoding time in language are theoretically unrelated and methodologically different from the others.

We found this state of affairs unfruitful and thus our aim in designing this book was to bring to light potential commonalities among these bodies of research, by presenting a wide scope of studies in a single volume. Of course, unrelated studies do not become integrated because they are placed side by side. However, bringing them together may, we believe, highlight common elements that have been studied or that might be studied.

Our second aim was to illustrate how the study of a concept as rich as time can shed light on a wide variety of major issues in psychology. To mention but a few that are addressed in this volume: the relative dominance of perceptual modalities; the relation between thought and language; qualitative vs. quantitative concepts; competence and performance; strategy choice; modes of representation; models of attention; and context effects. This range of issues could make the book useful to psychologists in a variety of fields: those interested in development, cognition, perception, linguistics or education.

The chapters of the book are organized from a life-span perspective, with each focusing on a different age-level. They include analyses of time pereption in infancy; temporal systems in the developing language; the growing conception of time as a quantifiable dimension in young and middle childhood; time measurement and time telling in middle childhood; the acquisition of time-speed-distance interrelation at that age; representation of conventional time series in young adolescents; and various models of time perception in the adult. By and large, each chapter is devoted to a review of a line of work pursued by its author for several years, and many include recent developments, yet unpublished.

For a taste of what this book contains we offer a brief review of each of the chapters:

Lewkowicz provided an overview of the current studies in the literature concerning the influence of temporal factors on infant behaviour. He examined studies on infants' intrinsic biobehavioral rhythms, on the role of temporal factors in the social interactions of infants, on their ability to utilize temporal information in learning and on their perception of various aspects of temporality. He then focused on studies from his own laboratory showing that by the age of six months, infants detect intersensory equivalence on the basis of temporal factors such as rate and duration. In recent studies he showed that, infants of that age exposed to a beeping tone and a flashing checkerboard, respond to variations in the temporal attributes of the auditory, but not of the visual component of the stimulus. By the age of 10 months, the dominance of the auditory information decreases, but does not disappear. Lewkowicz concluded that it is important to consider the multisensory aspects of the infant's temporal experience and the possibility that the dominance of auditory vs. visual temporal information may change with development.

Weist studied the development of temporality in children aged 2–5 years by examining their encoding of time in language. He proposed that children undergo four temporal systems differing in the level of complexity of the temporal relations involved. Weist assumes that the development of the cognitive systems precedes their appearance in language. Further, he believes that the ages at which these cognitive systems emerge are universal and consequently suggests studying the issue in a cross linguistic context. He attempted to detect the age of transition from one system to the next through the way Polish children encode tense, aspect and modality. His conclusions frequently attribute higher competence to the young child than the analyses of children acquiring English have led us to believe.

Levin and Wilkening examined the question of when children come to treat time as a quantitative dimension. They asked children aged 5–10, to reproduce events of short durations and to integrate them, and analysed time estimation and integration via the pattern of reproduced durations. Further, they examined the strategies that the children invented on their own when trying to measure or integrate time. Findings indicated that, at least from preschool on, children quantify time. A minority of preschoolers and most of young school aged children used counting to measure time. Preschoolers who did not come up with the idea of measuring time by counting, knew how to apply it for time measurement when it was suggested to them. Older children still had trouble integrating durations embedded in complex structures.

Levin, again working with children aged 5–10, examined the development of an understanding of the principles underlying measurement. She focused on the principles of constancy and arbitrariness, in their application to time. The principle of constancy means that measurement must be done with a constant unit and a stable series of tags, while the principle of arbitrariness means that the unit size chosen and the particular tags applied are arbitrary. Children familiar with counting time for reproduction were interviewed about the appropriateness of various manners of counting and asked to count in different ways to measure time. Findings indicated that children understood the principle of constancy at a younger age than they did the principle of arbitrariness. Furthermore, the principles were applied earlier to tags than to rhythm of counting. Not all of the children who invented counting to measure time understood the principles underlying that strategy.

Siegler and McGilly analysed 8– and 9–year-olds' acquisition of skill at telling time on an analog clock. They focused on the strategies children use for reading time and on the choice procedure per se. They suggest that the children's choices of strategies can be accounted for by the distribution of association model, which had previously been proposed by Siegler for the performance of other skills, such as arithmetic, spelling, and word identification. This model circumvents the need to assume the application of metacognitive knowledge in strategy choice. In the current chapter, Siegler and McGilly supply new support for the model in the context of time telling. The strength of the model is apparent not only in the consistency of the data with the model's predictions but also in its ability to shed new light on peculiarities of the particular task being studied.

Acredolo analysed the development of an understanding of the interrelations of time, speed and distance, among both 6–10 year old children and adults. He proposes two new distinctions whereby recognising the correlation between any pair of the dimensions of time, speed and distance, is distinguished from viewing that relation as dependent on the third dimension, and generating the relative value of one of the dimensions from the other two, is distinguished from being able to judge whether only one such relative value is possible. These distinctions afford a more elaborate picture of the development than emerged from previous literature. The author emphasizes that it is still unclear whether the developmental trends he describes stem from the evolution of general cognitive processing abilities or from changes in the comprehension of the specific domain of time.

Friedman examined how adults represent and process the order of conventional temporal elements: the days of the week and the months of the year. Furthermore, he analysed how these representations and processes change from the age of eight years to late adolescence. He proposes a model of time representation composed of two systems. The verbal list system codes links between each element and its successor so that the elements are processed sequentially. The image system codes the position of each element and allows for simultaneous accessing of the "location" of several elements. In a rich series of studies adults were found to use both systems. The choice between them was found to be determined by task demands. The developmental studies showed that the image system emerged later than the verbal list system.

Poynter introduced the notion that perceptual time-keeping is the process of monitoring change. Judgement of interval duration by adults is explained as a remembering of the segments of experience delimited by both organismic and sensory changes "filling" the time interval. The "segmentation" idea is used to explain much of the published research on duration judgement, and the generality of this approach was compared to other approaches, including "processing time" and "storage time" models. These models are compared in terms of their ability to explain empirical phenomena of time perception and duration estimation. Finally, the similarity between duration judgement and distance judgement is discussed in relation to the segmentation idea.

Block presents a general contextualistic model of temporal experience. According to this model interactions among four kinds of factors influence temporal experiences, where each of the factors is a cluster of variables. These factors are: the kind of temporal behaviour under consideration; the characteristics of the time period which a person experiences; the characteristics of the experience; and the activities during the time period. Block's major thesis is that a complete understanding of any kind of temporal experience is possible only by considering complex interactions among all of these factors. His chapter reviews research showing the separate importance of each of these factors and the ways in which each interacts with the others. The contextualistic model helps in classifying experiments and in evaluating theories and models of psychological time.

Zakay presents an integrated cognitive model to explain the time estimation of short intervals. The integrated model is compatible with the contextualistic approach presented by Block. It introduces order into the domain of time estimation by showing that the contradictions between various models are illusory. The integrated model is based on the notion of resource allocation and defines the contextual conditions under which resources are allocated to process either nontemporal or temporal information. These conditions include the time estimation method, the measurement paradigm, and response delay. By analysing the influence of these factors on the time estimation process, it becomes clear that under certain conditions memory processes play a major role in time estimation, while under other conditions a cognitive timer is the major tool used for this purpose. Four empirical studies supporting the integrated resource allocation model are reported.

Whether these chapters can serve our aims, you the reader, will judge—and time will tell.

References

Aschoff, J. (1984). Circadian time. In: J. Gibbon & L. Allan (Eds.), Timing and time perception. *Annals of the New York Academy of Science, 423*, 442–468.

Carroll, L. (1920). *Alice's Adventures in Wonderland.* London: G. Bell & Sons. (Original work published in 1865).

Drever, J. (1952). *A dictionary of psychology.* London: Penguin Books.

Fraser, J.T. (1978). *Time as conflict: A scientific and humanistic study.* Basel: Birkhauser.

Hoagland, H. (1933). The physiological control of judgments of duration: Evidence for a chemical clock. *Journal of General Psychology, 9*, 267–271.

James, W. (1952). *The Principles of Psychology.* Chicago: University of Chicago press. (original work publisled in 1890).

Maimonides, M. (1942). *The Guide for the Perplexed.* (M. Friedlander, Trans.). London: Routledge & Sons. (original work published 1190).

Mays, W. (1959). *The Philosophy of Whitehead.* New York: Macmillan.

Michon, J.A. and Jackson, J.L. (1985). Introduction: the psychology of time. In: J.A. Michon and J.L. Jackson (Eds.). *Time, mind, and behavior.* Berlin: Springer-Verlag.

Navon, D. (1978). On a conceptual hierarchy of time, space and other dimensions. *Cognition, 6*, 223–228.

Ornstein, R.E. (1969). *On the experience of time.* London: Penguin Books.

Piaget, J. (1969). *The child's conception of time.* (A.J. Pomerans, Trans.). New York: Basic Books. (original work published 1927).

St. Augustine, (1949). *The confessions of Saint Augustine.* (E.B. Pussey. D.D. Trans.) New York: Random House. (original work published 400 AD).

Szamosi, G. (1986). *The twin dimensions: Inventing time & space.* New York: McGraw-Hill.

TIME AND HUMAN COGNITION
A Life-Span Perspective
I. Levin and D. Zakay (Editors)

CHAPTER 1

DAVID J. LEWKOWICZ

The Role of Temporal Factors in Infant Behavior and Development*

INTRODUCTION

Time is an ever-present property of sensory experience. Although temporal change may occur over vastly different orders of magnitude, organisms display a remarkable degree of adaptation to temporal variations. The study of the development of temporal information processing occupies an important niche in general considerations of perceptual and cognitive development (Friedman, 1982). A great deal of research has been done on this question. Most of this research, however, has dealt with higher-level aspects of temporal processing and has concentrated primarily on children. The three areas of concern in this work have been with (a) children's acquisition of the concepts of past, present, and future (Harner, 1982), (b) children's ability to integrate spatial and temporal information (Wilkening, 1982), and (c) children's ability to accurately measure temporal events (Goldstone & Goldfarb, 1966, Levin, Wilkening & Dembo, 1984). As

*The author's work reported in this chapter was supported in part by a Behavioral Sciences Research Grant from the March of Dimes Birth Defects Foundation.

a whole, this literature indicates that concepts of time emerge slowly during childhood and although there is considerable controversy regarding the specific nature of this developmental process, in general, children do not attain the adult-like concepts of time until quite late in childhood.

In stark contrast to this considerable body of knowledge, there is a paucity of information regarding the precursors of these abilities in infancy. In fact, as recently as 1982 Fraisse noted this lack of information by stating that "[b]etween the animal and the adult there is an important field of study to be developed" (1982, p. 177). Furthermore, referring to the way in which, during development, each level of adaptation to time contributes to the next level in the child's ultimate attainment of the concept of time, Fraisse (1984) noted that "[t]his development has not yet been properly explored" (p. 136). This paucity of data is surprising given that Piaget (1954) considered time to be one of the four fundamental categories of the infant's mental experience (the other being space, object, and causality). It is also surprising since the temporal regularity or patterning of events in the infant's world is laden with information that is important for adaptive functioning and his or her capacity to function in the temporal domain is critical for the development of affective, linguistic, cognitive, perceptual, and social behaviors.

In the first part of the chapter the available studies on infants' behavioral rhythmicities and responsiveness to temporally organized stimulation will be reviewed. In the second part of the chapter the author's own studies of infants' processing of temporal information within the visual modality and across the auditory and visual modalities will be reviewed. It is hoped that this will provide a useful review of the pertinent studies and that it will serve to stimulate greater activity in this much-neglected area.

INTRINSIC BIOBEHAVIORAL RHYTHMS

Periodicity in physiological and behavioral functions is a ubiquitous property of biological systems. In humans periodicity that ranges across orders of magnitude may be observed in a variety of functions even prior to birth. As early as the 21st week of gestation and continuing right to the end of gestation fetuses exhibit cyclicity in their movements. The dominant frequencies of their movements range between .13 and 1.91 cycles per minute and remain stable throughout gestation (Robertson, 1985). Newborn infants exhibit motility cycles in the same range (between .24 and

1.86 cycles/minute) with an average frequency of .69 cycles/min (Robertson, 1982). This means that newborn infants produce repetitive motions anywhere between every 30 seconds and 8 minutes. With regard to other periodic functions, a rhythmicity in sleep states can be observed as early as the 32nd week of life in preterm infants (Stern, Parmelee, Akiyama, Schultz & Wenner, 1969; Stern, Parmelee & Harris, 1973). The two distinct sleep states, quiet sleep and active sleep, exhibit a mean cycle length of 12 minutes at 32 weeks post-conceptional age and by the 36th week this changes to a cycle length in the 40–60 minute range which then remains constant during the first year of life. This basic rest-activity cycle changes to a length of 90 minutes by adulthood.

Studies of infants older than 1 month of age have shown that they exhibit a bewildering variety of movements that are rhythmical and stereotyped in character. In her naturalistic studies of infants between one month and one year of age Thelen (1979) observed 47 types of stereotyped rhythmical movements. These movements included such behaviors as kicking, bouncing, scratching, waving, banging, rubbing, rocking, swaying, thrusting, and twisting. Although the onset of stereotypies varied with age, Thelen found that the age at which stereotypical movements occurred with greatest frequency was 6–7 months. Thelen rejects Piaget's assertion that infants engage in such stereotypies (secondary circular reactions in Piagetian terms) because of their knowledge of causality or of the sequential consequences of their own actions. Instead she proposes that the stereotypies are the product of intrinsic temporal and spatial pattern generation in the nervous system. At the same time, however, she does admit the possibility that such rhythmical behaviors may come to serve instrumental functions. Their most obvious function is to serve as a precursor to the development of skilled behavior (Thelen, 1981). In addition, they may provide contingent control over caregivers and serve as a vehicle of communication. One way in which repetitive motions can be employed for other purposes is that infants can use them to time events. For example, Pouthas (1985) found that 10–24 month-old infants, who were trained to withhold a response for a minimum of 5 seconds before reinforcement for making the response would be available, used a variety of rhythmical motor behaviors to delay their responses. Thus, it seems that the intrinsic rhythms and temporal regularities observed in early human behavior provide a temporal framework for the infant that permits him or her to measure the duration of events. With regard to the developmental changes that might take place, the most reasonable and attractive hypothesis is that most behaviors are controlled by intrinsic timing mechanisms during early development but that as development proceeds there is a shift towards extrinsic control (see Miller & Byrne (1984) for a discussion of this idea).

TEMPORAL NATURE OF SOCIAL INTERACTIONS

Temporal Organization of Mother-Infant Interactions

Temporal factors play a critical role in social interactions, whether they involve communicative or non-communicative acts. In communicative acts, infants exhibit impressive capacities for regulating their behavior in social interchanges with their caregivers. Stern, Beebe, Jaffe, and Bennett (1977) studied the content and structure of an adult's behavior in the interactions of each of two adults with 3–month-old infants. Their basic unit of analysis was the phrase and it could be classified into one of two types. The vocal phrase was defined as a clearly demarcated period of vocalization, while a kinesic phrase was defined as a clearly demarcated period of facial and/or head motion unaccompanied by vocalization. Coding of these two types of phrases allowed Stern et al. to assess the length of vocal and kinesic phrases and the length of the pauses separating the phrases. The next larger unit of analysis was a run. One type of run was a content run which was defined as the number of times the same or very similar phrases (either vocal or kinesic) were repeated. The other type of run was a temporal run which was defined as the number of times the same or different phrases were produced at a constant tempo. The largest unit of analysis was the episode of maintained engagement, or EME, which was defined as a period when a series of clearly demarcated temporal or content runs occurred.

Although Stern et al.'s very limited sample makes it difficult to draw any firm conclusions, their data offer some fascinating insights into the regulation of behavior by the adult in her interaction with an infant. The results showed that the adult's vocal and kinesic phrases were both less than 1 second in duration and that the vocal and kinesic pauses were somewhat longer than the phrases, with a duration closer to 1 second. Over 60% of the adult's vocalizations were content and temporal runs, indicating that she engaged in a great deal of repetitive behavior. Seventy percent of the kinesic phrases were content runs, indicating that the adult tended to repeat the same motions, and 54% of the kinesic phrases were temporal runs, indicating that the adult tended to perform various types of motions at a constant tempo. Finally, although the length of an EME varied, within each EME the adult tended to emit vocal and kinesic phrases at a constant tempo. This last finding indicates that once an adult establishes a tempo within a given EME she continues to emit behaviors at that tempo.

It is Stern et al.'s contention that this constancy in tempo permits the infant to form temporal expectancies. At the same time, however, Stern and Gibbon (1979) point out that if the adult were to maintain a constant tempo all throughout the interaction the infant would stop attending. As a result, Stern and Gibbon (1979) argue that in order to maintain the infant's attention, the adult should vary his/her tempo around some mean. Thus, the presence of variations around the mean value forces the infant to continually attend to the stimulus and as long as the variations are not too discrepant the infant can form an expectancy. To determine whether mothers do in fact vary their tempo around some mean value and what form this variation takes, Stern and Gibbon (1979) studied three mother infant dyads. For this analysis they examined those EMEs which did not contain any repetitive runs and computed the time between the beginning of a given utterance and the beginning of the next utterance within each EME. This was referred to as the onset-to-onset interval.

The analysis showed that as the mean duration of the onset-to-onset intervals increased, the standard deviation of the onset-to-onset intervals also increased, and that this increase was in direct proportion to the increase in the mean duration of the interval. This suggests the operation of what they refer to as a scalar timing process. A scalar timing mechanism is based on a single time estimation distribution that is transformed when different values are being estimated. For example, when the mother produces a tempo with a mean onset-to-onset interval of 1 second the infant sets his unit timer to 1 second. If the mother changes her tempo and thus changes the value of the interval to 2 seconds, the infant changes the unit timer to 2 seconds. Since scalar timing involves a proportional increase in variability with increases in the mean value of the interval, the proportion of the intervals that the infants will underestimate or overestimate will be the same regardless of the mean value of the interval. Stern and Gibbon argue that the mother's use of a scalar timing process provides the infant with an opportunity to build up a temporal expectancy, but that, at the same time, when the scalar timing process is used by the mother the infant does not attend to the content of the message.

Scalar timing is not, however, used by the mothers when they produce a repetitive run. During repetitive runs the standard deviation remained fairly constant despite variations in the mean duration of onset-to-onset intervals. Stern and Gibbon referred to this as an absolute timing process since this is a timing process where the variance is insensitive to the actual duration of the interval. Stern and Gibbon argue that mothers shift out of the scalar process and into the absolute timing process when they want to re-engage the infant's attention. According to their argument, because a shift from scalar to absolute timing results in a diminution of interval variability and because the variability has such an unstructured relationship with the duration of the interval, the infant no longer attends to the deviations from expectancies and instead attends to the content of the message. They argue that mothers do not produce changes in the infant's attention by changing the tempo of their vocalizations but rather that they do so by shifting from a scalar timing process to an absolute timing process. There is evidence, however, that shows that changes in the tempo of play between an adult and an infant does reduce visual attentiveness and facial expressivity in 3– and 5–month-old infants (Arco, 1983). In sum, Stern and Gibbon suggest that the infant uses a scalar timing mechanism for processing ongoing events. While this is an interesting idea, their conclusion is based on very limited data and only on data from the mother.

A recent study by Jasnow & Feldstein (1986) examined the temporal patterning of vocal exchanges between 9–month-old infants and their mothers. Unfortunately, Jasnow & Feldstein did not perform the types of analyses of maternal and infant behavior that would further address the question of scalar timing mechanisms. They did, however, provide very interesting data on the temporal coherence of mother-infant dialogue. Mother-infant dyads were studied in a free-play situation and the temporal pattern of sounds and silences in an ongoing dialogue was examined. Similar to the results from Stern et al. (1977), the results from the analyses of maternal behaviors indicated that the mother emits vocal behaviors that have durations of approximately one second. Analyses of the vocal behavior emitted by the infant and the relationship between the mother's vocal behavior and the infant's vocal behavior were also performed. A time-series regression analysis of the exchanges indicated that the vocal exchanges exhibited temporal properties similar to those usually found in adults' conversational exchanges. Both the mother and the infant were capable of producing conversational pauses that had durations of less than one second and were able to use these pauses in a meaningful way. Their vocal exchanges consisted primarily of alternating rather than simultaneous vocalizations and each waited approximately .8 sec before allowing the other member of the dyad to speak. The infants' switching pauses (time between the end of an infant's vocalization and the beginning of a mother's vocalization) were significantly influenced by the mother's switching pauses thus indicating that the infants were able to monitor quite precisely the duration of the mother's switching pause and adjust theirs in accordance. It would be interesting to know whether 3–month-old infants (the age group studied by Stern and colleagues) are capable of such fine temporal tuning. Stern and colleagues certainly suggest that this is the case; however, given the major changes that are known to occur in sensory/perceptual mechanisms between these two ages (Aslin, Pisoni, and Jusczyk, 1983; Banks and Salapatek, 1983) it would be surprising if that were the case.

Interactional Synchrony

Originally, Condon and Sander (1974a; 1974b) reported that neonates exhibit precise synchrony between the movement of their various body parts and phoneme boundaries in both tape-recorded and live adult speech and that this synchrony occurred within 1/30 of a second. Rosenfeld (1981), however, has questioned these findings on methodological grounds. Specifically, his criticisms were that: (a) it is very difficult to determine phoneme boundaries, (b) interscorer reliability for delimiting phoneme boundaries was not reported, (c) Condon and Sander's failed to report whether the observers coding the body movements were blind with respect to the auditory information. This last problem raises the possibility that if they were not then it was possible that the process of auditory capture of visual information could have contributed to the finding of synchrony.

More recently, Dowd and Tronick (1986) re-examined the possibility that movements of different parts of the infant's body are synchronized and that there is a relationship between the neonates' arm movements and stressed vowels produced by an adult. Unlike Condon and Sander, Dowd and Tronick only scored arm movements. Also, instead of using a back-and-forth method of single frame analysis with an observer making a judgement about a given movement, Dowd and Tronick videotaped the infants with two cameras so as to be able to derive 3–D coordinates for various points on the infant's arms. The recordings were done while the infants were listening to either a speech signal from the mother, from a tape recorder, or when no speech was presented at all. The motion of each arm was then scored and digitized with the aid of a computer; in this way any possibility of observer bias was eliminated. For the analysis of synchrony between the arm movements and speech, Dowd and Tronick chose onsets of first vowels in all stressed syllables as their speech events – these are more clearly defined than are the phoneme boundaries chosen for analysis by Condon and Sander. Two lag sequential analyses were performed. One analysis was performed to search for a relationship between the movement time series of one arm with the movement time series of the other arm. The other analysis was done to search for a relationship between the movement time series of the arms and the time series of the speech signal.

No temporal synchrony was found for right and left arm movements or for arm movements and speech events. Although Dowd and Tronick admit that theirs was not a direct attempt to replicate the Condon and Sander study, they questioned the Condon and Sander findings because it is not only very difficult to demarcate phoneme boundaries but also because phonemes occur at unpredictable times and infants would therefore have to react to their occurrence. They repeat Rosenfeld's (1981) observation that such a feat would require the infant to have a reaction time of approximately 33 milliseconds, something that even adults can't come close to. Even if one assumes that infants are capable of reacting with such speed, given Condon and Sander's method of scoring frame-by-frame, the only way to obtain synchrony would be if the phoneme boundary occurred at the beginning of the frame and if the infant were able to react to it immediately. If the infant's reaction were to occur just slightly later, a reaction time of 33 milliseconds would cause the movement to occur on the next frame and thus be asynchronous with the phoneme boundary.

Another recent study by Lester, Hoffman, and Brazelton (1985) examined the temporal organization of mother-infant interactions in both term and preterm infants at 3 and 5 months of age. Each of 20 mothers interacting with her full-term infant and each of 20 mothers interacting with her preterm infant was videotaped for three minutes. For each second of the interaction an observer made separate ratings of the mother's and of the infant's affective involvement by coding for the presence of one of 13 units of behavior called monadic phases. These 13 monadic phases represented an expansion of a set of seven monadic phases used previously by Tronick, Als, & Brazelton (1980). The seven monadic phases defined separate and mutually exclusive constellations of behaviors and were: avoid, avert, monitor, elicit, set, play, and talk. For example, the monadic phase of avoid consisted of head, body, and gaze orientation away from the mother, a negative-to-neutral facial expression, and crying.

The analyses of the data were aimed at determining whether there were any temporal regularities in the occurrence of the infant's and the mother's behavior, and, if so, whether there was any relationship between the infant's and the mother's temporal regularity. The 13 monadic phases were assigned a score from 1 to 13 and spectral analysis was performed to determine whether the behaviors occurred with any degree of temporal regularity (i.e., whether they tended to repeat in a periodic manner) and their spectral density was calculated to determine what portion of the variance could be accounted for by each of the distinct frequencies identified by the spectral analysis. Results showed that there were significant periodicities in the behavior of both 3– and 5–month-old infants, as well as in the behavior of the mothers. These periodicities ranged between .022 and .10 Hz, which corresponds to a cycle time of between 45 and 10 seconds. There were no differences between the full-term and preterm infants and between their mothers in the degree of behavioral periodicities; however, the preterms did exhibit more variability in their periodicities. In addition, although the strength of behavioral periodicities (i.e., the amount of variance accounted for by the various periodicities) increased from 3 to 5 months in both groups of infants, only the full-term infants showed an increase in the number of distinct periodicities. Lester et al. suggest that the increase in the strength of periodicities probably reflects increasing cognitive and affective capacities in the infants to organize their rhythmic activity around the mother's rhythmic activity. Finally, although both preterm and term infants exhibited rhythms that were synchronous with the rhythms of their mothers, in general, only the full-term infants showed an increase in synchrony with their mothers' rhythms over age and only the full-term infants dominated the interaction at 3 months and increased that dominance at 5 months of age.

Lester et al. offer some interesting speculations concerning the origins of the observed rhythms. They propose that the source of these rhythms may be the autonomic homeostatic control mechanisms that mediate CNS arousal and that intrinsic neural oscillators or timing mechanisms may control the behavioral rhythms that they observed. They cite data from studies of cardiorespiratory rhythms and note that these rhythms correspond to the rhythms observed in their study and, as a result, suggest that cycles of attention and affect could reflect a synchronization with these intrinsic homeostatic rhythms.

LEARNING OF TEMPORAL INFORMATION

In one of the earliest descriptions of temporal conditioning, Marquis (1941) noted that newborns increased their motor activity prior to feeding. While this may be indicative of a timing process, there is the very likely possibility that biochemical and/or digestive processes may have been responsible for the observed effects. Modern studies of classical conditioning have attempted to produce temporal conditioning in infants of varying ages. Studies by Brackbill, Fitzgerald and associates have shown that temporal conditioning is possible in infants but that it depends on the response system used, on the sensory modality used, and on the complexity of the task. Fitzgerald, Lintz, Brackbill, and Adams (1967) attempted to produce temporal conditioning of the pupillary response in 1– to 2–month-old infants. Using change in illumination as the unconditional stimulus (UCS), Fitzgerald et al. compared conditioning of pupillary dilation and constriction in response to time (20 second intervals) as the conditional stimulus (CS), sound together with time, and sound alone presented at random intervals. The results indicated that time, and time with sound, were effective in establishing a conditional response (CR) but that sound alone was not. Brackbill, Lintz, and Fitzgerald (1968) attempted to condition the eyeblink response in 2–month-old infants and were unable to produce temporal conditioning even though they were able to obtain conditioning to a sound as the CS. Finally, Brackbill and Fitzgerald (1972) attempted to determine whether infants are capable of discriminating temporal patterns. Thus, 1–month-old infants' pupillary response was studied in response to a change in illumination (UCS) that occurred according to an alternating pattern of 20 and 30 sec. inter-UCS intervals. For half the infants the change in illumination involved the onset of a light and the expected pupillary response was constriction and for the other half the change involved the offset of a light and the expected pupillary response was dilation. On test trials the UCS was omitted and the infants' pupillary response was observed. Successful conditioning was only obtained for the pupillary dilation group of infants who were conditioned with light offset. This suggests that the learning of temporal patterns is more difficult, at least at one month of age.

Other studies have not only obtained evidence of differential conditionability of different response systems, but have also obtained evidence of sex differences. In a study of temporal conditioning of heart rate in neonates, Stamps (1977) presented a buzzer (UCS) every 20 sec. to determine whether an anticipatory heart rate response, as well as a response to the absence of the UCS, would occur. The only evidence of temporal conditioning was anticipatory deceleration in the girls. A similar result was obtained by Stamps and Porges (1975) in a study using a trace conditioning technique (which permits the assessment of anticipatory responses to the UCS since the CS and UCS do not overlap in time). Newborn infants were presented with a 2 sec. sound (CS) followed 12 seconds later by blinking lights (UCS) for 6 seconds for a number of trials. Results showed that only the girls decelerated in response to the CS and in anticipation of the UCS. Since Stamps (1977) did not find an orienting response (viz., deceleration) in the absence of the UCS, he concluded that the infants did not accurately perceive the 20 sec. interval. In a study of trace conditioning of heart rate in 4–month-old infants, Turco and Stamps (1980) paired a visual stimulus (CS) and a sound (UCS) with a 3 sec. interval separating the presentation of the two stimuli. Only boys exhibited anticipatory conditioning; that is, in the last block of conditioning trials they showed deceleration during the interval between the CS and the UCS. In contrast, only girls responded to the absence of the UCS during the test trials.

Taken as a whole, the data from classical conditioning studies are equivocal with regard to infants' ability to time events. Although some of the studies provide evidence that it is possible to condition an expectancy even in newborns, the success of the conditioning is dependent on such factors as the CS modality, the response system used for the conditional response, the subject's gender, and the subject's age. Thus, the presence of these complicating factors makes it difficult to arrive at any firm conclusions regarding temporal abilities in infants based on studies of respondent learning.

In addition to learning that various neutral signals predict the occurrence of an unconditional stimulus, there are many instances in the infant's world when he or she engages in some activity that has consequences. In order for the infant to appreciate the causal relationship between his or her action and its consequences, he or she must be able to span the temporal delay between the action and its consequences that is often present in such situations. Interestingly, the few studies that have examined the role of temporal factors in instrumental conditioning have shown that a delay of as little as 3 sec. in the delivery of reinforcement following the performance of a response prevents the acquisition of a new response (Millar & Watson, 1979; Ramey & Ourth, 1971)). Such a severe limitation on the infant's acquisition of new responses would obviously have disastrous effects on the development of behavioral competence. Yet, it is clear that infants do acquire behavioral competence rather quickly during early ontogeny, so there must be other factors besides temporal ones that help the infant acquire new responses. Watson (1979; 1984) has, in fact, proposed a theory to account for the infant's ability to analyze his personal causal efficacy by reference not only to the temporal information, but to the similarities in the sensory pattern of responses and stimuli as well. Specifically, he proposes that the infant arrives at his or her personal causal efficacy and at the general causal structure of the world in relation to him or her by relying on two temporally-based factors: (a) the probability that the stimulus will follow some behavior produced by the infant, and (b) the probability that the behavior of the infant precedes the occurrence of the stimulus. In addition, the infant relies on the sensory relations between his/her response and the stimuli that follow (i.e., the magnitude of response and the resulting effect of that response) and on the relationship between the spatial position of the behavior and the spatial position of the resulting stimuli. An example that might illustrate how an infant arrives at his or her personal causal efficacy might be one where he or she emits a series of four behaviors in a period of a minute and each behavior has a different magnitude and is emitted in a different location. According to Watson's theory, the infant compares the temporal distribution of the stimuli that are the result of his or her behavior, the relative magnitude of the stimuli, and the spatial distribution of the stimuli to determine whether these stimuli were produced by his or her actions.

PERCEPTION OF TEMPORAL INFORMATION

So far our examination of a number of diverse areas of investigation has shown that (a) a number of motor rhythmicities are present prior to birth and continue into postnatal life, (b) mothers provide their infants with a temporal structure during social interactions and that beginning at 3 months of age temporal coherence in the social interactions between the infant and the mother appears, and (c) young infants have some limited capacities for learning to anticipate events purely on the basis of time. In the remainder of this chapter the infant's ability to perceive temporal information will be discussed.

Piaget (1954) was the first to seriously and systematically consider the role of temporal cues in early ontogeny. In his constructivist account of the development of the time concept in infants, Piaget argued that "time, like space, is constructed little by little and involves the elaboration of a system of relations" (p. 362). The development of the temporal sense progresses through a set of distinct stages. During the first three months of life the infant is able to perceive primitive time (i.e., duration) but only when that duration is tied directly to his or her own action; perception of time independently of the infant's own actions is not possible. In the next two stages of cognitive development, roughly spanning the period from 3 months to 9 months, the infant can perceive a sequence of events but, as in the first stage, only when that sequence of events is engendered by the infant or when the before and after are related to his or her own activity; if the events occur independently of the infant's own actions he or she will disregard their occurrence. In these two stages the infant is incapable of objectively structuring time. Piaget clearly states that "... the child at the present stage is not yet capable of ... measuring the length of intervals" (p. 378). Finally, during the last stage of cognitive development in the first year of life, the infant's increasingly greater memorial abilities make it possible for him or her to reconstruct short sequences of events independently of the self; however, he or she still cannot retrace the chronology of the events perceived in the external world and is still incapable of discriminating the duration of intervals. While these ideas are interesting, as has already been seen in the work on mother-infant interaction and on temporal conditioning, infants appear to posses rather impressive temporal capacities that are present far earlier than Piaget proposed. The work on infants' perceptual capacities will further show that Piaget's assertions are unsupported by the evidence.

There are a number of basic discriminative capacities related to time perception. These include the ability to detect temporal frequency and duration differences. In addition, there are a number of higher-level perceptual capacities that depend upon the temporal domain for information about the environment. Among these are perceptual grouping, perceptual segregation, and object perception. Some of these basic, as well as, higher-level capacities will be considered in the next several sections.

Response to Temporal Information in the Auditory Modality

Discrimination of duration is one of the basic functions of the auditory system. In general, the data from studies of infants' linguistic discriminative abilities indicate that they are able to detect relatively small duration differences, although the actual discrimination thresholds may depend on contextual cues. For example, Jusczyk, Pisoni, Reed, Fernald, & Myers (1983) found that 2–month-old infants are able to discriminate differences in the duration of initial frequency transitions in a complex sinusoidal auditory pattern; these initial frequency transitions signal the difference between the synthetic versions of the sounds /ba/ and /wa/. The differences that were discriminable were as small as 25 msec. In addition, Jusczyk et al. showed that 2–month-old infants were sensitive to differences in the overall duration of the pattern in that they perceived the categorical change to be at a longer initial frequency transition within the context of a longer auditory pattern. Eilers, Bull, Oller, & Lewis (1984) showed that 5– to 11–month-old infants are able to detect vowel duration differences when these vowels are embedded in one-syllable (mad), two-syllable (samad), and three-syllable (masamad) stimuli. For example, the infant was presented with the syllable "samad" where the last vowel had a duration of 300 ms. and then on the test trial the infant was presented with the same syllable whose last vowel had a duration of 400 ms. The infants were able to detect a difference in vowel duration of as little as 33% (100 ms.), although their discriminative accuracy was better for greater differences. Moreover, their overall discriminative accuracy was far below that of adults whose discrimination was nearly perfect even for the 33% difference. This finding, combined with the fact that there is a significant increase in auditory temporal acuity in children between the ages of 6 and 12 years (Irwin, Ball, Kay, Stillman, & Rosser, 1985), suggests that important changes in duration discrimination thresholds occur in early development.

A number of other studies have examined infants' ability to process relational information by investigating their ability to discriminate rhythmic sequences of auditory stimulation. Chang and Trehub (1977a) investigated discrimination of auditory patterns in 5–month-old infants. Infants were habituated to a sequence of 6 tones where four of the intertone intervals were the same and one was longer. To test for discrimination, the infants were then presented with the same six-tone sequence but with the longer interval in a new ordinal position. Cardiac deceleration was obtained in the test trial indicating that the infants perceived these two sequences as different.

Demany, McKenzie, and Vurpillot (1977) investigated 2–month-old infants' ability to discriminate auditory patterns by presenting sequences of tones that differed either because the intervals separating the members of the sequence were different or because the order of identical intervals was changed. Results indicated that the infants were able to make both types of discriminations. It is important to note, however, that these data cannot be interpreted as evidence that the infants were processing the sequences as patterns as such. This is because in the first two experiments reported by Demany et al. (1977) the sequences differed in terms of an inter-element interval as well as in terms of element grouping. Thus, the discrimination could be made on the basis of either of these attributes and may not have involved the processing of the gestalt properties of the sequence. The last experiment, where only the order of the intervals was changed, is not conclusive evidence of gestalt processing either because in that experiment a three element sequence was used and a change in the order of the two inter-element intervals involved a change in the duration of the first interval. As a result, the infants may have based their discriminations solely on the difference in the duration of the first interval. Washburn and Cohen (1984) replicated the Demany et al. findings with regard to discrimination of the sequence involving the change in interval order. They also showed that this discrimination was not dependent on the starting point of the pattern; that is, regardless of at what point the stimulus sequence was started the infants were able to discriminate the different patterns but did not discriminate between similar patterns starting at different points. Although this suggests that the infants' response was indeed based on the relative order of the inter-element durations, a more definitive answer would require the use of sequences consisting of more than just three elements which would make it possible to change the inter-element order without having to change the first interval.

Morrongiello (1984) did in fact do that and found that the processing of temporal pattern constructed from more than just three elements is more difficult and is dependent on the infant's age. Both 6– and 12–month-old infants were able to discriminate 9–element rhythmic sequences which differed both in element grouping and in changes in the duration of inter-element intervals. In contrast, only 12–month-old infants were able to discriminate changes in rhythmic patterns when those changes involved just a change in the order of the inter-element intervals and where those changes were more internal to the pattern. In sum, the ability to perceive relative temporal order may appear by the third month of life but the ability to perceive the gestalt or global properties of a complex temporal pattern may not appear until the end of the first year of life.

Two other studies have investigated infants' processing of temporal order in stimulus sequences consisting of heterogeneous elements. Chang and Trehub (1977b) habituated 5–month-old infants to sequences of tones of different frequency that formed one melody and then tested them with the same tones whose order was changed resulting in a different melody. The infants' cardiac response recovered indicating discrimination of the change in melody. Demany (1982) not only replicated this finding with younger infants and with a different measure but also showed that 1.5– to 3.5–month-old infants are able to segment auditory streams in a manner similar to adults. Both adults and infants were presented with auditory sequences that consisted of four different tones spaced at equal temporal intervals. Subjects were first presented with one tone sequence and then a change in the tone sequence was made and the subjects' ability to detect the change was studied. Both adults and infants were able to discriminate changes in the order of the tones in auditory sequences where no segmentation occurred. To determine whether infants perform auditory segmentation in a manner similar to adults, both infants and adults were first presented with an auditory sequence where two of the tones tended to cluster together and form one spectral group and where two other tones tended to cluster and form a second and distinct group. During the test trial, the order of the tones in the second group was changed. If auditory segmentation were operating then the change in the order of these tones should have no effect because the groupings were preserved and as a result the subjects should not be able to discriminate the change. This was, in fact, the result that was obtained in both adults and infants, indicating that even very young infants are able to perform auditory segmentation. Although the segmentation process is primarily spectrally based, temporal factors play a role in this process too because segmentation is dependent on the temporal order of the stimuli and on the stimulus presentation rate. In addition, the operation of a segmentation process forces the subject to ignore the objective temporal order of the stimuli and instead compels him or her to group the stimuli on the basis of some common feature or fate. As will be seen in a later section, infants also appear to be capable of grouping on the basis of common motion in the visual modality, although it is not known whether they are capable of segregation in a manner similar to the auditory modality. A demonstration of such a process would require the presentation of a random dot display where some of the dots move as one group and where others move as another group.

Response to Temporal Information in the Visual Modality

RESPONSE TO SPATIALLY-STATIC INFORMATION

A number of studies have examined infants' response to variations in the temporal properties of visual stimulation. These studies fall into two categories, those that have examined infants' response to spatially-static temporal changes and those that have examined infants' response to spatially-dynamic temporal changes.

The studies that have examined infants' responsiveness to temporal changes in spatially-static visual displays have found that, in general, beginning at birth infants are differentially responsive to variations in temporal frequency. A study of visual preferences for white patches of light flashing at one of four temporal frequencies (.5, 1, 2 and 4 Hz) was carried out by Gardner and Karmel (1981) in preterm infants at 37 weeks gestational age. Using a paired-comparison technique, Gardner and Karmel presented all possible pairs of the four frequencies and scored the infants' visual fixations of each member of the pair. Results indicated that the faster the frequency of the visual stimulus the greater was the infants' visual fixation of that frequency.

In a subsequent study Gardner and Karmel (1984) showed that full-term newborn infants exhibit similar preferences. In addition, they showed that the infant's level of internal arousal has a marked effect on the nature of his or her response to variations in temporal frequency. Infants who were swaddled and tested after a feeding, and who were therefore in a low state of arousal, looked longer as temporal frequency increased. In contrast, infants who were unswaddled and tested prior to a feeding, and who were therefore in a high state of arousal, looked less as temporal frequency increased. This shift in visual fixation with increasing arousal was explained as reflecting the operation of an intensity-gating mechanism seeking to maintain an optimum amount of stimulation. According to this interpretation, the newborn infant's differential fixations are a measure of how closely a given range of stimulation approximates his or her optimal level of stimulation. If the optimum level of stimulation is determined jointly by the objective intensity of a given stimulus and the level of internal stimulation engendered by the infant's level of arousal, then the value of a set of stimuli varying along some quantitative continuum will increase when arousal is high and decrease when arousal is low. The infant must therefore modulate his or her looking in order to maintain a reasonably constant and optimum level of stimulation.

Nystrom, Hansson, & Marklund (1975) studied visual preferences for stimuli varying in temporal frequency in 1– and 2–month-old infants. Using the paired comparison technique, Nystrom et al. presented all possible pairs of intermittent light presented at 1, 5, 10, or 20 Hz. The 1–month-old infants looked longer at the faster stimulus in all pairs, except for the 10 – 20 Hz pair where they looked less at the 20 Hz stimulus, although no statistical analyses for these data are presented. The decrease in looking at the 20 Hz. stimulus cannot be explained by its being above the infants' critical fusion frequency (CFF) since Regal (1981) showed that 4–week-old infants' CFF is 40.7 Hz. The 2–month-old infants appeared to exhibit similar patterns of looking, although the differences at each pair were smaller and again no separate analyses of the data from the 2–month-old infants are reported. The only analysis that Nystrom et al. reported was an analysis of the combined data from the two age groups. As a result, it is impossible to know whether the average differences in looking for the different pairs reported in the paper for the older group were in fact statistically reliable. The fact that there was a highly significant age x frequency interaction, combined with the fact that the 1–month-old infants exhibited larger looking differences, suggests that the source of the interaction was the failure of the older infants to differentiate among the different temporal frequencies. In addition, the older infants paid far less attention overall;

the total amount of looking across all the pairs observed in the 2–month-old infants was nearly 2.5 times less than the total amount of looking observed in the 1–month-old infants. Although this finding appears anomalous, its source is not discussed by the authors.

Karmel, Lester, McCarvill, Brown, and Hofmann (1977) studied 3–month-old infants' visual and electrophysiological response to variations in temporal frequency. In the first study, infants were presented with all possible pairs of checkerboards flashing at one of the following frequencies: 1.0, 1.4, 2.0, 2.8, 4.0, 5.7, 8.0, and 20 Hz. The visual fixation measure indicated that an inverted U-shaped function described the relationship between the duration of visual fixation and the temporal frequency of the visual stimulus. That is, the infants looked longest at the middle frequencies and less so at the frequencies at either end. In a second study, on separate trials infants were presented with a single checkerboard flashing at 1, 2, 4, 6, 8, 10, and 12 Hz. and the amplitude of the visual evoked potential (VEP) was measured. As in the behavioral study, an inverted U-shaped function characterized the relationship between temporal frequency and VEP amplitude, and the magnitude of visual fixations observed in the behavioral study correlated with VEP amplitude.

It should be noted that in all of the studies discussed so far the ratio of stimulus on time to stimulus off time was always the same (50%) across variations in frequency. This was done to equate stimulus density and/or intensity across variations in temporal frequency. However, this method of stimulus presentation introduces the problem of concomitant changes in stimulus duration with changes in the frequency of the stimulus; as stimulus frequency increases there is a concomitant decrease in stimulus duration. Thus, the data discussed so far may reflect one of three processes: (a) a visual preference for increasingly faster stimulation, (b) a visual preference for increasingly shorter stimuli, or (c) a visual preference for shorter stimuli presented at faster frequencies.

The only way to find out which of these processes accounts for the findings is to carry out systematic studies where temporal frequency and duration are varied independently, as well as jointly. Lewkowicz (1985a) did just that in an investigation of the mechanisms underlying temporal discrimination and of developmental changes in infants' response to variations in temporal frequency. Three different studies were carried out. In one study temporal frequency and duration were varied jointly, in the second study temporal frequency was varied but duration was kept constant, and in a third study duration was varied while frequency was kept constant. In all three studies, 4– and 6–month-old infants were presented with pairs of checkerboards that flashed at different rates. All possible pairs of three temporal frequencies (2, 4, and 8 Hz.) were presented and the amount of visual fixation accorded to each frequency within each pair was measured.

In the first study, the duration of the stimulus was kept constant at 50 ms. across the three rates. Results showed that infants in both age groups responded differentially to the three temporal frequencies of stimulation by looking longer at faster frequencies. Although this finding might suggest that the infants detected differences in temporal frequency, the fact that there was a concomitant increase in the total amount of stimulation presented over time means that the infants' differential response might have been due to stimulus density differences.

To determine if stimulus density differences were responsible for the differential response observed, the same 3 frequencies were presented in the second study, but this time differences in stimulus density were equated by a 50% on/off stimulus ratio at each frequency. Results indicated that the 4–month-old infants' response was indeed based on stimulus density differences in that they no longer showed differential looking. In contrast, the older infants still responded differentially. These results suggest that a developmental shift from a response based on overall intensity differences to a response based on periodicity of stimulation occurs between 4 and 6 months of age. To further confirm this developmental shift, preferences for variations in stimulus intensity were examined in a third study by presenting stimuli flashing at the same rate (2 Hz) but for different durations. Younger infants responded differentially, whereas older infants did not. In sum, these data showed that younger infants attended to the overall quantitative aspects of stimulation but not to frequency differences, whereas older infants no longer attended to stimulus density and instead attended to frequency differences. Moreover, the data from the 4–month-old infants were consistent with prior work showing that young infants are primarily responsive to the quantitative aspects of stimulation (Lewkowicz & Turkewitz, 1980; Lewkowicz & Turkewitz, 1981; Lewkowicz, 1985b).

RESPONSE TO SPATIALLY-DYNAMIC INFORMATION

Although the basis for the infant's visual response to temporal variations of spatially-static displays may not be based on periodicity per se in early ontogeny, it is clear that the visual system is capable of responding to changes over time from birth on. A great deal of the temporally-based information that the visual system receives is, however, based in the motion of objects. Motion can occur in a variety of ways: it can be smooth or it can be uneven, and it can be fast or slow. Sometimes the motion of an object can describe a recurring temporal pattern. It is, therefore, advantageous for the infant to be able to extract the temporal characteristics of an object's motion because its particular temporal pattern may distinguish it from another object (Kellman & Spelke, 1983). In addition, although only peripherally germane to the question of temporal perception, motion serves other important functions. It allows infants to (a) learn about the invariant properties of objects (Ruff, 1985), (b) perceive objects that might otherwise not be visible because of camouflaging (Kaufmann-Hayoz, Kaufmann, and Stucki 1986), or to perceive objects that require that all parts move in common (Bertenthal, Proffitt, and Cutting, 1984; Bertenthal, Proffitt, Kramer, & Spetner, 1987), and to (c) learn about the spatial layout of the environment (Yonas and Granrud, 1985).

Very few studies have actually examined infants' response to motion per se. Kaufmann, Stucki, and Kaufmann-Hayoz (1985) investigated response to slow and rapid motions in 1– and 3–month-old infants. Infants of both ages were presented with rotating dot circles in a paired-comparison test. Each infant was tested in a slow velocity condition and in a rapid velocity condition. In the slow velocity condition, one of the dot circles remained stationary while the other rotated at one of 5 velocities ranging from 28 to 124 minutes of visual angle/sec. In the rapid condition, one of the dot circles rotated at a speed fast enough to produce fusion in adults while the other rotated at one of 4 velocities ranging from 118 to 232 degrees of visual angle/sec.

The 1–month-old infants were less sensitive than the 3–month-old infants in the slow velocity condition; the minimum velocity at which the 1–month-olds fixated the moving stimulus more than the stationary stimulus was 84 min. visual angle/sec., whereas the minimum velocity at which the 3–month-olds fixated the moving stimulus more than the stationary stimulus was 56 min. visual angle/sec. Nonetheless, the 3–month-olds' sensitivity was below that obtained with a group of adults. Both groups of infants were equally sensitive in the rapid velocity condition; their maximum velocity threshold was 118 degrees visual angle/second. In sum, these data show that there may be two different mechanisms for the detection of motion. One mechanism may be responsive to slow motion and this mechanism appears to undergo developmental changes. The other may be responsive to rapid motion and no developmental changes seem to occur in this mechanism. Kaufmann et al. speculate that responsiveness to slow motion may be mediated by a population of retinal ganglion cells known as x-cells. Although these cells have cortical connections at birth and appear to be functional at birth, they are assumed to undergo functional differentiation during development and Kaufmann et al. suggest that this might account for the improvement in sensitivity for low velocities. Another population of retinal ganglion cells known as y-cells, which are known to mediate rapid motion detection, are assumed by Kaufmann et al. to mediate responsiveness to the rapid motions in this study. Since the y-cells and their subcortical connections are present at birth, sensitivity to fast motions would not be expected to change between 1 and 3 months.

In addition to being able to discriminate velocity differences, it is also important for the infant to be able to discriminate motion-based temporal patterns. Mendelson (1986) investigated 4–month-old infants' ability to discriminate between two different recurring patterns of motion. Infants were first familiarized with one of two recurring motion patterns produced by a hand by watching a film. One group of infants saw a hand waving and the other group saw a fist pounding on a table. Half of each group of infants saw a pattern of motion that was dubbed the 2–2–2–2 pattern where the infant saw recurring clusters of two waves or two bangs. A .3 sec. interval separated the two motions within each cluster of motions and a .8 sec. interval separated each cluster of motions. The other half of each group of infants saw a pattern that was dubbed the 3–1–3–1 pattern. This pattern consisted of two alternating cluster of motions: the first cluster of motions consisted of three successive hand waves or bangs separated by .3 sec, while the second cluster consisted of a single hand or wave or bang. Again, a .8 second interval separated each cluster of motions.

Following familiarization, during which there was a significant decline in looking, the infants were given a paired-comparison test where the familiar rhythm was paired with a novel rhythm to determine whether they would discriminate the familiar motion from the novel one. For example, an infant familiarized with the 2–2–2–2 pattern of hand waving was shown a hand waving according to the 2–2–2–2 pattern on one side and a hand waving according to the 3–1–3–1 pattern on the other side and his/her visual preference was observed. The amount of time the infants spent looking at each of the two motions for every 10 sec. block of the 30 sec. test trial was compared and although the amount of looking at the familiar motion continued to decline, the amount of looking at the novel motion did not exhibit a statistically significant increase. Thus, these data do not provide clear evidence that 4–month-old infants are able to discriminate between different rhythmic motions.

In a second part of his study Mendelson investigated the possibility that developmental changes in infants' response to rhythmic motions occur. Rather than use the familiarization-test procedure, in this study

Mendelson used the paired-comparison technique and examined 4– and 8–month-old infants' visual preferences by presenting them with all possible pairs of three different motion patterns which were deemed as spanning a range of complexity. The motions in this part of the study were produced by a wooden puppet that popped vertically out of and into a cardboard cone. The puppet moved according to one of three repetitive rhythms which were deemed to represent three levels of complexity: (1) the low complexity pattern was the 2–2–2–2 pattern, (2) the medium complexity pattern was the 3–1–3–1 pattern, and (3) the high complexity pattern was a 3–2–1–2 pattern. The movement of the puppet out of and into the cone lasted .25 sec., the interval separating each member of a movement cluster was about .3 seconds, and the interval separating each of the clusters was .75 seconds. Results indicated that the 4–month-old infants preferred the medium complexity pattern over the low complexity pattern. They did not, however, prefer the medium complexity pattern over the high complexity pattern nor did they prefer the high complexity pattern over the low complexity pattern. In contrast, the 8–month-old infants looked least at the low complexity pattern, more at the medium complexity pattern, and most at the high complexity pattern. Mendelson argued that these data show differential responsiveness to different levels of motion pattern complexity and that there is a developmental shift in preferences towards more complex motion patterns.

Since a similar shift in the auditory modality was discussed earlier, it would be interesting if the same type of shift occurred in the visual modality as well. Because such a conclusion has major implications for our ultimate understanding of perceptual development, it is important to consider the data from Mendelson's study carefully. The conclusion that the 4–month-old infants were able to discriminate between all three rhythmic patterns is unwarranted by the data. As already noted, the only significant difference in looking when the pair data were analyzed was the difference in amount of looking at the low complexity and the medium complexity patterns. The claim that developmental changes in preferences for different levels of temporal motion complexity occur is also supported by very weak evidence. No differences in the proportion of looking were found in any of the three pairs in the 8–month-old infants. Although a significant age x complexity interaction was found when the total duration of looking at each of the temporal patterns was analyzed, this interaction was due to decreased looking at the medium complexity pattern only; in the older infants there was no decrease in looking at the low complexity pattern nor was there an increase in looking at the high complexity pattern.

The assumption that the three temporal motion patterns reflect three levels of complexity should also be called into question. It has been shown that in an ongoing sequence of stimuli, those stimuli that occur close together in time are perceived as belonging to one group and that the longest interval in an ongoing sequence of stimuli is perceived as a pause between the groups (Dowling, 1973; Handel, 1973). In the three temporal motion patterns used by Mendelson, only two intervals were used: .3 seconds (separating the successive motions within a cluster) and .8 seconds (separating the different clusters). As a result, the number of elements that comprised the clusters varied within two of the patterns and across all three patterns. Because of these differences, it is possible that the differential responsiveness that was found, as, for example, in the proportion of looking in the low-medium pair in the 4–month-old infants, was based on these cluster differences. In the low-medium pair, the low-complexity stimulus was composed of two-elements clusters, whereas the medium-complexity stimulus was composed of alternating three– and one-element clusters. As the infant looked back and forth, it may have been relatively easy for him to make this discrimination. The same cannot be said for the other two pairs involving the high complexity pattern. In that case, the infant had a more difficult task because he had to discriminate between two-element clusters and three–, two–, or one-element clusters.

A discrimination based on the number of elements within a rhythmic cluster is different from a discrimination based on complexity. In the case of the temporal motion patterns used by Mendelson, temporal complexity can be translated to mean temporal regularity or predictability. For example, there is no question that the 3–2–1–2 pattern is less regular than the other two patterns; however, it is debatable whether there is a difference in the temporal regularity between the 2–2–2–2 and the 3–1–3–1 pattern. Although the number of elements presented over time changes in the latter but not in the former pattern, the alternating nature of that change makes the regularity of the 3–1–3–1 pattern very much like that of the 2–2–2–2 pattern. Moreover, given that it is unlikely that the infants began their look precisely at the beginning of one temporal pattern and looked at it for 5.2 seconds (the time required to see a full cycle of the high-complexity pattern) and then shifted their gaze to the other pattern for another 5.2 seconds, it is very unlikely that the infants ever had the opportunity to sample the entire repeating sequence. Rather, it is more likely that the most they ever saw were the separate groups and that they responded on the basis of the number of elements comprising the groups. A response on this basis is different from a differential response made solely on the basis of the temporal distribution of equal-element patterns. In sum, the differential responsiveness that was found by Mendelson was most likely due to the differentiation of the "local" features of the stimulus pattern and did not involve the extraction of the gestalt properties of the temporal pattern. Thus, the question of whether the visual modality parallels the auditory modality in its ability to respond to increasingly more complex temporal patterns as development progresses is still unanswered.

Intersensory Response to Temporal Information

Stern et al. (1977) made the observation that because caregiver characteristics in all modalities share similar temporal patterns, it is possible that they are substitutable and that the modality of stimulation is less important than is the temporal patterning of that stimulation. Since that time there has been a burgeoning of interest in issues of intersensory organization in infants, the sizeable body of data that has now become available makes it possible to assess Stern's suggestion. Since temporal properties of stimulation are one of the primary amodal characteristics of stimulation, many of the studies of intersensory responsiveness in infants have in fact investigated the infant's use of some form of temporal information to integrate auditory-visual stimulation.

INTERSENSORY RESPONSE TO RHYTHM

Two studies have examined infants' ability to detect intersensory equivalence of rhythmic information across the auditory and visual modalities. Mendelson and Ferland (1982) familiarized 4–month-old infants with a syllable which was presented in either a regular or an irregular rhythmic pattern. Then a film depicting a puppet moving its mouth in either the familiar or a novel rhythm was shown to each infant. Those infants viewing the film depicting the novel rhythm looked longer at the film than those who viewed the film with the familiar rhythm. The novelty effect was interpreted as indicating recognition of the previously learned auditory rhythm in the visual modality. Allen, Walker, Symonds, & Marcell (1977) investigated 7–month-old infants' ability to transfer rhythmic information across modalities by habituating the infants to either a regularly or an irregularly occurring sequence of sounds or lights and then assessing their response when the other sequence was presented in the same or different modality. The infants' cardiac response recovered significantly, indicating discrimination, during the dishabituation trials regardless of whether the change in temporal sequence occurred within or across modalities.

Although these two studies suggest that infants are able to transfer temporal information across the auditory and visual modalities, there are some problems with both studies. In the Allen et al. study different temporal sequences, composed of three flashing lights or three sounds, were presented; in one sequence the three elements making up the sequence were separated by two .9 sec. intervals while in the other sequence, the first and second elements were separated by a .3 sec interval and the second and third elements were separated by a .9 sec. interval. As a result, it was possible for the infants to make the discrimination either on the basis of the difference in the first inter-element interval or on the basis of the different length of the entire sequence. The Mendelson & Ferland findings are also ambiguous. Cross-modal transfer was obtained in only one of two conditions. The authors reported that there was a significant novelty preference following exposure either to the regular or the irregular sound. The novelty preference was due, however, to increased looking at the irregularly-moving puppet following familiarization with the regular sound and *decreased* looking at the irregularly-moving puppet rather than an increase in looking at the regularly moving puppet, following familiarization with the irregular sound. Viewed in another way, the amount of looking at the regular film following familiarization with the two sounds was *not* different.

INTERSENSORY RESPONSE TO SYNCHRONY

Synchrony is a very important intersensory cue. For example, the temporal synchrony of a seen and heard speech message is very important for the accurate perception of that message. Introduction of a temporal delay of as little as 400 ms. between the seen and heard version of the message leads to an appreciable drop in adults' ability to correctly identify it (Dodd, 1977). Presumably, putting the heard and seen aspects of the message slightly out of phase with one another interferes with the subject's ability to extract and match the equivalent temporal information that is specified by the movement of the mouth and the temporal distribution of acoustic energy.

Several studies of intersensory functioning have investigated infants' detection of information about the simultaneous occurrence of multisensory events. Spelke (1981) presented 4–month-old infants with two side-by-side films of puppets moving at the same tempo but out of synchrony with each other. For the first 100 sec. the infants heard a sound which occurred every time one of the puppets came in contact with a surface and for the second 100 sec. they heard a sound in synchrony with the other puppet. During this familiarization phase no evidence was obtained that would indicate detection of synchrony. Following the familiarization phase, a search test was given where both films were shown again while each sound track, this time out of synchrony with either puppet, was played a number of times. The only measure yielding positive results was the finding that more infants directed their first look at the object which was previously in synchrony with the current sound. They did not, however, spend more time looking at the object that previously corresponded to the sound.

Equally equivocal evidence of infants' ability to detect temporal synchrony was provided by Humphrey, Tees, & Werker (1979). In their study, 4–month-old infants were first habituated to a compound auditory-visual stimulus where the auditory and visual stimuli were presented at the same rate and in synchrony with each other. Recovery of the habituated response occurred when the compound stimulus was changed so that the two stimuli were no longer in phase. However, because recovery of response was not obtained when the converse procedure (ie., habituation with the asynchronous compound stimulus and dishabituation with the synchronous compound stimulus) was used and because the change in phase relationships was confounded with a change in rate, no clear conclusions can be drawn from this study either.

INTERSENSORY RESPONSE TO RATE

Several studies have examined infants' ability to detect intersensory equivalence of rate information. The only study to examine detection of intersensory equivalence of rate in newborns was a recent one by Gardner, Lewkowicz, Karmel, and Rose (1986). Infants' visual preferences for different temporal frequencies of visual stimulation were studied in the absence of prior auditory or visual stimulation or following prestimulation with auditory and visual stimulation. The infants viewed all possible pairs of flashing white lights presented at one of three temporal frequencies: 2, 4, or 8 Hz. In one group of infants half of the visual preference trials were preceded by prestimulation with a 2 Hz visual stimulus and the other half were preceded with a white noise stimulus presented at 2 Hz. In another group of infants the prestimulation stimulus was presented at 8 Hz. The prestimulation period consisted of an initial 30 sec. period of auditory or visual stimulation followed by 10 sec. periods of stimulation interspersed between preference trials. The expectation was that if the infants were able to detect and respond to the specific temporal frequency of the stimuli presented during the prestimulation phase, then either a systematic preference for the familiar frequency or a systematic preference for the novel frequency would have been obtained in the visual preference trials. Rather than either of these two outcomes, however, a general effect of prestimulation was observed. As the amount of prestimulation increased from no prestimulation, to 2 Hz prestimulation, to 8 Hz prestimulation, there was a decrease in looking at the fast temporal frequency and a concomitant increase in looking at the slowest frequency.

As in the Gardner & Karmel (1984) study, these findings were interpreted as reflecting the operation of an intensity-modulation mechanism. Presumably, the effect of the prestimulation was to increase the effective intensity of the visual stimuli through changes in the infants' arousal. If infants' visual preferences reflect an underlying process seeking to find an optimal level of stimulation, the shift in visual preferences towards lower levels of stimulation most likely reflects an attempt to maintain the optimal levels of stimulation by modulating visual behavior. With regard to temporal processing, these data make it clear that newborn infants do not respond to the temporal characteristics of the stimulation; rather, they indicate that newborns respond to temporal variations in terms of their overall quantitative value and that this kind of responsiveness makes it impossible for them to detect intersensory equivalence of temporal frequency.

The newborn data from the Gardner et al. study are not all that surprising given that the functional and structural status of the central nervous system is quite immature at birth (Bronson, 1982). Data from older infants suggest that there is a major change in the infants' response to temporally-based intersensory equivalence by the fourth month of life. By this age, infants appear capable of detecting the equivalence on the basis of temporal characteristics. Thus, studies by Spelke (1976; 1979) have shown that 4–month-old infants are able to match the rate at which an object bounces and the rate at which a sound is presented. In these studies 4–month-old infants were presented with pairs of films depicting puppets moving at two different rates and a sound whose rate of occurrence corresponded to the rate of movement of one of the puppets. In general, results indicated that the infants detected the temporal correspondence of the auditory and visual stimuli by looking first towards the corresponding visual stimulus. They did not, however, look longer at the corresponding visual stimulus. In a subsequent study, Spelke, Born, and Chu (1983) showed that the bisensory matching behaviors found in the prior study resulted from infants matching sounds with discontinuities in the motion of objects, rather than from infants matching sounds with visible impacts of objects with a surface.

It should be noted, however, that the Spelke (1979) studies suggest that the effect is asymmetrical; that is, the matching may be dependent on the specific rate of the stimulus. For example, in Experiment 2 of the 1979 studies, infants were presented with two films of objects bouncing at different rates and heard a sound which corresponded in rate to one of those two objects. The results showed that, both, for the first look and for the eventual look measures, looking at the two films in the presence of the slow sound was *identical.* It was only in the presence of the fast sound that the infants increased their looking at the fast film. In addition, it is possible that stimulus density differences played a role in the observed behavior. Although the on/off stimulus ratio was not reported, it appears that the stimulus moved for a constant amount of time across the two different rates. If that was the case, then this means that differences in stimulus density were confounded with rate differences.

Assuming that 4–month-old infants can detect the correspondence between objects' motions and sounds present at points where the direction of motion changes, studies by Lewkowicz (1985b) suggest that the ability of 4–month-old infants to make auditory-visual matches based on temporal relationships may be limited to displays of moving objects. In a series of three studies that were similar in design to the Lewkowicz (1985a) studies, 4–month-old infants were presented with all possible pairs of checkerboards flashing at one of three temporal frequencies (2, 4, 8 Hz). On some trials only the visual stimuli were presented and on others the visual stimuli were accompanied by a 1000 cps. tone which was presented at an on/off frequency corresponding to the frequency of one of the members of the pair of visual stimuli.

In the first study, the stimuli were presented at a 50% on/off ratio. No evidence of bisensory matching was obtained. This suggests one of two things: either the lack of motion in the visual stimulus made it impossible for the infants to make bisensory matches, or the bisensory matching observed by Spelke was due to the infants responding to stimulus density differences. To investigate whether stimulus density differences are indeed necessary for bisensory matching, in the second study, the duration of the stimulus was set to 50 ms. across all three frequencies. Once again, no evidence of bisensory matching was found, but evidence of the operation of an intensity-based mechanism was found. That is, although the infants exhibited increased looking with increasing frequency in the silent and in the sound condition, the presence of the two fastest sounds (4 and 8 Hz) led to an overall shift in looking. This shift was characterized by decreased looking at the fastest frequency and increased looking at the slowest frequency. Given the finding of such generalized effects, a third study was run where only the duration of the stimulus was varied while frequency was kept constant at 2 Hz. If an intensity-based mechanism was in fact operating, then a similar generalized effect would be expected since increasing durations of stimulation represent different amounts of stimulation. Indeed, a shift in looking was found but this time only in the presence of the longest sound; the infants in this study reduced their looking at the longest visual stimulus and increased their looking at the shortest stimulus. In sum, the pattern of results found in these studies paralleled the results from the newborns in the Gardner et al. (1986) study and both sets of results suggest that an intensity-based response mechanism operates during the early months of life which prevents infants from responding to the specific temporal properties of the types of stimulation used in these studies.

INTERSENSORY RESPONSE TO DURATION

Two studies have examined infants' ability to detect intersensory equivalence of duration. Kuhl & Meltzoff (1982) examined 4–month-old infants' ability to perceive speech intermodally. When infants were presented with two faces side-by-side, one articulating the vowel /a/ and the other the vowel /i/, and a vowel sound emanating from a speaker placed between the two visual stimuli, they looked longer at the face articulating the vowel that was simultaneously presented auditorially. In an attempt to isolate the aspects of the auditory stimulus that permitted the infants to make the match, Kuhl and Meltzoff carried out a second study in which they presented the infants with the same vowel sounds, but this time the spectral information necessary to identify them (formants) was removed and only intensity and duration information was preserved. Results indicated that intensity and duration were not sufficient to permit the infants to make the bisensory matches, suggesting that the linguistically relevant information was essential for the bisensory matching to occur.

A study by Lewkowicz (1986) examined infants' detection of duration-based auditory-visual correspondence. Three–, 6–, and 8–month-old infants were presented with pairs of checkerboards. In each pair, the checkerboards flashed at the same rate but the duration of the flash differed for the two checkerboards. Visual preferences were studied in silence as well as in the presence of a tone whose duration and onset/offset characteristics corresponded to one member of the visual pair of stimuli. Three different pairs of durations were presented: 400–800 ms., 400–1600 ms., and 800–1600 ms.

Three-month-old infants did not make bisensory matches of

duration. In contrast, separate analyses of the data from each of the three pairs in both the 6– and 8–month-old infants revealed that, although there was no evidence of matching for the 400–800 ms. pair, there was clear evidence of bisensory matching for both the 400–1600 ms. pair and for the 800–1600 ms. pair. For the 400–1600 ms. pair, the mean proportion of looking at the 1600 ms. stimulus was greater when this stimulus was presented together with the 1600 ms. sound than when it was presented together with the 400 ms. sound or in silence. Likewise, for the 800–1600 ms. pair, the mean proportion of looking at the 1600 ms. stimulus was greater when this stimulus was presented together with the 1600 ms. sound than when it was presented together with the 800 ms. sound or in silence. Since the sound was always in synchrony with the onset and offset of the matching visual stimulus, a second experiment was run to determine whether synchrony played a part in the matching that was observed. This was done by presenting 8–month-old infants with the same exact stimuli except that the onset and offset of the sound was made to occur 300 ms. after the onset and offset of the visual stimulus that corresponded in duration. Results indicated that synchrony was indeed critical since its disruption led to a disruption of bisensory matching.

The failure of the 3–month-old infants in the Lewkowicz (1986) study to make bisensory matches of duration is not in itself surprising; however, the absence of an intensity-based effect is surprising given the finding of intensity-based effects in the Lewkowicz (1985b) studies. The absence of such an intensity-based effect in the current data is puzzling, especially since the infants in this study were a month younger than were the infants in the Lewkowicz (1985b) studies and should, therefore, have been even more predisposed to respond in this manner. In the previous study, durations of 50, 100, and 200 ms. were used and the results indicated that there was a generalized shift in visual preference in the presence of the longest auditory stimulus. What is puzzling is that in the current study the 3–month-olds were actually presented with longer, and presumably more intense, durations of stimulation. Yet, no intensity-based effects were found.

One possible resolution of this discrepancy may be that the effective intensity of a temporally modulated stimulus is determined jointly by the duration of the stimulus and the frequency of its presentation. Such an interpretation is consistent with the fact that the visual and auditory systems each possesses two separate types of cells (Cleland, Dubin, and Levick, 1971; Moller, 1969). One type, known as transient cells, responds only to the onset and offset of stimuli. The other type, known as sustained cells, responds with a sustained train of discharges which last as long as the stimulus lasts. Given the existence of these two types of cells, it would be possible to show that, for example, the effects of a 100 ms. long stimulus presented twice during one second would not be the same as the effects of a 200 ms. stimulus presented once during one second, even though the total length of stimulation is the same in both cases. The differential effect of these two methods of stimulus presentation would result from the fact that the 100 ms. stimulus would activate the transient population of neurons twice as often as the 200 ms. stimulus would, thus leading to the overall activation of a greater number of neurons. Since the stimuli in the prior study with the 4–month-olds were presented at a rate that was four times greater (2 Hz) than was the rate of stimulus presentation in the current studies (.5 Hz), it is entirely possible that the absence of the intensity-based effect in the 3–month-olds was due to the fact that the auditory stimuli were not effectively intense enough to produce the kind of shift observed in the other studies (eg., Lewkowicz, 1985b). In sum, what these results and the results from the prior studies show is that intensity differences may be produced in any one of three ways: (a) varying duration and keeping rate constant, (b) varying rate and keeping duration constant, and (c) varying rate and duration jointly.

It is interesting to compare the results from the Lewkowicz (1986) studies to the Kuhl and Meltzoff (1982) results. Kuhl and Meltzoff's finding that a duration-based correspondence of an auditory stimulus with the movement of the mouth was not sufficient for 4–month-old infants to exhibit evidence of matching is consistent with the findings from the 3–month-old infants in the Lewkowicz (1986) study. Although no direct data on 4–month-old infants' ability to make duration-based bisensory matches were obtained by Lewkowicz (1986), the finding of generalized, intensity-based effects and no evidence of bisensory matching in the third study in the Lewkowicz (1985b) report (where only durations were varied and where 4–month-old infants were tested) makes it likely that the ability of infants to make bisensory matches of duration appears sometime between the fourth and the sixth month of life. Furthermore, linguistically relevant information contained in social exchanges may actually aid the infant in making what appear to be temporally-based bisensory matches in early ontogeny. In other words, it is possible that social and linguistic experiences in early ontogeny may provide the infant with a foundation for the development of more "basic" intersensory abilities involving the detection of "pure" temporal intersensory relationships.

Response to Temporally Related Auditory-Visual Compounds and Sensory Dominance

In this last section, data from a series of recently completed experiments will be described. In these experiments, I set out to examine developmental changes in infants' response to timing in multisensory events. Under ordinary conditions infants are faced with multisensory events and one of their tasks is to detect the temporal information inherent in such events. For example, in an auditory-visual event such as the mother speaking to the infant, the infant must be able to detect the temporal aspects of the motion of the mother's mouth, the temporal aspects of the sound, and the relationship between these two. What is not clear is whether in such a situation the infant relies on the temporal aspects of just the auditory component, just the visual component, or on both components and the relationship between them.

It is clear from the Stern et al. (1977) and the Jasnow and Feldstein (1986) studies that an interaction between a mother and her infant is rich in temporal organization and that infants respond to its temporal properties. What is not clear, however, is to what extent young infants can utilize the temporal aspects of multisensory input in their interactions with their world. The data from the Kuhl and Meltzoff's (1982) study suggest that infants as young as four months of age can make matches between the auditory and visual aspects of a linguistic message. They also show, however, that when the linguistic character of the auditory stimulus is stripped away and when only the temporal information of the auditory stimulus is retained, the infants do not exhibit evidence of bisensory matching. This fact alone might suggest that young infants cannot integrate multisensory information purely on the basis of temporal factors. Yet, the Spelke findings that 4–month-old infants are able to detect rate equivalence in auditory and dynamic visual displays when only temporal cues are available refutes this conclusion. The failure of the infants in the Kuhl and Meltzoff study to make bisensory matches when the auditory stimulus was stripped of its linguistic properties may reflect the violation of a very powerful expectancy that is very difficult to overcome. That is, presenting an infant with a picture of a face with moving lips may set up an expectancy in the infant to hear a linguistically relevant auditory stimulus. Stripping the auditory signal of its unique linguistic properties may simply be a violation of the expectancy and may not truly reflect the infant's capacity to process intersensory relationships on the basis of temporal properties. In connection with the question of whether young infants can integrate multisensory information on the basis of temporal information, there is some disagreement as to the age at which this ability is manifest. Spelke's findings suggest that infants can detect temporally-based cross-modal equivalence at 4 months of age whereas Lewkowicz's (1985b; 1986) findings suggest that this is not the case until 6 months of age. This discrepancy may be due to the different visual stimuli used by the two investigators. The earlier bisensory matching behavior found by Spelke may reflect the fact that spatially-dynamic visual stimuli may make it easier for infants to detect the temporal information.

In addition to the question regarding the development of intersensory perception of temporally-based equivalence, another very important question concerns the functional priority of sensory systems. If one sensory system has functional priority over another then it is important to determine the effect that dominance may have on the processing of multisensory information. A number of years ago Birch and Lefford (1967) discussed the existence of sensory hierarchies in older subjects and pointed out that there were important relationships between sensory dominance hierarchies and intersensory processes. They proposed the operation of three related and concurrently active processes responsible for the development of afferent control of directed action: (a) a developmental shift in sensory dominance hierarchies characterized by a shift from proximoreceptor control to teloreceptor control, (b) increasing tendency for intersensory integration, and (c) intrasensory differentiation. Although some information about the development of intersensory integration and about intrasensory differentiation is already available, there is virtually no information about sensory hierarchies and possible shifts in these hierarchies during ontogeny. Until studies of sensory hierarchies are carried out a clear picture of intersensory development will not emerge.

The experiments described in this section represent the first known attempt to systematically investigate the possibility that sensory dominance operates in early human ontogeny. Since the available data indicate that temporally-based bisensory matching is present by six months of age, the first set of experiments (Lewkowicz, 1988a) examined responsiveness to multisensory information at this age. Since major changes in sensory/perceptual functioning are known to occur during infancy, a similar set of experiments was carried out with 10-month-old infants (Lewkowicz, 1988b) to investigate possible developmental changes in responsiveness to multisensory information. The general technique consisted of creating a temporal expectation first by repeatedly presenting an auditory-visual compound stimulus having certain temporal properties and then violating this expectancy by changing these temporal properties to determine what aspects of the multisensory compound the infants were attending to. In addition to being able to determine what aspects of the compound stimulus the infants were attending to, it was also possible to determine whether detection of temporal expectancy violation is affected by input from other modalities.

The general method used to study processing of temporally-related multisensory compounds was the habituation-dishabituation technique. Infants were habituated to an auditory-visual stimulus compound made up of a flashing checkerboard and a pulsing square-wave tone having a frequency of 330 cps. To find out what aspects of the compound the infants were attending to, three different types of test trials were administered following the habituation phase. One test trial involved a change in both components of the stimulus. Since a significant response recovery on this test trial could be due either to the detection of a change in both components or the detection of a change in just one of the components, two additional test trials were administered. In one of these trials, the rate of the auditory component was changed while the rate of the visual component remained the same, and in the other test trial, the rate of the visual component was changed while the rate of the auditory component remained the same. To specifically determine what processes were responsible for the infants' responses, the type of temporal relationship between the auditory and visual components and the number of cues signalling a change in either one or both components was varied across the different experiments.

SIX-MONTH-OLD INFANTS

In the first experiment 24 six-month-old infants were habituated to an auditory-visual compound whose components were presented at the same rate. Half the infants were habituated with an auditory-visual compound whose auditory and visual components were both presented at a rate of 2.0 Hz, and half were presented with a compound whose components were both presented at a rate of 4.0 Hz. During each cycle of stimulation, the stimulus was on for 150 ms., and this stimulus duration was used at both rates. An infant-control procedure was used to study discriminative responding. As long as an infant looked at the checkerboard pattern, the checkerboard flashed and the tone was pulsed. As soon as the infant looked away for more than 1 sec. the trial was terminated and the next fixation of the checkerboard initiated the next trial. A total of 24 trials was administered to each infant. The first 12 trials constituted the habituation phase and the remaining 12 trials constituted the test phase. Following the completion of the 12 habituation trials, three types of test trials, interspersed between a set of three re-habituation trials, were administered twice in succession. For those infants habituated with the 2.0 Hz stimulus, a change in any one of the three types of trials involved a change to 4.0 Hz, whereas for infants habituated with the 4.0 Hz stimulus the change was to 2.0 Hz.

Since there was a linear relation between the size of the mean duration of visual fixation and the standard deviation, the data were first transformed to common logarithms. All analyses were based on the transformed scores. Results from the first experiment indicated that as a group the infants habituated to the auditory-visual compound (Figure 1.1) and that the different rates used during habituation did not have any effects on the course of habituation. To find out whether the infants discriminated the changes in the test trials, the average duration of visual fixation for the two test trials of each type was compared to the average duration of visual fixation for the last two habituation trials. Response in the test trials was dependent on the type of change introduced. There was no significant dishabituation in the visual nor in the auditory test trial, but there was a significant dishabituation in the auditory/visual test trial (Figure 1.1).

This finding indicates that a maximal change in the compound stimulus was detectable but that a change in either component alone was not detectable. Moreover, these data suggest that the infants responded neither to the holistic properties of the compound stimulus nor to the intersensory relationship of the components. Holistic processing would have required that the infants exhibit discrimination in all three test trials since any change, whether in both components simultaneously or in a single component, resulted in a change in the compound stimulus as a whole. With regard to responsiveness to the intersensory relationship of the components, had the infants been able to detect the changes in the relationship of the components, they would have exhibited discrimination in the auditory and in the visual test trials. This is because the intersensory relationship changed from a concordant one to a discordant one in both of these trials. They would not, however, have been expected to exhibit recovery of response in the auditory/visual test trial since in that trial the intersensory relationship remained the same.

The infants' failure to respond to changes in each of the components may in part have been due to the fact that the temporal properties of the auditory and visual components were identical during the habituation phase. As a result, the infants may not have had an opportunity to learn about the specific temporal properties of each component. The purpose of the second experiment was to find out if this was in fact the case. Thus, in

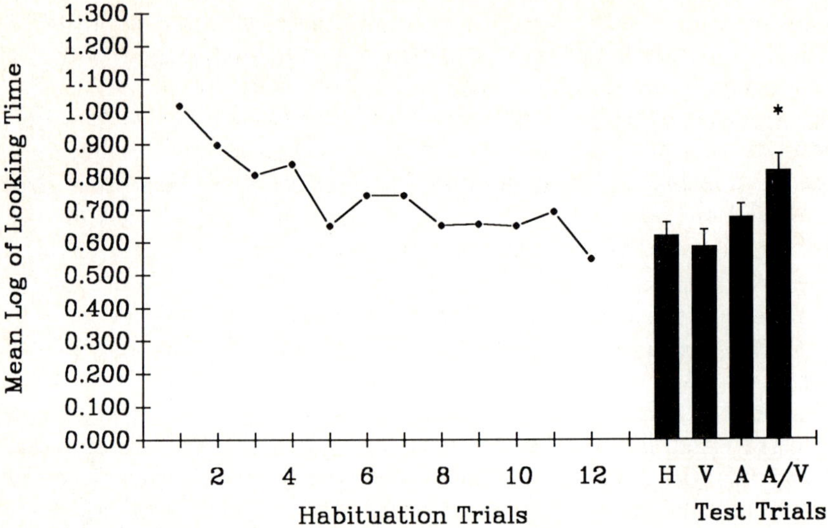

Figure 1.1. Six-month-old infants' response to the components of an auditory-visual compound following habituation with a compound that was temporally-concordant and when rate was the only discriminative cue available. The left part of the figure shows the decline in looking time during the habituation phase and the right part of the figure shows the mean looking times for the habituation trials (H) and for the three types of test trials: visual (V), auditory (A), and auditory/visual (A/V).

the second experiment 24 six-month-old infants were given an opportunity to learn about the specific temporal properties of each component. This was done by presenting a compound stimulus composed of temporally-distinct components during the habituation phase. Half the infants were habituated with a compound stimulus consisting of an auditory component presented at 2 Hz and a visual component presented at 4 Hz, and the other half were habituated with a compound stimulus consisting of an auditory component presented at 4 Hz and a visual component presented at 2 Hz. During the test trials, the rate of a given component was changed to the other rate. For example, if an infant was habituated with a compound stimulus consisting of a 2 Hz auditory and a 4 Hz visual component, in the auditory test trial the auditory component was changed to 4 Hz and the visual component remained at 4 Hz; in the visual test trial the visual component was changed to 2 Hz and the auditory component remained at 2 Hz.

As can be seen in Figure 1.2, the infants exhibited significant habituation, and in contrast to the infants in the first experiment, they not only discriminated the simultaneous change in both components of the compound, but also discriminated the change in the auditory component. They did not, however, discriminate the change in the visual component. Thus, it appears that the reason that the infants in the first experiment failed to discriminate the change in the single components was due to the two components being too temporally similar.

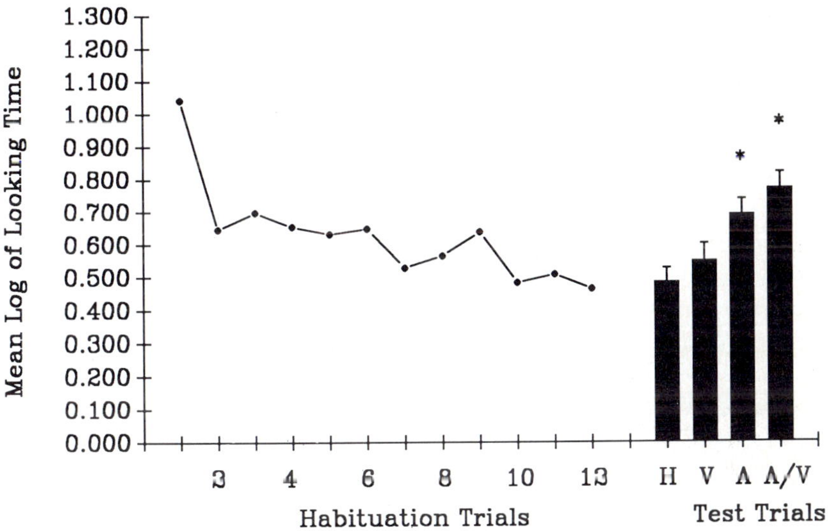

Figure 1.2. Six-month-old infants' response to the components of an auditory-visual compound following habituation with a compound that was temporally-discordant and when rate was the only discriminative cue available. The left part of the figure shows the decline in looking time during the habituation phase and the right part of the figure shows the mean looking times for the habituation trials and for the three types of test trials.

It is not clear from these results why the infants in the second experiment still did not respond to the change in the visual component. It may be that failure of infants in this experiment, as well as in the previous one, to respond to the change in the visual component reflects a form of auditory dominance when spatially-static visual information is presented in conjunction with auditory information. The possible operation of auditory dominance is supported by the fact that the response in the auditory/

/visual test trial was not greater than was the response in the auditory test trial. Had the infants been able to detect the changes in the visual component, the discriminability of the change in the auditory component alone would have been enhanced by a concurrent change in the visual component and would, therefore, have been evident in a greater magnitude of response in the auditory/visual test trial than in the auditory test trial.

Additional evidence in favor of an auditory dominance interpretation was sought in the third experiment. It was hypothesized that if the results from the previous two experiments do indeed reflect the operation of auditory dominance then providing the infants with an additional cue to help them discriminate the change in the visual component should not have any effect. Thus, in the third experiment, 24 six-month-old infants were habituated with a temporally-concordant auditory-visual compound stimulus, but this time the on/off ratio of the stimulus was kept constant at 50% across different rates. Half the infants were habituated with a compound stimulus whose auditory and visual components were presented at 0.5 Hz and the other half were presented with a compound stimulus whose components were presented at 2.0 Hz. Given the 50% on/off ratio, the "on" time for a stimulus presented at 0.5 Hz was 1000 ms. and the "on" time for a stimulus presented at 2.0 Hz was 250 ms. This meant that when the rate of a given component was changed, the duration of the component changed as well.

Following significant habituation, the infants in this experiment exhibited dishabituation to the change in both components, marginal dishabituation to the change in the auditory component, and no dishabituation to the change in the visual component (see Figure 1.3). Moreover, the response in the auditory test trial was greater than the response in the visual test trial, and the response in the auditory/visual test trial was also greater than the response in the visual test trial. There was no difference in response magnitude between the auditory/visual test trial and the auditory test trial. It is interesting to note that despite the fact that the infants in this experiment were habituated with a temporally-concordant compound, they, unlike the infants in the first experiment, exhibited limited evidence of discrimination when the auditory component changed. Although the infants' dishabituation was marginal, the magnitude of response to the change in the auditory component was greater than the magnitude of response to the change in the visual component. This suggests that the availability of a second discriminative cue helped the infants discriminate the change in the auditory component but that it was still not sufficient to detect the change in the visual component. This, together with the fact that the response to the change in both components was not greater than the response to the change in the auditory component, further suggests that the infants' failure to respond to the change in the visual component is due to auditory dominance.

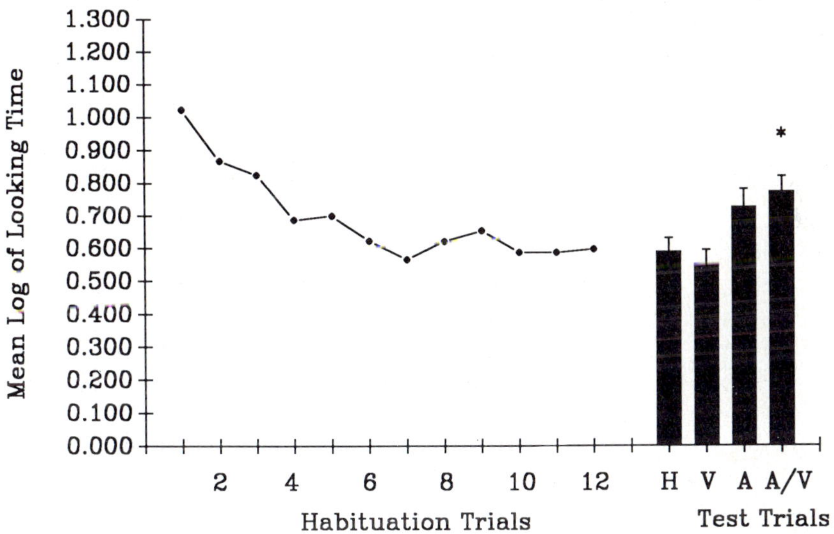

Figure 1.3. Six-month-old infants' response to the components of an auditory-visual compound following habituation with a compound that was temporally-concordant and when rate and duration were available as discriminative cues. The left part of the figure shows the decline in looking time during the habituation phase and the right part of the figure shows the mean looking times for the habituation trials and for the three types of test trials.

Despite the fact that the infants in the third experiment performed better than the infants in the first experiment, it is still possible that their failure to discriminate the change in the visual component was due to the fact that the two components were temporally indistinguishable during the habituation phase. To find out if this was the case, in the fourth experiment 24 six-month-old infants were habituated with a temporally-discordant compound stimulus; for half the infants the visual component was presented at 0.5 Hz and the auditory component was presented at 2.0 Hz, and for the other half the visual component was presented at 2.0 Hz and the auditory component was presented at 0.5 Hz. As in the third experiment, the on/off ratio was kept at 50% thus providing the infants with two discriminative cues both in the habituation and in the dishabituation phase. Although there was significant habituation, the results from the test trials were rather surprising. The infants only discriminated the simultaneous change in both components. Furthermore, the response in the auditory/visual test trial was significantly greater than the response in the visual and in the auditory test trials (see Figure 1.4).

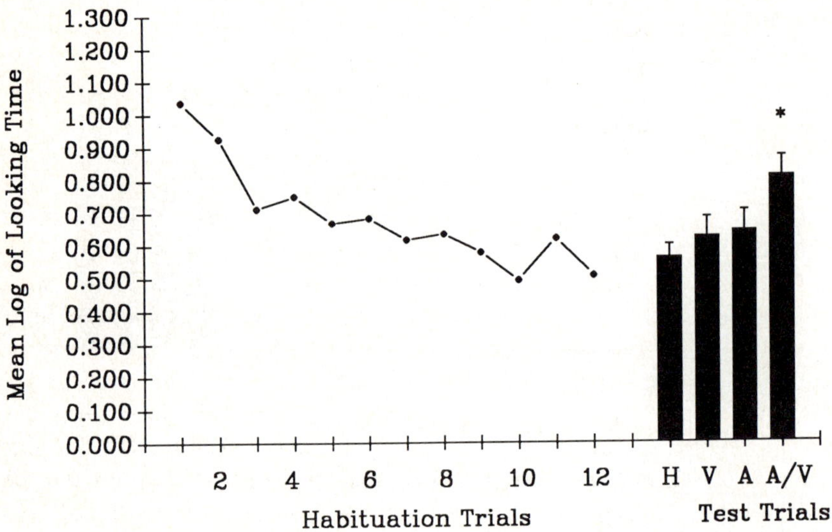

Figure 1.4. Six-month-old infants' response to the components of an auditory-visual compound following habituation with a compound that was temporally-discordant and when rate and duration were available as discriminative cues. The left part of the figure shows the decline in looking time during the habituation phase and the right part of the figure shows the mean looking times for the habituation trials and for the three types of test trials.

The results from this experiment can best be understood in the context of the results from the other three experiments. Although this experiment might be thought of as a way of highlighting the temporal distinctiveness of the components, the use of an equal on/off ratio introduced concomitant rate and duration differences in both the habituation and the dishabituation phases. It may be that variation in rate and duration at the same time during the habituation phase may exceed the infants' limited information processing capacities and may as a result make it more difficult to encode the temporal information. The infants' task in the test phase was equally difficult because they were faced with a simultaneous change in rate and duration and had to determine whether both of these attributes were the same or different from those experienced during habituation. In contrast, the infants in the second experiment only had to determine whether rate changed. In sum, these findings may reflect a response to greater information complexity and the operation of auditory dominance all at once.

One consistent finding across all four experiments is the failure of the infants to discriminate the change in the visual component. This was found across a range of frequencies and across a range of experimental manipulations designed to enhance the distinctiveness of the visual information. One possibility that had still not been examined was whether the rates of visual stimulation that were used in the prior experiments were discriminable from one another. A fifth experiment was therefore carried out with a group of 24 six-month-old infants where the infants' ability to discriminate between 0.5 Hz and 2.0 Hz was studied in the absence of concurrent auditory stimulation. Thus, half the infants were first habituated with the checkerboard flashing at 0.5 Hz and the other half were habituated with the checkerboard flashing at 2.0 Hz. Following the 12 habituation trials, the infants were administered two additional trials where the checkerboard flashed at the other rate. A comparison of the duration of the visual fixation in the last two habituation trials with the duration of visual fixation in the two test trials showed a highly significant recovery of response (see Figure 1.5). This indicates that the failure of the infants in the preceding experiments to respond to the changes in the visual component reflects auditory dominance rather than an inability to discriminate the visual changes in rate.

The last experiment was aimed at investigating the possibility that the auditory dominance observed in the prior experiments was due to the greater salience of the auditory component. Since the visual and auditory stimuli were not matched *a priori* to be of equal subjective intensity, it was possible that the visual stimulus was subjectively weaker than the auditory stimulus. To determine if this was in fact the case, Experiment 3 was repeated but this time the intensity of the visual component was increased. Infants were presented either with a 0.5 Hz or a 2.0 Hz temporally-concordant compound stimulus during the habituation phase. If the visual component was subjectively less intense, then an increase in its intensi ty might make the visual and auditory components more equivalent and, as a result, might lead to either a reduction in the differential responsive-

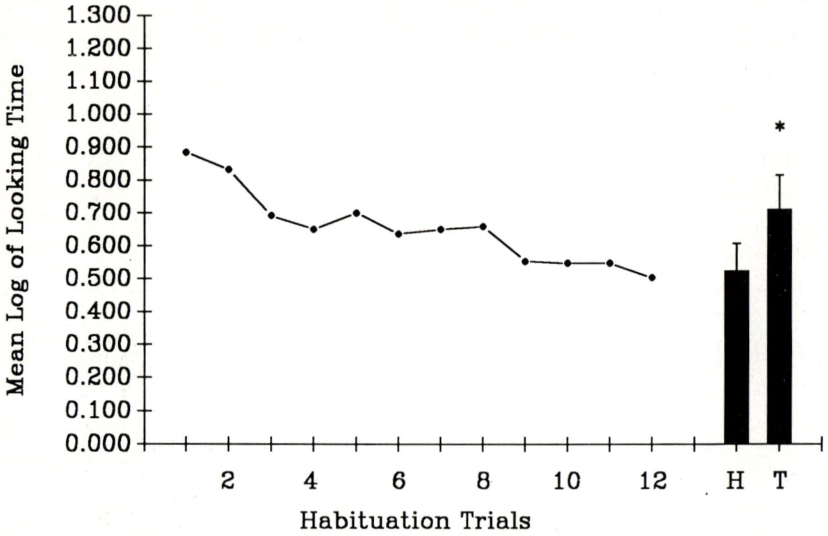

Figure 1.5. Six-month-old infants' response to temporal differences in visual information without competing auditory information. The line graph represents the visual fixation during the habituation trials and the bars represent the average visual fixation in the last two habituation trials (H) and in the test trial (T).

ness to the auditory and visual components, or to discrimination of the change in the visual component.

The results from this experiment were essentially a replication of the results from Experiment 3 (see Figure 1.6). Following significant habituation, the infants dishabituated to the change in the auditory component and to the simultaneous change in the two components, but not to the change in the visual component. This finding suggests that the infants' failure to respond to changes in the visual component were not due to the differential salience of the two components and offers additional evidence in support of an auditory dominance interpretation. It should be noted that there was one important difference between the results from this experiment and those from Experiment 3. In contrast to Experiment 3, in this experiment, the response in the auditory/visual test trial was greater than the response in the auditory test trial. This suggests that the change in the visual component enhanced the discriminability of the simultaneous change in the auditory component. In other words, even though the visual component was not discriminable when its temporal attributes were changed in the context of a constant auditory component, its greater intensity allowed it to enhance the discriminability of the concurrent change in the auditory component.

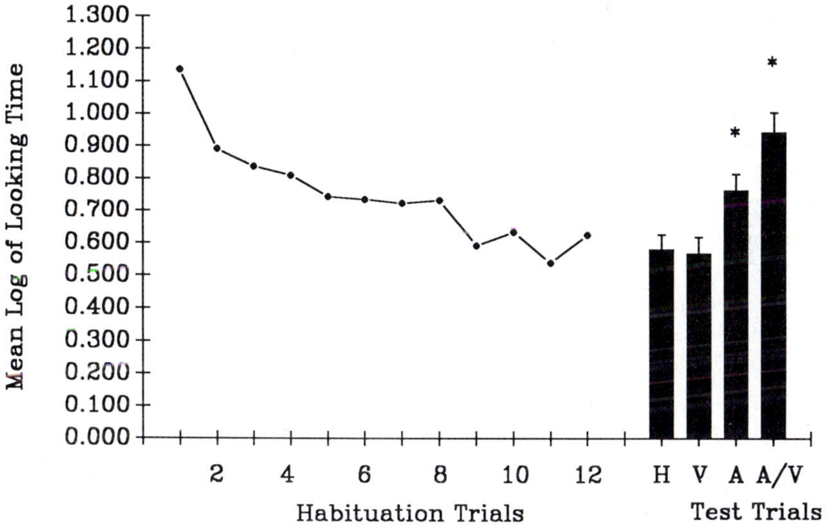

Figure 1.6. Six-month-old infants' response to the components of an auditory-visual compound with a brighter visual component following habituation with a compound that was temporally-concordant and when rate and duration were available as discriminative cues. The left part of the figure shows the decline in looking time during the habituation phase and the right part of the figure shows the mean looking times for the habituation trials and for the three types of test trials.

TEN-MONTH-OLD INFANTS

To determine whether developmental changes in the processing of temporally-related multisensory compounds occur, a similar, but not identical, series of experiments was conducted with 10–month-old infants. As a first step in determining the nature of the 10- month-old infants' response to multisensory compounds, in the first experiment half of the infants were habituated with the 2 Hz compound stimulus having a 150 ms. "on" time and the other half were habituated with the 4 Hz compound stimulus having a 150 ms. "on" time. Following significant habituation, the infants in this study dishabituated to the simultaneous change in both components and to the change in the auditory component (see Figure 1.7).

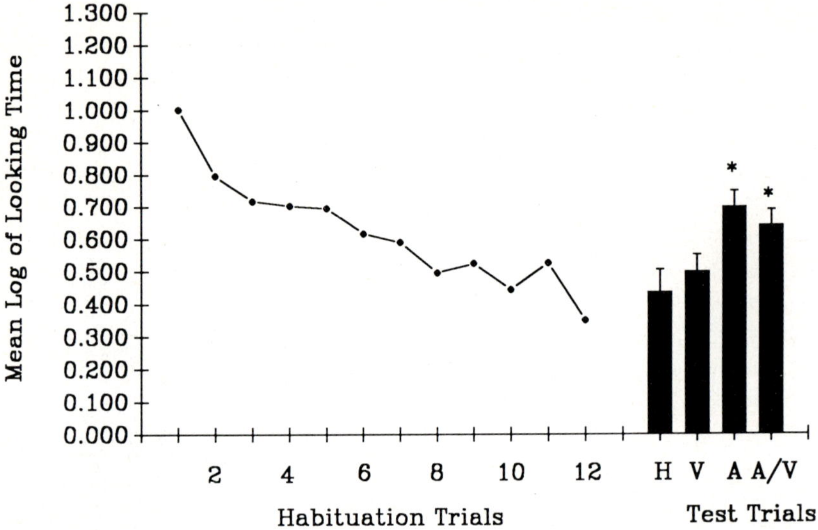

Figure 1.7. Ten-month-old infants' response to the components of an auditory-visual compound following habituation with a compound that was temporally-concordant and when rate was the only discriminative cue available. The left part of the figure shows the decline in looking time during the habituation phase and the right part of the figure shows the mean looking times for the habituation trials and for the three types of test trials.

This is different from the 6–month-old infants who in the same experiment only responded to the simultaneous change in both components. In addition, the response in the visual test trial was significantly smaller than the response in both the auditory and in the auditory/visual test trial. This suggests that the 10–month-old infants detected the temporal characteristics of the auditory component. The fact that the magnitude of response in the auditory/visual test trial was not greater than the magnitude of response in the auditory test trial suggests that the dishabituation in the auditory/visual trial was based on the infants' detection of the change in the auditory component alone. Like the 6–month-old infants, however, the 10–month-old infants also did not respond to the change in the visual component.

Since the infants failed to respond to the change in the visual component there was the question of whether the temporal similarity of the components in the first experiment made it impossible for the infants to learn about the temporal properties of the visual component. Thus, in a second experiment, a group of 24 ten-month-old infants was habituated with a temporally-discordant multisensory compound stimulus. Half of the infants were habituated with a compound stimulus consisting of a 2 Hz auditory and a 4 Hz visual component, and half were habituated with a compound stimulus consisting of a 4 Hz auditory and 2 Hz visual component. The stimulus "on" time was still 150 ms. for both rates. Results indicated that unlike the younger infants, the infants in the current experiment detected the change in the visual and in the auditory components, as well as in both components together (see Figure 1.8). There was no difference in the magnitude of response to the change in the visual and auditory components. The finding of discrimination of the change in the visual component suggests that the auditory modality no longer dominates responsiveness by 10 months of age.

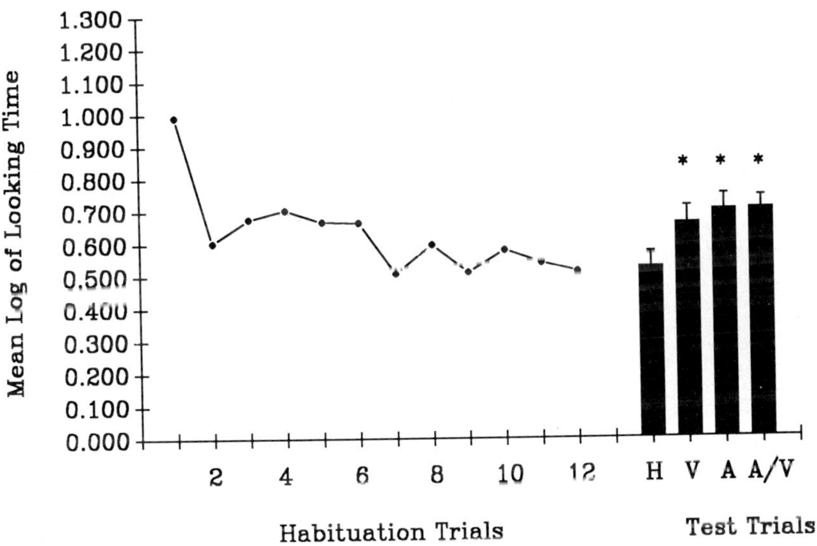

Figure 1.8. Ten-month-old infants' response to the components of an auditory-visual compound following habituation with a compound that was temporally-discordant and when rate was the only discriminative cue available. The left part of the figure shows the decline in looking time during the habituation phase and the right part of the figure shows the mean looking times for the habituation trials and for the three types of test trials.

To further confirm the developmental change found in the previous experiment, a third experiment was run with 24 infants where a temporally-concordant multisensory compound was presented during habituation, but this time the infants were provided with two discriminative cues. Half the infants were presented with a temporally-concordant compound stimulus whose visual and auditory components were both presented at 2 Hz, and half were presented with a compound stimulus whose visual and auditory components were presented at 0.5 Hz. For the 2 Hz compound, the stimulus "on" time was 250 ms. and for the 0.5 Hz compound the stimulus "on" time was 1000 ms. Following significant habituation, the infants dishabituated to the change in the visual and auditory components, as well as to the simultaneous change in both components (see Figure 1.9). There was no difference in the magnitude of response to the change in the visual and auditory components. Thus, once again, these data are different from the 6–month data and indicate that the

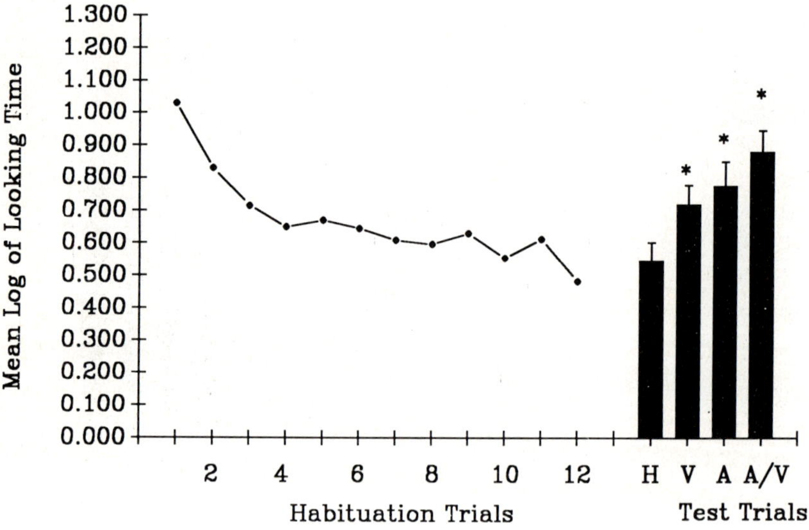

Figure 1.9. Ten-month-old infants' response to the components of an auditory-visual compound following habituation with a compound that was temporally-concordant and when rate and duration were available as discriminative cues. The left part of the figure shows the decline in looking time during the habituation phase and the right part of the figure shows the mean looking times for the habituation trials and for the three types of test trials.

10–month-old infants can detect changes in both the visual and the auditory components.

Although the 10–month-old infants detected changes in the visual component, it would be interesting to see whether they would be affected by information complexity during the habituation phase in a manner similar to that observed in the 6–month-old infants. Thus, in this fourth experiment, a group of 24 infants was habituated with a temporally-discordant multisensory compound; half of the infants were habituated with a compound consisting of a 2.0 Hz auditory and a 0.5 Hz visual component and half were habituated with a compound consisting of a 0.5 Hz auditory and a 2.0 Hz visual component. Since the on/off ratio was constant across rate changes, duration differences accompanied rate differences. Significant habituation was obtained. Results from the test trials indicated that complexity did indeed play a role in the infants' response since they only dishabituated to the simultaneous change in both components (see Figure 1.10).

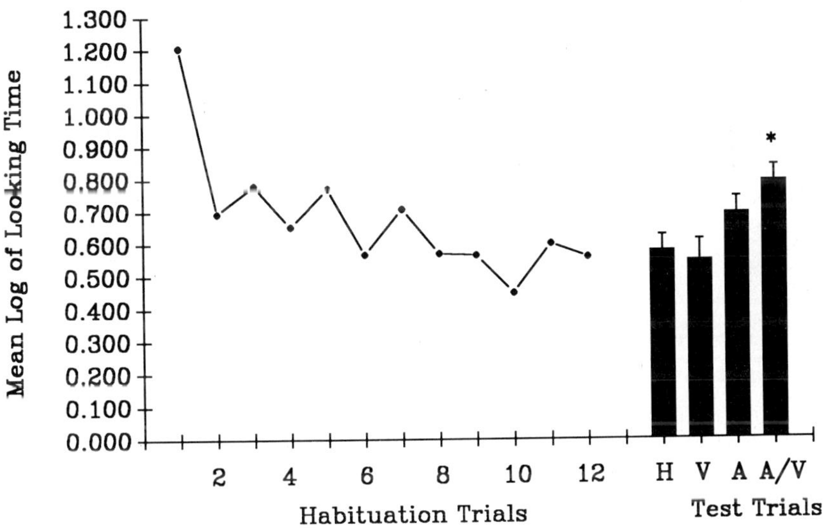

Figure 1.10. Ten-month-old infants' response to the components of an auditory-visual compound following habituation with a compound that was temporally-discordant and when rate and duration were available as discriminative cues. The left part of the figure shows the decline in looking time during the habituation phase and the right part of the figure shows the mean looking times for the habituation trials and for the three types of test trials.

Given that the older infants detected the change in the visual information when it was presented in a "simpler" information context, it is possible that enhancement of the visual component might just be enough to overcome the information complexity introduced in the fourth experiment. To see if that was indeed the case, the fourth experiment was repeated with a new group of 24 infants. The infants were once again habituated with the temporally-discordant compound; however, this time the intensity of the visual component was increased. Results from the test trials did indeed indicate that the increase in the intensity of the visual component affected processing. Following significant habituation, the infants dishabituated to the change in the visual and auditory components, as well as to the simultaneous change in both components (see Figure 1.11).

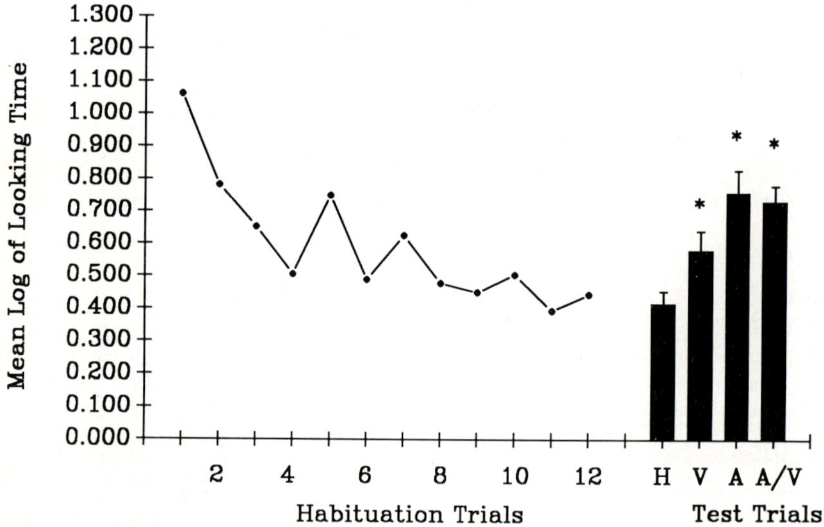

Figure 1.11. Ten-month-old infants' response to the components of an auditory-visual compound with a brighter visual component following habituation with a compound that was temporally-discordant and when rate and duration were available as discriminative cues. The left part of the figure shows the decline in looking time during the habituation phase and the right part of the figure shows the mean looking times for the habituation trials and for the three types of test trials.

Although the infants did respond to the change in the visual component, the data indicated that the visual information was not as easily discriminated since the magnitude of response in the auditory test trials was greater than in the visual test trials. Moreover, the magnitude of response in the auditory/visual test trial was greater than the magnitude of response in the visual test trial.

In sum, this series of experiments shows that in a task where auditory and visual information competes for the infant's attention, the auditory modality has functional priority over the visual modality at six months of age but that by ten months of age the visual modality is able to assert itself, although even then it appears to be the weaker one of the two. This is in marked contrast to adults who have been found to be strongly visually dominant across a variety of tasks where auditory and visual information competes for their attention (Colavita, 1974; Colavita & Weisberg, 1979; Egeth & Sager, 1977; McGurk & MacDonald, 1976; Radeau & Bertelson, 1977). As a result, it appears that a developmental shift in sensory dominance occurs somewhere between infancy and adulthood. This is consistent with Bronson's (1982) prediction that, based on the structural development of the nervous system, there ought to be an age X modality interaction in the infant's sensitivity to the sensory qualities of his or her environment. It is also consistent in its general aspects with Birch & Lefford's (1967) prediction of a developmental shift in sensory dominance. The implications of these findings for our understanding of the development of infants' response to temporal information are important. Given the existence of sensory dominance in infancy and given that changes begin to occur quite early in ontogeny, future models of the mechanisms underlying infants' response to temporal information must take the sensory modality used in the processing of the temporal information into account, particularly when responsiveness to multisensory information is of interest.

CONCLUSION

The foregoing review has shown that infants produce many behaviors in a temporally-organized fashion and that they are capable of responding to temporal variations in stimulation quite early in development. While it is clear that infants are capable of appreciating much finer aspects of their temporal environment than has earlier been believed (Piaget, 1954), many unanswered questions remain. Ultimately, we would like to understand how the intrinsic biobehavioral rhythms interact with temporal processing capacities, and how this reciprocal interaction contributes to the development of motor, linguistic, affective, and social aspects of the infant's behavior. Although it is tempting to postulate a single mechanism, such as a neural time keeper, to account for the many diverse temporally-based phenomena (e.g., Ashton, 1976, Stratton, 1982), it is not at all clear that this is the most parsimonious approach to take in an effort to understand the underlying mechanisms. For example, although it is possible that a common pacemaker may be involved in the production of such diverse behaviors as mother-infant interaction and the spontaneous production of motor behaviors, the mechanism responsible for these two types of behaviors and its ultimate organization is likely to be very different. Thus, the spontaneous generation of motor behaviors only requires the operation of a motor oscillator in the nervous system. In contrast, the production of the intricate rhythms observed in social interaction involves not only the generation of motor patterns that have precise temporal characteristics but also involves the operation of sensory, perceptual, affective, and cognitive mechanisms. Among the many things that these latter mechanisms must continuously assess are the nature of the information, its hedonic or affective value, its contextual meaning, its temporal character, etc. Since the flow of behavior is open to various influences on a continuous basis and since a pacemaker is only one element of such a system, it will obviously have very different properties from a system which is essentially a closed loop and one that is relatively impermeable to external influences. In sum, while it is relatively easy to speculate about mechanisms underlying temporally-determined behaviors, the conclusion drawn by Stratton in 1982 that a concentration on possible underlying mechanisms would be misplaced given the paucity of information in this area still holds today.

References

Allen, T. W., Walker, K., Symonds, L., & Marcell, M. (1977). Intrasensory and intersensory perception of temporal sequences during infancy. *Developmental Psychology, 13*, 225–229.

Arco, C. M. B (1983). Infant reaction to natural and manipulated temporal patterns of paternal communication. *Infant Behavior and Development, 6*, 391–399.

Ashton, R. (1976). Aspects of timing in child development. *Child Development, 47*, 622–626.

Aslin, R. N., Pisoni, D. B., & Jusczyk, P. W. (1983). Auditory development and speech perception in infancy. In M. M. Haith & J. J. Campos (Eds.), *Handbook of child psychology: Infancy and developmental psychobiology*, Vol. 2. New York: John Wiley & Sons.

Banks, M. S. & Salapatek, P. (1983). Infant visual perception. In M. M. Haith & J. J. Campos (Eds.), *Handbook of child psychology: Infancy and developmental psychobiology*, Vol. 2. New York: John Wiley & Sons.

Bertenthal, B. I., Proffitt, D. R., & Cutting, J. E. (1984). Infant sensitivity to figural coherence in biomechanical motions. *Journal of Experimental Child Psychology, 37,* 213–230.

Bertenthal, B., Proffitt, D. R., Kramer, S. J., & Spetner, N. B. (1987). Infants' encoding of kinetic displays varying in relative coherence. *Developmental Psychology, 23,* 171–178.

Birch, H. G. & Lefford, A. (1967). Visual differentiation, intersensory integration, and voluntary control. *Monographs of the Society for Research in Child Development, 32, No. 2.*

Brackbill, Y. & Fitzgerald, H. E. (1972). Stereotype temporal conditioning in infants. *Psychophysiology, 9,* 569–577.

Brackbill, Y., Lintz, L. M., & Fitzgerald, H. E. (1968). Differences in the autonomic and somatic conditioning of infants. *Psychosomatic Medicine, 30,* 193–201.

Bronson, G. W. (1982). Structure, status, and characteristics of the nervous system at birth. In P. Stratton (Ed.), *Psychobiology of the human newborn* (pp. 99–118). Chichester: John Wiley & Sons.

Chang, H. & Trehub, S. E. (1977a). Infants' perception of temporal grouping in auditory patterns. *Child Development, 48,* 1666–1670.

Chang, H. & Trehub, S. E. (1977b). Auditory processing of relational information by young infants. *Journal of Experimental Child Psychology, 24,* 324–331.

Cleland, B. G., Dubin, M. W., & Levick, W. R. (1971). Sustained and transient neurons in the cat's retina and lateral geniculate nucleus. *Journal of Physiology (London), 217,* 473–496.

Colavita, F. B. (1974). Human sensory dominance. *Perception and Psychophysics, 16,* 409–412.

Colavita, F. B. & Weisberg, D. (1979). A further investigation of visual dominance. *Perception and Psychophysics, 25,* 345–347.

Condon, W. & Sander, L. (1974a). Neonate movement is synchronized with adult speech: Interactional participation in language acquisition. *Science, 183,* 99–101.

Condon, W. & Sander. L. (1974b). Synchrony demonstrated between movements of the neonate and adult speech. *Child Development, 45,* 456–462.

Demany, L. (1982). Auditory stream segregation in infancy. *Infant Behavior and Development, 5,* 261–276.

Demany, L., McKenzie, B., & Vurpillot, E. (1977). Rhythm perception in early infancy. *Nature, 266,* 718–719.

Dodd, B. (1977). The role of vision in the perception of speech. *Perception, 6,* 31–40.

Dowd, J. M. & Tronick, E. Z. (1986). Temporal coordination of arm movements in early infancy: Do infants move in synchrony with adult speech? *Child Development, 57,* 762–776.

Dowling, W. J. (1973). Rhythmic groups and subjective chunks in memory for melodies. *Perception and Psychophysics, 14,* 37–40.

Egeth, H. E. & Sager, L. C. (1977). On the locus of visual dominance. *Perception and Psychophysics, 22,* 77–86.

Eilers, R. E., Bull, D. H., Oller, D. K., & Lewis, D. (1984). The discrimination of vowel duration by infants. *Journal of the Acoustical Society of America, 75,* 1213–1218.

Fitzgerald, H. E., Lintz, L. M., Brackbill, Y., & Adams, G. (1967). Time perception and conditioning an autonomic response in human infants. *Perceptual and Motor Skills, 24,* 479–486.

Fraisse, P. (1982). The adaptation of the child to time. In W. J. Friedman (Ed.)., *The developmental psychology of time.* New York: Academic Press.

Friedman, W. J. (1982). Introduction. In W. J. Friedman (Ed.), *The developmental psychology of time.* New York: Academic Press.

Gardner, J. M. & Karmel, B. Z. (1981). Preferential looking at temporal frequencies in preterm infants. *Child Development, 52,* 1299–1301.

Gardner, J. M. & Karmel, B. Z. (1984). Arousal effects on visual preferences in neonates.

Developmental Psychology, 20, 374–377.

Gardner, J. M., Lewkowicz, D. J., Rose, S. A., & Karmel, B. Z. (1986). Effects of visual and auditory stimulation on subsequent visual preferences in neonates. *International Journal of Behavioural Development, 9*, 251–263.

Goldstone, S. & Goldfarb, J. L. (1966). The perception of time by children. In A. H. Kidd & J. L. Rivoire (Eds.), *Perceptual Development in children.* New York: Academic Press.

Handel, S. (1973). Temporal segmentation of repeating auditory patterns. *Journal of Experimental Psychology, 101*, 46–54.

Harner, L. (1982). Talking about the past and future. In W. J. Friedman (Ed.), *The developmental psychology of time.* New York: Academic Press.

Humphrey, K., Tees, R. C., & Werker, J. (1979). Auditory-visual integration of temporal relations in infants. *Canadian Journal of Psychology, 33*, 347–352.

Irwin, R. J., Ball, A. K. R., Kay, N., Stillman, J. A., & Rosser, J. (1985). The development of auditory temporal acuity in children. *Child Development, 56*, 614–620.

Jasnow, M. & Feldstein, S. (1986). Adult-like temporal characteristics of mother-infant vocal interactions. *Child Development, 57*, 754–761.

Jusczyk, P. W., Pisoni, D. B., Reed, M. A., Fernald, A., & Myers, M. (1983). Infants' discrimination of the duration of a rapid spectrum change in nonspeech signals. *Science, 222*, 175–176.

Karmel, B.Z., Lester, M.L., McCarvill, S.L, Brown, P., & Hofman, M.J. (1977). Correlation of infants' brain and behavior response to temporal changes in visual stimulation. *Psychophysiology, 14*, 134–142.

Kaufmann, F., Stucki, M., & Kaufmann-Hayoz, R. (1985). Development of infants' sensitivity for slow and rapid motions. *Infants Behavior and Development, 8*, 89–98.

Kaufmann-Hayoz, R., Kaufman, F., & Stucki, M. (1986). Kinetic contours in infants' visual perception. *Child Development, 57*, 292–299.

Kellman, P. J. & Spelke, E. S. (1983). Perception of partly occluded objects in infancy. *Cognitive Psychology, 15*, 483–524.

Kuhl, P. K. & Meltzoff, A. N. (1982). The bimodal perception of speech in infancy. *Science, 218*, 1138–1140.

Lester, B. M., Hoffman, J., & Brazelton, T. B. (1985). The rhythmic structure of mother-infant interaction in term and preterm infants. *Child Development, 56*, 15–27.

Levin, I., Wilkening, F., & Dembo, Y. (1984). Development of time quantification: Integration and nonintegration of beginnings and endings in comparing durations. *Child Development, 55*, 2160–2172.

Lewkowicz, D. J. & Turkewitz, G. (1980). Cross-modal equivalence in early infancy: auditory-visual intensity matching. *Developmental Psychology, 16*, 597–607.

Lewkowicz, D. J. & Turkewitz, G. (1981). Intersensory interaction in newborns: Modification of visual preferences following exposure to sound. *Child Development, 52*, 827–832.

Lewkowicz, D. J. (1985a). Developmental changes in infants' response to temporal frequency. *Developmental Psychology, 21*, 858–865.

Lewkowicz, D. J. (1985b). Bisensory response to temporal frequency in 4–month-old infants. *Developmental Psychology, 21*, 306–317.

Lewkowicz, D. J. (1986). Developmental changes in infants' bisensory response to synchronous durations. *Infant Behavior and Development, 9*, 335–353.

Lewkowicz, D. J. (1988). Sensory dominance in infants: 1. Six-month-old infants' response to auditory-visual compounds. *Developmental Psychology, 24*, 155–171.

Lewkowicz, D. J. (1988). Sensory dominance in infants: 2. Ten-month-old infants' response to auditory-visual compounds. *Developmental Psychology, 24*, 172–182.

Marquis, D. P. (1941). Learning in the neonate: The modification of behavior under three feeding schedules. *Journal of Experimental Psychology, 29*, 263–282.

McGurk, H. & MacDonald, J. (1976). Hearing lips and seeing voices. *Nature, 264*, 746–748.

Mendelson, M. J. (1986). Perception of the temporal pattern of motion in infancy. *Infant Behavior and Development, 9*, 231–243.

Mendelson, M. J. & Ferland, M. B. (1982). Auditory-visual transfer in four-month-old infants. *Child Development, 53*, 1022–1027.

Millar, W. S. & Watson, J.S. (1979). The effect of delayed feedback on infant learning reexamined. *Child Development, 50*, 747–751.

Miller, C. L. & Byrne, J. M. (1984). The role of temporal cues in the development of communication. In L. Feagans, C. Garvey, & R. Golinkoff (Eds.), *The origins and growth of communication*. Norwood, N. J.: Ablex.

Moller, A. R. (1969). Unit responses in the rat cochlear nucleus to repetitive, transient sounds. *Acta Physiologica Scandinavica, 75*, 542–551.

Morrongiello, B. A. (1984). Auditory temporal pattern perception in 6– and 12–month-old infants. *Developmental Psychology, 20*, 441–448.

Nystrom, M., Hansson, M. B., & Marklund, K. (1975). Infant preference for intermittent light. *Psychological Research Bulletin, Lund University, 15*, 1–11.

Piaget, J. (1954). *The construction of reality in the child.* New York: Basic Books.

Pouthas, V. (1985). Timing behavior in young children: A developmental approach to conditioned spaced responding. In Michon, J. A. & Jackson, J. L. (Eds.) *Time, Mind, and Behavior.* New York: Springer-Verlag.

Radeau, M. & Bertelson, P. (1977). Adaptation to auditory-visual discordance and ventriloquism in semirealistic situations. *Perception and Psychophysics, 22*, 137–146.

Ramey, C. T. & Ourth, L. L. (1971). Delayed reinforcement of vocalization rates in infants. *Child Development, 42*, 291–297.

Regal, D. M. (1981). Development of critical flicker frequency in human infants. *Vision Research, 21*, 549–555.

Robertson, S. S. (1982). Intrinsic temporal patterning in the spontaneous movement of awake neonates. *Child Development, 53*, 1016–1021.

Robertson, S. S. (1985). Cyclic motor activity in human fetus after midgestation. *Developmental Psychobiology, 18*, 411–419.

Rosenfeld, H. (1981). Whither interactional synchrony? In K. Bloom (Ed.), Prospective issues in infancy research (pp. 71–97). Hillsdale, N.J.: Lawrence Erlbaum.

Ruff, H. A. (1985). Detection of information specifying the motion of objects by 3– and 5–month-old infants. *Developmental Psychology, 21*, 295–305.

Spelke, E. S. (1976). Infants' intermodal perception of events. *Cognitive Psychology, 8*, 553–560.

Spelke, E. S. (1979). Perceiving bimodally specified events in infancy. *Developmental Psychology, 15*, 626–636.

Spelke, E. S. (1981). The infants' acquisition of bimodally specified events. *Journal of Experimental Child Psychology, 31*, 279–299.

Spelke, E. S., Born, W. S. & Chu, F. (1983). Perception of moving, sounding objects by four-month-old infants. *Perception, 12*, 719–732.

Stamps, L. E. (1977). Temporal conditioning of heart rate responses in newborn infants. *Developmental Psychology, 13*, 624–629.

Stamps, L. E. & Porges, S. W. (1975). Heart rate conditioning in newborn infants: Relationships among conditionability, heart rate variability, and sex. *Developmental Psychology, 11*, 424–431.

Stern, D. N., Beebe, B., Jaffe, J., & Bennet, S. L. (1977). The infant's stimulus world during social interaction: A study of caregiver behaviours with particular reference to repetition and timing. In H. R. Shaffer (Ed.), *Studies in mother-infant interaction.* New York: Academic Press.

Stern, D. N. & Gibbon, J. (1979). Temporal expectations of social behavior in mother-infant play. In E. B. Thoman (Ed.), *Origins of the infant's social responsiveness.* Hillsdale, N.J.: Erlbaum.

Stern, E., Parmelee, A. H., Akiyama, Y., Schultz, M., & Wenner, W. H. (1969). Sleep cycle characteristics in infants. *Pediatrics, 43,* 65–70.

Stern, E., Parmelee, A. H. & Harris, M. (1973). Sleep state periodicity in prematures and young infants. *Developmental Psychobiology, 6,* 357–365.

Stratton, P. (1982). Rhythmic functions in the newborn. In P. Stratton (Ed.), *Psychobiology of the human newborn.* New York: J. Wiley & Sons.

Thelen, E. (1979). Rhythmical stereotypies in normal human infants. *Animal Behavior, 27,* 699–715.

Thelen, E. (1981). Rhythmical behavior in infancy: An ethological perspective. *Developmental Psychology, 17,* 237–257.

Tronick, E., Als, H., & Brazelton, T. B. (1980). Monadic phases: A structural descriptive analysis of infant-mother face-to-face interaction. *Merrill-Palmer Quarterly, 26,* 3.

Turco, T. L. & Stamps, L. E. (1980). Heart rate conditioning in young infants using a visual conditional stimulus. *Journal of Experimental Child Psychology, 29,* 117–125.

Washburn, K. J. & Cohen, L. B. (1984). *Infant perception of rhythmic form.* Paper presented at the International Conference on Infant Studies, New York.

Watson, J. S. (1979). Perception of contingency as a determinant of social responsiveness. In E. Thoman (Ed.), *The origins of social responsiveness.* (pp. 33–64). Hillsdale, N.J.: Lawrence Erlbaum Associates.

Watson, J. S. (1984). Bases of causal inference in infancy: Time, space, and sensory relations. In L.P. Lipsitt & C. Rovee-Collier (Eds.), *Advances in infancy research,* Vol. 13, 152–165. Norwood, N.J.: Ablex Publishing Corp.

Wilkening, F. (1982). Children's knowledge about time, distance, and velocity interrelations. In W. J. Friedman (Ed.), *The developmental psychology of time.* New York: Academic Press.

Yonas, A. & Granrud, C. E. (1985). Development of visual space perception in young infants. In J. Mehler & R. Fox (Eds.). *Neonate Cognition: Beyond the Blooming and Buzzing Confusion.* Hillsdale, N. J.: Lawrence Erlbaum Associates.

TIME AND HUMAN COGNITION
A Life-Span Perspective
I. Levin and D. Zakay (Editors)

CHAPTER 2

RICHARD M. WEIST

Time Concepts in Language and Thought: Filling the Piagetian Void from Two to Five Years*

INTRODUCTION

In his 1978 review of the developmental literature concerning time concepts, Friedman stated that, "there is no research that fills the gap between Piaget's infant work and his studies of temporal seriation of 6 to 10–year-olds" (p. 274) and in a similar vein "information about cognitive development in the important growth period of 1–4 years is either completely lacking or unreliable" (Campbell, 1986, p. 38). While recent research has closed the gap somewhat (see Friedman 1982a), very little is known about the period from about 1;6 to about 4;6. Friedman (1978) partitioned the research on the development of temporality into the areas of experiential, logical and conventional time. Experiential time, "refers to the subjective impression of the passage of time" (p. 269); logical time, "pertains to the Newtonian scheme of correlating a given event with a unique position

*I would like to acknowledge the support of the National Science Foundation (grant BNS–8617776), the Kościuszko Foundation, the National Academies of Science in Poland (Grant 157/I) and the United States, and State University of New York – College at Fredonia.

on a temporal continuum" (269); and conventional time, "refers to the knowledge of socially shared systems which organize temporal phenomena" (269). Friedman's review of the literature within the framework of these distinctions led him to the following conclusion: "... experiential time is a primitive mode, while conventional and logical time are poorly developed before the age of about 8 years" (p. 294). The claims that experiential time is primitive and that conventional time develops relatively late appear to be well founded (e.g. Fraisse, 1982 and Friedman, 1982b). In this chapter, I plan to take issue with the assertion that logical time is poorly developed before 8 years of age.

The prototypical research on the topic of logical time involves two vehicles which move along a parallel course at variable speeds starting and stopping with a variety of time-space relationships. Even the most sensitive research requiring f fewer inferences (e.g. Levin 1982), has failed to breach the developmental period from 1;6 to 4;6. In this chapter, I will approach the problem of logical time indirectly by drawing inferences about what children know about temporality from what they say. If an adult were to make a statement such as, *While waiting at the doctor's office yesterday from 3 to 5 P.M., I became extremely bored*, we could infer that the speaker understands conventional time and can express experiential time. Concerning logical time, the speaker is able to establish a temporal reference of a specific duration during the daily cycle prior to the speech time cycle. The speaker can also specify that some event involving a change of state occurred within the context of that interval, also prior to the time of the speech act. How do children get from their initial here-and-now system of communication to this level of complex temporal expression?

Based on theoretical work in philosophy and linguistics (e.g., Comrie, 1985, Reichenbach, 1947, and Smith, 1980 & 1983) and observations of the acquisition of a large variety of languages (see Slobin, 1985), I formulated a theory of temporal systems in child language (Weist, 1982 & 1986). The theory outlines a developmental sequence of four temporal systems where each system contains a network of interrelated time concepts. As children acquire language, the configurations of time concepts which they can comprehend and produce become increasingly complex. The purpose of this chapter is to develop and to expand the previous hypothesis (see Weist, 1985 & 1986) that innovations in the evolution of temporal systems have indirect implications for the nature of conceptual schema. The form of the argument is that the emergence of temporal relations in child language provides a sufficient (*not* a necessary) condition for inferring changes in the child's conceptual framework. Hence, if there are dramatic changes in temporal systems between 1;6 and 4;6 (and there are!), the analysis of those changes can tell us something about the child's understanding of time concepts during a period of development which is void of direct research. My strategy in this chapter is to outline the evolution of four temporal systems, to present a hypothetical set of language-thought inferences, and then to develop an argument for each inference. I will define linguistic concepts with increasing detail as the argument requires.

At this point, a few background remarks will be useful. The speaker acts in the center of a spatio-temporal-personal context. Relationships established between the speaker and the components of this context are called deictic relationships, e.g. *here* is near the speaker, *yesterday* is the cyclic interval prior to the time of speech, and *you* is the listener. While the focus of this chapter is on temporal deixis, spatial and personal deixis are inescapably relevant. Tense (more specifically absolute tense) morphology codes the deictic relationships between the time of the speech act and the time of some event. In English, for example, the second morpheme in the word *jumped* specifies that the action occurred prior to the time of speaking. Not all languages code tense, but when they do, it is likely to interact with aspect and modality. It is not possible to ignore this fact when investigating temporal development. Aspect (more specifically viewpoint aspect) refers to the temporal perspective that the speaker takes concerning a situation. When the speaker views the situation from an internal perspective, properties such as ongoing and incomplete are potentially salient, and when the speaker views the situation from an external perspective, properties such as complete and punctual are available. In English, the property of ongoing (or continuous) is coded with the progressive aspect, e.g. *is jump-ing*. Modality refers to the concepts of necessity and possibility which are coded in English by modal verbs such as *must* and *might*. In order to determine the conceptual implications of linguistic development, we will have to tease apart modality, aspect, and tense.

It is assumed that the quality of inferences which are made about conceptual development from the observations of linguistic development depends to a large degree on the quality of cross-linguistic perspective which is included in the inquiry. The reason for this is relatively clear. The child's capacity to express temporal distinctions depends on the relationship between the way in which the distinction is coded and the way in which children process information. If there is a match, the distinction will be relatively easy to process (see Slobin 1973, 1982, & 1985). Hence in Polish, it is relatively easy for children to discover the code for past tense because the past tense morpheme is perceptually salient, phonetically stable, consistently positioned, and obligatory in a well defined context.

The child must not only discover the code for temporal distinctions, the child must also construct the system of rules which controls their use. Again language specific factors come into play. The rule system which embodies the distinction may be transparent or opaque for the child. In Polish, the relationship between tense, aspect, and modality is relatively clear. This makes it easy for the child to use a distinction such as past tense. As a result children will express some distinctions in some languages more rapidly than in others.

Some general typological factors are also relevant to the acquisition process and our capacity to detect the emergence of important innovations will depend partly on the overall form of the language. The contrast between analytic and synthetic languages is quite relevant in this regard. A language is considered relatively analytic to the extent to which the words contain relatively few morphemes, and it is considered relatively synthetic to the extent to which the words contain a relatively large number of morphemes. In English, past tense is formed in a synthetic manner by combining the stem and a suffix in a single word, e.g. *walk* plus–*ed* equals *walked*, and in contrast, future tense can be formed in an analytic way by using the modal verb *will* plus the main verb, e.g. *walk*. In general, English is closer to the analytic end of the continuum, and languages like Finnish and Polish are closer to the synthetic end of the continuum. In a highly synthetic language, there is no such thing as a bare stem (c.f. English–*boy*, *walk*, and *large*) that the child can use while waiting to analyze the morphology. The child is forced to deal with the morphology from the earliest phases of development. Hence, cross-linguistic perspective should include a contrast between analytic and synthetic languages.

Temporal Systems in Child Language

My argument is that children progress through a series of four temporal systems; the speech time (ST) system, the event time (ET) system, the restricted reference time (RT_r) system, and the free reference time (RT_f) system. In the speech time system, the child's language is relatively, but not exclusively, limited to the child's immediate perceptual environment. The system is primarily a here-and-now communication system. Speech time, which is the time of the speech act, is the only functional time concept within this linguistic system. Initially, children code events as if they occurred during the speech time interval, and the child's point of temporal reference is also at speech time. The modal distinction between statements and requests is expressed, but typically within a frozen morphology.

During the interval from about 1;6 to 2;0, children begin to express some fundamental aspectual concepts which reflect the basic contrast between internal and external perspective on situations, e.g., ongoing versus completed. At 1;9, Marta, one of the children in our study of the acquisition of Polish, was describing an encounter with some cows on a farm.[2] First she said, *Wystraszy-ł-y-∅ (się' te krówki*, got:frighten:PFV-PAST-NVIR–3:P (REF) these cows, 'These cows got frightened'. The verb *wystraszyć* is perfective in aspect and the utterance codes a completed situation. Later, after a turn in the conversation, Marta was asked who frightened the cows, *kogo*? 'of whom'. She replied, *∅–straszy-ł–a–∅ krówki*, IPFV-frighten-PAST-FEM–3:S cows, '(Marta) was frightening the cows', and she walked around the room showing how she had done it. In the second utterance, Marta took an internal perspective on the situation and used the imperfective aspect (see Sentences 3 & 4 below).

During a similar phase of development (but depending to some extent on the specific tense, aspect, modality system), children begin to express deictic relationships between speech time and event time; where event time refers to the time relative to speech time which is established for some event. These distinctions are initially coded by a past versus nonpast contrast. Because reference time remains frozen at speech time, the second temporal system, identified as the event time system, has two functional time concepts; i.e., event time and speech time. At 1;8, Eva (see Bowerman, 1981 p. 34) said, *Ernie fell off* when commenting on the fact that she had just dropped the finger puppet named Ernie. When Daniel (2;2) (see Fletcher 1979 p. 272) remarked that, *Mummy painted the wall*, he was making reference to a situation which occurred two months earlier. However, neither Daniel nor Eva established an explicit point of reference. We only know that the children were placing some situation anterior to speech time.

During the period from 2;6 to 3;0, children begin to shift reference time away from speech time. Here, reference time is defined as the temporal context for an event. Initially, the temporal configurations which children are able to express are limited. Reference time either remains at speech time, as it does with a present perfect form, or it incorporates the time of the event, as it does with a simple past form. While three time concepts are functional, only two intervals of time are coordinated. Therefore, this system was referred to as the restricted reference time system. During this period, children begin to use temporal adverbs and adverbial clauses. Hence, children are now capable of expressing a point of reference such as 'yesterday' or 'tomorrow' and then talking about an event within that context.

By the time Finnish children are about 2;6, they demonstrate the capacity to use present perfect as well as simple past. At 2;5, Katja said, *Kuka se vetä–nyt*, Who this pull:off-PAST:ACTIVE:PART, 'who (has) pulled (the arms off the doll'? This is a prototypical use of the present perfect since Katja's question shows that she did not personally experience the prior situation. The results of the situation were present during speech time, and Katja's point of reference was at speech time (see Toivainen, 1980 p. 68). When Peter (3;2) said, *It's not anywhere. You better look for it when you get back home*, he used an adverbial clause to establish reference time at an interval subsequent to speech time and proposed that a specific event will occur within this temporal context. (Bloom, Lahey, Hood, Lifter, & Fiess, 1980 p. 244).

From about 4;0 to 4;6, the free reference time system emerges, at which time children can manipulate the concepts of speech time, event time, and reference time independently. They begin to contrast the temporal prepositions '*before*' and '*after*' and to use past perfect which requires the coordination of three temporal intervals. One of the children in a current research project of ours constructed the following two temporal configurations: 1) When asked what she had done earlier in the day, Monica (4;5) said: *I just played with something and after that I just walked around a little.*; and 2) While explaining when she played with her doll last and when she planned to play with her doll again, Monica (4;5) said: *This last weekend when I comed back home, and then I'm gonna this week, and then when I get home I'm going to play.* In the first utterance, Monica used the activity of playing as a reference to be followed by the walking around activity. In contrast, the terminal point of the achievement *arrival-at-home* marks the point of reference for playing in the second utterance.

Temporal Systems and Conceptual Development

In this paper, I want to explore the relationship between the evolution of temporal systems and conceptual development. The specific proposal is that the evolution of temporal systems in child language provides indirect evidence for the following conceptual developments: 1) ST system – object permanence, 2) ET system – displacement, 3) RT_r system – nonegocentric temporal perspective (or decentration) and, 4) RT_f system – seriation and reversibility.

THE ST SYSTEM AND OBJECT PERMANENCE

The focus of this chapter will be on the transitions from the ST to the ET system and from the ET to the RT systems. The ET system includes the relationship ET precedes ST. I will argue below that in order for a child to utilize the logic of the ET system, she must be able to retrieve the representation of some situation from memory and understand that this situation occurred prior to speech time. The capacity to conceptualize such a temporal relationship requires that children have the ability to construct relatively permanent representations of objects and events. If, at this phase of development, "out of sight" still meant "out of mind", there would be no representation to retrieve. Hence, in this section the goal is to demonstrate that children achieve object permanence during a phase in their linguistic development in which deictic relations between ST and ET are not yet coded. In fact, this is the least controversial part of this chapter. However, it can be taken as axiomatic that there are no claims about relationships between language and thought which are without controversy (e.g., see Corrigan, 1979).

To begin with, we can not count on two of the most often cited slogans concerning this period of development. At about 0;5, when children are failing Stage 4 tests of object permanence, "out of sight" does not mean "out of mind" and during the period from about 1;0 to 1;6 when child language is described as concerning the "here-and-now," children make reference to objects and events which are not part of the immediate perceptual environment. In other words, objects have a sense of permanence before children solve Piagetian hide-and-seek tasks, and children make reference to prior situations and anticipate subsequent situations prior to coding those relationships in their language. Bower and his colleagues (see Bower's 1974 review) demonstrated that infants of about 0;5 anticipate the reappearance of an object occluded by a screen and demonstrate a kind of visual tracking "double take" when the occluded object reappears in a different form. Spelke and her colleagues (see Spelke's 1985 review) presented children with a rotating screen which first occluded a block situated behind it, and then passed through the space formerly occupied by the block. Five month old infants were surprised by this "impossible" movement. Concerning the notion of identity, Spelke concluded that, "infants perceive an object to maintain its identity if it is displaced as a unit and if its displacement is continuous in space and time" (p. 108).

Recognition memory research with five month old children suggests that the five month old child's sense of object identity is not restricted to systematic perceptual transformations. In paired comparison tests of recognition memory, Fagan (1973) has found that five month old children show signs of facial recognition which persists for two weeks. Children have at least five or more months of conceptual development to expand on their infant conceptualizations of objects before the onset of holophrastic speech.

With hindsight, it is not surprising that there is little correspondence between general measures of early language development such as vocabulary size and the capacity to solve increasingly difficult hide-and-seek tasks (see Corrigan, 1979). The searching behavior required to solve hide-and-seek tasks is apparently neither a necessary nor a sufficient condition for the construction of conceptual representations.

During the period of language development which involves a ST temporal system, there are two particularly salient behaviors which correspond to Piagetian measures of object permanence and which demonstrate that this phase of child language is not restricted to the immediate spatio-temporal environment. They are the use of words such as "gone" and "more" and the recounting of past experiences. While Corrigan (1978) failed to find a significant partial correlation between an adjusted MLU score and levels of the Uzgiris-Hunt scale of object permanence, she did find that her three informants solved the most difficult Stage 6–serial-invisible-displacement task before using the words *more* and *gone* to spontaneously comment upon the recurrence and disappearance of objects.

Gopnik (1984), Gopnik and Meltzoff (1984), McCune-Nicolich (1981), and Tomasello and Farrar (1984) probed further into the relationship between the level of object permanence and the use of relational words. Tomasello and Farrar considered both "present" and "absent" relational words referring to "transformations of objects/persons" which occur within versus partially or totally outside the child's perceptual field, e.g., *bye* in contrast to *gone*. Present relational words emerged at about 1;1 to 1;2 during or after Stage 5 (which entails visible displacements) and absent relational words at about 1;5 to 1;10 during or after Stage 6 (which requires invisible displacements).

Gopnik (1984) concentrated on the word *gone* and its variants (e.g., *all gone*). Children said *gone* when: 1) watching an object disappear, 2) searching for missing objects, 3) commenting on empty containers and 4) observing a sudden transformation (see Table 1, p. 277). Gopnik and Meltzoff (1984) compared the use of *gone* to performance on the Uzgiris & Hunt (1975) scale of object permanence. They found that all of the children who failed to find an object following one invisible displacement with three screens (i.e., failed Level 13) did not use *gone*. The children who passed Level 13 and failed Level 14 were evenly distributed in their use of *gone*. All but one of those who were able to find an object following a series of invisible displacements (i.e., pass Level 14) used *gone.* The authors concluded that the most parsimonious explanation "proposes a more thorough going interaction between linguistic and cognitive development than either the classical Piagetian or Vygotskyan accounts" (p. 511). The idea is that children acquire a moderate understanding of objects and object transformations, then they learn words to express this knowledge. They advance their conceptual development through the interaction of new experiences with perceptual transformations and with the use of the words which code these transformations.

In addition to using relational terms prior to the transition from ST system to the ET system, children also recount previous experiences. Subsequent to Stage 6 object permanence Piaget (1962, p. 222) observed Jacqueline at 1;7 saying, 'Hopper, hopper jump boy' while drawing an analogy between the activity of a grasshopper and a situation which occurred two days earlier with her cousin (see also Ingram's, 1978 review). Piaget put a great deal of emphasis on this recounting behavior stating that, "these behaviors are an illustration of the turning point at which language in process of construction ceases to be merely an accompaniment to an action in progress, and is used for the reconstruction of past action" (p. 222).

The fact that children talk about prior situations before they begin to use past tense morphology has been reasonably well documented. Bowerman's daughter Christy (1;6) said, *man shout* when her mother came to get her in the morning. One hour earlier, the voices of the garbage men were heard from the alley. Christy repeated the utterance and demonstrated shouting noises between repetitions. In addition to commenting on past events, Christy also reported on past events at 1;7, for example, she told her mother, *No no mouth! /oeni/daddy mouth*, which referred to the fact that her father had told her not to put beads in her mouth. Christy did not begin to use irregular past forms until 1;10 and the regular past tense inflections were not considered productive until about 2;5. Bowerman's daughter Eva also made references to past events well before the relationship of anteriority was coded in her morphology. After climbing to the top of a bunk bed to look at some party balloons from three weeks earlier, Eva (1;6) said, *Balloon. Pop. Balloon. Balloon.* Eva's first irregular past forms were found at 1;8 and she established the regular past inflection at 1;11 (Bowerman, 1981). Sachs's Naomi began to make reference to immediate past situations at 1;5 and the regular past tense morphology emerged at 1;11 (Sachs 1983). Roger Brown made a similar observation in the development of Adam, Eve, and Sarah (Brown, 1973).

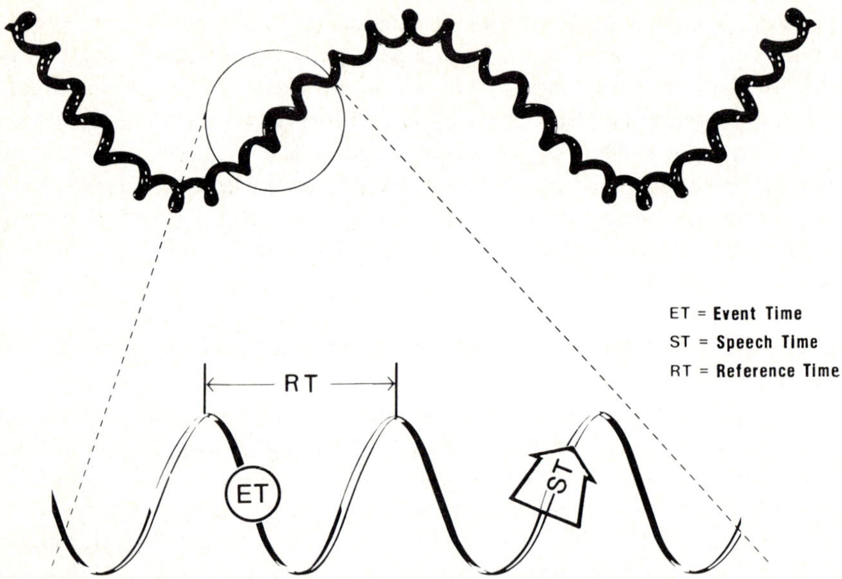

Figure 2.1. The recoiling coil represents a model of the adult's concept of time flow.

THE ET SYSTEM AND DISPLACEMENT

It is assumed that perception involves the construction of a representation of some selected component of the here-and-now environment. Displacement refers to the capacity to retrieve the representation of some prior situation which has been stored in episodic memory and to understand that the representation corresponds to a situation which occurred prior to the time interval of the current stream of consciousness. Furthermore, displacement refers to the capacity to use information which is stored in long-term memory (i.e. concepts and processing rules as well as episodic representations) to construct the representation of a situation with the expectation that the situation has the potential of occurring subsequent to the time interval of the current stream of consciousness. Thus, displacement refers to the capacity to think about situations which are remote in time and space, either recollections or anticipations. It requires that children understand the relationships anterior and posterior to the time of ongoing perceptual processing.

The adult's representation of time flow can be modeled by a coil which forms higher order coils, i.e. a recoiling coil as shown in Figure 2.1 (see also Weist 1985). The model can not be a simple time line because it must have cyclic properties as well as the property of consistent progress. When adults retrieve a representation of some prior situation, they have the capacity to locate (precisely or vaguely) the situation along the time coil. Hence, when an adult uses *yesterday* as his/her reference time interval, s/he is referring to the prior daily cycle. The adult can then use the prior daily cycle as a frame of reference to locate some event. Displacement, as the term is used here, entails only the primitive capacity to locate a situation prior to or subsequent to the current/ongoing frame of temporal reference, i.e. the deictic center, and it does *not* entail the location of some situation within some interval along a time coil. Yet the capacity for displacement signals a major breakthrough in the child's thought processes releasing the child from the constraints of the here-and-now.

Figure 2.2 contains a representation of two models of time flow which correspond to the ST and ET phases in the evolution of temporal systems.

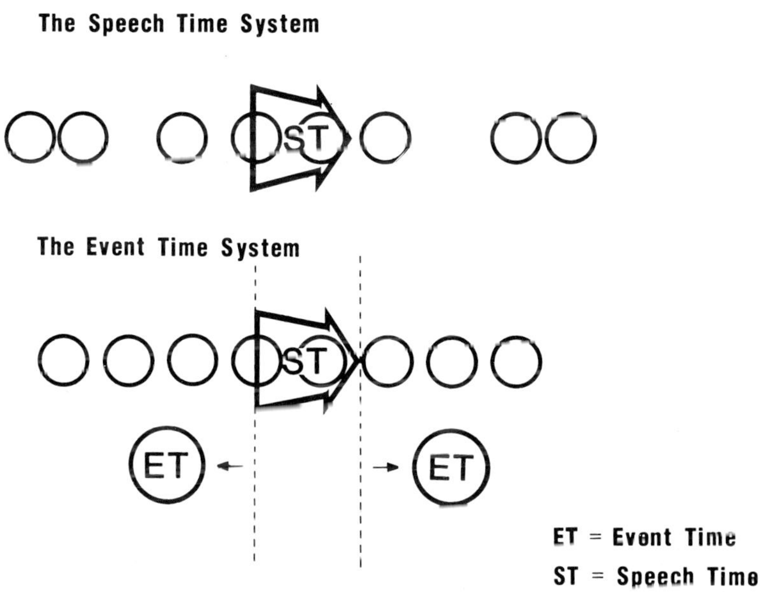

Figure 2.2. Time flow models for children during the phases of development corresponding to the ST and the ET temporal systems.

Both models contain a series of dots which portray the child's fuzzy conceptualization of time flow at this point in development. Clearly the child's model of time flow can not be a coil, much less a recoiling coil, since it lacks the property of cyclicity. Keeping in mind that these models pertain to child language, the initial system contains only the concept of ST. When the children shift into the ET system at about 1;6 to 2;0, they only locate events prior to and subsequent to speech time. As yet there is no evidence that they are able to code even relative remoteness, much less defining such intervals as yesterday, in the summer, or next week. However, we do not yet have data on the acquisition of languages with remote tenses (see Comrie 1985 Ch. 4).

What can we look for in child language which will enable us to infer that children have the capacity for displacement? Since absolute tense codes the relationships ET prior to ST, ET simultaneous with ST, and ET subsequent to ST, the language-thought inference should be transparent; i.e. when absolute tense is observed, displacement can be inferred. The inference is not so simple because there is a complex interaction of tense with aspect and modality. A dominant argument has been that past tense morphology does not code the deictic relationships ET prior to ST but the aspectual property of completion or result (e.g. Antinucci & Miller 1976 and Bronckart & Sinclair, 1978) and that future tense does not code ET subsequent to ST but some modal meaning of intension or desire (e.g. Aksu, 1978 and Stephany, 1981). Furthermore, some investigators have argued that tense does not code deictic relationships because children can not conceptualize these relationships, i.e., they lack the capacity for displacement (see Antinucci & Miller, 1976). In the next two sections, we will look at this argument closely and determine if tense in child language can be used to make inferences about displacement.

Past Tense and Aspect

In order to determine if tense morphology codes tense or aspect, the concept of aspect requires further explanation. There are two types of aspect; situational (or lexical) aspect (also called *aktionsart*) and viewpoint aspect (often simply referred to as aspect). The notion of situational aspect is based on a classification of situation types which has been elucidated in recent years by Vendler (1967), Dowty (1979), Smith (1986) and others. In general, aspect concerns the temporal (or dynamic) structure of situations. Some intrinsic situational properties are particularly relevant to language. Accordingly, the set of situations can be partitioned into static (or states) versus dynamic (or events), with the dynamic set further divided into atelic (or activities) versus telic, and finally telic into accomplishments and achievements.

States are stable situations, such as *to be compulsive*, *to know Polish*, or *to love sunshine.* A state will remain stable unless something happens to change it. The stages are neither differentiated nor successive, and there are no inherent boundaries, i.e., initial or final points. Activities involve pure action such as to *cycle*, to *ski*, or to *drink beer.* The stages are homogeneous and successive and the activity can end on any stage. Accomplishments (like achievements) have a clear terminal point such as to *build a wheel*, to *cook a steak*, or to *read an article.* The stages are successive but heterogeneous and there are natural initial and final points. Achievements involve processes which are "intimately bound up" (Comrie, 1976 Ch. 2) with the terminal point such as *to notice Gretchen*, *to reach the summit*, or *to win the race.* There may be preliminary stages but the initial and final points are simultaneous. This classification system has been very influential in the analysis of aspect in a large variety of languages and it has played a key role in the debate about temporal development (see Smith & Weist, 1987).

Whereas distinctions such as activity and accomplishment are coded in the lexicon, viewpoint aspect is likely to be coded in the morphology. The semantic domain of aspect includes such concepts as completion, duration, and repetition. Within this domain the most fundamental distinction contrasts the external with the internal viewpoint of situations. When a situation is viewed externally, either completion or result is potentially a salient property; when viewed internally, either continuation or duration may be salient. Let us consider the accomplishment of building a house. From an external perspective, we can conceptualize the situation as having a beginning, an interpolated phase, and an end, i.e. as complete, or we can focus on the termination or the resulting product. In English, the simple tense form is used to obtain this perfective viewpoint, e.g. *He built the house.* From the internal perspective, the activities of building extend through time and are potentially available to be coded. In English, the progressive form is used for this viewpoint, e.g. *He was building the house when something happened.* Some situations, such as the activity of taking a walk, leave no result which excludes resultative from the properties which can be coded given an external perspective. Other situations occur in an instance, such as the achievement of noticing someone, and a sequence with repeated occurrences is needed for internal perspective, i.e. an iterative aspectual value. In Slavic languages, the distinction between external and internal perspective is made with perfective and imperfective aspect. The distinction is pervasive in the world's languages (see Dahl, 1985 and Bybee, 1985).

A number of investigators of child language have argued that the equivalent of the distinction between perfective versus imperfective is made by children during the period from about 1;6 to 2;0 (e.g., Aksu 1978 for Turkish, Antinucci & Miller 1976 for Italian, Bronckart & Sinclair 1973 for French, Erbaugh 1982 for Mandarin, Fletcher 1979 in a review of English, Stephany 1981 for Greek, etc.). However, according to many of these investigators the distinction between perfective and imperfective is coded in child language with past versus nonpast tense morphology. This hypothesis was called the defective tense hypothesis based on the claim that the tense morphology of the child and the adult have different functions.

Why do children use tense morphology defectively? The answer to this question is one of the critical points of this chapter. According to Antinucci and Miller (1976), "at this point in his development (1;6 to 2;5), in fact, the child lacks an abstract conception of time that would allow him to construct, between any two events x and y, the relation *Event X precedes Event Y . . .* (p. 184)." Hence, the child could not construct the relationship ET precedes ST. Children use tense morphology defectively because they lack the basic conceptual capacity to do otherwise.[3] Instead of locating events in time, they code aspectual properties of situations.

More specifically, Antinucci and Miller (1976) argued that Italian children refer to states which exist during the speech time interval. These states are the result of a prior change of states. In order to do this, Italian children use the *passato prossimo* form which consists of an auxiliary and a past participle. In the adult language, the past participle agrees with the direct object only if it is pronominalized. Italian children invent a general agreement rule whereby the past participle *always* agrees with the direct object, e.g., (1;10) *La signora ha chius – a la port – a* (c.f. adult *ha chius – o*), 'The woman closed the door.' In this example the child's form of the past participle *chiusa* agrees in gender with the direct object *porta.* They observed that children used the *passato prossimo* in reference only to telic situations such as fall, arrive, break, and close. According to the argument, the children could not refer to atelic (or activity) situations in this way because activities do not leave resultative products which can linger through time into the speech time interval. As their argument was related to Piagetian theory, children presumably can not construct a representation unless, "the past event (process) and present moment (end-state) are related not simply by an abstract temporal relation but by a more concrete effectual relation" (p. 183). In summary, Antinucci and Miller's (1976) major empirical contribution to the defective tense hypothesis was in the domain of situational aspect, i.e., children only use *passato prossimo* to refer to telic situations.

Stephany (1981) added the observation that Greek children never use the imperfective past form. From 1;8 to 1;11, the children she observed contrasted the imperfective nonpast with the perfect past without using the imperfective past form. It could be argued that children are contrasting perfective with imperfective aspect and tense differences are simply redundant.

What if we found children using imperfective as well as perfective past forms? Could we finally be guaranteed that the deictic use of tense has evolved? Stephany (1986) and others have argued to the contrary. Imperfective past forms may code an epistemic modal meaning where epistemic modality generally concerns the notion of possibility. Stephany presented data from a variety of languages to support the position that "the first use of the imperfective past has been observed to be not a temporal, but a modal one, serving to describe simulated activities and states, and to set the stage and assign character roles in pretend play" (p. 393). It is important to note that most of the examples cited by Stephany were from three-year-old children.

It would not be difficult to get the impression that there is no linguistic evidence for deictic past reference until after three years of age. In fact, when we began our research on child Polish about ten years ago, the only thing some investigators were relatively sure about was that deictic tense evolves before *six* years of age, e.g. "Although the two-year-olds in the present study did not appear to be using the inflectional morphemes as tense markers, it is *probably* not true that such learning would wait until age 6, as claimed by Bronckart & Sinclair" (Bloom, Lifter, and Hafitz 1980 p. 407 emphasis mine).

Table 2.1.
THE INTERACTION OF TENSE AND ASPECT IN POLISH

	PREFIXATION	
TENSE	ASPECT	
	IPFV	PFV
PAST	robi-ł–a-ś do/make-PAST-FEM–2:S	z-robi-ł–a-ś PFV-do/make-PAST-FEM–2:S
PRES	robi-sz do/make:NPAST–2:S	
FUT	będzie-sz robi-ł–a be:FUT–2:S do/make-PP-FEM	z-robi-sz PFV-do/make:NPAST–2:S
	SUFFIXATION	
TENSE	ASPECT	
	IPFV	PFV
PAST	Sięga-ł–y-ś–m y reach-PAST-NVIR–1:P	Sięg-nę–ł–y-ś–my reach-PFV-PAST-NVIR–1:P
PRES	Sięga-my reach:NPAST–1:P	
FUT	będzie-my sięga-ł–y be:FUT–1P reach-PP-NVIR	Sięg-nie-my reach:NPAST-PFV–1:P

Evidence for Temporal Deixis

In the Poznań research project, Hanna Wysocka, Ewa Buczowska, Emilia Konieczna-Tou, Katarzyna Witkowska-Stadnik and I conducted a cross-sectional and longitudinal analysis of the development of the tense-aspect-modality system of Polish with the focus on aspect and tense. We simultaneously looked at viewpoint aspect, tense, situational aspect, relative remoteness, and realism. In Polish in the indicative mood, there are five possible combinations of three tenses and two aspects. There is no present-perfective. Viewpoint aspect is coded by prefixation, suffixation, full or partial suppletion, vowel alternation, and various combinations of these means. The brief summary shown in Table 2.1 was designed to be a minimal presentation of the tense-aspect system of Polish, and as such only the prefixation and one of the suffixation patterns were included. Concerning prefixation and the example *robi-ć/z-robi-ć*, do/make-INF/PFV-do/make-INF, 'to do/make', the perfective form is produced by adding the prefix *z–* to the imperfective stem *robi–*. In a similar pattern, the perfective form of the pair *sięga-ć/sięg-ną–ć*, reach-INF/reach-PFV-INF, 'to reach' is formed by adding the suffix *–n* to the imperfective stem *sięg–* (some facts about stem final linking vowels are omitted).

First, I will discuss what Polish children *might do* if they were to behave in a manner which would be consistent with the hypothesis that they code aspect first and tense later. They *might* begin by using the imperfective nonpast forms to talk about the here-and-now e.g. *robisz* 'you are doing' or *sięgamy* 'we are reaching'. At some point in development, they might attempt to code the aspectual concept of a completed situation. The simplest morphological solution would be to add a prefix or a suffix, and therefore, code perfective aspect e.g. *zrobisz* or *sięgniemy*. According to this hypothesis, aspect would be coded before tense, but aspect would be coded with aspect morphology and not with tense morphology. This simple solution would cause conversational havoc since the newly formed perfective nonpast forms would have future meaning to their caregivers (as can be seen in Table 2.1). This simple aspect before tense hypothesis does not make any pragmatic sense and Polish children do not consider it.

Alternatively, it is possible that Polish children start again with the imperfective nonpast form and use the past tense morpheme *ł* to code a completive aspectual meaning. Thus, the children might start with *robisz* 'you are doing/making' or *sięgamy* 'we are reaching' and then shift to *robiłaś* or *sięgałyśmy*. This would again put quite a strain on the conversation since imperfective past forms do not have a completive aspectual value. There is no evidence that children entertain this hypothesis. To be consistent with the defective tense hypothesis, the children would have to shift tense and aspect simultaneously using only the imperfective nonpast forms and the perfective past forms. However, the tense shift would have to be redundant with only the aspect morphology carrying information.

In contrast to these proposals about what Polish children *might* do, what they *do do* is to shift tense and aspect simultaneously using the tense morphology to code deictic relationships and the aspect morphology to code viewpoint aspect. The same pattern can be found in children learning other Slavic languages (e.g. Gvozdev, 1961 on Russian; Radulovic, 1975 on Serbo-Croatian; and Stojanova, 1987 on Bulgarian). There is a number of ways to support this argument (see Weist, 1983; Weist & Konieczna,

1985; and Weist, Wysocka, Witkowska-Stadnik, Buczowska & Konieczna, 1984). In this paper, I will concentrate on a descriptive analysis with the focus on the contrasting uses of individual verbs. This provides the strongest argument for productivity. All of the examples were taken from the children in our project. These children were recorded twice a month over a period of several months with the following starting ages: Marta 1;7, Bartosz 1;7, Wawrzon 2;2 and Kubuś 2;1.

VIEWPOINT ASPECT

Sentences 1–8 contain aspectual contrasts between perfective and imperfective verb forms where tense was a constant. Marta (1;9) produced Sentence 1 after listening to her father describe a situation in which she spilled coffee grounds on herself. Hence, Marta used the perfective form of the verb to ask a question about this completed situation, i.e., *z-robi-ł–a–∅*, PFV-do-PAST-FEM–3:S. In the context for Sentence 2, Marta's mother was explaining that Marta's voice was recorded on a tape-recorder. Marta touched the tape-recorder and asked what she was doing. In this context, she used the imperfective form of the verb, i.e. *∅–robi-ł–a–∅*, IPFV-do-PAST-FEM–3:S. The difference between Sentences 1 and 2 lies in the presence versus absence of the prefix *z*–(see also Table 2.1). As mentioned briefly above, Sentences 3 and 4 were produced by Marta (1;9) when she was asked to name some animals that she had seen in the country. After mentioning cows, she proceeded to explain that the cows became frightened. She used the past perfective verb from *wystrasz-y-ł–y–∅* (*się*). After a few turns in the conversation, Marta began to creep around the room demonstrating what she had been doing to the cows and describing that she had been frightening them. For this purpose she used a causative form of the verb and a secondary imperfective form. Marta's nonverbal actions confirmed the internal linguistic perspective that she was taking on the situation.

S1 – Marta (1;9) : Co z-robi-ł–a–∅?
What PFV-do-PAST-FEM–3:S?
'What did (Marta) do?'

S2 – Marta (1;10) : Co tam ma–∅? Co ∅–robi-ł–a–∅ Mart-usi-a
What there have:IPFV–3:S? What IPFV-do-PAST-FEM–3:S Marta-DIM-F:N:S
'What does (she) have there? What was Marta doing?'

S3 – Marta (1;9) : Wystrasz-y-ł–y–Ø (się)
Frighten-PFV-PAST–3:P (REF)
'(They/the cows) got frightened'.

S4 – Marta (1;9) : Ø–straszy-ł–a–Ø krów-k-i
IPFV-frighten-PAST-FEM–3:S cow-DIM-F:A:P
'(Marta) was frightening the cows'.

S5 – Bartosz (1;11) : Na-pisa-ł–e-m
PFV-write-PAST-MASC–1:S
'(I) wrote (it)'.

S6 – Bartosz (1;8) : Kto to tu Ø–pisa-ł–Ø–Ø?
Who this here IPFV-write-PAST-MASC–3:S
'Who was writing this here'?

S7 – Wawrzon (2;2): I będzie-my może Ø–budowa-ć
And be:FUT–1:P maybe IPFV-build-INF
'And maybe (we) will build'.

S8 – Wawrzon (2;2): Z-buduje–Ø ogrodzeni-e
PFV-build:NPAST–3:S fence-N:A:S
'(Daddy) will build the fence'.

In Sentence 5, Bartosz (1;11) responded to a question containing a verb in the perfective aspect, i.e. *Co z-robi-ł–e-ś*? What PFV-do-PAST-MASC–2:S, 'What did you do?, using a perfective verb form. He was confessing that he had written on the experimenter's notebook. In Sentence 6, Bartosz's father had called attention to the fact that Bartosz had some "drawings" on his stomach, and possibly in the hope of avoiding the blame for this art work, Bartosz (1;8) asked the naive question 'Who was writing here' pointing to his stomach. The absence of the prefix *na–* in the verb form *pisał* signals that the aspectual value was imperfective. Sentences 7 and 8 are interesting because the aspectual contrast is in the future tense. In Sentence 7, Wawrzon (2;2) is contemplating something that he and his friend might do, and there is clearly no sense of expected completion. The imperfective future is formed paraphrastically with the future form of *być* 'to be', i.e., *będzie-my*, plus the imperfective infinitive *budować*. In contrast, Sentence 8 contains the nonpast form of the perfective verb *z-budowa-ć* PFV-build-INF 'to build'. The nonpast perfective form has future meaning. This is an indirect request and Wawrzon is telling his father what he expects him to build, i.e., the fence.

ABSOLUTE TENSE

S9 – Marta (1;8)	:	Tam włoży–Ø There put:in:PFV:NPAST–3:S '(She) will put (it) in there.'
S10 – Marta (1;8)	:	Włoży-ł–a–Ø Put:in:PFV-PAST-FEM–3:S '(She) put (it) in.'
S11 – Marta (1;9)	:	Tam palusze-k–Ø wkłada –ł–a–Ø There finger-DIM-M:A:S put:in:IPFV-PAST-FEM–3:S '(She) was putting (her) finger in there.'
S12 – Bartosz (1;8)	:	Nie ma. Tu nie. Ø–id-ę Not have. Here no. IPFV-go/walk:NPAST–1:S 'It is not here. I am going.'
S13 – Bartosz (1;8)	:	Bącze-k–Ø po-szed –ł–Ø–Ø Top-DIM-M:N:S PFV-go/walk-PAST-MASC–3:S 'The top went (away).'
S14 – Bartosz (1;11)	:	Ja pó – jd – ę I PFV-go/walk:NPAST–1:S 'I will go.'

The best evidence for a productive morphology derives from examples where children contrast both tense and aspect as shown in Sentences 9–14. For Marta the examples involve the aspectual pair *włoży-ć/wkłada-ć*, put:in:PFV-INF/put:in:IPFV-INF, 'put in'. Marta used past and nonpast forms of the perfective member of the pair and the past form of the imperfective. Bartosz used the perfective member of the aspectual pair *pó–jś–ć/Ø–iś–ć*, PFV-go-INF/IPFV-go-INF, 'to go/walk' in the past and nonpast and the imperfective verb in the nonpast. The hypothesis that Polish children use tense morphology productively to code deictic relationships between 1;6 and 2;0 is confirmed by other research on Polish (see Smoczyńska, 1985) and research on other Slavic languages (see Weist's review 1986).

In comparison, children learning English seem somewhat slow (e.g. Brown 1973 or Fletcher, 1979); e.g. the following estimates of the evolution of irregular and regular past forms: Brown's Eve 2;3 & 2;2, Leopold's Hildegarde 2;3 & 2;4, and Fletcher's Daniel 2;0 & 2;2. In the most typical pattern, children learning English code the progressive aspect first, followed closely by the irregular past, with regular past forms occurring somewhat later.

It is worth considering this pattern more closely, and Bowerman's (1981) very careful observations of Christy and Eva make this possible. Christy and Eva began to make unmarked references to the past at about 1;6, and both children showed a pronounced increase in past references at about 1;9; e.g. 1) Mother: P (a friend) went on a trip; Christy (1;9): *P Mama.*; Mother: P's mommy went too. Who did P go to visit?; Christy: *P... visit... grandma.*; Context (Christy had been told a few days earlier that P had gone to visit her grandparents), and 2) Eva (1;9) *I break doll*; Context (Eva was holding a doll whose foot she had broken two days earlier). The morphological and lexical pattern of development for the two children was as follows:

	Christy	*Eva*
Irregular Past	1;10	1;8
Progressive	1;10	1;8
Future adverbials, e.g. soon	1;10	1;8
Regular Past	2;5	1;11

Like children learning Slavic languages, Christy and Eva code tense and aspect simultaneously between 1;6 and 2;0. In contrast to children learning Slavic and other highly synthetic languages such as Finnish, they take longer to come to grips with the inflectional morphology. This delay makes sense since the children are learning a relatively analytic language where bare stem forms are commonly encountered, e.g. the use of *go* and *visit* in Christy's mother's question about the past. A useful source of evidence for displacement in an analytic language like English is some marked increase in references to the past which Christy demonstrated prior to the morphological evidence.

SITUATIONAL ASPECT

Even though aspect and tense morphology are productive, it is still concievable that children use this morphology to code components of the speech time situation, e.g. in Sentences 5 & 6 the products of Bartosz's prior writing activities remained and were the topic of conversation during speech time. This line of argument can easily be dismissed by looking at a few more examples such as Sentences 3 & 4 where nothing of the cows remained in the speech situation. The best way to counter the argument that past tense morphology codes speech time products of past situations is to find references to prior *activities*, i.e. atelic situations. Atelic situations can not leave speech time remains by their intrinsic nature.

In Discourse Segment 1, Marta (1;8) made reference to a past activity with the verb *lecieć* 'to fly'. Marta used the imperfective form of the verb in contrast to the perfective *polecieć*, and the reference was obviously to a real world situation. While 'flying around the world' is an accomplishment (hence telic) 'flying by the building' is clearly an activity. The present tense of the verb *lecieć* was used earlier in the discourse segment, but the past form *leciał* was spontaneous. Discourse Segment 2 also involved an imperfective verb inflected for the past tense (from the infinitive *odpoczywać* vs. *odpocząć*), and the reference was to a past activity. In her question, grandmother used the imperfective verb *robić* 'to do/make' in the past tense (c.f. perfective *zrobić*). Thus, she established the context for an imperfective-past reply. From the context, it appears that Marta was making a reference to something she actually saw in the moderately remote past.

Discourse Segment 1:
Context – Marta (1;8) is playing with a teddy bear and a plane can be heard in the background.

Grandmother	: Co to leci? 'What is flying?'
Marta	: Samolot 'Plane'
Context	: The sound of the plane is getting quieter.
Marta	: ∅ – lecia – ł – ∅ – ∅ samolot IPFV-fly-PAST-MASC–3:S plane 'The plane was flying.'
Grandmother	: Widziałaś samolot? Gdzie leciał samolot? 'Did you see the plane? Where was it flying?'
Marta	: Na 'To'
Grandmother	: na . . . lotnisko 'To . . . the airport.'

Discourse Segment 2:
Context – Marta (1;8) is talking with grandmother about a bath and the topic changes.

Marta	: Gołąbki 'Pigeons'

Grandmother : Gołąbki. I co robiły gołąbeczki?
'Pigeons. And what were the little pigeons doing?'

Marta : Poci-wa-ł–y–∅ (c.f. odpoczywały)
Rest-IPFV– PAST-NVIR–3:P
'(They) were resting.'

Grandmother : odpoczywały.
'They were resting.'
(Grandmother continues with an expansion.)

The Defective Tense Hypothesis Revisited

It is quite clear that children learning Slavic languages use tense morphology to express deictic relations between about 1;6 and 2;0 (see also Smoczyńska, 1985). If children learning other languages such as Romance languages use tense morphology defectively to code the temporal properties of situations; i.e., aspect, rather than relations between ST and ET, this can *not* be so because children all over the world are slow to develop the conceptual capacity for displacement. Having demonstrated this fact, we have not explained why young Italian or French children do what they do. That issue was left unresolved by Weist et al. (1984) and Weist (1986).

Thanks to some recent work in linguistics by Bybee (1985) and Dahl (1985), it is possible to offer a potential explanation. Let me start by reviewing exactly what was claimed: 1) "The meaning of the child's past tense is at this point rather limited. He is able to encode a past event, but only if it results in a present state. Looking at this fact from a linguistic point of view, we could say that the past 'tense' has more of an aspectual than a temporal value" (Antinucci & Miller, p. 183) and 2) "Before the age of 6, however, the distinction between perfective (*meaning telic*) and imperfective (*meaning atelic*) events seems to be more important than the temporal relation between action and the moment of enunciation. Imperfective (*meaning atelic*) actions are almost never expressed by past tenses, . . . " (Bronckart & Sinclair 1973, p. 126 & 127, underlined translations mine, see their definitions p. 112). The point I want to emphasize is that these authors claimed that child language is different from adult language. According to them, *passato prossimo* and *passé composé* are used by adults to specify tense and by children to specify aspect.

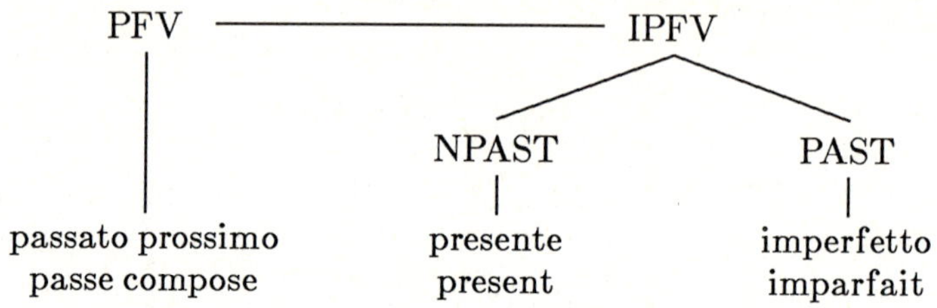

Dahl (1985) has recently completed an extensive cross-linguistic study of tense and aspect. A review of this project is beyond the scope of this paper (see, Bybee 1985). I will focus on the distinction between perfective and imperfective aspect and the interaction of these categories with tense. According to Dahl, the most common relationship between tense and aspect is shown above in the hierarchical arrangement of PFV vs. IPFV and NPAST vs. PAST. The distinction between perfective and imperfective aspect is fundamental and the nonpast versus past distinction is dominated by the category imperfective. According to Dahl, "A PFV verb will typically denote a single event seen as an unanalyzed whole, with a well-defined result or end-state, located in the past. More often than not, the event will be punctual, or at least, it will be seen as a single transition from one state to its opposite, the duration of which can be disregarded" (p. 78). Romance languages fit into this pattern and Slavic languages do not. Assuming that Dahl is correct, when Italian children contrast *passato prossimo* with *presente*, the contrast is between perfective and imperfective aspect. Hence, the children are not doing anything which adults do not do. They are simply developing the tense-aspect system in a hierarchical fashion. The child's use of *passato prossimo* as perfective aspect is *no more* defective than the adult's usage. In fact, the argument can be turned completely around. Since we know from the Slavic research that 1;6 to 2;0 year old children can express deictic relations, which presupposes conceptual displacement, Italian children have to use perfective aspect to express past because they have not yet constructed the past/nonpast distinction dominated by the imperfective category of aspect. In this respect, they may be like children learning Mandarin who must use the aspectual system to code temporal relations prior to the emergence of temporal adverbs because there is no tense system (see also Weist, 1986).

Experimental Observations

The Poznań project involved an integrated research design which included experimental along with naturalistic observations. Both methods have their strong and weak points. The major problem with experimentation for us was that we were unable to work successfully with children younger than 2;6. Our procedures were designed to evaluate the child's understanding of the tense and aspect distinctions which are at the core of the ET system. We know now from the naturalistic observations of a large variety of languages that children shift into this system somewhere between about 1;6 and 2;0 (Slobin 1985 & Weist 1986). The experimental evidence is still relevant for a few reasons. It is important to establish that children can contrast the imperfective versus the perfective forms and past versus nonpast forms of the same verbs. We find these contrasts in the naturalistic data (see Sentences 1–14), but only if we are fortunate. In the experimental situation, the contrasts are under control and the issue of productivity is resolved. Furthermore, we are able to integrate facts about comprehension with production.

In one component of our research, we used a sentence-picture matching task (Weist, 1983). The pictures that were used for the aspect problems contrasted a complete with an incomplete situation, e.g., a man finishes/does not finish eating lunch before leaving. The test sentence contrasted perfective verbs such as *z–jeś–ć*, PFV-eat-INF, or *zamk–n(ą)–ć*, close-PFV-INF, with their imperfective counterparts *∅–jeść*, IPFV-eat-INF, or *zamyk(a)–∅–ć*, close-IPFV-INF. There were 12 aspect problems with half of the problems involving prefixation and half suffixation. In order to limit the contrast to aspect, the verbs were presented in the past tense, e.g., *z–jad–ł*, PFV-eat-PAST, versus *∅–jad–ł*, IPFV-eat-PAST, or *zamk–n(ą)–ł*, close-PFV-PAST, versus *zamyk(a)–∅–ł*, close-IPFV-PAST. The following problems were typical: 1) *Pan (zjadł/jadł) chleb i jabłko i poszedł do pracy*, 'The man (ate/was eating) bread and an apple and went to work.' or 2) *Pan (zamknął/zamykał) okno kiedy zaczęło padać*, 'The man (opened/was opening) the window when it started to rain.' (see also Weist, 1983 pp. 90–91, Figures 1 & 2).

There were two kinds of tense problems. In one type of problem, the pictures contained a contrast between ongoing versus anticipated action, e.g., a girl is in the process of building a small house versus a girl is moving toward a basket of blocks. The sentences contained the nonpast form of the verb, e.g., *∅–buduj–e*, IPFV-build–3:S, versus *z–buduj–e*, PFV-build–3:S. The imperfective member of the pair has present tense meaning and the perfective counterpart has future meaning, i.e., 'is building' versus 'will build'. Thus, the problem contains a present versus future contrast which is accomplished by a contrast in aspect. The second type of tense problem contained one picture in which the result of some action was portrayed, in contrast to the situation in which action was anticipated, e.g., mother is leaving a store with a loaf of bread versus mother is picking up and squeezing a loaf of bread in a store. In these problems, the sentences contained the contrast between the past versus the nonpast form of a perfective verb, e.g., *kup(i)–∅–ł–a–∅*, buy:PFV-PAST-FEM– 3:S, '(She) bought' versus *kup(i)–∅–∅*, buy:PFV:NPAST–3:S. '(She) will buy.' This contrast creates a distinction between past and future tense. The following sentences exemplify the two tense problems: 1) *Dziewczynka (buduje/zbuduje) domek z klocków*, 'A girl (is building/will build) a small house of blocks.' and 2) *Mama (kupiła/kupi) chleb*, 'Mother (bought/will buy) bread'.

The procedure began with a complete description of the two alternative picture sets. Two sentence alternatives were read, then one of the sentences was repeated. The child was asked to choose the picture which matched the sentence. Ten $2\frac{1}{2}$ and ten $3\frac{1}{2}$ year-old children participated. The youngest group passed both tense and aspect tests with averages of 69 and 75 percent correct responses (i.e., their behavior deviated from a binomial model with $p=1/2$ and $n=6$). The older group was significantly better with averages of 88 and 90 percent correct. In other words, by $2\frac{1}{2}$ years of age Polish children can process the tense-aspect contrasts of their language, and they can cope with the procedures of a sentence-picture matching test.

In another experimental phase of the Poznań project (see Weist, et al. 1984), we used an elicitation procedure which was adapted from the previous work of Bronckart & Sinclair (1973), DiPaolo & Smith (1978) and Harner (1981). In contrast to previous studies, we presented children with the obligatory context for past and future tense. In the past-tense problems, the experimenter used toys to act out a sequence of two events and simultaneously described the events using the present tense, e.g., *Chłopiec biega po pokoju, potem kładzie się*, 'The boy is running around the room, and then he lies down.' The experimenter then asked a question using the imperfective past form of the verb, i.e., *Co x robił/robiła najpierw*? 'What was he/she doing first?' We used the imperfective form of the verb to encourage a reply in the imperfective form.

For the future-tense problems, we acted out a sequence of events building up to an impending event. Having described the action using the present tense, we asked the elicitation question with the perfective future form, i.e., *Co się stanie*? 'What will happen?' The following problem was typical: *Pan wsiada do samochodu, zapala silnik a potem . . .* 'The man gets in the car, starts the engine, and then . . . '. The mean percentage of correct past and future tense responses was 92% past and 66% future for the 2½ year-old children and 99% past and 83% future for the 3½ year-old children. Hence, it is possible to encourage 2½ year-old children to do something they do in the natural conversational context about a year earlier. In retrospect, this is not very surprising; however, at the time the research was conducted and even today in some circles, people did/do not think that the 2½ year-old child is capable of expressing deictic relations.

Future Tense and Modality

Earlier in this chapter, I argued that past tense morphology in child language codes the deictic relationships ET prior to ST. In order to make this argument we had to analyze tense and aspect simultaneously and to discriminate between coding a deitic relationship and coding an aspectual relationship. This section contains an argument of a parallel form. The argument here is that children express modality and futurity. The latter can not be *reduced* to the former.

DEONTIC MODALITY

Modal distinctions appear quite early and deontic modality is expressed before epistemic modality (Stephany, 1986). Deontic modality concerns the concept of necessity including at least intention, desire, obligation, and permission. In the prototypical case, deontic modality specifies constraints on the agent and is expressed by free grammatical morphemes such as clitics, particles, and auxiliaries. In English, for example, the sentences, *I want to go*, versus, *I have to go*, contrast the agent's desire with the agent's obligation. While moods, such as the imperative, have propositional scope (rather than agent scope), they can have deontic meaning; e.g. the illocutionary force of, *Go home!*, is that of necessity.

In contrast to deontic modality epistemic modality expresses the idea of possibility. It is used to qualify propositions and therefore has the entire proposition in its scope. Epistemic modality is usually coded by inflectional morphemes, e.g. in Polish the conditional enclitic particle–*by*. This type of modality reflects the speaker's commitment to the truth of an assertion and is referred to as mood, e.g., subjunctive, conditional, potential, etc. The sentence, *If it snows, then we might go*, includes a condition for an event and the possibility of the event (see Bybee, 1985 and Lyons, 1979).

Starting at about 1;9, Greek children contrast the indicative, subjective and imperative moods with the subjective mood having a desiderative function and the imperative mood having an instrumental function (Stephany, 1986, see also Lyons, 1977 p. 836). In child Polish during the initial phase of productive morphology (around 1;6 to 1;9), children contrast the indicative with the imperative mood. Discourse Segment 3 contains a particularly good example because Marta (1;10) used the imperative and the indicative form of the same verb within the span of a few turns. Marta started with the imperative form of the perfective verb *wypluć*, 'to spite out' (c.f. imperfective *wypluwać*). The imperative form *wypluj* is related to but distinct from the indicative nonpast form which is *wypluje* in the third singular. As the dialog continued, Marta's mother used the infinitive, *wypluć*, in her question. After providing a demonstration, Marta described what she had just completed with the same perfective verb in the past tense, i.e. *wypluła*.

Discourse Segment 3:
Context – Marta (1;10) hands an apple to her mother.

Marta	: Wypluj – ∅ mamuniu! Spit:out:PFV-IMP mommy 'Spit (it) out mommy!'
Mother	: Co mam zrobić? What am I to do?
Marta	: Wypluj! 'Spit out!'
Mother	: Wypluć? Jak mam wypluć? 'To spit out? How am I to spit out?'
Context	: Marta bites off a piece of an apple and then spits it out.
Marta	: Wyplu – ł – a – ∅ Spit:out:PFV-PAST-FEM–3:S 'Marta spit (it) out.'
Mother	: No! 'Hey!'

While child language investigators are often reluctant to give children credit for the capacity to express deictic future forms, the argument that children can express deontic modality is readily acceptable. When children produce a future form, a strong argument must be made that the future form has some deictic value above and beyond whatever modal meanings the utterance expresses. Part of the reason for this is that everyone knows that children are capable of wanting things and of trying to cause people to do things. In contrast, people are reluctant to accept that children of this age can think about an event which lies outside the domain of speech time. An important point is missing in this argument. Lyons (1977 p. 824) and others have pointed out that, "there is an intrinsic connexion between deontic modality and futurity." When children express a desire, obligation, or command, they have an expectation which concerns a state of affairs subsequent to speech time. When Marta told her mother to spit, it is clear from the overall discourse segment that she expected her mother to take a bite of the apple and to spit it out. In fact, when her mother failed to do so, she demonstrated what she had in mind.

FUTURE TENSE

It is possible that all references to the future have some modal value, i.e. some sense of necessity or possibility. Some future utterances are indirect speech acts with an obvious instrumental illocutionary force; e.g. Marta (1;7) said to her mother, *Mamusi-a wyjmie–∅*, Mommy-F:N:S take:out:PFV:NPAST–3:S, 'Mommy will take it out.' Marta's mother replied, *Mamusia wyjmie, oczywiście. Proszę bardzo*, 'Mommy will take it out, certainly. Here you are.' Obviously, Marta's mother understood Marta's future indicative statement as a request. In contrast, many of the future tense utterances simply concern something which the child anticipates subsequent to speech time. At 1;8, Bartosz was returning to his room to get some more toys, and he said, *Przyniesie-m*, bring:PFV:NPAST–1:S, '(I) will bring (something).' to which Zofia replied *Co przyniesiesz*? 'What will you bring?' This was clearly a statement and both members of the conversation expected that Bartosz would get some toy from his room and bring it back into the living room. At 1;7, Marta was moving a pram and it almost fell over. She said, *Przewróci–∅*, turn:over:PFV:NPAST–3:S, '(Marta) will turn (it) over.' Marta's mother expanded on her statement and asked why, i.e., *Przewróci Martusia wózek? Dlaczego*? 'Marta will turn the pram over? Why?' Here Marta's mother clearly expected her to do something. Whatever their modal value, statements like these express the deictic relationship ET subsequent to ST.

TRANSITION FROM THE ET TO THE RESTRICTED RT SYSTEM

Before discussing the introduction of RT into the child's temporal systems, I would like to summarize some of the properties of the ET system and to consider the dynamics of the transition from the ET system into the initial RT system. Our Polish data show that when the children were between 1;6 and 2;0, they could talk about situations which occurred prior to and subsequent to speech time. The typical reference to past (or future) situations involved a single proposition. These utterances were either spontaneous or prompted and they referred to situations which were either relatively recent or moderately remote (see Weist, et al. 1984). Scaffolding (Bruner, 1975) on the part of adults was neither necessary nor sufficient to produce references to the past or to the future. Bowerman (1981) has made an even stronger case for the spontaneity of displaced references; "Spontaneous reference to both past and future (and nonactual) events was well established from the one-word period long before the child responded in any way to adult questions and remarks about these events. And when temporal markers such as past tense,–*ing*, and *will* came in, they appeared first only in purely spontaneous comments, only later spreading to contexts of answering adult questions about past, future, etc" (p. 2).

Sachs (1983) found a different pattern of development. Between 1;8 and 2;1, Naomi only made reference to the immediate past, i.e. to prior events within two hours of speech time. At 1;10, adults began to ask about earlier past situations, but Naomi didn't reply to this prompting until 2;2. Sachs concluded that, "these parental references to Earlier PAST (*more remote than 2 hours*) served to introduce the child to a new idea through linguistic interaction" (p. 20). According to Sachs, when conceptual development has progressed to some unspecified level, children are conceptually ready to benefit from linguistic interactions about the past. Linguistic interaction creates the opportunity "for learning to use past in the more abstract sense: reference to earlier time." However, the spontaneous past references to which Bowerman referred were "Earlier" as well as "Immediate" according to Sachs's definitions. Hence, linguistic interaction is not required to introduce children to the idea of remote past reference. They can and do arrive at this idea on their own.

Does this mean that adult scaffolding is superfluous? While I do not think scaffolding is superfluous, it is difficult to isolate its function. Our data are consistent with those of both Sachs and Bowerman in the general sense that children make references to the past first and scaffolding follows. These references typically contain a simple proposition. It appears that after adults notice that children can make reference to the past, they begin to probe the child's ability to talk about these past experiences. Since Polish children express deictic relationships between 1;6 and 2;0, the frequency of scaffolding observations increases during the transition period from 2;0 to 2;5. Since there are relatively few examples available in the literature, it is worth considering three concrete examples.

Discourse Segment 4:
Context – Magda (2;5) and Hanna are talking and mother is preparing tea.

Hanna	: A co ty robiłaś dzisiaj ciekawego w przedszkolu? 'What of interest were you doing in kindergarten today?' Byłaś w przedszkolu? 'Were you in kindergarten?'
Magda	: By – ł – a – m be-PAST-FEM–1:S '(I) was (there)'
Hanna	: I co robiłaś? 'And what were you doing?'
Magda	: Bawi – ł – a – m (się) Play:IPFV-PAST-FEM–1:S (REF) '(I) was playing.'
Hanna	: Bawiłaś się? 'Were you playing?'
Magda	: Tak 'Yes'
Hanna	: Z kim się bawiłaś? 'Who were you playing with?'

Discourse Segment 5:

Father	: Ale powiedz co tam zrobiłeś sobie ciekawego? But tell us what you did to yourself?
Kubuś	: (2;4) Ja z-jad-ł –e –m piasek–∅, wiesz. I:NOM:S PFV-eat-PAST-MASC–1:S sand-A:M:S, you know. 'I ate sand, you know.'

Emilia : Smakował ci?
Did you like it?

Kubuś : Nie
No

Father : Co było później?
What happened next?

Kubuś : Tatuś–∅ mnie z-bi –ł –∅ –∅ wiesz,
Father-N:M:S Me:ACC:S PFV-
spank-PAST-MASC–3:S you know
'Daddy spanked me, you know.'

Emilia : A co było później?
What happened next?

Kubuś : Po-szed-ł –e –m do dom-u
PFV-go-PAST-MASC–1:S to home-G:M:S
i pokaza-ł –e –m jak buzi-a wygląda–∅
and show:PFV-PAST-MASC–1:S how face-N:F:S
look:IPFV:NPAST–3:S
'(I) went home and showed how my face looked.'

Mother : Komu pokazałeś?
'To whom did you show (it)?'

Kubuś : Mam-us-i
Mother-DIM-D:F:S
'Mother'

Discourse Segment 6:
Context – Kubuś's (2;4) mother asks him a question.

Mother : Opowiedz, jaki miałeś rowerek. O kuzynkach coś opowiedz.
'Tell us what kind of small bike you had and about your cousins, tell us something.'

Kubuś : Ja mia – ł – e – m o kuzinkach te lowelki.
'I have-PAST-MASC–1:S about cousins these bikes.'
(c.f. ja miałem od kuzynków te rowerki)
'I had from (my) cousins these bikes.'
Ja jeździ – ł – e – m
I ride:IPFV – PAST – MASC – 1:S
'I was riding around.'

Emilia	: Gdzie jeździłeś? 'Where were you riding around?'
Kubuś	: Do takiego wilka. To such a wolf.
Emilia	: A gdzie był ten wilk? And where was this wolf?
Kubuś	: W lasu (c.f. w lesie), ja jeździłem. 'In the forest, I was riding.'
Emilia	: No i co? Przyjechałeś do wilka i co? 'Yes and what? You came to the wolf and what?
Kubuś	: Ja ziabai – ł – e – m (c.f. zabiłem) tym najfem (c.f. nożem). I kill:PFV-PAST-MASC–1:S with this knife. 'I killed the wolf with this knife.'

Discourse Segment 4 not only contains scaffolding but also a routine which may be universal. The adult initiates the exchange and the child responds. The adult persists and the child responds again. The form of the individual utterances is the same as that of a typical child of 1;8 or 1;9, i.e. single word utterances inflected for aspect, tense, gender, number and person. Our only access to reference time and place is through the adult's utterance. Discourse Segments 5 and 6 are important because they demonstrate that children can talk about unique as well as routine (or scripted) past experiences. At 2;4, Kubuś was clearly more advanced in his linguistic development than Marta and Bartosz during the 1;7 to 1;11 period, and he was somewhat precocious for his age, e.g., the third sentence in Discourse Segment 5 contains both coordination and subordination. In spite of his precocity, he did not establish RT in his sentences. In this context, it could be argued that he did not establish RT because his parents had already done so; however, he did not use expressions such as 'yesterday', 'last week', 'in the summer' etc., in the context of self-initiated references to the past. What adults do when scaffolding is to guide the child to some episodic memory representation which has at least fuzzy time and space referents. Once the child retrieves the representation, the adult encourages the child to reveal some of its components. These linguistic interactions may facilitate the development of the capacity to shift RT away from ST, and set the stage for the emergence of the initial RT system.

THE RESTRICTED RT SYSTEM

The Restricted RT System and Nonegocentric Perspective

The restricted reference time (RT_r) system is characterized by the ability to establish reference time at a different point in time than speech time and to specify relative tense relations which employ reference time. Cromer (1974) argued that a system with these properties will not emerge until about 4½ or later because of "a late-developing ability to consider the relevance of another time to the time of the utterance" (p. 223). The RT_r system requires a degree of decentration. Very little has been written about temporal decentration, but much more is known about spatial decentration. I plan to evaluate the developmental course of spatial decentration, and then argue that a similar course can be inferred for temporal decentration.

If Piaget and Inhelder's (1956) conclusions were currently valid, Cromer's argument would have indirect corroboration. They concluded that the child, "appears rooted in his own viewpoint in the narrowest and restricted fashion so that he cannot imagine any perspective but his own" (p. 242). However, Borke (1975) demonstrated that Piaget and Inhelder's conclusions had more to do with the unique requirements of their famous three mountain test, than they did with egocentrism. Borke used visual displays of common objects such as a sailboat, a horse, and a house and a revolving display to obtain the child's responses. Three-year-old children were about 80% correct in their capacity to judge the perspective of an observer in a different spatial location.

Some of the ingredients of nonegocentric perspective can be found even in the one-year-old child. The one-year-old child will look where other people point and when they themselves point to objects they usually accompany their pointing with vocalizations and/or looking at the interlocutor (see Leung & Rheingold, 1981). The behavior indicates that children are aware that the interlocutor has a point of view which can be directed, but it does not show that the child can appreciate the alternative perspective. This appreciation clearly comes later as John Flavell and his colleagues have shown (e.g., Masangkay, McCluskey, McIntyre, Sims-Knight, Vaugh & Flavell, 1974). Flavell and his colleagues have identified two stages in the decentration process; 1) three-year-old children can infer *what* object a person does or does not see, but 2) the four-year-olds can infer *how*, i.e., with what perspective, another observer experiences a common scene.

(See also Loveland, 1984 on the relationship between personal deixis and spatial decentration and the general review by Gelman & Baillargeon, 1983).

Further evidence for noneogocentric spatial perspective in three-year-old children comes from research on personal and spatially deictic pronouns and locative adverbs (e.g., deVilliers & deVilliers, 1974 and Tanz 1980). According to the deVilliers, "children aged 3 years and older are performing with 80–90% accuracy in comprehension of these terms" (p. 442). Hence, it would be difficult to argue today that a general egocentric perspective inhibits the three year-old from shifting the temporal point of reference away from the deictic center of speech time (see reviews by Johnston 1984 & 1985).

Before continuing with Cromer's argument, it would be a good idea to review what *perfect* means (see Comrie 1985). Perfect codes the relationship ET prior to RT. Since it relates ET to RT and not ST, it specifies a relative tense relationship rather than an absolute tense relationship. In English perfect is always used in combination with absolute tenses. Thus, English has past perfect, e.g. *He had arrived*, present perfect, e.g. *He has arrived*, and future perfect *He will have arrived.* Perfect is emphatically *not* the same concept as perfective aspect (c.f. Quirk & Greenbaum 1978 p. 40 & 41). Present perfect is a form of past tense. The major difference between present perfect and simple past is the location of RT, i.e., RT is at ST in the former and at ET in the latter. This is what it means to say that present perfect indicates present relevance.

Part of Cromer's reluctance to credit children with variable reference time came from his observations of the late acquisition of the present perfect in American English. Since we know today that children learning British English do not exhibit this retarded acquisition (see Wells, 1979 and Gathercole, 1985) it is not possible to attribute the delay to failure to conceptually decentrate. According to Gathercole, three-year-old Scottish children use the present perfect in the following three ways: 1) specifying possession in *have got* constructions; 2) when the result of a recent event is still relevant at speech time, and 3) when referring to "an event or state that occurred or existed at some unspecified time in the past." (see also the use of the present perfect in Finnish, Toivainen 1980).

The Restricted RT System: Temporal Adverbs

One of the major linguistic sources of evidence for the claim that children have shifted from an ET to a RT_r system at about 2;6 to 3;0 is the use of temporal adverbs during this period by children acquiring varied languages (see Weist, 1986). The adult English speaker can make reference to a situation which occurred prior to ST and explicitly specify RT prior to speech time with a temporal adverb or maintain RT at ST with the present perfect, e.g., *The skier hurt his leg yesterday* versus *The skier has hurt his leg.* When someone uses the simple past with no temporal adverb, by default RT is interpreted as coincident with ET, e.g., *The skier won the race.* Since we know that children start with a here-and-now system where ET and RT coincide with ST, the conservative decision was *not* to give children credit for the capacity to shift RT away from ST until they can specifically identify other temporal points of reference.

It is possible that this decision was too conservative. When children use imperfective aspect, they take an internal perspective on a situation. When a child takes an internal perspective on a situation, which is also coded as occurring prior to or subsequent to speech time, s/he has in some sense shifted his/her temporal reference point away from speech time. Typically, the imperfective aspect in Slavic languages is thought of as the unmarked form (c.f. Dahl, 1985). As such, it can have a variety of meanings e.g., progressive, iterative, incomplete, etc. (Majewicz, 1982 a & b). A stronger case can be made for flexible RT when aspect is used to specify some specific property of the internal structure of situations. In Polish, motion verbs usually have three forms perfective, imperfective, and non-determined (or habitual), e.g., *pojechać*, *jechać*, and *jeździć* 'to go by vehicle'. When Bartosz was 2;0, he used all of these motion verb forms in the past tense, and Kubuś used them all in the past by 2;4 (see Discourse Segment 6). In Polish, this kind of aspectual evidence for flexible RT is found at about the same time as temporal adverbs. In contrast, internal perspective on past situations, marked by the past progressive in English, emerges after temporal adverbs (e.g., Fletcher 1979). At present, it appears that the decision to make claims for variable RT contingent on temporal adverbs was not in error. However, more cross-linguistic data on aspect is needed.

Forty years ago, Ames (1946) showed that children begin to express temporal adverbs between about 2;6 and 3;0. However, it is also well known that children make errors, e.g., while Bloom's (1970) Kathryn was correctly specifying ET prior to or subsequent to ST with tense morphology at 2;6, her use of temporal adverbs was, "usually inaccurate or superfluous" (p. 229). The limited data on temporal adverbs indicates that they are initially found around 2;0 but errors persist at least until 3;0 (e.g., Clark 1985, on Romance Languages).

In our analysis of the emergence of temporal adverbs in child Polish from 2;4 to 3;2, we identified three different categories: 1) immediate, 2) remote, and 3) cyclic (Weist & Buczowska, 1987). The immediate set consists of the following adverbs: *już* 'already', *teraz* 'now' and *zaraz* 'soon'. The three children observed during this period consistently used these temporal adverbs correctly. *Już* 'already' is used with past, present, or future tense, *teraz* 'now' with present and future, and *zaraz* 'soon' with future. To say that children use *już* correctly sounds like an empty claim since a correspondence between the temporal adverb and the tense is guaranteed. However, when *już* is used with a verb in the past tense, the verb will be in the perfective aspect, with few exceptions. Hence, there is a coordination of tense, aspect, and the adverb, *już*.

S15 – Tunia (2;7)	: No, tu jest, Ja chcę taką kitkę. 'Well, here (it) is. I want such a pony tail.' Już, już, ja zrobiłam. Tu załóż! Już ja, ja już. Already, already, I have made (it). Here, put (it) on! Already I, I already.
S16 – Magda (2;9)	: Już jestem mama. Kupiłam mleczko. 'Already (I) am mommy. (I) bought some milk!'
Context – Emilia	: No, nagrywam ale to ty musisz mówić. 'Yes, I am recording but you have to talk."
S17 – Tunia (2;10)	: Już będę gadała. 'Already (I) will be chatting.'
Context – Father	: Jedziemy jutro? 'Are (we) going tomorrow?'
S18 – Wawrzon (2;7)	: Teraz. Z ciociami do Łodzi. 'Now. With the aunts to Łódź.'
S19 – Wawrzon (2;6)	: Teraz wejdę do łóżka 'Now (I) will go into bed.'
S20 – Tunia (2;7)	: Jeszcze tu, uczeszę, zaraz. 'Still here, (I) will comb (your hair) soon.'

Sentences 15–20 contain examples of the usage of the adverbs *już*, *teraz*, and *zaraz*. Sentence 15 demonstrates the prototypical use of the adverb, *już* 'already' with a perfective verb in the past tense i.e. *z-robi-ł-a-m*, PFV-do/make-PAST-FEM–1:S, 'to do/make.' Tunia (2;7) was combing her doll's hair and making a pony tail which required a rubber band. When Emilia asked if she was supposed to put the rubber band on the pony tail, Tunia replied that she had already made the pony tail, and it was ready

for the rubber band. Polish has no perfect tenses and therefore no present perfect combination. In the context of Sentence 15, *już* plus a verb with perfective aspect and past tense yields a temporal configuration which conveys the same meaning as the English present perfect, i.e. ET prior to RT equals ST. The fact that the pony-tail making activity was completed was relevant to the time interval of the speech act. The rubber band was required during the speech time interval, and Tunia used the imperative verb form *załóż–∅* put:on-IMP 'put (it) on!' to make the current relevance of the completed situation more salient. When *już* is used with a verb in the present tense, as it is in Sentence 16, it ties a past situation into the present time frame. With the future tense, *już* emphasizes that something is about to happen and it can be used with either perfective or imperfective verbs. In Sentence 17, the verb is imperfective and Tunia was commenting on the fact that she had already started to speak. The use of *teraz* is shown in Sentences 18 and 19. In Sentence 18, it is clear that Wawrzon understood that *jutro* means sometime in the future since he was arguing with his father that they should leave at the current moment and not sometime later. Prior to uttering Sentence 19, Wawrzon went to the kitchen, returned to his room, and jumped up on his bed. He said, *Now I will go to bed* as he was in the process of doing so. With the perfective verb in Sentence 20, Tunia was stating her plan to do the combing in the immediate future.

Members of the remote set begin to appear later at about 2;9. When a remote adverb makes a general temporal reference, such as *dawno* 'long ago', *później* 'later' or *kiedyś* 'sometime in the past,' it appears to have a meaning which resembles the adult meaning, e.g., Sentence 21. In Sentence 22, it can be seen that children appear to understand the kinds of things that can happen during seasons like summer and winter, and they refer to such events. This, however, does not imply that they have demonstrated an understanding of the sequence of seasonal cycles (see Friedman, 1982b but also Ames, 1946).

Context – Wawrzon and Hanna are comparing tape recorders.

S21 – Wawrzon (3;2): A mój był, ile był, kiedy był wyprodukowany.
And mine was, how many was, when was (it) produced.
Już bardzo dawno, kiedy ja się nie urodziłem.
'Already very long ago, when I was not born yet.'

S22 – Tunia (3;0) : One w lato (c.f. lecie) będą porzeczki dla mnie do jedzenia.
In the summer, there will be currents for me for eating.

The cyclic set includes *dzisiaj* 'today', *wczoraj* 'yesterday', *jutro* 'tomorrow', and specific references to the days of the week. These were initially found at about 2;7, and they invariably caused problems. Initially *wczoraj* and *jutro* entered into contradictions with the tense of the sentence, e.g., Wawrzon (2;8) –*jutro bawi–ł–e–m tymi zabawkami.* Tomorrow play:IPFV-PAST-MASC–1:S with these toys, 'I played with these toys tomorrow' or Magda (2;10) –*A wczoraj pó–jd-ę do przedszkolu*, And yesterday I PFV-go:NPAST–1:S to kindergarten, 'Yesterday I will go to kindergarten.' It is possible to determine from the larger discourse context that *dzisiaj* does not consistently refer to the current daily cycle. When children refer to a specific day of the week, they are simply referring to someday or maybe only sometime, as shown in Discourse Segment 7.

Discourse Segment 7:

Emilia : Mhm, kiedy dziadek wróci?
'I see, when will he be back?'

Tunia (2;11) : W piątek
'On Friday'

Emilia : Też w piątek, a nie dzisiaj?
'Also on Friday, and not today?'

Tunia : Dzisiaj nie
'Today no'

Emilia : Czemu? Tak daleko pojechał do pracy?
'Why? Did he go so far to work?'

Tunia : Tak
'Yes'

Emilia : Dokąd?
'Where to?'

Tunia : Do, pół (c.f. Za pół) godziny wróci – ∅
To, half hour return PFV:NPAST–3:S
'He will return in half an hour.'

Emilia : Za pół godziny?
'In half an hour?'
Ale to nie wobec tego w piątek.
'So it won't be on Friday.'

Tunia : W piątek nie, ale za pół godziny.
'On Friday no, but in half an hour.'

Discourse Segment 8:
Context – Tunia (2;11) and Emilia are looking at a coloring book.

Tunia : Ja też już po – malowa – ł –a – m to.
I also already PFV-color-PAST-FEM–1:S it.
'I have already colored it.'

Emilia : A kiedy po – maluje – sz tę stronę?
And when PFV-color:NPAST–2:S this page?
'And when will you color this page?'

Tunia : Tę stronę jutro.
This page tomorrow.

Emilia : Jutro, dobrze. A tę stronę kiedy po – malowa – ł – a – ś?
Tomorrow, good. And this page when PFV-color-PAST-FEM–2:S
'Tomorrow, good. And when did you color this page?'

Tunia : Wczoraj
'Yesterday'

During this period from 2;6 to 3;0, the cyclic set is less and less likely to enter into contradictions with tense (see Discourse Segment 8). *Wczoraj* means sometime in the past and *jutro* means sometime in the future. This period may or may not correspond to the cycle prior or subsequent to the current daily cycle. Hence, *wczoraj* and *jutro* are deictic but not cyclic during this period (Weist & Buczowska, 1987).

In spite of the fact that the past tense morphology in English develops somewhat late in comparison to Slavic languages, temporal adverbs emerge at about the same time. Bowerman's (1981) Christy and Eva produced the immediate set, i.e. *already, now,* and *soon* by 1;11 and 1;9 respectively. In the data summarized in Bowerman, the arrival of the cyclic set of adverbs, i.e. *yesterday, today,* and *tomorrow,* was not specified but it was probably not until after 2;6. Sachs (1983) reported that Naomi introduced *yet*, *already*, *still*, *in a minute*, and *yestermorning* (any time in the past) at 2;2. Contrasts between *tomorrow* and *yesterday* were not mentioned.

The Restricted RT System: Adverbial Clauses

As the children we observed approached 3;0, they began to use temporal adverbial clauses introduced with *jak* 'when'. They seldom used *kiedy* 'when' although they certainly heard the word. This finding is consistent with other observations of child Polish (see Smoczyńska 1985 p. 658 & 659). Discourse Segments 9 and 10 demonstrate the use of *jak* to introduce temporal adverbial clauses. Discourse Segment 9 is interesting because Magda (2;11) also uses *wtenczas* 'then/at that time'. This is an unusually complex set of sentences including *żeby* 'so that' clause as well. Discourse Segment 10 is interesting because Mateusz (3;4) corrects himself to make the verb *być* 'to be' agree in gender with the season *zima* 'winter' which is feminine, i.e., *był* is changed to *była*. He does not state the season explicitly, but his mother's follow-up question brings it out.

Discourse Segment 9:
Context – Magda's (2;11) mother is talking to Hanna about the weather. They agree that it will be nice soon and the children will be able to play outside. It is late March.

Mother	: Tak. To już będzie pogoda. 'Yes. Already it will be good weather.'
Magda	: Jak będzi-e pada – ł – ∅ deszczyk to na głowę When be:FUT–3:S fall-PP-MASC rain on head załozy – my czarny parasol duży. put:up:PFV:NPAST–1:P black umbrella large. Będ – ę wtenczas za mamą ∅–trzyma – ł – a. be:FUT–1:S then behind Mommy IPFV-hold-PP-FEM, bo mama nie będzi – e pozwoli – ł – a because mommy not be:FUT–3:S permit:PFV-PP-FEM ten parasol zakłada-ć na czapeczkę this umbrella put:up:IPFV-INF on cap żeby na czapeczkę nie pada – ł – o – ∅ deszczyk

so that on cap not fall:IPFV-PAST-NEUT–3:S rain.
'When it will rain on the head, we will put up the large black umbrella. Then/at that time, I will be holding (it) behind mommy, because mommy will not allow this umbrella to be put up, on a cap, so that the rain will not fall on a cap.'

Hanna : Acha
'I see.'

Discourse Segment 10:
Context – Mateusz (3;4) and his mother are looking at pictures and they see a snowman. They start talking about snowmen. It is April.

Mother : A kiedy lepiliśmy bałwanki?
And when were we making snowmen?

Mateusz : Jak by – ł – ∅ – ∅, jak by – ł – a – ∅, jak pada – ł – ∅ – ∅ śnieg.
When be-PAST-MASC–3:S, when be-PAST-FEM–3:S, when fall-PAST-MASC–3:S snow
'When (he) was, when (she) was, when snow fell.'

Mother : Jak padał snieg, to jaka wtedy jest pora roku?
'When it was snowing, what season of the year is it then?'

Mateusz : Zima
'Winter'

The age of the emergence of *jak* clauses in Polish corresponds to the onset of *when* clauses in English; according to some estimates between 2;6 and 3;0 (see Bloom, Lahey, Hood, Lifter & Fiess, 1980). There is also a sequential similarity to English in that temporal adverbial clauses are preceded by causal adverbial clauses in both languages. Furthermore, the Polish data corresponds with the cross-linguistic comparison which was carried out by Clancy, Jacobsen, and Silva (1976).[5]

THE TRANSITION FROM A RESTRICTED TO A FREE RT SYSTEM: TEMPORAL SEQUENCING

In Weist 1982 & 1986, I claimed that the set of temporal configurations which can be expressed within the restricted RT system is limited. It was proposed that when RT is established outside the domain of ST, ET will be coterminous with RT, e.g., Discourse Segments 9 & 10. Thus, the restricted RT system was viewed as a two-time-system in contrast to the free RT system in which temporal intervals are freely coördinated. In our data, the constraint on two temporal intervals *lasts only for about six months.* As I have already pointed out, children learning Polish begin to produce temporal adverbial clauses at about 3;0. They are most likely to introduce these clauses with the conjunction *jak.* With temporal clauses, *jak* means 'when or while'. The precise meaning depends on the aspect of the verbs in the two clauses. Let us consider the following four sentences.

S23 – Wawrzon (3;1): Jak będzi-e ten gra –ł –Ø tamten (będzie) gra-ł–Ø
While be:FUT–3:S this play:IPFV-PP-MASC that play:IPFV-PP–3:S
'While this one is playing, that one will be playing.'

S24 – Wawrzon (3;1): Jak je Lejek znalaz –ł –Ø –Ø a tam po-ucieka-ł–y–Ø(c.f. uciekły)
When them Lejek find:PFV-PAST-MASC 3:S and there PFV-run:away-PAST-NVIR–3:P
'When Lejek found them and there (the puppies) ran away.'

S25 – Tunia (3;0) : Jak Ø–je –m, jak ja stoj –ę z kubkami to on mie Ø–bij-e
While IPFV-eat:NPAST–1:S, while I stand:IPFV:NPAST–3:S with cups he me IPFV-hit:NPAST–3:S
'While (I) eat, while I stand with cups, he hits me.'

S26 – Tunia (2;9) : Jak po-gryzi-e jeden się to wariat dostani –e.
When PFV-bit:NPAST–3:S one REF crazy-man get:PFV:NPAST–3:S.
'When it bites itself, it will become a "crazy-man."'

S27 – Tunia (2;9) : Ja ziuci –ę (c.f. rzucę) potem podniosi-ę (c.f. podniosę)
I throw PFV:NPAST–1:S then

pick:up:PFV:NPAST–1:S
'I will throw (it) then I will pick (it) up.'

In Sentences 23 and 25, the children describe coterminous events and in Sentences 24 and 26, the temporal configuration is sequential. Absolute tense varies freely. The coterminous relationship was constructed with the future tense in Sentence 23 and with the present tense in Sentence 25. The sequential constructions are situated in the past in Sentence 24 and in the future in Sentence 26. Sentences 24 and 26 contain configurations with ST, ET, and RT at different temporal locations. In Sentence 24 the verb *znaleźć* 'to find' refers to an achievement situation. Hence, the initial stage of the event situation (i.e. running away) occurs at the same point as the final stage of the referent situation (see Figure 2.3 below). Instead of using the past form of the perfective verb *uciec* 'to run away', Wawrzon invents a perfective with a prefix *po*, i.e., *pouciekać*. In Sentence 26, 'becoming crazy' occurs as a result of having been bitten and therefore follows in time. In addition to *jak* clauses, we have also found the occasional use of *potem* 'then' and *najpierw* 'first' to sequence two clauses as shown in Sentence 27. Hence, our data shows that children have a temporal system in which they can coordinate three different temporal locations a year before my original estimate of 4;0 (Weist, 1986).

During the past ten years, Katherine Nelson and her colleagues have been involved in a series of studies concerning the acquisition of scripts (see Nelson, 1986 and Nelson & Gruendel, 1981). They start with Schank and Abelson's (1977) definition of a script as "a structure that describes an appropriate sequence of events in a particular context" (p. 41). Nelson and Gruendel argue that scripts grow out of routine activities in the child's life. As a child repeatedly experiences the same episode, the independent experiences "fuse" into the generalized knowledge of the event structure. Nelson and Gruendel claim that scripts (or more specifically Generalized Event Representations) "are basic building blocks of the cognitive organization." Their research is particularly relevant for two reason; a) "scripts represent events that occur over time and thus the links between their component acts are temporal links" (p. 138) and b) they studied children in the pertinent two to five year old range although three was the youngest age group in most of the studies. When three-year-old children were asked to retrieve potential scripts such as what happens at a birthday party: 1) they recalled an ordered set of events using sequencers like *and then*; 2) they employed a present narrative style with the personal pronoun *you* (in the sense of the impersonal *one*), and 3) they recalled more information.

In child language, around 3;0 when children begin to sequence events, the order of their clauses in the sentence often matches the order of events in the world. Three-year-old children describe past and anticipate future experiences involving event sequences. It is certain that some of these reports involve scripts and some do not, but very often it is difficult to make the discrimination. Sentence 28 appears to be a good example of a script related utterance, whereas Sentence 24 was undoubtedly based on a unique experience. While scripts may play a role in early clause sequencing, they are not necessary for it. This observation is consistent with Nelson's research. Scripts may facilitate the temporal location of events in a larger episodic structure.

S28 – Wawrzon (3;1): Potem a jak się przełoży–∅ tym to
Then and when REF switch: PFV:NPAST–3:S this
∅–jedzie–∅ na tym torze
IPFV-go:NPAST–3:S on this truck
'Then, and when this gets switched, (the train) goes on this track.'

In summary, most of the data which is available at this point indicates that the concept of reference time emerges in child language around 2;6. Initially there are constraints on the variety of temporal configurations which children can express, i.e., ET is at RT, ST is at RT, or both ET and ST are at RT. By 3;0, children can express sequences requiring three unique temporal intervals. These sequences are often restricted by event order, and some may evolve from script structures.

TEMPORAL LOCATION: RT VERSUS ET SYSTEMS

When children are communicating within constraints of the ET system, they locate events prior to, simultaneous with, subsequent to speech time. The children do not specify other temporal reference points (their model of time flow was shown in Figure 2.2). When children incorporate reference time into their temporal system, they begin to locate events in time. However, they still have a very fuzzy model of time flow. As yet, their model of time flow has no metric. They contrast remote with immediate past or future, but there is no linguistic evidence for units such as a day or a year. Figure 2.3 contains a general model of time flow in the top panel

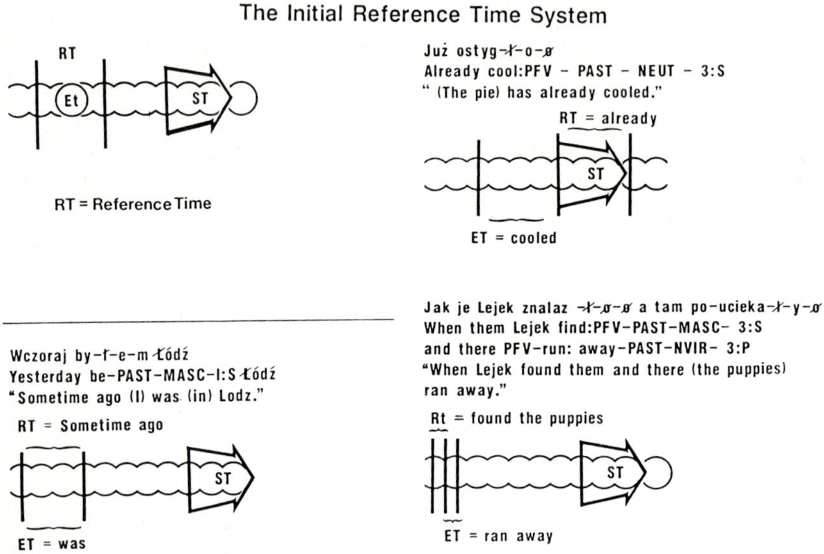

Figure 2.3. A time flow model for the initial RT system and three examples of typical temporal configurations.

and the remainder shows three temporal configurations which correspond to the following three sentences:

S29 – Wawrzon (2;9): Wczoraj byłem Łódź.
'Yesterday (=sometime ago) I was in Łódź.'

S30 – Wawrzon (2;6): Już ostygło. Już jest.
'It has already cooled down. It is ready (to eat).'

S24 – Wawrzon (3;1): Jak je Lejek znalazł a tam pouciekały (c.f. uciekły).
'When Lejek found them and there (the puppies) ran away.'

In Sentence 29 and the second panel of Figure 2.3, Wawrzon used the word *wczoraj* to locate RT. *Wczoraj* means yesterday to the fluent speaker but 'sometime in the past' to Wawrzon. Sometime within the scope of this period, he went to the city *Łódź.* This configuration contrasts with one in which RT is specifically located (not a default) at ST. In Sentence 30 and the third panel of Figure 2.3, Wawrzon used the word *już* to express the idea that some event has just occurred and the result has relevance for the ST interval. In Sentence 24 and the fourth panel of Figure 2.3, Wawrzon located RT in the past with the adverbial clause, 'when Lejek found them.' The nature of this referential location depends on the situational aspect of the verb phase. In this case, the verb *to find* is an achievement, and RT corresponds to the terminal point of the situation. The event (the running away of the puppies) was places right after this point of reference. This third configuration is more advanced than the first two since it involves the coordination of three different temporal locations.[6]

THE FREE RT SYSTEM AND SERIATION AND REVERSIBILITY

A good deal of evidence indicates that it is not until about 4;0 to 4;6 that children freely coordinate the three concepts of ST, ET, and RT (e.g., Bowerman's 1979 review). At this phase in development, past perfect forms are found at least in Finnish, and the temporal propositions *before* and *after* are attested in many languages including Polish (see Smoczyńska 1985 p. 659). Since most of the research has concentrated on *before* and *after* as temporal conjunctions my remarks will have to be limited to this usage. I know of only two studies which have directly evaluated the relationship between the capacity to comprehend sentences with *before* and *after* and conceptual development; Ferreiro and Sinclair (1971) and Trosborg (1982). I will focus on the latter. In the *before* and *after* tests, Trosborg used the four sentence types which are typical of this kind of research. The only relevant distinction here is whether clause order matches event order; e.g., 1) Matching order *Soren washed the car, before he polished his bicycle.* and *After Mette baked the cake, she peeled the potatoes* versus 2) Mismatching order – *Before Soren cleaned his boots, he polished his shoes* and *Mette drank the milk, after she ate the cake.* Trosborg used two comprehension tasks. In one task, she asked which event occurred first and in the other one, the children were required to act out sentences with colored objects which varied in shape. When the sequence of action was arbitrary such as washing a car and polishing a bicycle, children who were on the average 5;4 showed a clear advantage of matching orders over mismatching orders on both tasks. Six-year-olds were still having difficulties with mismatching problems in the verbal judgment task. When the test sentences contained a logical sequence such as brushing teeth and going to bed, *only* the younger groups, i.e., 3;5 and 4;6, found the mismatching orders difficult. On problems of seriation, e.g., picture arrangement, and on conservation problems, e.g., continuous quantity with two containers of liquid, children did not reach the 80–90% level of correct performance until over six years of age. Trosborg made relatively strong claims for cognitive prerequisites (Trosborg 1982, p. 399).

In a variety of languages, children begin to use 'before' and 'after' around 4;6. A closer look at the spontaneous production of sentences with 'before' and 'after' will undoubtedly show a strong tendency to match the order of events referred to and the order of events in the world. While the children are demonstrating the freedom to express ST, ET, and RT at different temporal locations, they still may not be totally free to compose their sentences with clauses in any order. In my opinion, more research is needed to establish the relationship between cognitive development and the emergence of the free RT system.

CONCLUSION: TEMPORAL SYSTEMS AND CONCEPTUAL DEVELOPMENT

The argument has been made that it is possible to make inferences about the child's conceptualization of time from innovations in child language. Between the ages of 1;6 and 4;6 children say some remarkable things about time, e.g., a Brazilian child at (3;11) – 'No. I gonna take a long time to wake up because tomorrow I gonna wake up in yesterday today.' (a translation from Portuguese, deLemos & Bybee 1981). With statements such as this one, we might be predisposed to think that temporal relationships are muddled in the preschool child's mind. In child language research it is possible to learn a great deal about the child's understanding of temporal relationships by analyzing the form of what they say as well as the content.

After ruling out a number of alternative explanations, we can conclude from our research on child Polish that the initial past versus nonpast contrasts specify a deictic relationship sometime between 1;6 and 2;0. Since children can construct the relationship ET prior to ST, it is inferred that they have the capacity to retrieve the episodic representation of some prior experience and appreciate its anterior property. When the initial deictic relationships are expressed, there is very little evidence that children can locate prior or subsequent situations along the time line as RT remains at

ST. Within one year's time, around 2;6, contrasting temporal locations emerge. In Polish, children contrast past imperfective statements having internal perspective on an anterior situation with statements containing the adverb *już* and a past perfective verb form e.g., Discourse Segment 6 versus Sentence 15. The exact interval along the time line is not specified in either utterance, but the former is relatively remote in contrast to the latter.

Between about 2;6 and 3;0 children use adverbs to specify intervals along their conceptual model of time flow, but the intervals do not always correspond to the fluent speakers interpretation of the meaning of these adverbs. It is now clear that the child's point of reference can be placed prior to, simultaneous with, or subsequent to ST, but it is seldom clear where in terms of calendar time the point of reference is. Hence, 'yesterday' comes to mean sometime in the past, and the time span referred to may or may not be within the prior daily cycle. During the same developmental phase, children begin to use temporal adverbial clauses. They describe their temporal frame of reference with these clauses. At this point, they express an experiential (or episodic) referential location, but there is still no specific placement along a metrical model of time flow. When Wawrzon (2;9) said, 'Now, in a year when I grow up,' there is no reason to suspect that Wawrzon's year has 365 daily cycles or 12 monthly cycles. Furthermore, Wawrzon's perception of when he would become sufficiently mature to do many things was very much different from that of his parents. The discrepancy in the placement of temporal intervals may be explicit in the child's utterance; for example, when Bloom's Kathryn (2;6) said, *You came here last night when my mother was ironing*, the time was not last night but six weeks prior (Bloom 1970 p. 229).

In Harner's (1975) experimental analysis of *yesterday* and *tomorrow*, children played with separate sets of toys on successive days. On the second day, there were three sets of toys; 1) yesterday's—the old ones, 2) today's—the current ones, and 3) tomorrow's—the ones the child hasn't played with yet. Harner asked two, three, and four-year-old children to show her the toys from yesterday and those for tomorrow. The two-year-old children failed to match the toys with the temporal modifiers, and four-year old children succeeded. The three-year-old children were un likely to make an error by choosing the current/today's set, and they made fewer errors on yesterday's set of toys. These data are consistent with the pattern of development outlined in Section 5.2.

In general, Harner (1982) interpreted the difficulty with cyclic adverbs as: "a) understanding the meaning of the temporal adverbs, and b) coordinating two temporally marked linguistic forms (verbs and adverbs) rather than either a conceptual confusion of past and future verbs with each other" (p. 154). We agree with Harner (see Weist & Buczowska, 1987). It is worth adding that Harner did not require children to discriminate yesterday's toys from another *anterior* set such as the day before yesterday. We predict that a requirement of this form would cause three-year-old children considerable problems.

When RT is initially integrated into the child's temporal system, there are constraints on its use. In Weist 1986, I argued that the restricted RT system is limited to two temporal intervals; allowing the configurations (RT=ET) prior or subsequent to ST and ET prior or subsequent to (ST=RT). It still appears that the system may emerge with this constraint, but the constraint is rapidly overcome. By 3;0 to 3;5, children have sufficient control over sequencing mechanisms to place ET, RT, and ST at unique intervals in time. This fact provides additional support for the claim that nonegocentric temporal perspective is within the capacity of three-year-old children.

In spite of some evidence to the contrary, most of the research indicates that the sequence of clauses is restricted by the sequence of events in the world, and that constraint remains until at least 4;6 when a free RT system has been attested. I expect to see that more sensitive tests of seriation and reversibility will place these conceptual developments prior to the evolution of the free RT system.

When the theoretical framework found here was presented for the first time in 1982, our estimates of the integration of ET and RT into the emerging temporal systems of child language were precocious to say the least. The following two quotations represented *good* estimates of the course of development at that time:

> "Data from the youngest children studied suggest that nonpresent verb forms are first used to refer to *aspects* of an extended present. Data gathered from children over 2;6 years suggest that children are able to refer to both the present consequences of past events (completive aspect) and the past as an event preceding and separate from the present (tense)" (Harner, 1982 p. 153).
>
> "At Stage 1, children can refer to times other than the present but always from the point of view of the present. At Stage II, children can narrate a sequence of times from a point of view other than the present. Probably this stage begins for most children by the fourth year" (Smith, 1980 p. 276).

These statements were largely shaped by research on English with a secondary influence from French and Italian. By looking at a language with a very different tense-aspect-modality system, my colleagues in Poland and I were able to revise these estimates downward. It is now possible to make cross-linguistic comparisons with a variety of languages (see the chapters in Slobin 1985). This measure by cross-linguistic perspective is substantial but still only a drop in the bucket. We need a full range of observations (1;6 to 5;6) on languages which are presently being studied, including Polish, and we need data from languages which have unusual temporal systems, e.g., Bamileke-Aschang and Bamileke-Ngyemboon which are Bantu languages with rich systems of remote tense (Comrie, 1985). The study of such languages would, for example, help us to understand when the property of cyclicity becomes part of the child's model of time flow. This is relevant to the development of the concept of seriation. If we are seriously interested in making language-thought inferences, in my opinion cross-linguistic perspective is essential. This chapter contains numerous examples of how the contrastive process (e.g., Slavic versus Romance languages) can lead to important insights, and the expansion of cross-linguistic perspective in the future will continue to improve our understanding of the conceptual development of temporal concepts and relationships.

Footnotes

[2]The grammatical code is the same as the code used in Slobin (1985). It is as follows: ACC (A)=Accusative 1, 2, & 3=first, second, & third person; COND=conditional; DIM=diminutive, FEM (F)=feminine; FUT=future; IMP=imperative; IPFV=imperfective; MASC (M)=masculine; NEUT (N)=neuter; NOM (N)=Nominative; NPAST=non-past; NVIR=non-virile; PP=past participle; PAST=past; PFV=perfective; P=plural; PRES=present; REF=reflexive; S=singular; VIR=virile; and VOC=vocative.

The Polish examples in this chapter were sometimes simplified in that we did not present the phonologically precise child forms, e.g., Marta's [Klufki] versus [Krufki] in Sentence 4.

[3]A review of the development research on memory process is beyond the scope of this paper (see Brown, Bransford, Ferrara, & Campione, 1983). In fairness to Antinucci and Miller, ten years ago the developmental research jumped from infants to kindergarteners. Due primarily to the work of DeLoache, Brown, Wellman and Perlmutter we have direct evidence for the two-year-old's capacity to remember locations and objects, and we know that children from 1;6 to 2;0 can utilize rudimentary mnemonic strategies (e.g., DeLoache, Cassidy, & Brown, 1985).

[4]Whenever children use some regularity in their language to invent a new form, they provide evidence for productivity e.g. children learning English overgeneralize the rule for regular past tense formation producing *comed, doed*, etc. Slavic children invent new forms

as well (see Chmura – Klekotowa, 1967 & 1988). The formation of the past tense is so regular in Polish that there is no room for overgeneralization of the rule for past tense formation (see also Smoczyńska 1985 p. 648).

[5]In Reilly's (1982) extensive study of the acquisition of conditionals, she found hypothetical conditionals produced at three years of age (see also Kuczaj & Daly 1979), but not fully comprehended until four, at which time counterfactuals are also understood. As Reilly (1982) pointed out the conditional mood requires decentration "the ability to detach oneself mentally from the real world and the real time continuum" (p. 234). The emergence of hypothetical conditionals at about 3;0 in a number of languages provides more evidence that the child's point of temporal reference is no longer frozen at ST.

[6]By 2;2 Bowerman's (1981) Christy was able to express a wide range of temporal configurations; e.g.

1) I be right back down *after* I relax.
2) We haf' read a book *'fore* you go.
3) First I get some. *Then* you can sniff.
4) Daddy hafta fix it *when* he come home.
5) This don't work *when* I hold it.
6) We can fix breakfast *while* Daddy sleeps.

These all appear to involve two events which Christy anticipates in the future. At this phase of development, Christy was only using the "immediate set" of temporal adverbs. In other words, she was showing only the most rudimentary signs of establishing RT. Her precocious temporal sequencing appears to precede well defined temporal location along a time line.

[7]Ames's (1946) research shows that the child's capacity to express concepts of calendar time develops significantly between 4;0 and 5;0.

References

Aksu, A.A. (1978). *Aspect and modality in the child's acquisition of the Turkish past tense.* Unpublished Ph.D. dissertation, University of California, Berkeley.

Ames, L.B. (1946). The development of the sense of time in the young child. *Journal of Genetic Psychology, 68,* 97–125.

Antinucci, F. & Miller, R. (1976). How children talk about what happened. *Journal of Child Language, 3,* 167–189.

Bloom, L. (1970). *Language Development.* Cambridge, Massachusetts; MIT Press.

Bloom, L., Lahey, M., Hood, L., Lifter, K. & Fiess, K. (1980). Complex Sentences: acquisition of syntactic connectives and the semantic relations they encode. *Journal of Child Language, 7,* 235–262.

Bloom, L., Lifter, K. & Hafitz, J. (1980). Semantics of verbs and the development of verb inflection in child language. *Language, 56,* 386–412.

Borke, H. (1975). Piaget's mountains revisited: Changes in the egocentric landscape. *Developmental Psychology, 11,* 240–243.

Bower, T.G.R. (1974). *Development in Infancy.* San Francisco: Freeman.

Bowerman, M. (1979). The acquisition of complex sentences. In P. Fletcher & M. Garman (Eds.), *Language Acquisition.* Cambridge: Cambridge University Press.

Bowerman, M. (1981). *Notes for the Nijmegan Workshop,* Max-Planck-Institut, The Netherlands.

Bronckart, J.P. & Sinclair, H. (1973). Time, tense, and aspect. *Cognition, 2,* 107–130.

Brown, R. (1973). *A First Language: The Early Stages.* Cambridge MA: Harvard Univ. Press.

Brown, A., Bransford, J., Ferrara, R. & Campione, J. (1983). Learning, remembering, and understanding. In J. Flavell & E. Markman (Eds.), *Handbook of Child Psychology.* New York: Wiley.

Bruner, J. (1975). The Ontogenesis of Speech Acts. *Journal of Child Language, 2,* 1–20.

Bybee, J. (1985). *Morphology.* Amsterdam: Benjamins.

Campbell, R. (1986). Language acquisition and cognition. In P. Fletcher & M. Garman (Eds.), *Language Acquisition.* Cambridge: Cambridge University Press.

Chmura-Klekotowa, M. (1967 & 1968). Neologizmy słowotwórcze w mowie dzieci I & II (Morphological neologisms in the speech of children). *Poradnik Językowy, 10,* 433–445, & 1, 19–25.

Clancy, P.M., Jacobsen, T. & Silva, N. (1976). The acquisition of conjunctions: A cross-linguistic study. *PRCLD, 12,* 71–80.

Clark, E.V. (1985). Acquisition of Romance, with special reference to French. In D.I. Slobin (Ed.), *The Crosslinguistic Study of Language Acquisition.* Hillside, New Jersey: Erlbaum.

Comrie, B. (1976). *Aspect: An Introduction to the Study of Verbal Aspect and Related Problems.* Cambridge: Cambridge University Press.

Comrie, B. (1985). *Tense.* Cambridge: Cambridge University Press.

Corrigan, R. (1978). Language development as related to stage 6 object permanence development. *Journal of Child Language, 5,* 173–189.

Corrigan, R. (1979). Cognitive correlates of language: Differential criteria yield differential results. *Child Development, 50,* 617–631.

Cromer, R.F. (1974). The development of language and cognition: the cognitive hypothesis. In B. Foss (Ed.), *New Perspectives in Language Development* (pp. 184–252). Harmondsworth, England: Penguin Books.

Dahl, O. (1985). *Tense and Aspect Systems.* Oxford: Blackwell.

de Lemos, C. (1981). International processes in the child's construction of language. In W. Deutsch (Ed.), *The Child's Construction of Language.* New York: Academic Press.

de Lemos, C. & Bybee, J. (1981). The acquisition of past reference in Brazilian Portuguese. Max-Planck Institut: The Netherlands.

De Loache, J., Cassidy, D.J., & Brown, A. (1985). Precursors of mnemonic strategies in very young children's memory. *Child Development, 56,* 125–137.

de Villiers, P.A. & de Villiers, J.G. (1974). On this, that, and the other: Nonegocentrism in very young children. *Journal of Experimental Child Psychology, 18,* 438–447.

Di Paolo, M. & Smith, C.S. (1978). Cognitive and linguistic factors in the acquisition of temporal and aspectual expressions. In P. French (Ed.), *The Development of Meaning.* Tokyo: Bunka Hyoron.

Dowty, D. (1970). *Word Meaning and Montague Grammar.* Dordrecht: Reidel.

Erbaugh, M.S. (1982). *Coming to order: Natural selection and the origin of syntax in the Mandarin-speaking child.* Unpublished Ph.D. dissertation, University of California, Berkeley.

Fagan, J.F. (1973). Infant's delayed recognition memory and forgetting. *Journal of Experimental Child Psychology, 16,* 424–450.

Ferreiro, E. & Sinclair, H. (1971). Temporal relationships in language. *International Journal of Psychology, 6,* 39–47.

Fletcher, P. (1979). The development of the verb phrase. In P. Fletcher & M. Garman (Eds.), *Language Acquisition.* Cambridge: Cambridge University Press.

Fraisse, P. (1982). The Adaptation of the Child to Time. In W.J. Friedman (Ed.), *The Developmental Psychology of Time.* New York: Academic Press.

Friedman, W.J. (1978). Development of time concepts in children. In H.W. Ruse & L.P. Lipsitt (Eds.), *Advances in Child Development and Behavior* (Vol. *12*) (pp. 267–298). New York: Academic Press.

Friedman, W.J. (1982a). *The Developmental Psychology of Time.* New York: Academic Press.

Friedman, W.J. (1982b). Conventional time concepts and children's structuring of time. In W.J. Friedman (Eds.), *The Developmental Psychology of Time.* New York: Academic Press.

Gathercole, V. (1985). *On present perfect in Scottish and American English. SRCD* meeting, Toronto.

Gelman, R. & Baillargeon, R. (1983). A review of some Piagetian concepts. In J.H. Flavell & E.M. Markman (Eds.), *Cognitive Development.* New York: Wiley.

Gerhardt, J. (1987). *From discourse to semantics: The development of the verb morphology and forms of self-reference in the speech of a 2 year old.* Unpublished manuscript.

Gopnik, A. (1984). The acquisition of *gone* and the development of the object concept. *Journal of Child Language, 11*, 273–292.

Gopnik, A. & Meltzoff, A.N. (1984). Semantic and cognitive development in 15– to 21–month-old children. *Journal of Child Language, 11*, 495–513.

Greenfield, P.M. & Smith, J.H. (1976). *The Structure of Communication in Early Language Development.* New York: Academic Press.

Gvozdev, A.N. (1961). *Voprosy Izucheniya Detskoy Rechi.* Moscow: Izdvo Akademii Pedagogicheskikh Nauk RSFSR.

Harner, L. (1975). Yesterday and tomorrow: Development of early understanding of the terms. *Developmental Psychology, 11*, 864–65.

Harner, L. (1981). Children talk about time and aspect of actions. *Child Development, 52*, 498–506.

Harner, L. (1982). Talking about the past and the future. In W.J. Friedman (Ed.), *The Developmental Psychology of Time.* New York: Academic Press.

Ingram, D. (1978). Sensorimotor intelligence and language development. In A. Lock (Ed.) *Action, Gesture, and Symbol: The Emergence of Language.* New York: Academic Press.

Johnston, J.R. (1984) *Children's Verbal Representation of Location.* Paper presented at the Salk Institute Workshop on Spatial Cognition.

Johnston, J.R. (1985). Cognitive Prerequisities: The Evidence from Children Learning English. In D.I. Slobin (Ed.), *The Crosslinguistic Study of Language Acquisitions.* Hillsdale, N.J.: Erlbaum.

Kuczaj, S. & Daly, M. (1979). The development of hypothetical reference in the speech of young children. *Journal of Child Language, 6*, 563–579.

Leung, E. & Reinhold, H. (1981). Development of pointing as a social gesture. *Developmental Psychology, 17*, 215–220.

Levin, I. (1982). The nature and development of time concepts in children: The effect of interfering cues. In W. J. Friedman (Ed.) *The developmental psychology of time.* N.Y.: Academic Press.

Loveland, K.A. (1984). Learning about points of view: Spatial perspective and the acquisition of 'I/You'. *Journal of Child Language, 11*, 535–556.

Lyons, J. (1977). *Semantics.* Cambridge: Cambridge University Press.

Majewicz, A.F. (1982). Understanding aspect I & II. *Lingua Posnaniensis, 14*, 19–61 & *15*, 15–40.

Mandler, J. (1983). Representation. In J.H. Flavell & E.M. Markman (Eds.), *Cognitive Development.* New York: Wiley.

Masangkay, Z.S., McCluskey, K.A., McIntyre, C.W., Sims-Knight, J., Vaughn, B.E., & Flavell, J.H. (1974). The early development of inferences about the visual percepts of others. *Child Development, 45*, 357–366.

McCune-Nicolich, L. (1981). The cognitive bases of relational words in the single word period. *Journal of Child Language, 8*, 15–34.

Nelson, K. (1986). *Event Knowledge: Structure and Function in Development.* Hillsdale, N.J.: Erlbaum.

Nelson, K. & Gruendel, J. (1981). Generalized event representation: Basic building blocks of cognitive development. In M.E. Lamb & A.L. Brown (Eds.), *Advances in Developmental Psychology, vol. 1.* Hillsdale, New Jersey: Lawrence Erlbaum.

Piaget, J. (1962). *Play, Dreams and Imitation in Childhood.* New York: Norton.

Piaget, J. & Inhelder, B. (1956). *The Child's Conception of Space.* London: Routledge & Kegan Paul.

Quirk, R. & Greenbaum, S. (1978). *A Concise Grammar of Contemporary English.* New York: Harcourt Brace Jovanovich.

Radulovic, L. (1975). *Acquisition of language: Studies of Dubrovnik children.* Unpublished Ph.D. dissertation, University of California, Berkeley.

Reichenbach, H. (1947). *Symbolic Logic.* Berkeley: University of California.

Reilly, J.S. (1982). *The acquisition of conditionals in English.* Dissertation. University of California at Los Angeles.

Sachs, J. (1983). Talking about the there and then: The emergence of displaced reference in parent-child discourse. In K.E. Nelson (Ed.), *Children's Language, Vol. 4.* Hillsdale, New Jersey: Erlbaum.

Schank, R.C. & Abelson, R.P. (1977). *Scripts, plans, goals, and understanding.* Hillsdale, New Jersey: Erlbaum.

Slobin, D.I. (1973). Cognitive Prerequisities for the Development of Grammer. In C.A. Ferguson & D.I. Slobin (Eds.), *Studies of Child Language Development.* New York: Holt, Reinhart & Winston.

Slobin, D.I. (1982). Universal and Particular in the Acquisition of Language. In E. Wanner & L.R. Gleitman (Eds.) *Language Acquisition: The State of the Art.* Cambridge: Cambridge Univ. Press.

Slobin, D.I. (1985). *The Cross-linguistic Study of Language acquisition.* Hillsdale, New Jersey: Erlbaum.

Smith, C.S. (1980). The acquisition of time talk: Relations between child and adult grammars. *Journal of Child Language, 7*, 263–278.

Smith, C.S. (1983). A theory of aspectual choice. *Language, 59*, 470–501.

Smith, C.S. (1986). Aspect as a parameter. In S. Choi, D. Devitt, W. Jais, T. McCoy & Z. Zhang (Eds.), *Proceedings of the Second East Coast Conference on Linguistics.* Columbus, Ohio: Ohio State University Press.

Smith, C.S. & Weist, R.M. (1987). On the temporal contour of child language: A reply to Rispoli & Bloom. *Journal of Child Language*, 14, 387–392.

Smoczyńska, M. (1978). Wczesne stadia rozwoju skƚadni w mowie dziecka. (The early phases of development of syntax in the speech of children). Dissertation, Uniwersytet Jagiellońoki, Kraków.

Smoczyńska M. (1985). Acquisition of Polish. In D.I. Slobin (Ed.), *The Cross-linguistic Study of Language Acquisition.* Hillsdale, New Jersey: Erlbaum.

Spelke, E.S. (1985). Perception of unity, persistence, and identity: Thoughts on infant's conception of objects. In J. Mehler & R. Fox (Eds.), *Neonate Cognition.* Hillsdale, New Jersey: Erlbaum.

Stephany, U. (1981). Verbal grammar in Modern Greek early child language. In P.S. Dale & D. Ingram (Eds.), *Child Language: An International Perspective.* Baltimore: University Park Press.

Stephany, U. (1986) Modality. In P. Fletcher & M. Carman (Eds.), *Language Acquisition.* Cambridge: Cambridge University Press.

Stojanova, J. (1987) *The Emergence of Temporality in Bulgarian Child Language.* Paper presented at the Fourth International Congress for the Study of Child Language. Lund, Sweden.

Tanz, C. (1980). *Studies in the Acquisition of Deictic Terms.* Cambridge: Cambridge University Press.

Toivainen, J. (1980). *Inflectional Affixes Used by Finnish-speaking Children Aged 1–3 Years.* Helsinki: Suomalaisen Kirjallisuuden Seura.

Tomasello, M. & Farrar, M.J. (1984). Cognitive bases of lexical development: Object permanence and relational words. *Journal of Child Language, 11,* 477–493.

Trosborg, A. (1982). Children's comprehension of 'before' and 'after' reinvestigated. *Journal of Child Language, 9,* 381–402.

Uzgiris, I. & Hunt, J. (1975). *Assessment in Infancy: Ordinal Scales of Psychological Development.* Urbana: University of Illinois Press.

Vendler, Z. (1967). Verbs and times. In Z. Vendler, *Linguistics in Philosophy.* Ithaca, New York: Cornell University Press.

Weist, R.M. (1982). Temporal systems in child language: A crosslinguistic study. Paper presented at the 15th Annual Meeting of Societas Linguistica Europea, Athens.

Weist, R.M. (1983). Prefix versus suffix information processing in the comprehension of tense and aspect. *Journal of Child Language, 10,* 85–96.

Weist, R.M. (1985). Cross-linguistic perspective on cognitive development. In T.M. Schlechter and M.P. Toglia (Eds.), *New Directors in Cognitive Science.* Norwood, New Jersey: Ablex Press.

Weist, R.M. (1986). Tense and aspect: Temporal systems in child language. In P. Fletcher & M. Garman (Eds.), *Language Acquisition.* Cambridge: Cambridge University Press.

Weist, R.M. & Buczowska, E. (1987). The emergence of temporal adverbs in Polish. *First Language, 7,* 217–229.

Weist, R.M. & Konieczna, E. (1985). Affix processing strategies. *Journal of Child Language, 12,* 27–35.

Weist, R.M. & Witkowska-Stadnik, K. (1986). Basic relations in child language and the word order myth. *International Journal of Psychology, 21,* 363–381.

Weist, R.M., Wysocka, H., Witkowska-Stadnik, K., Buczowska, E. & Konieczna, E. (1984). The defective tense hypothesis: On the emergence of tense and aspect in child Polish. *Journal of Child Language, 11,* 347–374.

Wells (1979). Learning and using the auxilliary verb in English. In V. Lee (Ed.), *Language Development* (pp. 250–270). London: Croom Helm.

Zarębina, M. (1965). Kształtowanie się systemu językowego dziecka (The formation of the language system of a child). Kraków: Wydawnictwo Polskiej Akademi Nauk; Wrocław: Ossolineum.

TIME AND HUMAN COGNITION
A Life-Span Perspective
I. Levin and D. Zakay (Editors)

IRIS LEVIN
FRIEDRICH WILKENING

CHAPTER 3

Measuring Time via Counting: The Development of Children's Conceptions of Time as a Quantifiable Dimension*

INTRODUCTION

> And yet, Lord, we perceive intervals of times, and compare them, and say, some are shorter, and others longer. We measure also, how much longer or shorter this time is than that; and we answer "this is double or treble;" . . . This same time then, how do I measure? do we by a shorter time measure a longer, as by the space of a cubit, the space of a rood? . . . Thus measure we the spaces of stanzas, by the spaces of verses, and the spaces of verses, by the spaces of the feet, and the spaces of the feet, by the spaces of the syllables, and the spaces of long, by the space of short syllables; . . . But neither do we this way obtain any certain measure of time; because it may be, that a shorter verse, pronounced more fully, may take up more time than a longer, pronounced more hurriedly . . . Whence it seemed to me that time is but a protraction; but of what, I know not. (*The Confessions of Saint Augustine, 400 AD*)

*This chapter is based on Working Paper No. 74 of the Tel Aviv Study Group on Human Development and Education. We wish to thank Orit Krispin and Lily Levy for their significant contributions to the studies they had taken part in. Thanks are extended also to Dan Zakay for his helpful comments on the manuscript.

The nature of time and the ways to measure it have intrigued the human mind from early history—and still puzzle us when contemplating the laws of modern physics. Nevertheless, at least two notions nowadays seem self evident: (a) that physical time passes in a constant pace, irrespective of the events occuring in it, and (b) that the progression of time is measurable, so that the numbers applied to its units are amenable to mathematical operations.

The conception of time as a quantifiable and uniform entity, independent of the motions taking place in it, appears to be a relatively late invention in human history (Szamosi, 1986, pp. 88–111). It emerged around the 12th century, with the construction of musical notations coordinating different intervals. It took another five centuries until the concept of time became systematically integrated into a more general model of the physical world, which was Galileo's accomplishment. He worked out how the laws of motion can be described when distance and time are conceived of as dimensions that are independent from each other. This paved the way to Newton, whose theory still serves as the framework in contemporary physics for the macroscopic world of perceived objects and events (Capec, 1971).

This cultural evolution of reasoning about time implies that the way we conceive of time should not be taken as self evident. It seems highly plausible that the child has to work out step by step a metric concept of time. Piaget held this view and devoted two major books (and several later discussions) to this issue (Piaget, 1946/1969, 1946/1970). Although various aspects of his analysis have been critically examined and his conclusions have been reformulated (e.g., Acredolo & Schmid, 1981; Montangero, 1979; Siegler & Richards, 1979), his major conclusion that young children can grasp time only on a qualitative level has generally been accepted (for an exception see Wilkening, 1981).

The aim of this chapter is to examine, in light of recent data from our laboratories, the questions of when children come to treat time as a quantifiable dimension and what strategies they invent on their own when trying to measure the duration of short events.

QUALITATIVE VERSUS QUANTITATIVE REASONING: INTEGRATION OF DURATIONS

For several decades, an adequate investigation of children's developing capability to quantify time had been impeded by the reliance on Piaget's choice-task paradigm. The adherence to this specific paradigm was an almost natural outcome of Piaget's theory.

Piaget (1946/1969) assumed that the ability to quantify duration was a late achievement in the course of development. Young children were claimed to have only an ordinal concept of time: They could decide which of two durations was the longer one, but not how much longer it was. Children's judgments were said to be based on the relation between duration and succession. With such an ordinal concept, "preoperational" children could reason that if two events started together, the one that stopped last must have been the one with the longer duration. Similarly, they were able to recognize that if the two events stopped simultaneously, the first to start must have extended for the longer time.

Partially Overlapping Events

In accordance with this theoretical view, the choice paradigm always included two events to be compared. In most instances, the two events either started or stopped simultaneously; never did one event come to an end before the other had started. Thus, there was always a partial duration overlap between the two events. As a rule, the events to be compared were motions in space, involving intermixed cues of time, speed, and distance. For instance, two cars were running on parallel tracks, at the same or at different speeds, covering identical or different distances. The child's task was to determine which car ran for the longer time.

The inclusion of speed and distance cues was intentional: Piaget believed that young children cannot have a concept of time independent of speed and distance, because they do not clearly distinguish between these dimensions. In the choice task, accordingly, children until the age of 8 or 9 years tended to attribute more time to the slower car, or to the car covering the longer distance. Only after time is seen as separate entity, differentiated from speed and distance, are children in the Piagetian view in a position to relate duration to succession, which then leads to time quantification in a later stage of development.

Piaget's notions have been supported in many followup studies (e.g., Acredolo & Schmid, 1981; Lovell & Slater, 1960; Siegler & Richards, 1979). These studies retained the choice paradigm and found, in accordance with Piaget, that children before the age of 10 (or even older) did not succeed in basing their time judgments solely on the relevant cues of succession. A typical error of the younger children was that they chose the car that stopped farther ahead (distance cue) as the one that had travelled for the longer time. The main departure from Piaget's original findings was that, in some of the followup studies, the concept of time appeared to be mastered even later than Piaget had thought.

Piaget's analysis was challenged, however, in a series of studies by Levin and her colleagues (see Levin, 1982, for a summary). They showed that when the interfering cues of speed and distance were eliminated, children by the age of five years are well aware of the logical relation that exists between duration and succession. Preschoolers succeeded, for instance, in comparing the burning time of two lamps. But, in the same study, children could not cope successfully with comparing the running times of two cars. Hence, speed and distance were claimed to function as interfering cues that mask children's competence to relate the time-relevant cues of duration and succession.

The results of Levin's studies show that, contrary to Piaget, children's understanding of time can be meaningfully investigated without intermixing time cues with speed and distance cues. However, the choice paradigm used by Levin was again incapable of telling apart qualitative from quantitative reasoning. A child could have arrived at a correct choice by processing only the succession of the beginning and ending points of the durations, and/or by processing the metric duration information. Hence, this task would have been incapable of assessing a quantitative time concept, if it had been there.

Children's time quantification as such was first studied by Wilkening (1981, 1982). Using a paradigm derived from Anderson's (1981) information integration theory, Wilkening investigated children's and adults' ability to quantify and integrate time, speed, and distance information. Subjects were told that an animal was fleeing over a footbridge from a barking dog. Different durations were the barking times of the dog; different distances were the length of the path covered by the fleeing animal; and different speeds were represented by pictures of animals which are known to have different maximum speeds (e.g., turtle and cat).

Subjects were shown factorial combinations of values on two dimensions and had to estimate a value on the third. For example, when the task was to infer a quantitative value of time, an animal (speed level) was presented at a certain distance level on the footbridge. Judgments were made by turning on a record of a barking dog for the desired time. The pattern of these judgments suggested that 5-year-old children integrated speed and distance information by a subtractive rule to infer time, Time = Distance − Speed. Although this rule does not agree with the normative ratio rule, Time = Distance/Speed, it reveals that children at this age were able to recognize all three variables as distinct entities, a conclusion corroborated by a set of converging additional data in the same study. In particular, a time concept appears to be present on a metric level already by 5 years, far earlier than stated by Piaget.

Would children also be able to quantify time when comparing durations with different starting and ending times? As discussed earlier, Levin (1982) had shown that 5–year-olds can make use of this ordinal information in a meaningful way, when no interfering cues are presented. What would happen if Wilkening's (1981) methodology was applied to the choice paradigm? Would the rules underlying young children's durations comparisons prove to be qualitative ones, just taking into account the ordinal succession information, or would the children employ a quantitative approach, processing the metric time information? A study by Levin, Wilkening, and Dembo (1984) addressed these questions.

The duration information was presented by two faucets, each of which poured water into an opaque jar for specified times. The two events started and/or ended either together or one after the other, so that there was always some duration overlap. The child was to decide which, if either, jar had received less water and to equalize the amount by restarting the appropriate faucet. These adjustment responses, in conjunction with the factorial beginnings x endings design, allowed the diagnosis of qualitative and quantitative processing rules. For example, it was possible to study whether children followed the normative metric rule—adding or subtracting the duration differences—or whether they employed less sophisticated nonmetric approaches. First, fourth and seventh graders took part in the study. They were 7, 10 and 13 years old.

The predominant finding was that children shifted with age from nonmetric to metric rules. All 13–year-olds and most 10–year-olds followed the normative rule, adding an amount of water proportional to the differences in duration at the beginning and/or end of the two events. This quantitative rule was virtually absent in the 7–year-olds. They reduced the information to an ordinal level. Four different qualitative rules emerged:

Rule 1 was a pure centration rule. These children took only the ending times into account. When the two events ended together, children claimed that the durations were the same, regardless of the beginning times; and when one event ended later, the children chose to add water to the one with the earlier stop time, again disregarding the beginnings.

Rule 2 was an advance over Rule 1 in that these children took into account the beginning differences, but only when the stop times were equal. Neither of these rules involved any quantification. The amount of water added was unrelated to the actual time differences.

Rule 3 involved first signs of quantification. These children made greater adjustments for differences in ending time than for differences in beginning time. However, different degrees of time lags were again not discriminated.

Rule 4 exhibited the beginnings of true quantification in problems that differed only in stop times. In these cases, the judged duration differences were linearly related to the actual differences. In contrast to the three less sophisticated rules, start times were always taken into account. However, when one event both started and stopped before the other, the durations were judged to be the same, irrespective of the degree of beginning and ending differences. Quantification was thus again absent in most conditions.

Rules 3 and 4, incidentally, validate findings of earlier studies, which had shown that, if at all, ending differences are more salient than beginning differences in the durations choice paradigm (Levin, Gilat, & Zelniker, 1980; Levin, Goldstein, & Zelniker, 1984; Montangero, 1981).

The shift from qualitative rules to quantitative algebraic rules found in the study reported here appears to conform with what had been suggested by Piaget (1946/1969) and implied by Siegler and Richards (1979) and Richards (1982). The question is raised, however, whether the present findings imply that, at the age of 7 years, children still have a nonmetric concept of time. This conclusion would conflict with Wilkening's (1981) findings, which showed that even 5–year-olds have a metric concept of time.

It seems highly plausible that the nonalgebraic rules cannot be taken as representations of children's knowledge. Rather, they seem to be induced by peculiarities of the task used by Levin, Wilkening and Dembo (1984). One possibility is that the choice-task format per se induces the nonalgebraic rules, as suggested by Wilkening and Anderson (1982, p. 235).

Another possibility is that a more specific difficulty inherent in the task presented by Levin, Wilkening & Dembo (1984) might have led the young children to "fall back" on qualitative rules. The difficulty might have been that there was a time overlap in each problem, during which water poured from both faucets together. The easiest way to arrive at a correct solution required the child to ignore this overlap interval, that is, the very "busiest" part of the whole event. This may be counterintuitive for young children, leading them to adopt a strategy that simplifies the problem.

It seemed to be useful, therefore, to eliminate the overlap and to study children's integration of successive durations. This was the purpose of the following experiment.

Integration of Successive Events

Young children's failure to process the metric time information in the Levin at al. (1984) study cannot be attributed to a general deficiency in quantification and integration capacity. In many recent applications of information integration theory, children from the age of 4 years have been found to coordinate various physical dimensions —including time—according to algebraic rules, which imply quantification (e.g., Anderson, 1980; Cuneo, 1982; Wilkening, 1982). Specifically, young children were found to even have a preference for adding-type rules, that is, for the very rules that are prescribed by the normative rules for determining the result of duration combinations. Addition and subtraction, which were required in our time problems, are accessible to young children—and probably even privileged. Would these rules be used when the specific difficulties that are inherent in the time overlap paradigm are circumvented?

Wilkening, Levin, and Druyan (1987) presented successive events and asked the children to judge their overall duration. Actually, to combine the duration of successive events seems to be more closely tied to the daily experiences of the child than to operate on durations of events that partially overlap. Moreover, the integration of successive durations seems to be easier because the irrelevant information that should be ignored is the "empty" interval between the two events, not a "full" interval as in the overlap paradigm. For these reasons, we expected time quantification to appear earlier in the successive duration task.

A more general source of difficulty in attempts to quantify time may lie in its continuity. Virtually every physical device for measuring time, be it a sundial or an atomic clock, segments time into units and counts them (Jespersen & Fitz-Randolph, 1978). To the young child, it may not be obvious that time can be segmented into units, and that the segmentation can be useful for measuring it. In our previous study (Levin et al., 1984), we had observed that, from the age of 10 years, the majority of the children spontaneously counted to estimate the durations. Therefore, our followup study was also designed so that children's use of counting strategies could be explored in a more elaborate way.

The two durations, the overall duration of which had to be judged, were presented in a factorial design, first x second duration. Values on each factor were 2, 4, and 6 seconds. These were presented as lighting times of a red bulb. On each factorial combination, the bulb was lit twice, with a constant pause of 2 seconds, and the child's task was to let the bulb burn for the same time it lit in the two intervals together. Each child judged the nine duration combinations in two different random orders. For half of the children, the presentation of the lights was accompanied by rhythmic beats of a metronome. We expected that this hint would enhance children's counting and quantification of time.

Kindergartners, first and second graders participated in the study. They were 5, 6 and 7 years old.

The major finding was that, from the age of 6 or 7 years, children integrated the two durations by the correct additive rule. This rule, of course, implies quantification—as prescribed by any metric concept of time. At each age, the frequency of additive integration was higher in the rhythm than in the non-rhythm condition. This was even true for the 7–year-olds: 29 out of 30 children in the rhythm condition employed the correct integration rule, while only 16 out of 30 employed it in the non rhythm condition.

The results were less clear for the youngest children in this study. The judgments of the 5–year-olds were often unsystematic and unreliable, as indicated by a relatively low correlation between first and second judgment obtained for the majority of the children at this age. It should be noted, however, that in this study the statistical criteria for rule diagnosis on the individual level were relatively conservative. Hints of an additive integration, though not statistically significant over the whole range of durations, appeared in several 5–year-olds. Thus, there was a tendency to quantify time from the youngest age on.

Nevertheless, it remains unclear why the youngest children were relatively unsuccessful in this task, compared with 5–year-olds' performance in other tasks of information integration. One reason could be that the judgment of single durations per se may be too difficult. Alternatively, children may be able to reliably estimate single durations but fail to integrate the single estimates into a value of overall duration. It seemed desirable, thus, to investigate young children's capability of estimating single durations.

Estimating Single Durations

It has already been reported in the literature that children of preschool age succeed in estimating single durations (Crowder & Hohle, 1970; Fraisse, 1982; Friedman, 1977). However, in each of these studies just one fixed time interval was presented, typically around 10 seconds long, and the children had to reproduce that duration. Our question, though, goes further: We asked if children can reliably distinguish between durations that differ from each other in only a few seconds.

In an unpublished study, Levin and Levy asked 128 children 5 to 8 years of age, from preschool to third grade, to reproduce the lighting times of a bulb, 2, 4, or 6 seconds, presented in three different random orders. After each presentation, the child's task was to reproduce the duration by pressing a key that made the bulb burn. Half of each age group got special instructions and will be considered in a later section.

The means of the three judgments of each duration were found to be in the correct order for almost all children. Only 2 out of 16 preschoolers and 2 children from the other three age groups together (N = 48) failed to produce this order. Additional analyses revealed, however, a remarkable age trend in the reliability of the single judgments: There were only two preschoolers and two first graders whose judgments of all three judgments of the 2–s duration were below those of the 4–s duration and all those, in turn, were below all judgments of the 6–s interval. In the age groups of the 7– and 8 year-olds, in comparison, as many as 9 and 12 out of 16 children respectively, reached this criterion. Nevertheless, it seems safe to assume that even the 5–year-olds can differentiate between single durations in the range of interest here. This conclusion is corroborated by the analysis of variance, which yielded a significant effect for duration only, but neither for age nor for the age-duration interaction.

Converging data have recently been provided by Janke and Kanigowski (1988). They used five different time intervals from 4 to 16 seconds. These were presented as durations of sunlight, and the children were asked how high a magic flower would have grown in that time. Thus, a graphic rating scale was used. Children 7 and 8 years of age participated in this experiment. Again, the analysis of variance yielded a significant effect of duration, but neither of age nor of the age-duration interaction. Additional trend analyses revealed that the (normative) linear component accounted for more than 90% of the variance in both age groups. Furthermore, the reliability of the ratings was remarkable, the mean value being above $r = .80$ even for the 7–year-olds.

Taken together, these data suggest that children as young as 5 years do not have major problems in differentiating between single durations and giving quantitative estimates of them. What seems to be difficult, at least for the younger children investigated here, is to perform the task reliably across all durations. The similarity in achievement on the single duration task and the integration of successive durations task suggests that integration under these conditions does not pose an additional difficulty for children who are able to quantify single durations. The child probably just ignores the short pause in the succession of the two events and immediately connects the second duration to the first. Alternatively, the child may add the two estimates in a procedure he or she is well acquainted with. In any case, the present data again warrant the conclusion that children at least from the age of 5 years on have the potential to conceive of time as a quantitative dimension.

Integrating Successive versus Overlapping Events

There seems to be a developmental lag of about 2 years from children's integration of successive events to the integration of overlapping ones, as a comparison of the results of the cited studies by Wilkening, Levin & Druyan (1987) and Levin, Wilkening, & Dembo (1984) indicate. It has already been mentioned that one reason for this discrepancy could be children's difficulties in ignoring the "full" interval in the overlap paradigm, which seems to be less natural than to ignore the "empty" interval in the successive duration task.

However, the tasks differed in other aspects as well. First and foremost, they differed in the physical medium by which the events were presented. In the overlap paradigm, time was presented as running water, whereas in the succession task it was presented as the illumination of a bulb. These differences may have had consequences as to children's use of time measurement strategies. In the running-water experiment, time could be measured—at least potentially—by imagining the amount of water accumulated in the beakers. One might expect this feature to have a facilitating effect. In comparison, to imagine the accumulating of the bulb's light seems to be much harder, if not impossible. This very difficulty, however, may have led the children in the successive-duration task to invent their own measurement strategies (as will be detailed later) and this, in turn, might explain the higher level of quantification observed in that experiment.

Various other differences between the tasks may have also been of importance, all of the following pointing to greater difficulties of the time overlap task. In that task, the duration differences in beginning and ending times were varied in steps of 1.5 seconds and thus were probably harder to discriminate than those in the succession task, in which the duration levels differed by 2 seconds. In the same vein, the time interval that should be ignored was always the same between the successive durations (pause of 2 seconds), whereas in the overlap paradigm the irrelevant interval took different values. Similarly, the overlap paradigm could have been more attention demanding because the events were presented by two separate devices (faucets), whereas in the successive-duration task childern had to watch one and the same device (bulb) throughout all trials. Finally, only 9 different factorial combinations were included in the succession task, whereas the overlap task had 16 problems.

To reexamine the effects of problem structure on children's ability to add durations, it seemed desirable to create equivalent tasks, one for the integration of overlapping events, the other for the integration of successive events. This was the purpose of the following unpublished study by Levin and Krispin.

The durations were presented as illuminations of two small red bulbs, varied in a 3 x 3 factorial design. Each of the nine problems was presented twice in two different random orders. In the successive duration task, each bulb was lit for 2, 4, or 6 seconds. The pause between the two durations was 1, 2, or 3 seconds, randomly distributed over the nine factorial combinations. In each trial, the child was asked to light the first bulb for the same time the two bulbs had burned together.

In the duration overlap task, the bulb that burned first always stopped burning after the other had finished, so that the shorter duration was completely included in the longer one. Beginning and ending lags were 2, 4, or 6 seconds, and the joint time (i.e., the shorter duration) was 1, 2, or 3 seconds. These intervals were again randomly distributed over the nine problems. The child was asked to equalize the burning times by restarting the bulb that had started second and stopped first, for the time the other bulb had burned longer. As in the succession task, a correct response could be reached by adding two durations, each of 2, 4, or 6 seconds, and ignoring the intermediate interval of 1, 2, or 3 seconds.

A total of 120 Israeli children of both sexes participated in this study, with 40 children in each of three age groups: 6, 8, and 10 years. Half of each age group received the overlap, the other half the successive duration task. Only the data of half of the children will be reported in the following. The other half in each group got special instructions and will be considered in a later section.

Individual rule assessments showed a clear developmental progression: Whereas no 6–year-old integrated the durations according to the normative adding rule, neither in the successive nor in the overlap condition, almost all 10–year-olds clearly followed that rule in both conditions. The difference between the two tasks emerged only in the intermediate age group, the 8–year-olds. Of them, 70% integrated the successive durations by an adding rule, but only 30% used that rule for integrating the duration differences in the overlap task. The great majority of the judgment patterns that did not follow the adding rule was unclassifiable because the data were unreliable, which was particularly true for the youngest age group.

Figure 3.1 shows the judgments averaged over children in each group. The data are plotted as a function of the first duration, with one curve for each level of the second duration. The effects of the task are evident: At each age, mean judgments of successive durations follow more closely the normative pattern of parallel lines than is true for the judgments in the overlap paradigm. An effect of age is also clearly visible: the older the children, the better the approximation to parallelism in their judgment patterns. On the group level, the 3 x 3 analysis of variance (first by second duration) yielded two significant main effects and a nonsignificant interaction in all but one of the six age-task conditions, in line with an additive model. The exception were the data of the 6–year-olds in the overlap condition, for which only the second duration lag was found to have a significant effect. The results obtained at the group level suggest that the indivi-

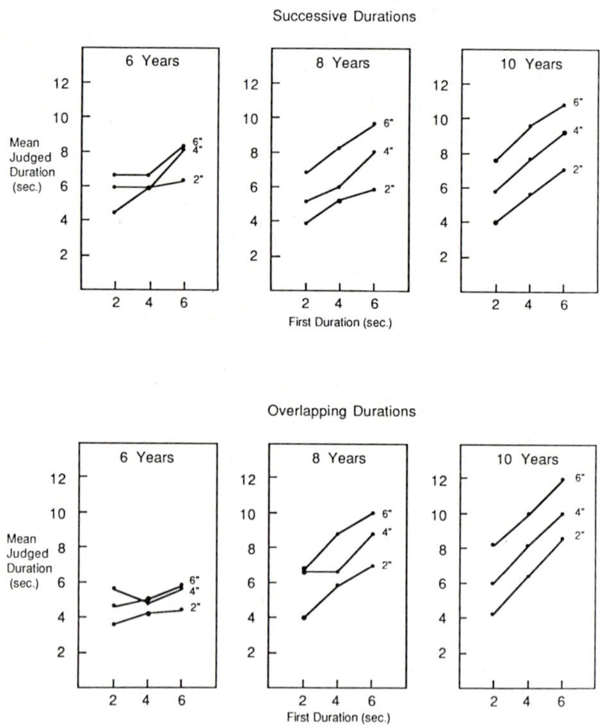

Figure 3.1. Mean judged duration for the three age groups in successive-duration and in duration-overlap tasks. (Curve parameter is second duration.)

dual rule assessments were rather conservative. In light of these data, it seems likely that tendencies towards an additive rule were present even in at least some of the single-subject judgment patterns that had been classified as unreliable.

The data from the study by Levin and Krispin show, again, a developmental lag of children's behavior in the time overlap task. Responses in this task reach the level of those in the successive duration task about 2 years later. For example, only by the age of 10 years were the individual adding rules in the overlap task about as frequent as they were for the 8–year-olds in the succession task. When the judgments were averaged over children on the group level, a similar developmental lag emerged. These data thus validate the findings of the two separate studies discussed earlier (Levin et al., 1984; Wilkening et al., 1987). A closer look at the strategies that children use to measure time may shed more light on the question why the levels of time quantification in children's time productions differed as a function of the task. Counting, a special strategy to measure time, will be considered next.

COUNTING: A TIME MEASUREMENT STRATEGY

Man has invented ingenious instruments to measure time. When objective devices such as clocks are not immediately available, we often resort to "counting" the time. For example, we may count to measure the time that passes from lightning to thunder. Children can be observed measuring time by counting from an early age on when they play hide-and-seek. It seems questionable, however, whether they really understand that they are measuring time in this situation, namely the maximum time allotted for hiding.

There is now ample evidence that counting is a surprisingly early achievement in the development of the child. With certain constraints, children as young as two and a half years have been reported to count in a sensible way (e.g., Fuson, Richards, & Briars, 1982; Gelman & Gallistel, 1978). These findings, however, apply to the counting of discrete objects. Several authors have argued that the type of units has an effect on the age at which children consider them to be countable: the less concrete the units are, the higher the age at which children start counting them (e.g., Steffe, von Glasersfeld, Richards, & Cobb, 1983).

Realizing that the passage of time can be measured by counting

—and to do so successfully—seems to be particularly demanding. Unlike as with discrete objects, the units of time are not naturally given but have to be created by the counting itself. Forthermore, measuring time by counting requires keeping a constant rhythm. Only then do we preserve the units—a prerequisite for any sensible quantification. In this respect, time is fundamentally different from other continuous dimensions such as distance in space, which can also be segmented into countable units. Moreover, the time units are gone as soon as they are counted. No restart is possible, in contrast to spatial, visible dimensions. For all these reasons, it seems to be of interest to investigate children's use of counting as a time measurement strategy. The following study was a first attempt.

In the successive-duration experiment partly reported earlier in this chapter (Wilkening, Levin, & Druyan, 1987), half of the children were exposed to a rhythmic beat throughout the presentation of each duration. These beats of a metronome were introduced to suggest a segmentation of the durations and thus were supposed to enhance the use of counting. No child was explicitly instructed to count. Children were encouraged, however, to continue with counting—and to do so aloud—when they had initiated this strategy on their own in the preliminary practice trials. In other children, information on their "covert" use of counting could be obtained by lip reading in the course of the experiment and/or in subsequent interviews.

Five different counting strategies were observed. The first three were considered to be sensible ones, because all of them accomplished an addition of the durations. The last two of the five strategies to follow were nonsensible, in comparison, because they do not bring about an additive integration. (1) *Addition*: These children counted during both sucessive durations, each time starting from 1. Then, they added the two cardinal numbers reached in each presentation and counted up to their sum when reproducing time. (2) *Two separate countings*: These children also counted from 1 in each of the two durations. In the reproduction, they again counted twice from 1, only without ceasing between the two counts. (3) *Counting-on*: These children counted from 1 during the first duration, ceased in the interstimulus interval, and then continued with the number following the one they had reached for the first duration. In the reproduction phase, they counted up to the final cardinal number without interruption. (4) *Single-duration counting*: The children counted each duration. But during reproduction they counted only up to one of the cardinal numbers. Often, the children were systematic as to the duration they chose to reproduce: always the first, the second, or the longest one. (5) *Irrelevant counting*: These children counted during each of the two durations. In the reproductions, however, their countings did not match the prior counts in any obvious way.

Counting clearly increased with age. Whereas the majority of the 5–year-old children did not count at all, almost every 7–year-old employed one of the sensible counting strategies. Counting-on was the predominant one in the 6–year-olds. Two separate countings was the most frequently used strategy by the 7–year-olds; nonsensible counting strategies were virtually absent by this age.

At all ages, counting was performed more frequently when the successive events were accompanied by the rhythmic beats. This effect appeared most clearly for the 5– and 6–year-olds: Of the 30 children in each condition, only 8 counted in the non-rhythm, but 17 counted in the rhythm task among the 5–year-olds. Among the 6–year-olds 15 children counted in the non-rhythm condition, and almost all, 29, counted in the rhythm condition.

The developmental progression observed here—from noncounting over non-sensible to sensible counting of time—can be interpreted in line with other findings that have been reported in the literature. For example, Case, Kurland, & Daneman (1979) have shown that by the age of 6 years children can count two sets of objects successively and report their numerosities, whereas 4–year-olds still fail on this task (see also Fuson et al., 1982). The strategy of two separate countings generally seems to be less advanced than the addition of two cardinal numbers, as could have been predicted from data presented by Carpenter (1986) and Carpenter and Moser (1983). It should be noted, however, that the previous studies on children's counting abilities did not refer to measurement of time. The cited experiment by Wilkening et al. was the first to reveal young children's surprising potential to spontaneously utilize counting for measuring and integrating time.

Counting Successive versus Overlapping Durations

The following study by Levin and Krispin further examined children's use of counting in measuring time. Two questions were addressed. The first concerned the limits of knowledge of those children who do not count. These children may not know at all how counting can be applied to time quantification. Alternatively, they may know how to quantify time by counting, but not know how to use numbers for integrating the durations. Another possibility is that the children may know how to apply counting to time quantification and integration, but fail to access their counting competence in this context. In this case, once the option of counting is suggested to the children, they may carry out the task in the same manner as those who came up with the idea on their own.

In the present study, the experimenter suggested to half of the sample to count aloud, by saying: "If you'll count, it can help you. Count aloud so I can hear you counting." No further instructions as to when or how to count were provided. A few practice trials were included to provide the children with an opportunity to familiarize themselves with the problem and to coordinate time reproduction with counting.

The second question referred to factors affecting the choice of strategies. More specifically, we examined whether the problem structure—successive versus overlapping durations—affected the counting strategy. As discussed earlier, adding the beginning and ending lags of overlapping durations demanded ignoring the "full" interval of co-occurrence of the two events. In contrast, adding two successive events required ignoring the "empty" interval between them. Therefore, integrating overlapping events was expected to be harder and, indeed, was less well performed in terms of duration production.

Accordingly, we expected non-sensible counting strategies to emerge more often for overlapping durations. These strategies were assumed to arise from children's confusion as to which parts of the events should be considered for integration. Particularly, we expected a further non-sensible strategy: *counting-all.* A child using this strategy would count throughout the presentation of the two events, not ceasing to count when appropriate, that is, when the two bulbs lit together. An analogous strategy for the successive-duration task would be to count from the beginning of the first event to the end of the second, not ceasing in the pause between them. Such a strategy never appeared in the previous study, which had used successive events only (Wilkening et al., 1987).

Because the boundaries between the events can be perceived more readily with successive than with overlapping durations, we expected that the use of "two separate counts" and "addition," which count the two durations separately from each other, would appear more frequently with successive events. "Counting-on," which fuses the two durations into a single event, may more likely be enhanced in overlap problems.

The study by Levin and Krispin found all the aforementioned counting strategies, except irrelevant counting. An additional, unexpected strategy appeared: *partial counting.* Children who used this strategy admitted that they had sometimes counted and sometimes not; they gave no reason for this inconsistent behavior.

Half of the 120 children, 6–, 8–, and 10–year-olds, were instructed to count aloud, the other children were interviewed about their strategy at the end of the session. In the latter groups, covert counting was frequently observed by the children's lip movements or by their use of fingers. Table 3.1 presents the number of children employing different counting strategies in both task conditions.

Table 3.1.
NUMBER OF CHILDREN USING DIFFERENT COUNTING STRATEGIES FOR SUCCESSIVE AND OVERLAPPING DURATIONS AMONG 6–, 8– AND 10–YEAR-OLDS (N = 120)

PROBLEM STRUCTURE	COUNTING STRATEGY						NO COUNTING
	ADD	SC	CO	SDC	CA	PC	
SUCCESSIVE	19	10	16	3	1	4	7
OVERLAPPING	11	3	17	7	13	1	8

Note:
ADD = Addition; SC = Separate counts; CO = Counting-on; SDC = Single duration counting; CA = Counting-all; PC = Partial counting.

The data show that counting or noncounting as such was unrelated to the task, successive or overlap problems. However, the counting strategies of those children who did count were affected by the task. As expected, "counting-all" appeared almost exclusively for overlapping durations. The other non-sensible strategy, "single duration counting," was also somewhat more frequent for overlapping durations. "Addition" and "separate countings," in contrast, were more frequent for successive durations, as expected, but "counting-on" was used in both tasks to almost the same extent. The effect of problem structure on the choice of strategies indicates that children can access more than one single strategy for adding durations, the choice being partly determined by the structure of the problem.

Induced versus Spontaneous Counting

Additional analyses in the Levin and Krispin study dealt with the differences in strategy choice between the induced-counting and the spontaneous-counting conditions. We compared the strategies of the children who counted on their own with those of the children who had been instructed to count. The strategies were classified into "sensible counting" (the three strategies accomplishing addition), "non-sensible counting," and "no counting." Table 3.2 presents the number of children using a strategy from one of these categories in both task conditions, successive and overlapping durations, and in both treatment groups, instructed and not instructed to count.

Table 3.2.
NUMBER OF CHILDREN USING DIFFERENT CATEGORIES OF COUNTING WITH AND WITHOUT INSTRUCTION TO COUNT IN THE SUCCESSIVE AND OVERLAP DURATION TASK

GROUP	COUNTING		NO COUNTING
	SENSIBLE	NON-SENSIBLE	
OVERLAPPING DURATIONS			
6–YEAR-OLDS			
UNINSTRUCTED	0	3	7
INSTRUCTED	1	9	0
8–YEAR-OLDS			
UNINSTRUCTED	7	2	1
INSTRUCTED	7	3	0
10–YEAR-OLDS			
UNINSTRUCTED	8	2	0
INSTRUCTED	8	2	0
SUCCESSIVE DURATIONS			
6–YEAR-OLDS			
UNINSTRUCTED	2	2	6
INSTRUCTED	9	1	0
8–YEAR-OLDS			
UNINSTRUCTED	7	2	1
INSTRUCTED	9	1	0
10–YEAR-OLDS			
UNINSTRUCTED	9	1	0
INSTRUCTED	9	1	0

The data in Table 3.2 reveal that the performance in successive and in overlap problems was very similar, as long as the children were not instructed to count. Under this condition, the use of sensible strategies increased with age in both tasks, especially from 6 to 8 years. The instruction to count had a notable effect on strategy choice in the 6–year-olds, this effect being quite different for the two tasks: When faced with successive durations, these children switched from no counting to sensible counting. When exposed to overlapping durations, in contrast, children of the same age shifted to non-sensible counting strategies. This means that young children who do not discover counting as a time measurement strategy on their own apply a sensible counting strategy to the quantification of successive durations. But these children apparently do not know when to count and how to add durations that are embedded in a more complex stimulus configuration, such as overlapping durations.

The youngest children in this study, the 6–year-olds, thus appear to have a limited ability to access counting as a strategy for time quantification. They rarely initiate counting for this purpose. This conclusion, however, is based on studies that required children to process two durations. The relative complexity of this task could have interferred with the accessibility of counting. In a further study by Levin and Levy, parts of which have already been reported earlier, we looked therefore at counting of single durations. Half of the sample of 128 children was instructed to count and half was not, when asked to estimate and reproduce single durations of 2, 4, and 6 seconds (illuminations of a bulb).

A comparison of the results of the two studies, one dealing with two successive, the other with single durations, revealed that the proportion of children who counted was very similar, when only the non-rhythm condition is considered for the successive-duration task. In that condition, counting was spontaneously employed by 27%, 50% and 90% of the 5–, 6–, and 7–year-olds, respectively. For the single duration task, when children were not instructed to count, the respective percentages were 31%, 44%, and 81%—and 100% for the 8–year-olds. These results support the previous conclusion that the spontaneus use of counting as a strategy for measuring time is unaffected by problem structure, single or successive durations, and is frequently used by the age of 7 years.

COUNTING AND JUDGING TIME

So far, children's reproductions of durations and their counting strategies to measure time have been considered separately from each other. It seems of great interest, however, to investigate whether and how children's counting strategies and their integration rules for time productions are related. In particular, the counting data can provide converging evidence for the interpretation of the integration and nonintegration rules assessed by functional measurement methods. If, for example, an adding rule for duration judgments would appear together with the counting strategy of addition in the same child, it seems safe to assume that the process underlying the duration judgments really was one of addition, integrating two separate estimates on the dimensions defined by the experimenter.

Wilkening, Levin, and Druyan (1987), in their successive duration study, found a remarkably strong relation between counting strategies and integration rules. Of the children for whom an additive rule was assessed for duration productions, 97% were found to use one of the sensible counting strategies eliciting addition: addition, two separate countings, or counting on. In contrast, of the children who gave unreliable time productions or followed a nonadditive rule, only 32% used a sensible counting strategy. On the other hand, 73% of the children who did not count in a sensible way produced unreliable duration judgments, whereas this was true of only 17% of the children with a sensible counting strategy (see Wilkening et al., 1987, for additional data).

However, sensible counting did not guarantee the judgments of the durations to obey the normative integration rule. Of the children who counted in a sensible way, about one third did not succeed in integrating the durations according to the additive rule. This could be due to children's failure to keep a constant rhythm of counting. They may either not know that rhythm is important for measuring time, or be unable to perform a constant rhythm of counting.

The relation between counting strategy and time productions was further analyzed in the cited study by Levin and Krispin. They examined whether the strong strategy-production connection could be replicated under two new conditions: in other problem configurations, and when the instruction to count was varied. This was studied for both overlapping and successive durations.

Table 3.3 presents the cross-classifications of counting strategies and integration rules in the different task conditions, collapsed over age, which was 6 to 10 years. Because of the low frequencies of many individual strategy and rule categories, a distinction is made only between additive integration and the remaining other approaches for the time productions, and only between the sensible and non-sensible strategies for the countings.

In the group of children who had not been instructed to count, an adding rule for time judgments was practically always (96%) associated with a sensible counting strategy, both with successive and overlapping durations. On the other hand, 79% of the children whose judgments did not follow the correct integration rule either did not count at all or counted in a non-sensible way. This relation was less strong for the overlapping dura-

Table 3.3.
NUMBER OF CHILDREN USING DIFFERENT CLASSES OF STRATEGIES FOR SUCCESSIVE AND OVERLAPPING DURATIONS, BY INTEGRATION RULE AND PRESENCE/ABSENCE OF COUNTING INSTRUCTION (N = 120)

PROBLEM-STRUCTURE /RULE	COUNTING INSTRUCTION			
	UNINSTRUCTED		INSTRUCTED	
	SENSIBLE STRATEGY	NON-SENSIBLE STRATEGY	SENSIBLE STRATEGY	NON-SENSIBLE STRATEGY
SUCCESSIVE				
ADDITION	16	0	23	2
OTHER	2	12	4	1
OVERLAPPING				
ADDITION	10	1	11	8
OTHER	5	14	5	6

tions. Here, one third of the children who used one of the sensible counting strategies failed to exhibit the correct integration rule for duration judgments. This may, again, have been due to those children's difficulties with keeping a constant counting rhythm, which seems to be harder in this more complex and more attention demanding task.

For the children who were instructed to count, the strategy-production connection was less clear. For successive durations, by far the most frequent cross-classification was obtained for an additive integration associated with sensible counting; the other cell frequencies are almost negligible. For the overlap task, quite a different result emerged. Of those children who counted sensibly, only 69% followed an additive rule in the time production, a similar frequency as obtained in the condition without a counting instruction. The most surprising inconsistency appeared for the children who did not count in a sensible way in the overlap task. Of these, more than half succeeded in reproducing the durations by an additive rule. How was this possible?

Seven out of these eight children were found to employ the strategy of "counting-all". They started counting when the first bulb lit and stopped only when that bulb went out, not having ceased during the time the other bulb lit (overlapping duration). Their apparent success in producing judgments following an adding rule could have been due to the fact that the overlapping durations were relatively short, 1, 2, or 3 seconds. These levels were relatively hard to distinguish, in comparison with the beginning and ending lags, which were 2, 4, or 6 seconds. Their sums ranged from 4 to 12 seconds. Therefore, to erroneously count during the time both bulbs burned together added only a little effect to the estimates of the intervals to be integrated. This effect, apparently, could sometimes not be detected in the individual analyses of variance. An additional explanation for this unexpected result is based on our coincidental observation that some children who "counted all" counted at a slower pace during the interval of duration overlap. They may have been uncertain as to whether it was appropriate to count during that period, and ended up counting more slowly.

The close relationship between counting strategies and integration rule for time production can also be demonstrated on the group level. In the factorial plot of the duration judgments, the data of the children who employed one of the sensible counting strategies followed the pattern of parallelism indicative of addition in each counting group. Except for the children with the counting-all strategy just discussed, the parallel pattern of time productions was not found for the non-sensible counting strategies. In light of these findings, it appears that a sensible process of counting almost always underlay the duration productions following the normative adding rule.

The question arises whether counting is necessary for integrating durations, or whether it is necessary for the prior process of quantifying each of the single events involved. On the one hand, it seems possible that the single durations, at least in the range presented here, can be discriminated and quantified without counting, and that counting is mainly employed to aid integration. On the other hand, sensible counting may be necessary for quantifying the single durations, and just for this reason be employed in the integration task. This question was addressed in the study by Levin and Levy already mentioned.

In that study, children 5 through 8 years of age had to reproduce single durations. Half of the children were instructed to count aloud, and did so appropriately. Of those children, some already had started counting on their own during the practice trials, even before having explicitly been instructed to count. Hence, a distinction could be drawn between spontaneous and induced counting. Of the children not instructed to count, in the other half of the sample, there were also some who initiated counting on their own. In this group, therefore, we could distinguish between children who counted and those who did not.

All groups, spontaneous counters, induced counters, and noncounters, were similarly successful in reproducing the single durations according to their objective order. However, the error variance in these judgments was lower for the children who counted than for those who did not, pointing again to a better discrimination of the intervals in the former group. In an analysis of variance, only the factor of counting, not the age, was found to have a significant effect on the quality of the time productions. Nevertheless, even the children who did not use any counting strategy showed a capability of discriminating between the single durations. For those children who employed counting, it seemed to have made no difference whether they had been instructed or not: Those children who did not access counting on their own were just as capable of applying it to the problem at hand as were the children who discovered the strategy spontaneously.

DEVELOPMENT OF TIME MEASUREMENT: SUMMARY AND GENERAL CONCLUSIONS

The present chapter dealt with two interrelated questions: When do children come to treat time as a quantifiable dimension, and when do they employ special strategies, particularly counting, to measure time?

As to the first question, the findings reported here converge on the conclusion that children as young as 5 years can conceive of time as a quantitative entity. Metric concepts of time at this early age had already been found by Wilkening (1981). That study, however, focused on children's understanding of time in relation to speed and distance. The present data show that the children can also quantify durations on the basis of "pure" time information in events that do not involve speed and distance information.

Children's quantification of time comes out most clearly in the algebraic addition rules for the integration of successive events. The quantification can be read off directly from the factorial plots of the judgments. Not only did these children discriminate different levels of durations, but they also integrated them as prescribed by the normative adding rule. This finding, incidentally, could be of methodological benefit for future work on children's perception of time: The adding rule can be used to yield validated scales of subjective time, according to the logic of functional measurement. This issue, however, goes beyond the questions addressed here.

Children's quantification of time was not perfect, to be sure. Most important, it did not appear in every task at the same age. When the events were partly simultaneous, in a problem designed after Piaget's overlap paradigm, qualitative rules for time judgment were found to predominate until the age of about 10 years. When the events were presented successively, in contrast, the correct algebraic integration rule was already employed by most 6–year-olds. And when the duration of single events had to be judged, quantification of time appeared at about the same age. In light of these data, it seems clear that the findings reported by Piaget and by other researchers who adopted his choice paradigm must be task-specific, too. Their claims that a metric concept of time is absent in children below the age of 10 years or even more can no longer be accepted.

The quality of children's time judgments—and of their integration rules—did not only vary with the problem structure but also with the strategies they used to measure the passage of time. Counting was of particular interest. When it was applied in a sensible way, it raised both the reliability of the judgments and the likelihood of a correct integration rule.

In our tasks, we deliberately created a context that encouraged quantification by counting. Several counting strategies were observed, sensible and non-sensible ones. Any of them implies that the child understands two important aspects: that time is basically quantifiable and that it can be segmented into units. When the pace of counting is held constant, which was true for many children, counting can provide a very reliable tool for recording and reproducing time. The three sensible counting strategies found here could accomplish even more: They almost automatically lead to an integration of the durations by addition. Thus, the counting data provided converging evidence for the interpretation of the integration process: The adding rules assessed for time productions were not merely surface descriptions of the data. A true integration by adding was evident in many cases.

The employment of the various counting strategies also varied as a function of the task, as already shown for time productions. Not only did the implicit hint of the rhythm and explicit instruction to count enhance the use of counting. The structure of the problem had also an impact. For example, different strategies were preferred for successive than for partly simultaneous durations. Furthermore, when counting was induced by rhythm or explicit instruction, it tended to be more sensibly applied to successive than to overlapping durations. For the problems and for the age range investigated here, it appears that children's use of a sensible counting strategy is the more likely the less complex the attentional demands of the task are. This interaction may, however, be more intricate, which remains an interesting question for future research.

Certainly, counting per se is not a major problem for most 5–year-old children in several contexts. However, to spontaneously realize that it can be applied to measurement of time requires a high level of abstraction, as would follow from the problem taxonomy proposed by Steffe et al. (1983; see also Levin, 1989). As an alternative to counting, some of the younger children, 5– and 6–year-olds, invented idiosyncratic methods to measure time.

These noncounting strategies were of two kinds. Some were attempts to segment the time into units, such as listening to their own heart beats, breathing rhythmically, or imitating the sound of a clock ("tik-tak, tik-tak, . . . "). Other approaches were mainly an attempt to record and represent the accumulation of time, such as humming a song or delineating an imaginary window in the air. Even if these methods may be less efficient than counting, they nevertheless imply that those children, too, had an appreciation of time as a quantitative, measurable entity. These findings thus contribute to the overall picture that emerged here: the young child being highly adaptive in finding methods to measure and judge time.

References

Acredolo, C., & Schmid, J. (1981). The understanding of relative speeds, distances, and durations of movement. *Developmental Psychology, 17*, 490–493.

Anderson, N. H. (1980). Information integration theory in developmental psychology. In F. Wilkening, J. Becker, & T. Trabasso (Eds.) *Information integration by children* (pp. 1–45). Hillsdale, NJ: Erlbaum.

Anderson, N.H. (1981) *Foundations of information integration theory.* New York: Academic Press.

Capec, M. (1971). Bergson and modern physics. In *Boston Studies in the Philosophy of Science* (vol. 7). Dordrecht-Holland: Reidel.

Carpenter, T.P. (1986). Conceptual knowledge as a foundation for procedural knowledge. In J. Hiebert (Ed.). *Conceptual and procedural knowledge: The case of mathematics.* Hillsdale NJ: Lawrence Erlbaum Associates.

Carpenter, T.P. & Moser, J.M. (1983). The development of addition and subtraction problem-solving skills. In T. P. Carpenter, J. M., Moser, & T. A. Romberg (Eds.). *Addition and subtraction: A cognitive perspective.* NJ: Lawrence Erlbaum Associates.

Case, R., Kurland, M., & Daneman, M. (1979). *Operational efficiency and the growth of M-Space.* Paper presented at the Biennial Meeting of the Society for Research in Child Development, San Francisco.

Crowder, A. M. H., & Hohle, R. H. (1970). Time estimation by young children with and without informational feedback. *Journal of Experimental Child Psychology, 10*, 295–307.

Cuneo, D. O. (1982). Children's judgements of numerical quantity: A new view of early quantification. *Cognitive Psychology, 14*, 13–44.

Fraisse, P. (1982). The adaptation of the child to time. In W. J. Friedman (Ed.). *The developmental psychology of time*, (pp. 113–140). New York: Academic Press.

Friedman, E. R. (1977). Judgements of time intervals by young children. *Perceptual and Motor Skills, 45*, 715–720.

Fuson, K. C., Richards, J. & Briars, D. J. (1982). The acquisition and elaboration of the number word sequence. In C. J. Brainerd (Ed.). *Children's logical and mathematical cognition: Progress in cognitive development research.* New York: Springer-Verlag.

Gelman, R., & Gallistel, C. R. (1978). *The child's understanding of number.* Cambridge, MA: Harvard University Press.

Janke, B. & Kanigowski F. (1987). *Time estimation by children: Integrating successive durations.* Unpublished manuscript. University of Frankfurt.

Jesperssen, J., & Fitz-Randolph, J. (1978). *From sundials to atomic clocks: Understanding time and frequency.* Washington D.C.: National Bureau of Standards.

Levin, I. (1982). The nature and development of time concepts in children: The effects of interfering cues. In W. J. Friedman (Ed.). *The developmental psychology of time* (pp. 47–85). New York: Academic Press.

Levin, I. (1989) Principles underlying time measurement: The development of children's constraints on counting time. In I. Levin & D. Zakay (Eds.). *Time and human cognition: A life-span perspective,* (pp. 145–183). Amsterdam: North Holland Publishers.

Levin, I., Gilat, I., & Zelniker, T. (1980). The role of cue salience in the development of time concepts: Duration comparisons in young children. *Developmental Psychology, 16,* 661–671.

Levin, I., Goldstein, R., & Zelniker, T. (1984). The role of memory and integration in early time concepts. *Journal of Experimental Child Psychology, 37,* 262–270.

Levin, I., Wilkening, F., & Dembo, Y. (1984). Development of time quantification: Integration and non-integration of beginnings and endings in comparing durations. *Child Development, 55,* 2160–2172.

Lovell, K., & Slater, N. (1960). The growth of the concept of time: A comparative study. *Child Psychology and Psychiatry, 1,* 179–190.

Montangero, J. (1979). Les relations du temps, de la vitesse et de l'espace parcouru chez le jeune enfant. *L'Année Psychologique, 79,* 23–42.

Montangero, J. (1981). Les relations entre durée et succession: Étude d'une "prélogique" enfantine appliquée au temps (The relations between duration and succession: A study on a "prelogic" in children applied to time). *L'Année Psychologique, 81,* 287–308.

Piaget, J. (1969). *The child's conception of time.* (A. J. Pomerans, Trans.) New York: Basic Books. (Original work published 1946).

Piaget, J. (1970). *The child's conception of movement and speed.* (G. E. T. Holloway & M. J. Mackenzie, Trans.) New York: Basic Books. (Original work published 1946).

Richards, D. D. (1982). Children's time concepts: Going the distance. In W. J. Friedman (Ed.) *The developmental psychology of time,* (pp. 13–45). New York: Academic Press.

Siegler, R. S., & Richards, D. D. (1979). The development of time, speed and distance concepts. *Developmental Psychology, 15,* 288–298.

St. Augustine. (1949). *The confessions of Saint Augustine* (E. B. Pussey, Trans.) New York: Random House. (Original work published 400 AD)

Steffe, L. P., von Glasersfeld, E., Richards, J., & Cobb, P. (1983). *Children's counting types.* New York: Prager.

Szamosi, G. (1986). *The twin dimensions: Inventing time & space.* New York: McGraw-Hill.

Wilkening, F. (1981). Integrating velocity, time, and distance information: A developmental study. *Cognitive psychology, 13,* 231–247.

Wilkening, F. (1982). Children's knowledge about time, distance and velocity interrelations. In W. J. Friedman (Ed.). *The developmental psychology of time* (pp. 87–112). New York: Academic Press.

Wilkening, F., & Anderson, N. H. (1982). Comparison of two rule assessment methodologies for studying cognitive development and knowledge structure. *Psychological Bulletin, 92,* 215–237.

Wilkening, F., Levin, I., & Druyan, S. (1987). Children's counting strategies for time quantification and integration. *Developmental Psychology, 23,* 823–831.

TIME AND HUMAN COGNITION
A Life-Span Perspective
I. Levin and D. Zakay (Editors)

CHAPTER 4

IRIS LEVIN

Principles Underlying Time Measurement: The Development of Children's Constraints on Counting Time*

INTRODUCTION

Measurement, the assignment of numerals to properties of objects or events according to rules, is a major activity in the scientific endeavor. Many among us tend to endorse the view that no mature science is possible without measurement. Lord Kelvin (1824–1907), the British mathematician and physicist, who introduced the absolute scale of temperature, blatantly expressed this view: "When you can measure what you are speaking about, and express it in numbers, you know something about it; but when you cannot measure it, when you cannot express it in numbers, your

*This chapter is based on Working Paper No. 75 of the Tel Aviv Study Group on Human development and Education. I wish to thank Orit Krispin and Lily Levy for their significant contributions to the studies they had taken part in. I am also very grateful to Sara Druyan, William Friedman, Rochel Gelman, Robert Siegler, Sidney Strauss, Liliana Tolchinsky Landsmann, and Dan Zakay for their helpful comments on a previous version of this chapter.

Partial support for the preparation of this manuscript came from a grant from the Sloan Foundation to the Cognitive Science Program at the University of Pennsylvania.

knowledge is of a meager and unsatisfactory kind: it may be the beginning of knowledge, but you have scarcely, in your thoughts, advanced to the stage of science, whatever the matter may be" (Popular Lectures I 73). Such an extreme view may be too limiting, in that it devalues highly significant contributions to human thought, like Darwin's theory of evolution or even Freud's psychoanalytic theory. Moreover, it may imply that measurement is the only way leading to theoretical breakthroughs.

Another view is provided by Kuhn (1977) who claims that "the route from theory or law to measurement can almost never be travelled backwards. Numbers gathered without some knowledge of the regularity to be expected almost never speak for themselves." (pp. 197–198). Nevertheless, he admits that measurements invited by one theory pave the way for the next. Without attempting to decide which comes first "the chicken or the egg", it seems a defendable argument that the evolution of science frequently goes hand in hand with progress in measurement.

In spite of the significance attributed to measurement, little is known about children's understanding and use of measurement. If we agree that a major goal of education is the cultivation of scientific thought, children's measurement should interest us. Intriguing, but scattered, beginnings have been undertaken in the realm of how children measure spatial properties such as length or area (Beilin & Franklin, 1962; Bryant & Kopytynska, 1976; Hiebert, 1979; Inhelder, Sinclair & Bovet, 1974; Miller, 1984, 1987). Other studies dwell on children's measurement of time (Case, Sandieson, & Dennis, 1986; Levin & Wilkening, 1989; Piaget, 1969). The present chapter focuses on children's comprehension and use of general principles underlying measurement in their application to time.

The use of a particular procedure for problem solving does not guarantee that the principles underlying that procedure are understood by its user, either explicitly or implicitly (Fuson & Hall, 1983). A series of studies on time measurement (Wilkening, Levin & Druyan, 1987; Levin & Wilkening, 1989) show that very young children devise an efficient strategy for measuring time. When asked to reproduce events lasting for a few seconds, second graders used counting to measure the time elapsed. About half of the first graders, and a few kindergartners also initiated counting for that purpose. Moreover, even the youngest children knew how to apply counting to time. When the experimenter suggested counting to help in duration reproductions, children of the entire age range knew how it should be done. They counted from the beginning to the end of the event displayed, and counted again in the same manner, up to the same cardinal number when reproducing the event. The question arises as to whether children at such a young age understand the principles underlying time measurement in its application to counting time.

PRINCIPLES UNDERLYING TIME MEASUREMENT: CONSTANCY AND ARBITRARINESS

Measurement, at least on interval and ratio scales, is composed of counting units. Unit size is arbitrary, but must be constant. For instance, length can be measured by cubits, inches, feet, yards, centimeters, or by derived units such as light-years. It is, however, obligatory to use the same units throughout an act of measurement. In the same vein, if two lengths are measured so as to be compared, added, subtracted or the like, the same units must be used for both. The arbitrariness of units implies that the number derived through measurement is only symbolically related to the measured entity. The same length can be described by different cardinal numbers, depending on the units of measure.

The principles of equal units and arbitrariness of units have the following implications for the procedure of counting time.

a) Constant rhythm: Counting time must be carried out in a constant rhythm. The same rhythm must be used in counting two durations to allow for mathematical operations to be performed on these measurements.
b) Arbitrariness of rhythm: The particular rhythm chosen in counting time is irrelevant.

Since measurement involves counting, it is also based on the principles underlying counting in general. Gelman & Gallistel (1978), and later Gelman, Meck & Merkin (1986), analyzed young preschoolers' counting procedures. They argue that children as young as three years old have an implicit skeletal understanding of the principles underlying counting. An important member of this set of principles is stable order. Understanding of this principle directs the child to use the same tags in the same order on repeated counts. Even children who use a non-conventional series of tags, practically never apply an entirely different set. Rather, they use the conventional series of numbers with omissions, repetitions, or the like (Wagner & Walters, 1982).

Gelman and Gallistel do not require that the child use the conventional series of numbers without omissions or repetitions in order to be credited with the knowledge of how to count. The child has only to use the same series of tags repeatedly in the same order. The authors' disregard for the particular tags used is based on the notion that, in principle, any series of ordered tags can serve for counting. They do not, however, question whether children realize that counting can be done appropriately with a series of tags that includes omissions as long as the same omissions appear in repeated countings.

We examined the question of whether children understand that counting can be done with different sections of the conventional scale of tags. The use of a "random" section of tags taken from the conventional scale appears frequently in actual acts of measurement. When we measure length, for instance, we sometimes start from some value other than zero. Try and use a ruler to measure the width from left to right of the paragraph you are now reading in order to see if it can be fitted into a box. Chances are you will start your measurement some value other than zero. For certain purposes (e.g., how wide is the paragraph?) such a measurement needs adjustment. For others, (e.g., which of two paragraphs is wider?) no adjustment is required.

The use of a certain section of tags (e.g., counting 3,4,5 instead of 1,2,3), implies a distinction between the cardinal meaning of a number, which is determined by the number of counted tags and the conventional meaning of that number.

The principles of constancy of tags and arbitrariness of tags have the following implications for counting time:

a) Constant tags: The same tags must be used in counting two durations to allow for mathematical operations to be carried out on the measurements.
b) Arbitrariness of tags: The particular tags chosen in counting time are irrelevant.

CONSTANCY AND ARBITRARINESS: ORDER IN DEVELOPMENT

An attempt to predict the order in which the different principles would emerge employed the distinction between obligatory and permissible constraints. Obligatory constraints refer to the obligation to count time in a constant manner: in a fixed rhythm and with the same tags. Permissible constraints relate to the tolerance towards counting time in various manners: in any constant rhythm and with any stable series of tags.

We suggest that obligatory constraints may be easier to acquire than permissible constraints, within the limits of equal complexity. An obligatory constraint is vulnerable to violation, and such violations may lead to inconsistencies which shed light on the constraint involved. Permissible constraints cannot be violated and hence may be less noticeable. Consequently, we expected questions relating to constancy to be successfully answered at a younger age than those relating to arbitrariness.

The hypothesis that children grasp the principle of arbitrariness of time units relatively late, could also be based on features specific to time.

Measurement of time is carried out conventionally using units of a particular size. The most frequent goals of measuring time are time telling and determining how much time was taken or will be taken by an event. To achieve these purposes, people overwhelmingly use a small class of units, each of which serves for certain unit sizes. Very short durations are described by seconds, longer intervals by minutes, and still longer by hours. In contrast, the measurement of other dimensions such as length and temperature, is carried out by means of a variety of units (inches and centimeters, Fahrenheit and Celsius), both within and across cultures. Moreover, even if young children are unfamiliar with different conventional units for measuring dimensions other than time, they frequently encounter the use of "local units" for these dimensions. Tiled floors are measured by counting tiles, untiled floors by counting foot steps, and furniture by counting the number of hand spans covering the estimated length. Time, however, is almost always measured by timers, be they analogical or digital, wrist watches or pendulum clocks, all of which use the same units. Hence, the culture at large does not provide many opportunities that suggest the principle of arbitrariness in relation to time. This must be logically constructed by the child despite the uniqueness of units conventionally used for time measurement.

Children's difficulty in realizing the arbitrariness of time units might derive from another source as well. Units of time of longer intervals, the day, the month and the year, are not entirely arbitrary. To a large extent, they approximate external and internal natural cycles (e.g., Aschoff, 1981; Gallistel, in press). Consequently, there may be a tendency to regard units measuring shorter intervals as not arbitrary either. Attempts to change the conventional units of time, for instance to decimal units so as to facilitate time computations and notations, have always met with strong objections, partly because conventional time units are perceived as natural (Vij, 1982).

Children who fail to recognize that for the purpose of reproducing durations, time can be counted using any series of ordered tags may believe that this should be done only with conventional numbers. This notion could stem from the overgeneralization of a principle which applies to counting in other contexts. Counting for various purposes, such as cardinality, ordinality, addition or subtraction (see Fuson, Richards & Briars, 1982 for uses of counting) frequently requires the use of the conventional series of number words. For instance, the question "How many?" cannot be answered directly by counting from a number other than 1 or by use of the alphabet. Other goals, however, such as comparing numerosities, can be achieved directly by employing a non-conventional scale of tags, without any need for transformation. For instance, two sets can be compared directly ("Are they the same?") by counting each with the a, b, c or from 3 rather than 1. Hence, to respond correctly to a question concerning the arbitrariness of tags, children have to analyze the particular goal of counting. For time reproduction they must conclude that any series of ordered tags would do.

COMPARISON WITH PRINCIPLES PROPOSED BY PIAGET

The purported developmental order in which the comprehension of constancy precedes that of arbitrariness might be said to be in line with Piaget's model. Piaget (1969) provided the only literature, except for the present chapter, to deal with children's growing knowledge of principles underlying time measurement. Piaget, however, studied the principles underlying the child's interpretation of information provided by timers, "since it is exceedingly difficult to get children to make spontaneous measurements of time" (p. 176). In our tasks children did measure time spontaneously, so that we could use their invented procedure rather than ready-made timers as a context for probing principles. Before commenting on the relationship between these sets of principles, let us first consider Piaget's contribution.

The essence of measurement, according to Piaget, consists of the extraction of a unit and the counting of repetitive displacements of that unit throughout the quantity to be measured. To get hold of a time unit, we equate it with a particular motion. By repeating the same motion throughout a duration, we are able to measure it.

The use of recurrent motions to measure time implies the understanding of two principles, termed isochronism and synchronism by Piaget. The principle of isochronism means that the same motion recurring under the same conditions necessarily lasts the same amount of time. For instance, when no change is introduced, the durations of the swings of a metronome are all equivalent to each other. Moreover, the durations of the recurrent motions are constant, regardless of the events they measure.

The second principle, synchronism, means that two motions which start simultaneously and end simultaneously necessarily last the same amount of time. Their synchronicity is independent of their relative velocity or amount of output. Thus, when the measuring motion coincides with a measured event, both are of the same duration, whether or not they are equal in speed, distance covered, or other output factors.

We would argue that the principles proposed by Piaget are related, at a very high level of abstraction, to the principles we are suggesting. This is not to say that these two sets of principles are equivalent, or that comprehension of one set implies understanding of the other. Nevertheless, generally speaking the sets may show parallel developmental courses, and understanding of one set may contribute to the understanding of the other.

The isochronic principle seems to be related to the principle of constancy. Understanding that the same physical motion recurring under the same conditions lasts the same duration is related to recognizing that equal intervals are created by counting rhythmically. In addition, isochronism may be related to an awareness that two durations are equal if they include the same number of the same events. Hence, if two durations are counted in the same rhythm with the same scale of tags up to the same number, they should be equal.

Synchronism seems to be related to the principle of arbitrariness. Understanding that two different motions starting together and ending together last for the same time regardless of their relative velocity, implies that counting in different rhythms or starting and ending the count with different numbers can cover the same duration. Hence, counting of a particular duration can be done appropriately in different rhythms and with different tags.

Piaget concludes that isochronism is recognized at a younger age than synchronism. This conclusion is in line with our hypothesis that constancy is grasped before arbitrariness. However, Piaget assessed each of the principles with a different type of task presented to a different group of children. (See similar criticism of Piaget's investigation of another developmental order in: Siegler & Richards, 1979). We attempted to assess the two principles by tasks as similar as possible, and in repeated measures with the same children.

GENERAL FRAMEWORK FOR THE REPORTED STUDIES

The current chapter presents two unpublished studies of children's acquisition of principles of measurement in their application to time. The studies by Levin and Levy and by Levin and Krispin share the same two aims, one major and the other minor. The primary aim was to investigate the developmental changes in children's comprehension of principles concerning time measurement. Within this framework, Levin and Levy focused on the order in which children became aware of the principles of constancy vs. arbitrariness, while Levin and Krispin analyzed the order in which the principle of arbitrariness was applied to rhythm vs. tags. The secondary aim in both studies was to examine the relationship between comprehension of principles underlying time measurement and children's actual acts of time measurement. Levin and Levy analyzed acts of measurement through children's choice of strategy for reproducing single durations. Levin and Krispin examined children's algebraic integration of durations.

Awareness of principles was tapped on somewhat different levels in the two studies. The first study assessed an explicit level of awareness using a semi-structured interview. Children were asked to judge the appropriateness of different ways of counting time to afford time reproduction. The second work examined a more implicit level of awareness by asking children to reproduce durations under novel constraints and then analyzing their strategy. They, however, also assessed explicit awareness by asking the children to explain what they did.

INTERVIEW FOR ASSESSING FOUR PRINCIPLES OF TIME MEASUREMENT

The development of understanding of the four principles – constant rhythm, arbitrariness of rhythm, constant tags and arbitrariness of tags – was assessed in an interview held after children had completed a task involving the reproduction of durations. The children were presented with a light bulb which was lit for 2, 4, or 6 seconds. Each of these durations was presented three times, in a random order affording nine trials. The children's task was to relight the bulb for the same amount of time by pressing a key for the required duration.

A total of 128 subjects, equally divided by grade and sex, were recruited from schools situated in an upper-middle class suburb of Tel Aviv. They came from kindergarten, first, second and third grades, and were about 5, 6, 7 and 8 years old, respectively. Half of the subjects in each grade were instructed to use counting for the time reproduction. They were told "if you count it will help you." They were further encouraged to count aloud "so I can hear you." No additional instructions were given as to what or how to count. The second half of the subjects were not guided on the strategy they were to use. However, counting was detected in many of them by lip reading, as well as by a short interview immediately following the testing session.

The interview on principles, to be analyzed hereafter, started by telling the subjects that the "bulb game" they had just finished playing had also been played in another school. Each problem in the interview consisted of a story told about two children playing the game. They were described as having counted differently, and the interviewee was asked to decide whether either of them had been more successful in lighting the bulb for exactly the same amount of time as the experimenter, or whether both had succeeded to the same extent. The subjects were then asked to justify their answers.

The interview consisted of four stories. In the first story, the children were described as counting in a different rhythm: one fast, the other slowly. The correct response as dictated by the principle of arbitrariness of rhythm, is that they both succeeded in time reproduction to the same extent. In the second story, the children differed in constancy of rhythm: one counted slowly while the experimenter lit the bulb, and quickly while he himself lit it. The other child counted quickly on both occasions. According to the principle of constancy of rhythm, the child who counted in the same rhythm both times should be judged to have succeeded better. In the third story, the children counted with different tags: One counted from 1 up and the other from 3 up. The correct response following the principle of arbitrariness of tags is that both succeeded to the same extent. In the fourth story, one child counted from 1 when the experimenter lit the bulb, and from 3 when she lit the bulb. The other girl counted from 3 on both occasions. The correct response as dictated by the principle of the constancy of tags is that the second child did better. In sum, judgments on constancy questions were classified as correct if the child who counted in the constant manner was judged as having done better. On arbitrariness questions, the judgment that both children did equally well was considered correct.

Developmental Trends Revealed by Interviews

JUDGMENTS

The number of children providing correct judgments for each question are presented, by grade, in Table 4.1.

Table 4.1.
NUMBER OF CHILDREN PROVIDING CORRECT JUDGEMENTS, BY QUESTION AND GRADE (n=128)

GRADE	RHYTHM CONSTANCY	TAG CONSTANCY	RHYTHM ARBITRARINESS	TAG ARBITRARINESS
K	11	15	6	4
1 st	16	10	7	3
2 nd	24	27	10	10
3 rd	25	27	22	21

The data shows an increase with age in the number of correct judgments. The change with age, however, is not monotonic. On the questions relating to constancy, the major improvement occurs in the second grade. At that age, about three quarters of the children responded correctly. In contrast, the dominant progress on the issue of arbitrariness emerges in the third grade. But even in the third grade only about two thirds answered correctly on arbitrariness. The difference between grades was found to be significantly by ANOVA. Post-hoc analyses revealed a significant difference between the first and second grade on the constancy problems, and between the second and third grade on the arbitrariness problems. On constancy of tags, there was also a significant difference between the second and third grade. A comparison drawn by sign test between judgments on arbitrariness vs. constancy problems, on tags and on rhythm, showed the performance was significantly better on constancy in each grade, except for third graders on rhythm. These results suggest that understanding of the two types of principles – constancy of units and arbitrariness of unit – develop sequentially rather than synchronically. The earlier acquisition of constancy than of arbitrariness, is in line with our expectations.

FOUR LEVELS OF EXPLANATIONS

The explanations provided by the interviewees lent themselves to classification into four levels. The levels differed in the criteria used by the children to determine successful performance of the task at hand. The lowest level explanations consisted of describing successful performance as reaching a high number in counting. On the second level, successful counting was equated with counting conventionally. On the third level, successful counting was confined to counting by the "correct" units, rhythm or tags, as determined by the measured event. On the fourth level, the criterion for successful counting was correct. It consisted of counting in constant rhythm and tags and was indifferent to the particular rhythm or tags chosen. The levels are more fully described herewith from lowest to highest, along with illustrative explanations provided by our subjects:

a) *Racing:* The higher the number you reach, the better you do. It is therefore better to count quickly than to count slowly, and starting from 3 is preferable to starting from 1.
"It is better to count fast, because then you pass the second child" (kindergartner).
"The girl who counted from 3 gets there faster and beats the first one" (kindergartner).

b) *Conformity to convention:* Counting should be done in the regular manner, otherwise it is "confusing". Technical difficulties rather than principled limitations are suggested for preferring regular counting.
"It is difficult to count from 3. You can get confused and not succeed" (1st grader).
"It is more correct to count slowly, because you can pay more attention" (1st grader).

c) *Objective units:* In counting time, objective units are being counted. Counting should therefore be done with the right numbers and in the right rhythm. The "right" numbers and rhythm are determined by the event (the "counting by the bulb"), or by the cause of the event (the "counting by the experimenter", who did not in fact count).
"The boy who counted slowly did better, because the boy who counts fast does not reach the right number, your (the experimenter's) number" (2nd grader).
"You should count at a medium pace (neither quickly nor slowly) to match the rhythm of the bulb" (3rd grader).

d) *Correct explanation:* Rhythm or numbers used are immaterial to reproducing the required durations, as long as they are constant.
"It does not matter if you count quickly or slowly, as long as you count in the same way both times" (3rd grader).
"The name of the number does not matter. One-two is like three-four. You have to count at the same pace when you (the experimenter) light (the bulb) and when he (the child) lights it" (3rd grader).

The explanations provided were classified independently by the authors, who were unaware of the child's grade or other performances. Any disagreement was resolved through discussion. A graduate psychology student, experienced in research on time, served as an independent judge and reclassified all responses for reliability. The consistency between the two classifications was found to be quite satisfactory. The percentages of consistent classifications were: 78%, 77%, 91%, and 76% for the first to the fourth story, respectively.

Table 4.2 displays the number of subjects in each grade who gave explanations at the different levels for each of the problems. Results were similar for all four problems: first and second level responses decreased with age. Responses at the third level increased and then decreased, and at the fourth level increased with age. As before, the major increase in correct explanations for the constancy problems was at the second grade. On the arbitrariness issue, it appeared at the third grade.

Table 4.2.
NUMBER OF CHILDREN PROVIDING DIFFERENT LEVELS OF EXPLANATION, BY QUESTION AND GRADE (n=128)

	RHYTHM CONSTANCY				TAG CONSTANCY				RHYTHM ARBITRARINESS				TAG ARBITRARINESS			
LEVEL	1	2	3	4	1	2	3	4	1	2	3	4	1	2	3	4
GRADE																
K	6	16	4	6	12	10	6	4	8	10	11	3	12	8	10	2
1st	1	12	7	12	8	5	11	8	5	5	15	7	5	6	18	3
2nd	0	6	5	21	5	1	6	20	0	3	19	10	2	1	20	0
3rd	0	1	6	25	0	0	5	27	0	2	10	20	0	1	13	18

Interview Qualifications

The interview shed light on the children's ability to use principles underlying time measurement to generate judgments of hypothetical situations and to explain these judgments. However, it suffered from a number of limitations that should not be overlooked. First, the interview imposed high demands on the subjects' verbal competence. The children had to comprehend and coordinate the details of each story. Furthermore, they had to understand the meaning of the question posed to them. In particular, they had to grasp that "success" in the "bulb game" meant accurate time reproduction rather than appropriate or conventional counting. Needless to say an attempt was made to clarify our intentions. The fact that young children did not comprehend what determined success, could stem either from their limited comprehension of the ontological category of time, of their limited access of general principles of measurement or from misinterpretation of our intentions. The significant role of communication difficulties in children's problem solving has recently been pointed out in a convincing manner (Siegal, Waters & Dinwiddy, in press). Similar problems are evident in studies asking children to decide if counting in a novel manner is correct. It is difficult to decide whether children comprehend that they should relate to appropriateness rather than to conventionality of counting (Gelman, Meck & Merkin, 1986).

Secondly, the classification of a judgment as correct or incorrect is not necessarily always valid. A correct judgment may stem from the wrong reasoning, and vice versa. This has already been persuasively shown (Richards & Siegler, 1982). Third, the level of explanation provided was determined by the content analysis of open verbal responses. Such a method, as becomes obvious to anyone who has ever attempted to use it, must rely on interpretation of the child's intentions, an inherently fallible procedure.

Finally, the interview as such tapped an explicit level of awareness of the target principles. In the following study an attempt was made to assess children's recognition as evidenced primarily by problem solving rather than by explanations. By this method, we expected to discover the awareness of the principles on a more implicit level, and perhaps at a younger age level.

CONSTRAINED TASK FOR ASSESSING PRINCIPLES

Children's understanding of the principles concerned was reexamined by Levin and Krispin using behavioral problem solving. A total of 120 children, equally divided by grade and sex, were recruited form first, third, and fifth grades, and were about 6, 8 and 10 years old, respectively. They came from two neighboring schools in the center of Tel Aviv, an area inhabited by low to middle class families. Each age and sex group was divided in half, and each half was presented with a different task involving adding durations and reproducing their sum. Details of these tasks will be presented below. Half of each of these groups was instructed to count to help them in estimating durations (in the same manner as in the previous study), and half were not.

Upon completion of the adding duration task, the task concerned with measurement principles was presented. It started with a few practice trials in which children were required to reproduce single durations. They were asked to light a bulb for the same amount of time that it was lit by the experimenter. They were all instructed to do so by counting aloud, and they all counted appropriately. The test phase consisted of four problems. Children's understanding of arbitrariness of tags was examined in the first two problems, and of arbitrariness of rhythm in the last two. The problems were presented in two counterbalanced orders, 1,2,3,4, and 3,4,1,2:

1) Children were asked to count starting from 1 when the experimenter lit the bulb, and then to count starting from 3 when they lit the bulb. However, they had to light the bulb for exactly the same amount of time as the experimenter.
2) Children were asked to count from 1 while the experimenter lit the bulb. Upon completion, they were asked to light the bulb themselves and to count starting from 3 until they reached the same final number that they had reached when the experimenter lit the bulb. They were then asked to judge whether the bulb was lit both times for the same amount of time, or whether it was lit longer on either of the occasions.
3) Children were asked to count fast when the experimenter lit the bulb, and then to count slowly when they lit the bulb. However, they had to light the bulb for exactly the same amount of time as the experimenter.
4) Children were asked to count fast when the experimenter lit the bulb. Upon completion they were asked to light the bulb themselves and to count slowly until they reached the same final number they had reached when the experimenter lit the bulb. Then, they were asked to judge whether the bulb was lit both times for the same amount of time, or whether it was lit longer on either of the occasions.

Componential Analysis of Tasks

Analysis of the components involved in solving each of these problems suggests the developmental order in which they should be solved. The first question involved understanding of three components:

a) that counting from 3 up to the same cardinal number as counting from 1 entails fewer tags.
b) that there is a direct relation between number of tags and length of time taken to count. Hence, counting fewer tags covers less time.
c) that time lost at the beginning (due to skipping the first two tags) could be compensated for by adding tags at the end (two more tags).

The second problem investigated the understanding of the first two of these components, but not the third. In this problem, children had to acknowledge that by counting from 3, they covered less time. No compensation was required. The addition of a component raises the difficulty of the problem, since some of the children may fail in applying this component. Moreover, for all children the higher the number of components the greater the difficulty to integrate them. (see, similar analysis in Wilkinson, 1984). Therefore, it was predicted that more children would perform correctly on the second than on the first problem. Furthermore, children failing in the first problem were expected to detect their own error at times and either be able to correct it or not. We shall return to this later.

The third problem involved three components parallel to those of the first problem:

a) that there is an inverse relation between speed of counting and time covered. Hence, counting slowly covers more time than counting fast up to the same number.
b) that there is a direct relation between number of tags and length of time taken to count at any given speed.
c) that time gained by counting slowly could be compensated for by dividing the tags counted, in proportion to the relative speeds of counting.

The fourth problem investigated the understanding of the first two components, but not the third. In the fourth problem, children had to realize that counting slowly covers more time than counting fast. But, again, no compensation was required. Consequently, we predicted that more children would perform correctly on the fourth than on the third problem.

The order of difficulty of the tag problems (1,2) vs. the rhythm problems (3,4) could also be predicted. Each of the tag problems was expected to be easier than its counterpart concerned with rhythm. The main difference between tag problem 2 and rhythm problem 4 is that problem 2 requires understanding of a direct relation while problem 4 of an inverse relation. Remember that in problem 2 the child has to consider the direct relation between the number of counted tags and the duration covered. In problem 4 he or she has to recognize the inverse relation between speed of counting and duration. The claim that direct relations are grasped earlier in development than inverse relations has already been suggested in the literature (Acredolo, Adams & Schmid, 1984; Strauss & Stavi, 1982; Wilkening, 1981).

The major difference between tag problem 1 and the rhythm problem 3 is that problem 1 requires additive compensation, while problem 3 demands multiplicative compensation. In problem 1 the child has to grasp that if two tags are missing at the beginning, two should be added to the end. In contrast, in problem 3 the child must realize that counting slowly multiplies counted time, and could be compensated for by dividing the number of tags. Studies carried out within the functional measurement approach suggest that additive integration of information emerges earlier in development than multiplicative integration (Anderson & Cuneo, 1978; Wilkening, 1979, 1981) consequently, since problem 2 requires understanding the effect of addition and subtraction on time, while problem 4, the effect of multiplication and division, we expected problem 2 to be solved earlier than problem 4.

Problem 2 can be expected to be easier than problem 4 on another ground as well. Problem 2 requires compensating for loss of tags by means of adding tags. In contrast, problem 4 demands compensating for change in rhythm by means of subtracting tags. To understand that tags compensate for tags is expected to be easier than grasping that tags compensate for rhythm. Hence, the rationale underlying the compensation is more complex on problem 4.

In sum, we expected problem 2 to the easiest, problem 3 the most difficult, and problems 1 and 4 of an intermediate difficulty. No expectation could be formulated as to the relative difficulty of problems 1 and 4. These expectations were based on whether or not a component of compensation was required by the problem; on whether a direct or an inverse relation was involved; and on whether the compensation required was additive or multiplicative. These considerations are all related to the type of information processing involved in the target problems and not to the epistemological meaning of the concepts examined. It is possible that this latter factor also has an effect, that we are as yet unaware of.

Developmental Trends Revealed by the Constrained Task

ARBITRARINESS OF TAGS: PROBLEM 1 – DEMANDING COMPENSATION

Performance on the first problem, which required counting from 1 while the experimenter lit the bulb and from 3 while reproducing the same time, improved with age. However, very few children in the age range examined added exactly two tags to the first cardinal number obtained. Many added three tags. Adding three tags indicates that the children understood they had to add as many tags as they had lost by starting to count from 3 but they failed to grasp that they had skipped only 2 tags.

Hence, it was decided that counting up to 2 or 3 tags more than the previous cardinal number would be considered correct counting.

Following time reproductions, the children were asked to evaluate whether they had lit the bulb for the same time as the experimenter, or whether one of them had lit it longer. Despite the fact that the children were previously requested to relight the bulb for the same amount of time, they could still judge that they had lit the bulb for either more or less time. This would be the case if they failed to compensate because they either did not know how to, or they failed to coordinate this with the other components. Whenever a child answered that he or she had lit the bulb for either more or less time, he or she was asked again to light it for the same time as the experimenter, and the trial was repeated from the beginning.

The combination of reproduction and its evaluation yielded three major patterns:

a) *Cardinal number determines duration:* The child counted up to the same cardinal number, once from 1 and once from 3, and judged the two durations to be equal.
b) *Inaccessible compensation:* The child counted up to the same cardinal number, once from 1 and once from 3, and judged the second duration to be shorter. Thus, the child was aware of the components relating starting number to the number of tags, and number of tags to duration. But he or she failed to compensate by adding to the end the tags omitted at the beginning.
c) *Compensation:* The child added 2 or 3 tags in the second counting and judged the two durations to be equal.

Table 4.3 presents the frequency of the three patterns of response as a function of grade. All other patterns of response are included in "other". Results show that the majority among first graders counted up to the same number. This response decreased among third and fifth graders. This type of counting suggested a certain lack of discrimination between the time measured and the measuring numbers. The child believed that to reproduce the same time he or she was obliged to count up to the same cardinal number. However, among those who counted up to the same number, about 50% in each grade were aware that the way they counted was wrong. Moreover, they could tell that by counting from 3 to the same final number, a shorter duration was covered. Their problem lay in accessing or in integrating the component of compensation within the algorithm required. When given a second chance to view the experimenter light the bulb, and asked to light it for exactly the same time, about half (10 out of the 24 described as "same CN, Evaluate Exp. more) of the children who were aware they had erred corrected their counting. A similar proportion of

Table 4.3.
NUMBER OF CHILDREN USING DIFFERENT PATTERNS OF COUNTING TYPES AND EVALUATIONS ON PROBLEM 1, BY GRADE (n=120)

GRADE	CORRECT	INCORRECT		
	ADD 2/3 EVALUATE: SAME TIME	SAME CN EVALUATE: EXP. MORE	SAME CN EVALUATE: SAME TIME	OTHER
1 st	8	12	11	9
3 rd	17	5	4	14
5 th	22	7	4	7

Note:
ADD 2/3 = Counting up to 2 or 3 more than the previous cardinal number.
Same CN = Counting up to the same cardinal number.
Evaluate same time = Judging the two durations to be equal.
Evaluate Exp. more = Judging the time the bulb was lit by the experimenter to be longer.

children (9 out of these 24) counted again up to the same number. These results are in line with a modular model of component, to be discussed later.

The data also indicates that correct control of all components, evidenced by correct compensation (even accepting the addition of 3 rather than 2 tags, as correct) was not achieved by a vast majority of any of the age groups examined. Among fifth graders, only 55% responded correctly. Younger children performed less well.

ARBITRARINESS OF TAGS: PROBLEM 2 – WITHOUT COMPENSATION

In the second problem on the constrained task all the children were instructed to count once from 1 and once from 3 to the same cardinal number. They were asked to compare the two durations.

The number of children of each grade giving each response, is presented in Table 4.4. Results show that the correct response, stating that counting from 1 took more time, was given frequently from the youngest age on. Among first graders 78% responded correctly, and the proportion increased with age. Analysis by chi square showed that the effect of grade was reliable. Of the 16 who erred, 88% said that the two durations were equal.

Table 4.4.
NUMBER OF CHILDREN GIVING DIFFERENT JUDGEMENTS ON PROBLEM 2, BY GRADE (n=120)

GRADE	CORRECT	INCORRECT	
	COUNTING FROM 1: MORE TIME	SAME TIME	COUNTING FROM 3: MORE TIME
1 st	31	9	0
3 rd	34	2	4
5 th	39	1	0

ARBITRARINESS OF RHYTHM: PROBLEM 3 – DEMANDING COMPENSATION

Recall that the third problem required the child to count quickly during time presentation, and then to count slowly during time reproduction. However, the durations were to be equal. Quite a few children divided the first cardinal number by two to determine the cardinal number of the second count. Many explained that counting two tags quickly takes the same amount of time as counting one tag slowly. A few divided the number by 3 providing a similar explanation. This type of counting was considered correct. Not only did it indicate understanding of the inverse relation between speed and time, but also that counting for the same time at different speeds can be performed only if the proportion between the speeds of counting is taken into account.

Counting up to a lower number during reproduction was considered a partially correct response. Although these children counted up to a lesser number the second time, the two cardinal numbers were not related in any interpretable way, and the children were unable to justify the particular number at which they chose to end the second count. Hence, it was assumed that they were unaware of the fact that there is a simple rule governing transformation between the durations covered by fast and by slow countings. It could also be the case that they were aware of the rule but unable to execute the transformation.

Following time reproductions, the children were asked to evaluate whether they had lit the bulb for the same time as the experimenter, or whether one of them had lit it longer. In spite of the fact that the children were previously requested to relight the bulb for the same amount of time, they could still judge that they had lit the bulb for either more or less time. Whenever a child answered that he or she had lit the bulb for either more or less time, he or she was asked again to light it for the same duration as the experimenter, and the trial was repeated from the beginning.

Four patterns of responses were distinguished:

a) *Cardinal number determines duration:* The child counted up to the same cardinal number, once quickly and once slowly, and judged the two durations to be equal.
b) *Inaccessible compensation:* The child counted up to the same cardinal number, once quickly and once slowly, and judged correctly the second duration to be longer. Thus, the child was aware of the components relating speed to time and number of tags to duration, but failed to compensate by dividing the number of tags.
c) *Global compensation:* The child counted up to a lower number when counting slower. But no interpretable relation was established between the two cardinal numbers. The two durations were judged to be equal.
d) *Elaborate compensation:* The child divided by 2 or 3 the cardinal number in the second counting, and judged the two durations to be equal.

Table 4.5.

NUMBER OF CHILDREN USING DIFFERENT PATTERNS OF COUNTING TYPES AND EVALUATIONS ON PROBLEM 3, BY GRADE (n=120)

GRADE	CORRECT	PARTIAL CORR	INCORRECT		
	DIVIDE 2/3 EVALUATE: SAME TIME	LOWER CN EVALUATE: SAME TIME	SAME CN EVALUATE: S. MORE TIME	SAME CN EVALUATE: SAME TIME	OTHER
1 st	1	4	4	9	22
3 rd	7	8	10	6	9
5 th	13	5	8	2	12

Note:
Divide by 2/3 = Counting up to half or one third of the previous cardinal number; Same CN = Counting up to the same cardinal number; Lower CN = Counting up to a lower cardinal number; Evaluate same time = Judging the two durations to be equal; Evaluate S. more = Judging the time the bulb was lit by the subject as longer.

Table 4.5 presents the frequency of the four patterns of response as a function of grade. All other patterns of response are included in "other". Counting up to the same number was the most frequent response among first and third graders. It decreased among fifth graders. Moreover, even among fifth graders counting correctly and judging the resultant durations to be equal was rare. Only 33% of them succeeded in doing this. Even if we assess as correct those who counted slowly up to a lower number, whatever particular number it was, and judged the two durations to be equal, only 45% of the fifth graders can be said to have responded correctly. Younger children performed less well.

Among those who counted both times up to the same number 44% evaluated the two durations as equal. The rest judged correctly that counting slower covered more time. When given a second chance to reproduce the time displayed, 10 out of the 22 children counted again up to the same cardinal number. Hence, they repeatedly failed to compensate. All the rest, except for one child, counted correctly on the second trial, i.e., dividing the cardinal number by 2 or 3. This finding coincides nicely with the modular model.

ARBITRARINESS OF RHYTHM: PROBLEM 4 – WITHOUT COMPENSATION

The fourth problem on the constrained task required all of the children to count twice up to the same number, at two different paces. They counted quickly while the experimenter lit the bulb, and slowly while they lit it. The question posed to them was whether the two durations were equal or whether one was longer. The correct response would be to state that they had lit the bulb for a longer time than the experimenter. The two incorrect responses were to claim that the bulb was lit twice for the same length of time, or that the experimenter had lit it for longer. The number of children who produced different responses by grade, is presented in Table 4.6.

Analysis by chi square, after combining the two categories of incorrect responses, revealed the effect of grade to be reliable. The data in Table 4.6 shows that correct responses increased with age. The major incorrect response was to state that the durations were equal. Of all children who erred, 67% committed that error.

Table 4.6.
NUMBER OF CHILDREN GIVING DIFFERENT JUDGEMENTS ON PROBLEM 4, BY GRADE (n=120)

GRADE	CORRECT	INCORRECT	
	COUNTING SLOWER MORE TIME	SAME TIME	COUNTING FASTER MORE TIME
1 st	11	21	8
3 rd	30	7	3
5 th	36	1	3

Developmental Order of Tasks

Problem 2 was expected to be the easiest and problem 3 to be the most difficult. Problems 1 and 4 were predicted to be of intermediate difficulty but could not be ordered a priori in terms of the relative difficulty between them. To examine the reliability of the predicted orders, the responses to each problem were classified as correct or incorrect (partially correct responses were considered incorrect). On the reproduction problems, 1 and 3, correct counting was considered correct. Evaluations were not taken into account since different children evaluated different responses, their own responses. On the comparison problems, 2 and 4, the right comparisons were graded as correct.

Two Guttman scale analyses were carried out. The first excluded problem 1, and the second problem 4. On both analyses, problem 2 was expected to be the easiest, and problem 3 the most difficult. Problems 1 and 4 were predicted to be of intermediate difficulty.

Both analyses strongly supported the predicted order. In both, the coefficients of reproducibility (R) and scalability (C) were above the criteria for approximation to a perfect Guttman scale. These criteria are R=.90 and C=.60 (SPSS Manual, 1975). On the first scale the coefficients were found to be: R=.97 and C=.89, and on the second scale: R=.93 and C=.75. The conclusion to be drawn is that on the individual level, successful performance on a difficult problem substantially guarantees success on an easier one.

PRINCIPLES UNDERLYING TIME COUNTING AND THE USE OF COUNTING TO MEASURE TIME

The issue raised here is whether children's understanding of principles underlying time measurement is related to the strategy they use when required to measure and integrate durations. In our studies, both principles and strategies were assessed within the context of measuring time by counting.

Interview Scores and Single Duration Counting

The following analysis examined the relationship between the spontaneous use of counting for measuring time and the explicit awareness of the principles underlying time measurement. Remember that Levin and Levy asked children to reproduce single durations of 2, 4 or 6 seconds. Half of the children in each grade were instructed to count. Since spontaneous counting was the issue concerned, the analysis took into account only those children who were not instructed to count, but were left to choose their own strategy.

The primary strategy which emerged among children not instructed to count, and the only useful one for time quantification, was that of counting. The few other strategies selected (e.g., humming a song or listening to one's own heart beat throughout the estimated duration) were idiosyncratic, rarely used, and inefficient. The majority of children who did not count did not use any explicit systematic strategy. They simply stared intently at the burning bulb throughout the time it was lit, as though trying to sense the length of time elapsing. (For more details see Wilkening, Levin, & Druyan, 1987; Levin & Wilkening, 1989).

Following the reproduction task, principles were assessed by the interview described above on the suitability of various manners of counting for reproducing durations. They were asked if counting time for reproduction could be done successfully in different rhythms, with different tags, in non-constant rhythm or with non-constant tags.

Each child received a score of 0–4, according to the number of problems he or she solved correctly. Two scores were given: One on judgments, the other on explanations. An explanation was considered correct only if it accompanied a correct judgment. Table 4.7 displays the number of children who counted spontaneously vs. those who did not count, by score on the interview. The upper and lower rows present scores based on judgments and on explanations, respectively.

Table 4.7.
NUMBER OF CORRECT JUDGMENTS AND EXPLANATIONS ON INTERVIEW, BY PRESENCE/ABSENCE OF SPONTANEOUS COUNTING AMONG K, 1st, 2nd, AND 3rd GRADERS (n=64)

	NUMBER OF PROBLEMS SOLVED CORRECTLY				
JUDGMENTS	0	1	2	3	4
COUNTING	5	4	14	8	9
NON-COUNTING	9	4	8	1	2
EXPLANATIONS	0	1	2	3	4
COUNTING	8	6	10	8	8
NON-COUNTING	15	4	2	1	2

Chi square analyses indicated a reliable relation between the tendency to count and understanding of principles underlying counting. Among the 40 children who counted spontaneously, a lower proportion than among the 24 non-counters did not judge any question correctly or judged only one question correctly. The proportion of counters who solved two questions only was practically the same as that of non-counters. In contrast, a higher proportion of counters than non-counters solved three or four questions correctly. Hence, in general, the higher the number of problems answered correctly, the higher the proportion of counters vs. non-counters. The same trend appeared in regard to the children's explanations.

It should be noted, however, that several children who counted did not reveal any understanding of the principles underlying the strategy they used. Fewer children revealed a thorough understanding of the constraints on counting but still did not count spontaneously. Hence, there seems to be a slight indication that the use of strategy precedes the comprehension of its constraints, at least as assessed here.

Constrained Task Scores and Counting/Adding Durations

Levin and Krispin assessed children's strategies for adding durations. Not only were they required to measure time, but they also had to manipulate the measures algebraically. Two tasks were used, both calling for the addition of two durations and replication of their sum. In the first task, two bulbs were lit successively with an interval between them. The child was asked to light one bulb for the total time that both bulbs had been lit. In the second task, two overlapping durations were displayed. The shorter duration was completely included in the longer one, since the first bulb to be lit was the last bulb to go out. The child was asked to relight the bulb which had been lit for the shorter time for the amount of time it would take to equal the duration of the other bulb. A correct response on this task required adding the beginning gap to the ending gap and ignoring the intermediate interval in which both bulbs were lit together. On both tasks the right response could be achieved by adding two durations, each composed of 2, 4 or 6 seconds, and ignoring the intermediate time of 1, 2 or 3 seconds. Half of the children were instructed to count, and the other half were left to choose their own strategy. Many of them counted. (for more details see Levin & Wilkening, 1989.)

Two types of integrative rules were discerned: addition and other. In the problems composed of successive durations addition meant adding the counts of the two durations. In the problems with overlapping durations it meant adding the beginning gaps to the ending gaps. In both cases addition was the correct strategy.

Several incorrect strategies were termed "other": Counting All involved counting from 1 throughout the two durations. In the case of the two successive durations this meant continuing to count during the empty interval between them.In the case of the overlapping durations it meant counting while the two bulbs were both lit. In Single Duration Counting, children counted each duration from 1, but during reproduction, they counted up to only one of the cardinal numbers. An incorrect strategy was also attributed to children who admitted that they had counted only on some of the trials, and to those who did not count at all. Obviously counting on some of the trials and no counting could only be observed in children who were not instructed to count.

Understanding of the principles of time measurement was then examined through the constrained counting task. Recall that here children were asked to count in different rhythms, or with different tags, and to reproduce the same duration. They were also asked to judge whether they replicated the same time when rhythm or counting tags varied. Each child received a score of 0–4 according to the number of tasks, out of 4, which he or she performed correctly.

Table 4.8.
NUMBER OF TASKS PERFORMED CORRECTLY BY COUNTING STRATEGY AMONG 1st, 3rd AND 5th GRADERS INSTRUCTED AND UNINSTRUCTED TO COUNT (n=120)

STRATEGY TYPE	NUMBER OF TASKS PERFORMED CORRECTLY				
	0	1	2	3	4
INSTRUCTED TO COUNT					
ADDITION	1	5	12	15	10
OTHER	3	7	5	2	0
UNINSTRUCTED TO COUNT					
ADDITION	3	1	10	10	7
OTHER	3	9	5	8	2

Table 4.8 presents the number of children who performed correctly on the different number of tasks, by two rules of integration: addition and other, separated by presence vs. absence of instruction to count. Chi square analysis could not be carried out in each of the separated groups due to the low expected values in many of the cells. Since the two groups revealed similar trends they were combined for the statistical analysis. The relation between strategy and principled understanding by level of performance, in the two groups combined, was found to be significant by the chi square analysis.

Children using addition revealed a better understanding of the principles underlying time measurement. Of 76 children who added (43 instructed to count and 33 uninstructed), a lower proportion performed on no task or one task correctly, than among the 44 children who did not add. A similar proportions of children who added and who did not add performed well on two of the tasks only. In comparison, a higher proportion of those who added performed correctly on three or four tasks. Generally, the higher the number of tasks solved correctly, the higher the proportion of children who added.

There were few children who added but did not exhibit any understanding of the principles underlying counting. Similarly, few children who revealed a thorough understanding of the principles did not add. These findings suggest that the appropriate use of counting time for adding durations neither clearly precedes nor follows the understanding of constraint on counting time.

These findings should be viewed with a degree of caution since they were obtained with samples of a wide age range. Kindergartners to third graders were interviewed by Levin and Levy, and first to fifth graders were examined with the constrained task by Levin and Krispin. Since all the performances involved improved with age (see Levin & Wilkening, 1989), the relationship between them may have been mediated by age or schooling. Statistical analyses of the data within each age group were impossible due to the small number of children per grade.

GENERAL CONCLUSIONS: PRINCIPLES UNDERLYING TIME MEASUREMENT

The two studies reported had two aims, one major the other minor. The first aim was to analyze the developmental changes in children's recognition of principles underlying time measurement. The minor one was to provide a preliminary examination of the relationship between comprehension of these principles and the choice of strategy for time quantification and integration.

Children's understanding of principles underlying time measurement was assessed by two types of tasks: a semistructured interview involving hypothetical stories, and a constrained counting test based on behavioral measures and their evaluation by the children. Hence, the first task tapped a more explicit level of recognition. While implicit awareness is expected at an earlier age than explicit, it is impossible to draw a direct comparison between performance on the two tasks, for reasons specified hereafter.

Principles can only be assessed in a particular context. The context provides a structure which calls for integration of the principles with a variety of skills, be they domain-specific or general (see, Anderson, in preparation; Siegler, 1981 Reply to commentary, for similar claims). Each of our tasks invited the use of skills not shared with the other task. Consequently, different developmental aspects of the use of principles were illuminated. Rather than viewing the situation as hopelessly confusing, we would argue that development can be richly described only by employing different tasks, which converge on some aspects and diverge on others. The use of different tasks, inviting the use of different strategies on the part of the subject and calling for integration with various skills can, thus, shed light on the complexity of the use of principles.

Constancy vs. Arbitrariness

We assessed children's understanding of two types of constraints imposed on counting time, obligatory and permissible. The former constraints relate to the restriction that counting time must be done in a constant manner: in a fixed rhythm and with the same tags. Violation of constancy of either rhythm or the scale of tags renders counting an inappropriate device by which to measure time for various goals: reproducing durations, comparing intervals and the like. Permissible constraints refer to the liberty to count time arbitrarily: in any fixed rhythm and with any stable series of tags.

The procedural constraints on counting time are derived from principles underlying measurement in general, not only the measurement of time. Measurement must be done with a constant unit and a stable series of tags. Counting time in a constant rhythm and with the same series of tags guarantees the preservation of these principles. Similarly, the unit size chosen and the particular tags applied are arbitrary in measurement. Hence, counting time can be done at various rhythms and with different tags.

Let us mention in this context, however, that although counting can be done, in principle, in any rhythm and with any series of tags, the appropriate choice may be constrained by the features of the task at hand. For example, the more exact the measure of time required, the faster the counting should be. This is equally true for technological counting. Processes measured by atomic clocks cannot be measured by an ordinary watch. Similarly, any stable series of tags can be used as long as it is long enough to suit the given set of objects to be counted.

We assumed obligatory principles to precede in development permissible principles of a similar level of complexity. This assumption was derived from the Piagetian notion that contradictions provide the opportunity for cognitive change (Inhelder, Sinclair & Bovet, 1974; Piaget, 1980), and the supposition that obligatory principles are more vulnerable to violation. Violations as such may bring about contradictions which can be transcended by awareness of the underlying principles. For instance, using different units to measure quantities which are perceived as equal, leads to unequal measures which contradict perceived equality (Carpenter, 1975; Hiebert, 1979; Inhelder, Sinclair & Bovet, 1974).

In line with this assumption, we found that children grasp the principle of constancy at a younger age than they do the principle of arbitrariness, both for rhythm and for tags. This finding may, however, be an outcome of factors specific to time. Time in contrast to other dimensions, is conventionally measured with a small class of unique units: seconds for short durations, hours for longer ones. We do not mean to imply that young children are necessarily aware of the inclusion relation between these time units. They may view them as unrelated to each other, each uniquely adapted to intervals of a certain size. In addition, conventional time units for measuring time may be grasped as absolute since longer time units such as the day or the year, are "natural units" in the sense that they correspond to natural cycles and inner clocks (e.g., Aschoff, 1981; Gallistel, in press).

Children's Four Levels of Criteria for Successful Counting: Possible Sources

The explanations Levin and Levy found on all four questions dealing with constancy and arbitrariness of rhythm and of tags, were classified into four levels. The levels differed in the criteria employed for determining successful performance of the task at hand. On the lowest level, successful performance was described as reaching a high number in counting. Such a response may stem from young children's notion that counting well consists of counting up to a higher number, since a major difficulty they are aware of in counting is of having a limited retrievable series of tags. This criterion, however, is irrelevant to the goals of reaching a correct cardinal number or of measuring. Its use indicates that for these children counting does not serve for quantification. This kind of explanation was provided by our youngest children only, i.e., kindergartners. Even among them it was rare. We might expect it to appear among younger children who grasp counting as a string, rather than a chain of numbers used for quantifying sets of objects (see distinctions in: Fuson & hall, 1983).

On the second level, successful counting was equated with conventional counting. Counting was considered conventional if it started from 1 and was of a regular rhythm, neither too fast nor too slow. The fact that counting was done on the dimension of time was ignored at this level. Indeed, by counting conventionally the child usually reaches the general goal of counting correctly. His or her major difficulty in counting may be to count regularly, without omitting numbers. This criterion overlooks the particular features of the task at hand. The goal of time reproduction can, of course, be achieved by counting from any number, by omitting numbers, by counting backwards, etc. as long as counting is consistent. Children may fail to analyze the particular constraints of the task and consequently view unconventional counting as wrong. Findings which suggest that young children tend to grasp unconventional but correct countings as inappropriate have already been reported. (Briars & Siegler, 1984; Gelman & Meck, 1986).

On the third level, children perceived successful counting as counting by the "correct" units, rhythm, or tags. It seems as though they assumed that either the passing time, or the event occurring during that time, i.e., the burning of the bulb, constrained the way counting should be done. Some children gave the impression of viewing time as composed of separate "objective" units. To quantify time appropriately one should count these units, and so counting has to be done in the correct rhythm, the rhythm of time. Similarly, it should be done with the correct numbers. Otherwise, the appropriate quantification of time fails. Other children mentioned the counting of the experimenter or of the bulb, as the model of counting they should replicate in order to reproduce the same time. This claim ignored the fact that neither the experimenter nor the bulb gave any hint that they were involved in counting. These children seemed to view the passage of time as related to the kind of events occupying it. Counting the time of the burning bulb is constrained by that event, and is qualitatively different from counting any other event. Third level children failed to see the arbitrariness of counting time, i.e., that it can be done in any rhythm. They also missed the peculiarity of the task of reproduction, i.e., that it can start from any number.

On the fourth level, the criterion for successful counting was correct. It consisted of counting in a constant rhythm and a stable series of tags, and was indifferent to the particular rhythm or tags chosen. To sum up, the four levels of explanations utilize different criteria, each suiting the particular constraints of the task at hand better than the preceding one, and revealing a more advanced concept of counting of measurement and of time. This analysis indicates that the emergent evolution of principles underlying counting time is partly determined by the child's analysis of the particular constraints of the task served here by counting. Nevertheless we would tend to expect a similar pattern of explanations were children to use counting for measuring time for purpose other than time reproduction, such as comparing or adding durations.

Cognitive Structure Underlying Counting Time in Constrained Tasks

In the second study, children's understanding of the principle of arbitrariness was further analyzed by directing them to count in novel ways while reproducing an event. We examined two questions. First, whether they know that counting fast, or counting from 3, to the same number covers less time, and second, whether they know how to compensate their fast or from–3 counting to reproduce the same time. Compensation was granted when they divided the cardinal number reached by counting quickly by 2 or 3, to determine the cardinal number to be reached when counting slowly. Similarly, children were recognized as compensating when they added 2 or 3 to the first cardinal number obtained, when counting from 3 to the second final number.

Our results suggest that the cognitive structure underlying counting time in the constrained tasks changes with age. Four structures could be discerned:

a) *a fixed coordinated partial knowledge structure*
b) *a fixed uncoordinated partial knowledge structure comprised of separated components*
c) *a variable structure, comprised of modular components, vacillating in coordination*
d) *a fixed coordinated complete knowledge structure*

The first group of children, described as having a fixed, coordinated, partial knowledge structure, grasped the amount of time as a direct function of the cardinal number reached in counting it. They believed that if the same cardinal number was reached by two different counts, the durations they covered must be the same. When asked to count in two different ways and cover the same time, they counted up to the same number ignoring rhythm of counting or the number at which counting had started. When asked to compare the durations that had elapsed during the two different counts, they judged them to be equal. Hence, their knowledge can best be described as partial but consistent.

By systematically ignoring the rhythm of counting they conveyed that they conceived of counting time as quantifying the numerosity of time units, each treated as "a singular individual entity" (Fuson & Hall, 1983, p. 83) rather than as a unit of a certain size. In other words, these children attributed a cardinal rather than a measuring meaning to counting time. Thus, the "numerosity" of the time reproduced was grasped as independent of the rhythm and as dependent on the cardinal number. Similar phenomena have been shown by Soviet and Genevan psychologists in the measurement of other dimensions (Davydov, 1975, 1982; Gal'perin & Georgiev, 1969; Inhelder, Sinclair & Bovet, 1974; Minskaya, 1975). Indifference to unit size is a limitation in children's comprehension of measurement in general, not only of the measurement of time.

By disregarding the fact that counting started from different numbers, they revealed that they view the number of units counted as equivalent to the last number that was counted. Hence, they failed to coordinate ordinality and cardinality. This failure exhibits the general limitation of their knowledge of counting, not specifically that related to time. It is, however, an empirical question whether the same children, or at least children of the same age groups, would show this limitation for unit counting of discrete objects.

The second group of children, were described as having a fixed but uncoordinated partial knowledge comprised of separated components. When asked to reproduce the same duration by counting differently, they counted up to the same number, just as was done by the previous group of children. However, when asked to evaluate whether the two durations were equal, they realized that the rhythm of counting or the starting number does matter. Moreover, the majority of these children acknowledged that counting slower to the same number covers more time, or that counting from 3 covers less time. When asked again to reproduce the same time, they again failed to do so and persisted on counting to the same number. Their knowledge structure is best described as including separate and uncoordinated components.

The third group of children were described as having a variable structure, comprised of modular components, vacillating in coordination. To reproduce the same amount of time by counting differently, they counted up to the same cardinal number, just as the two previous groups did. When asked to compare the two durations, they realized that counting slowly to the same number covers more time, or that counting from 3 amounts to less time. In this respect they acted like the previous group. However, when asked again to count differently and reproduce the same time, they managed to do so. When counting slower, they counted half or a third of the number of tags. When counting from 3 they increased the cardinal number by 2 or 3. Thus they succeeded in coordinating components that were uncoordinated in the first trial.

Their behavior could have been interpreted as a case of a set of modular components, of the kind examined by Wilkinson (1984) for counting in general. The modularity of components is evident in the manner they are applied in performing a task. The components are retrieved from memory as separate units and need to be coordinated to produce the requested algorithm. Failure to integrate the known components produces errors that are, at times detectable, thus leading to fresh attempts at coordination of components. (Wilkinson, 1984; p.31). Alternatively, their behavior could be viewed as showing that they had reached a new level of stable coordination during the experiment. In this case we could not have claimed a variable knowledge structure. To provide clear evidence that the ability of such children to coordinate the components concerned is indeed variable, their performance should be reassessed with the same or similar tasks.

The fourth group of children counted differently up to a different tag to reproduce the same time. Their knowledge can be described as a fixed, coordinated, complete knowledge structure.

The four level model we propose is not very different from cognitive development as described by Siegler's (1981) rule assessment approach, according to which children improve with age in their ability to integrate information. When asked to solve a problem which required the coordination of two dimensions (e.g., balance beam) young children were found to take only one dimension into account. Older children related to the two dimensions but failed to integrate them. They "muddled through" when integration was demanded. These children can be described as having a "variable knowledge structure" in Wilkinson's (1984) terminology. Still older children, took into account the two variables and coordinated them appropriately.

Tags vs. Rhythm

The four different structures emerge at somewhat different ages when applied to counting tags and to counting rhythm. The knowledge structure evolves sooner for tags than for rhythm. The first two groups consisted mainly of first graders when tags were considered, and third graders when rhythm was taken into account. The third group included mostly first and third graders in regard to tags and fifth graders in regard to rhythm. The last group contained mostly fifth graders, but more of them on tags than on rhythm. The conclusions specifying age levels should be taken as rather preliminary, however, since they are based on too small a number of subjects.

The discrepancy between tags and rhythm is also apparent in the more general results of this study. By first grade (and maybe even earlier), most children know that counting from 3 covers less time. This means that they acknowledge the direct relation between number of tags counted and duration covered. They also know that counting up to the same final number does not necessarily imply covering the same duration. But only by the third grade (or perhaps by the second), do most children recognize that counting slower covers more time. This indicates that they acknowledge the inverse relation between time and speed. By the fifth grade (or maybe by the fourth) children can compensate by adding to the end the same number of tags that were left out at the beginning. They thereby show that they recognize that counting up to a different number can cover the same time. It is the number of counted numbers that matters. Only later, (perhaps by the sixth grade) do most children become able to compensate for speed of counting by number of tags, taking into account the proportions involved.

We attributed the application of principles earlier to tags than to rhythm to the issue of additive vs. multiplicative integration and to direct vs. inverse relations. Number of tags is directly related to time: the more tags you count the longer the time it takes. In contrast, speed is inversely related to time: The faster you count up to a certain number, the shorter the time it covers. This is in line with the finding that children are able to relate distance to time at a younger age (direct relation) than speed to time (inverse relation) (Acredolo, Adams & Schmid, 1984; Wilkening, 1981).

The difference between tags and rhythm was not apparent in the results obtained by Levin and Levy (see Table 1). Children's explicit understanding that counting should be carried out in a constant manner developed simultaneously for both tags and rhythm. Similarly, the explicit understanding that the particular rhythm and the specific tags used are immaterial, also emerged hand in hand. We can suggest no definitive explanation for this inconsistency between the results obtained in the two studies. On the one hand it may be related to the fact that a more explicit level of principle recognition was assessed in the first study. On the other hand, it may stem from the fact that a clearer distinction between the cardinal number and the measured time was demanded in the second study. According to Piaget (1969) children's major difficulty with time, is to distinguish between the time and the features of the events occurring in it. The second study may have occasioned this difficulty to a greater extent than the first.

As stated above, many children who judge correctly that counting in different manners up to the same number does not cover the same time, do not know how to compensate for the difference. Their difficulty does not seem to focus on deciding what kind of algebraic manipulation to perform on the cardinal number (should I add? subtract? multiply? and how much?). Rather, it seems to lie in acknowledging that counting up to different numbers could cover the same time. Therefore, their major error is counting up to the same number. This difficulty could stem from children's approach to time as though it were a discrete rather than a continuous dimension, or from limitations in information processing evident in their failure to coordinate the various demands inherent in each of the problems. Such limitations in information integration were analyzed by Case (1985), who attributes them to maturational factors.

Comparison of the Current Model of Principles with Piaget's Model: Isochronism and Synchronism

Piaget proposed two principles, isochronism and synchronism, as the principles underlying understanding of time measurement. Isochronism means that the same motion recurring under the same conditions necessarily lasts the same duration, regardless of the events that are measured by the motions. Synchronism means that two motions which start simultaneously and end simultaneously necessarily last the same amount of time, whether or not they are of the same speed or bring about the same amount of output.

Piaget distinguished three stages in the development of the understanding of time measurement. He employed two major tasks to characterize them. The first task demonstrated the progression from the first to the second stage, and the second task, from the second to the third stage. In the first task, the child repeated the same activity twice (e.g., tapping on the table), one time faster than the other. Both times, however, the activity was timed, and the child had to watch the timer (e.g., an hourglass) attentively. The child was then asked if the timer ran both times at the same velocity. It should be noted that asking the child about velocity rather than time, renders that task as somewhat dubious for the assessing of understanding of time.

Until the age of 7 or 8, most of the children assumed an inverse relation between their own velocity and that of the timer. That is, the faster they acted, the slower they thought the timer ran. Piaget argued that because they lacked the isochronic principle, i.e., that the same motion under the same conditions preserves its velocity, the children were ready to accept as valid the perceptual illusion created by the pace of their own activity. In the second stage, children asserted that the timer's speed was independent of their own speed.

We suggest that isochronism is related to the principle of constancy. Understanding that under the same conditions recurrent motions are of the same duration is close to recognizing that counting rhythmically creates equal intervals of time. Consequently, the child acknowledges that counting time must be done in a constant manner. In our study constancy was recognized at about the same age that Piaget detected isochronism. This is quite surprising since the tasks we used differed in many ways from those devised by Piaget.

In the second task used by Piaget, the child watched two different timers (e.g., an hourglass and a stop watch) running together, each reaching a particular point (e.g., when the sand ran out or the watch hand completed half a circle). Then, only the first timer was started and the child drew a straight line in a fixed rhythm, till the timer reached its appointed point. The child was asked how long the line will be, if he were to draw it until the second timer reached its allocated point. Second stage children, about 8 to 10 years old, tended to respond that the lines drawn would differ in length. Lacking the principle of synchronicity, the child is unaware the the two timers, which differ in velocity as well as in the distances they cover, must run for the same duration, if they start and stop running simultaneously. In the same vein, the child does not appreciate that the timer's time and his or her drawing time must be equal, whenever they co-occur. Consequently, the child either has no idea what length of line should be expected on the second drawing, or decides that the lines should differ in length. In the third stage, understanding of isochronism and synchronism, as well as the transitivity of the relations involved, implies, for Piaget, understanding the principles underlying time measurement.

We propose that synchronism is related to arbitrariness. Recognizing that two timers measure the same time in spite of the fact that they run at different speeds and produce different outputs, is related to knowing that the same duration can be covered by counting in different speeds or with different tags. Here again, the age level at which arbitrariness was evidenced by our subjects is close to the age level at which Piaget's subjects displayed an understanding of synchronism, despite the difference in the tasks employed. An elaborate comparative analysis of the two sets of principles and their developmental course awaits future research.

A major difference between our model and that of Piaget, is that he proposed principles specific to time while the principles we described are of measurement in general. Nevertheless, no assumption is made that these principles will emerge in the same sequence and in the same age levels when applied to dimensions other than time, such as length. However, we consider the question of the developmental relation between the understanding of the same principles when applied to different dimensions, as highly important. It may enhance our understanding of factors contributing to the conception of time and of measurement.

In contrast to Piaget, we do not consider the principles we analyzed, constancy and arbitrariness, as the only principles involved in time measurement. Since measurement involves counting, principles underlying counting are part of the evolution of measurement. In addition, since measurement involves algebraic operations, principles underlying these are also part of that evolution. In this respect, we view the present studies as a modest beginning for a new domain of research, about which very little is yet known.

References

Acredolo, C. Adams, A. & Schmid, J. (1984). On the understanding of the relationships between speed, duration and distances. *Child Development, 55,* 2151–2159.

Anderson, N. H. (in preparation). Adaptive Thinking. In: N. H. Anderson (Ed.). *Contributions to information integration theory.*

Anderson, N. H., & Cuneo, D. O. (1978). The height and width rule in children's judgments of quantity. *Journal of experimental psychology: General, 107,* 335–378.

Aschoff, J. (1981). Handbook of behavioral neurobiology (Vol. 4). New York: Plenum Press.

Beilin, H., & Franklin, I. C. (1962). Logical operations in area and length measurement: Age and training effects. *Child Development, 33,* 607–618.

Briars, D. J., & Siegler, R. S. (1984). A featural analysis of preschoolers' counting knowledge. *Developmental Psychology, 20,* 607–618.

Bryant, P. E., & Kopytynska, H. (1976). Spontaneous measurement by young children. *Nature, 260,* 773.

Carpenter, T. P. (1975). Measurement concepts of first– and second– grade students. *Journal of Research in Mathematics Education, 6,* 3–14.

Case, R. (1985). *Intellectual development: Birth to adulthood.* Orlando: Academic Press.

Case, R., Sandieson, R., & Dennis, S. (1986). Two cognitive-developmental approaches to the design of remedial instruction. *Cognitive Development, 1,* 293–333.

Davydov, V. V. (1975). The psychological characteristics of "prenumerical" period of mathematics instruction. (A. Bigelow, Trans.) In L. P. Steffe (Ed.). *Soviet studies in the psychology of learning and teaching mathematics.* (Vol. 7). Chicago: The University of Chicago. (From Learning capacity and age level: Primary grades. D. B. El'Konin & V.V. Davydov (Eds.). Moscow: Prosveschenie, 1966).

Davydov, V. V. (1982). The psychological characteristics of the formation of the elementary mathematical operations in children. In T. P. Carpenter, J. M. Moser, & T. A. Romberg (Eds.). *Addition and Subtraction: A developmental perspective.* Hillsdale, NJ: Lawrence Erlbaum Associates.

Fuson, K. C., & Hall, J. W. (1983). The acquisition of early number word meanings: A conceptual analysis and review. In H. Ginsburg (Ed.). *The development of children's mathematical thinking,* (pp. 49–107). New York: Academic Press.

Fuson, K. C., Richards, J., & Briars, D. J. (1982). The acquisition and elaboration of the number word sequence. In C. J. Brainerd (Ed.). *Children's logical and mathematical cognition: Progress in cognitive development research.* New York: Springer-Verlag.

Gallistel, C. R., (in press). *The organization of learning.* Cambridge: Bradford Books/ MIT Press.

Gal'perin P. Ya., & Georgiev L. S. (1969). The formation of early mathematical notions. (D. A. Henderson, Trans.) In J. Kilpatrick, & I. Wirszup (Eds.), *Soviet studies in the psychology of learning and teaching mathematics*: Vol. 1. Chicago: The University of Chicago. (*From A series of four articles published in Reports of the Academy of Pedagogical Sciences in the USSR,* Vol. 1, 1960).

Gelman, R. & Gallistel, C. R. (1978). *The child's understanding of number.* Cambridge, MA: Harvard University Press.

Gelman, R. & Meck, E. (1986). The notion of principle: The case of counting. In: J. Hiebert (Ed.). *The relationship between procedural and conceptual competence* (pp. 29–57). Hillsdale, NJ: Erlbaum.

Gelman, R., Meck, E., & Merkin, S. (1986). Young children's numerical competence. *Cognitive Development, 1,* 1–29.

Hiebert, J. (1979). *The effect of cognitive development on first grade children's ability to learn linear measurement concepts.* (Tech. Rep. No. 506) Madison: Wisconsin Research and Development Center for Individualized Schooling.

Inhelder, B., Sinclair, H., & Bovet, M. (1974). *Learning and the development of cognition.* Cambridge, Massachusetts: Harvard University Press.

Kuhn, T. S. (1977). The function of measurement in modern physical science. in: Kuhn. T. S. *The Essential Tension.* Chicago: The University of Chicago Press.

Levin, I., & Wilkening, F. (1989) Measuring time via counting: The development of children's conceptions of time as a quantifiable dimension. In I. Levin, & D. Zakay (Eds.). *Time and human cognition: A life span perspective,* (pp. 119–144). Amsterdam: North Holland Publishing.

Miller, K. (1984). Child as the measurer of all things: Measurement procedures and the development of quantitative concepts. In: C. Sophian (Ed.). *Origins of cognitive skills* (pp. 193–228). Hillsdale NJ: Lawrence Erlbaum Associates.

Miller, K. (1987). *Measurement as a tool for thought.* Paper presented as part of the symposium Tools for Thought at the biennial meeting of the Society for Reaserch in Child Development, Baltimore, MD.

Minskaya, G. D. (1975). Developing the concept of number by means of the relationship of quantities. (A. Bigelow, Trans.) In L. P. Steffe (Ed.). *Soviet Studies in the psychology of learning and teaching mathematics*: Vol. 7. Chicago: The University of Chicago. (From Learning capacity and age level: Primary grades. D. B. El'Konin & V. V. Davydov (Eds.). Moscow: Prosveschenie, 1966).

Piaget, J. (1969). *The child's conception of time.* (A. J. Pomerans, Trans.) New York: Basic Books. (Original work published 1946).

Piaget, J. (1980). *Experiments in contradiction.* (D. Coltman, Trans.) Chicago: The University of Chicago Press.

Richards, D. D., & Siegler, R. S. (1982). U – Shaped behavioral curves: It's not whether you are right or wrong, it's why. In S. Strauss, & Stavi, R. (Eds.). *U – Shaped behavioral growth.* New York: Academic Press.

Siegal, M., Waters, L. J., & Dinwiddy, L. S. (in press) Misleading children: Causal attributions for inconsistency under repeated questioning. *Journal of Experimental Child Psychology.*

Siegler, R. S. (1981). Developmental sequences within and between concepts. *Monographs of the Society for Research in Child Development, 46* (2, serial no. 189).

Siegler, R. S., & Richards, D. D. (1979). The development of time, speed and distance concepts. *Developmental Psychology, 15,* 288–298.

Statistical Package for the Social Sciences (SPSS). (1975). McGraw Hill.

Strauss, S., & Stavi R. (1982). U. – Shaped behavioral growth: Implications for theories. In W. W. Hartup (Ed.). *Review of Child Development Research*: Vol. 6. (pp. 517–599). Chicago: University of Chicago Press.

Vij, B. B., (1982). *Towards a unified technology: If time standard went metric.* New Delhi: Soni Book Agency.

Wagner, S. H. & Walters, J. (1982). A longitudinal analysis of early number concepts: From numbers to number. In Forman, G. E. (Ed.). *Action and Thought: From sensorimotor schemes to symbolic operations.* (pp. 137–161). New York: Academic Press.

Wilkening, F. (1979). Combining of stimulus dimensions in children's and adults' judgement of area: An information integration analysis. *Developmental Psychology, 15,* 25–33.

Wilkening, F. (1981). Integrating velocity, time, and distance information: A developmental study. *Cognitive psychology, 13,* 231–247.

Wilkening, F. Levin, I., & Druyan, S. (1987). Children's counting strategies for time quantification and integration. *Developmental Psychology, 23,* 823–831.

Wilkinson, A. C. (1984), Children's partial knowledge of the cognitive skill of counting. *Cognitive Psychology, 16*, 28–64.

TIME AND HUMAN COGNITION
A Life-Span Perspective
I. Levin and D. Zakay (Editors)

ROBERT S. SIEGLER
KATE MCGILLY

CHAPTER 5

Strategy Choices in Children's Time-Telling*

INTRODUCTION

When just beginning to learn to solve a class of problems, people often know only a single problem-solving strategy. For example, when beginning to learn to add, children often can only solve problems by counting their fingers. By the time people have acquired a high degree of skill in the area, they often consistently use a single efficient procedure. Continuing with the addition example, adults and older children consistently solve simple addition problems by retrieving answers. During the transition period, however, people often use a variety of strategies. While in the midst of learning to add, children solve simple addition problems by counting from one, by counting from the larger addend, by decomposing problems into simpler forms, and by retrieving answers from memory (Fuson, 1982; Baroody & Ginsburg, 1986; Siegler, 1987a). A central assumption of the

*This research was supported in part by Grant #HD–19011 from the National Institutes of Health, in part by Grant #83–0050 from the National Institute of Education, and in part by a grant from the Spencer Foundation, and in part by a Natural Sciences & Engineering Research Council of Canada Scholarship awarded to the second author.

present research is that for many cognitive acquisitions, understanding of transitions demands understanding of the diverse strategies that children use in the transitional periods.

The fact that children who are in transitional periods often use diverse strategies raises a number of questions. What strategies do they use; what benefits do they obtain from using the diverse strategies; how do they choose among them? These issues have been addressed previously in the context of addition, subtraction, and multiplication (Siegler, 1987b; 1988; Siegler & Shrager, 1984; Siegler & Robinson, 1982). In the research described in this chapter, we extend the examination of strategy use and strategy choice to time-telling on a conventional analog clock.

Time-telling is of interest for both theoretical and practical reasons. Everyday observation indicates that children who are learning to tell time use several strategies. They sometimes count forward by 5's from the previous hour, sometimes count forward by 5's from other points on the clock, and sometimes retrieve the time from seeing the configuration of the hour and minute hands. Time-telling also is of interest because of its relation to the previously-studied arithmetic tasks. It is like them in that it unsolves numbers and counting, but differs in that it appears also to involve a substantial perceptual-recognition component. Thus, it provides a test of whether a model developed to account for strategy choices in arithmetic also is useful outside of the arithmetic domain. Finally, time-telling is a task of considerable practical importance, one to which children devote a large amount of time both in and out of school, and one about which little is currently known. The basic descriptive data on the development of time-telling skills should be valuable independent of the success of the model in accounting for them.

The chapter begins with a discussion of two literatures. One focuses on the general issue of how people choose strategies. The other focuses on the development of time-telling skills. Next, we describe an experiment intended to document which strategies children use to tell time, how often each strategy is used, how accurately and rapidly each one is used, and the conditions under which each strategy tends to be used. Finally, we examine the ability of the strategy-choice model to account for children's time-telling performance.

A SHORT REVIEW OF THE LITERATURES ON STRATEGY CHOICE AND TIME-TELLING

The Issue of Strategy Choice

Traditionally, cognitive and developmental psychologists have tried to determine *the* strategy that people use on a certain task. This approach has led to many influential models, among them models of sentence verification (Clark & Chase, 1972; Carpenter & Just, 1975; Trabasso, Rollins, & Shaughnessy, 1971), mental rotation (Cooper & Shepard, 1973; Shepard & Metzler, 1971), transitive inference (Clark, 1969, Huttenlocher & Higgins, 1971; Sternberg, 1977), and addition of numbers (Ashcraft, 1982; Groen & Parkman, 1972).

Recently, however, increasing numbers of researchers have recognized that people use diverse strategies on many tasks, including those where single strategies were previously assumed. Hunt and his colleagues demonstrated that different people use different approaches to verify sentences (MacLeod et al., 1978; Matthews, Hunt, & MacLeod, 1980). Cooper and her colleagues described alternative strategies that people use to perform mental rotation (Cooper & Regan, 1982; Glushko & Cooper, 1978). Egan and Grimes-Farrow (1982) and Sternberg and Weil (1980) identified several strategies that people use to draw transitive inferences.

It is not only true that people of different ages and abilities use different strategies to perform a single task; it also is true that individuals use multiple strategies. The majority of kindergarteners, first graders, and second graders have been found to use at least three addition strategies (Fuson, 1982). The majority of kindergarteners and first graders have been found to use at least three subtraction strategies (Siegler, 1987b). The majority of third graders have been found to use at least three multiplication strategies (Siegler, 1988). The phenomenon does not only reflect children using different strategies on different problems. When presented the identical subtraction problems a week later, kindergarteners and first graders used visibly different strategies on 34% of problems (Siegler, 1987b). Thus, variability of strategy use exists even within a single child solving the identical problem at two points close in time, when knowledge and general cognitive level are essentially constant.

To accurately represent what people are doing, cognitive models must incorporate this variable strategy use. Failing to do so can lead to severe distortions. For example, one of the best known and most extensively documented cognitive-psychological models is Groen and Parkman's (1972) min model. It posits that first and second graders solve essentially all single digit addition problems by counting up from the larger addend. Thus, they would solve 3+6 by thinking "6, 7, 8, 9". The min model predicts that solution times and percentage of errors on each problem will be a linear function of the smaller addend, because the smaller addend indicates the amount of counting-on from the larger number that needs to be done to solve the problem. This prediction has proved accurate for both groups of children and individuals, in both Europe and North America, in both standard and special education settings (see Ashcraft, 1987, for a review of this literature).

Despite all this support, the model is wrong. In a recent experiment, Siegler (1987a) examined young children's simple addition, using both the usual solution-time and error measures and children's verbal reports. The results were striking. When data were averaged over all trials, as in earlier studies, the results closely replicated the previous finding that solution times and percentage of errors were a linear function of the smaller addend. If these analyses were the only ones conducted, the usual conclusion would have been reached, namely that first and second graders consistently use the min strategy to add.

However, the children's verbal reports suggested a quite different picture. The min strategy was but one of five approaches that they reported using. This reporting of diverse strategies characterized individual as well as group performance; most children reported using at least three approaches. Not only did children not report using the min strategy on every trial, they only said they had used it on 36% of trials. At no age did they report using it on more than 40% of trials.

Dividing the error and solution time data according to what strategy children said they had used on that trial lent considerable credence to the children's verbal reports. On trials where they reported using the min strategy, the min model was an even better predictor of solution times than in past studies or in the present data set as a whole; it accounted for 86% of the variance in solution times. In contrast, on trials where they reported using one of the other strategies, the min model was never a good predictor of performance, either in absolute terms or relative to other predictors. It never accounted for as much as 40% of the variance. A variety of measures converged on the conclusion that children used the five strategies that they reported using, and that they employed them on those trials where they said they had. Thus, it appeared that the min model misrepresented what children were doing on almost two-thirds of trials.

The general point is that people in the process of learning often use multiple strategies and that failing to recognize this can lead to seriously incorrect conclusions. Only by taking seriously the diversity of strategy use, even within a single person, can cognitive models hope to characterize transition periods accurately.

THE ADAPTIVE VALUE OF USING DIVERSE STRATEGIES

Once the diversity of people's strategy use is recognized, the question immediately arises: What function does the diverse strategy use serve? Considering the patterns of speed and accuracy produced by each strategy suggests that children derive substantial advantages from using multiple strategies. This can be seen especially clearly in the choice of whether to state a retrieved answer or to use a *backup strategy.* A backup strategy is defined as any strategy other than retrieval; thus probability of backup strategy use is always 1 minus probability of retrieval. Examples of backup strategies include counting fingers to add, sounding out words to read, looking up a word's spelling in a dictionary, and so on. Both retrieval and use of backup strategies have clear, though different, advantages for someone in the process of acquiring a new competence. Retrieval can be executed much faster, but the backup strategies often yield high accuracy rates on problems where retrieval cannot. Ideally, children would use retrieval where that faster approach could be executed accurately, and would use backup strategies where the backup strategies were necessary for accurate performance. In fact, children's strategy choices have followed exactly this pattern in the domains we have studied. On easy problems children rely primarily on retrieval; on difficult problems, they rely primarily on backup strategies.

Comparing children's behavior under conditions where they are and are not allowed to use such backup strategies reveals just how adaptive the children's strategy choices are. Allowing children to use backup strategies leads to more accurate performance on all problems. However, the degree of the advantage for each problem is closely related to how often children use backup strategies on that problem when allowed to do so. That is, on problems where children are much more accurate when they use backup strategies, they use them often. On problems where children are only slightly more accurate when they use backup strategies, they use them much less often.

This pattern of strategy use allows children to strike an effective balance between concerns of speed and accuracy. They wind up using the fastest strategy, retrieval, when they can do so accurately, and using slower backup strategies when such strategies are necessary for accurate performance. The question is how children are able to make such adaptive strategy choices.

TWO APPROACHES TO HOW PEOPLE CHOOSE STRATEGIES

Given that people have a number of strategies at their disposal, *how* do they decide which one to use in a particular situation? Two approaches to this question can be contrasted: models emphasizing rational use of explicit, statable, metacognitive knowledge about cognitive capacity, available strategies, and task demands, and models emphasizing the adaptive products that fall out of the workings of basic cognitive processes.

APPROACHES EMPHASIZING EXPLICIT KNOWLEDGE. One way in which children could choose strategies would be to explicitly consider metacognitive knowledge about the difficulty of problems, their own memory capacity, and available strategies. For example, given the task of determining what time it was when an analog clock said 4:25, a child might judge the difficulty of the problem, ponder available strategies, and decide which strategy should be used given the characteristics of the problem and the available strategies.

Although depictions emphasizing such rational, top-down decision processes are appealing, their value as a general model of strategy choice has been increasingly questioned. The criticisms have focused both on the frequent lack of empirical connections between explicit, statable metacognitive knowledge and strategic behavior (Brown & Reeve, 1986; Chi & Ceci, 1987; Cavanaugh & Perlmutter, 1982; Sternberg & Powell, 1983), and on the vagueness of theoretical ideas about how metacognitive knowledge might exert its effect. Although children clearly have such metacognitive knowledge, it remains unclear when such knowledge is involved in strategy choices and what role it plays when it is involved.

The present approach is based on a different assumption: that at least some strategy choices are not based on such explicit metacognitive knowledge at all, but rather fall out from the basic workings of memory.

THE DISTRIBUTION OF ASSOCIATIONS MODEL. The distribution of associations model (Siegler, 1986; Siegler & Shrager, 1984) illustrates a way in which people could choose strategies effectively without being limited by their explicit knowledge about problem difficulty, cognitive capacities, and the characteristics of different strategies. The model's complexity precludes a full description of it in this context; extensive descriptions of it are available in the above-cited sources. However, the model's main mechanism for choosing between stating a retrieved answer and using a backup strategy is both relatively simple and critical to the present analysis of time-telling. Therefore, we will describe it here in some detail.

The strategy choice involves two interacting parts: a distribution of associations, and a process that operates on the distribution of association to produce behavior. The distribution of associations is made up of associations of varying strengths between particular problems and possible answers to the problem. As an example, the representation of the time when the big hand points to the 6 and the little hand is half way between the 12 and the 1 (12:30) would consist of associations of differing strengths between that configuration of the clock hands and times such as 12:00, 12:30, 1:30, and so on.

The process operates on this representation in the following way. First, the child sets a *confidence criterion*. This confidence criterion is a threshold that must be exceeded by the associative strength of a retrieved answer for that answer to be stated. It can assume any of a range of numerical values. Once this threshold is set, the child retrieves an answer. The probability of any given answer's being retrieved on a particular retrieval effort is proportional to the associative strength of that answer relative to the associative strengths of all answers to the problem. If the associative strength of whatever answer is retrieved exceeds the confidence criterion, the child states that answer. Otherwise, the child may either again retrieve an answer and see if it exceeds the confidence criterion or abandon efforts to retrieve and instead use a backup strategy to solve the problem.

HOW THE MODEL ACCOUNTS FOR THE DATA. The model accounts for the existence of different strategies, the variability of strategies and particular answers produced by individual children, the particular errors that are made most often, and the relations among percentage of errors, length of solution times, and percentage of backup strategy use. The way in which it does so has been described previously by Siegler and Shrager (1984) for addition, by Siegler (1987b) for subtraction, and by Siegler (1988) for multiplication. Here, the discussion will focus on how the model accounts for when children most frequently use backup strategies.

As noted above, children's pattern of strategy use seems very adaptive. One aspect of this adaptiveness involves when children use each strategy. The more difficult the problem, defined either in terms of high error rates or long solution times, the more often children use the relatively time-consuming backup strategies. In single-digit addition, subtraction, and multiplication, children's frequency of use of backup strategies on each problem has consistently correlated between r=.75 and r=.90 with the frequency of errors and length of solution times on that problem (Siegler, 1986). This pattern of strategy use is of considerable value to the child. It allows use of retrieval on relatively easy problems, where retrieval is likely to lead to correct answers, yet also leads to use of backup strategies on the more difficult problems where success would otherwise be unlikely. The pattern cannot be explained in terms of metacognitive knowledge leading to use of the more time consuming backup strategies on the more difficult problems. Siegler and Robinson (1982) found that children's explicit judgments of the difficulty of each addition problem did not correlate sufficiently highly with the problem's actual difficulty to allow this route to produce the high correlations that existed between the children's frequency of use of backup strategies on each problem and the problems' actual difficulty (with actual difficulty measured by the problem's mean RT and percent errors).

The distribution of associations model was generated to provide an alternative to metacognitive accounts of strategy choices, one that could produce adaptive choices among strategies even in the absence of explicit metacognitive knowledge. Within the model, the close associations among percentage of errors, length of solution times, and percentage of backup strategy use on each problem arise because all three variables are functions of the same independent variable: the peakedness of the distribution of associations linking a problem to associated answers. To understand the model it is useful to compare its workings on problems where most associative strength is concentrated in the correct answer (a *peaked distribution*) with its workings on problems where associative strength is distributed among several answers (a *flat distribution*).

Figure 5.1 depicts a peaked and a flat distribution. When the process operates on these two distributions, its operation on the problem with the peaked distribution (12:00) elicits 1) a higher percentage of retrieval (because the more peaked the distribution, the higher the probability that the answer with greatest associative strength within that distribution will be retrieved and the higher the probability that once the answer is retrieved, its associative strength will exceed the confidence criterion and thus allow the answer to be stated); 2) a higher percentage correct (since the more peaked the distribution, the more likely that the correct answer (the answer at the peak of the distribution) will be retrieved and the more likely that it will be stated if retrieved); and 3) shorter solution times (since the more peaked the distribution, the more likely that an answer whose associative strength exceeds the confidence criterion will be retrieved and stated on an early retrieval attempt). Thus, the model suggests that the reason that use of backup strategies consistently parallels problem difficulty is that the factor that determines percentage of errors and length of solution times, namely the peakedness of distributions, also determines how often backup strategies are used.

The model goes beyond this explanation for the general correlational

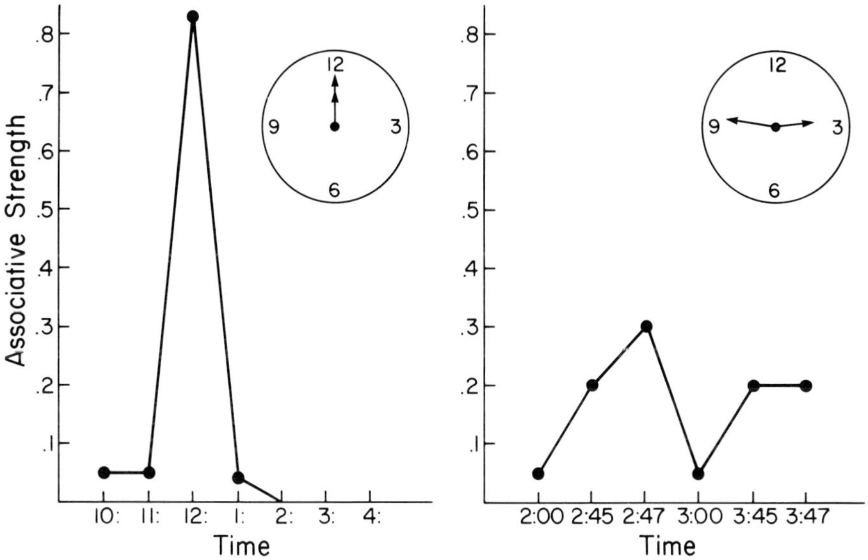

Figure 5.1. A peaked (left) and a flat (right) distribution of associations.

pattern to predict the types of trials most responsible for the correlations. It indicates that the correlation between percentage of backup strategy use on each problem and percentage of errors on that problem is primarily a correlation between percentage of backup strategy use on each problem and percentage of errors *on retrieval trials* on that problem. Similarly, the correlation between percentage of backup strategy use on each problem and solution times on that problem should be largely a correlation between percentage of backup strategy use on each problem and solution times *on retrieval trials* on the problem. As explained above, percent errors on retrieval trials, solution times on retrieval trials, and percent backup strategy use all are hypothesized to be functions of the peakedness of the distribution of associations. In contrast, the model suggests that when children use backup strategies, the peakedness of the distribution does not influence their responses (since at that point, they are no longer trying to retrieve the answer). Errors and solution times on backup strategy trials will be due to specific sources of difficulty that arise in trying to execute those strategies (such as the amount of counting to be done in the counting fingers strategy in addition). Because they depend on these specific sources of difficulty in executing the strategy—rather than on the distribution of associations—percentages of errors and lengths of solution times on backup strategy trials on each problem should be less highly correlated with percentage of backup strategy use on that problem.

The patterns of correlations in addition, subtraction, and multiplication all have followed the predictions of the model. Percent errors and length of solution times on retrieval trials on each problem have consistently more closely paralleled percent backup strategy use on that problem than have percent errors and length of solution times on backup strategy trials. The finding is consistent with the view that the children's adaptive patterns of strategy use are byproducts of the workings of the retrieval mechanism. Seen from this perspective, the distribution of associations on each problem determines what is retrieved, and thereby determines patterns of strategy use as well as patterns of errors and solution times. As summarized in Siegler (1986), the present strategy choice model has allowed us to account within a single framework for many additional aspects of children's behavior, including developmental changes in errors, solution times, and strategy use.

The Development of Time-Telling Skills

Surprisingly little is known about how children tell time. Most studies concerned with time have focused on children's understanding of duration (especially speed-distance-time relations), and on their conceptualizations of the various time systems such as the days, months, and years (e.g., Friedman, 1982; 1983; 1986; Levin, 1977; 1979; Levin, Wilkening, & Dembo, 1984; Piaget, 1946/1969, Richards, 1982; Siegler & Richards, 1979). In a society where so much is constrained by the time of day, it is surprising that time-telling is not a more researched domain.

Two initial issues concerning the development of time-telling skills are the ages at which the skills develop and the order in which they are acquired. Several studies have examined the percentage of 4– to 10–year-olds who can state the exact time given particular clock settings. The clock settings can be divided into three, and perhaps four or five, groups. The three clear groups are hour times (e.g., 3:00), 5–minute-times (e.g., 3:25, 3:50), and 1–minute-times (e.g., 3:27, 3:52). Beyond this, it may prove useful to divide 5–minute-times into those that are also quarter and/or half hours (e.g., 3:15, 3:30) and those that are not.

Not surprisingly, the first times that children can tell are typically hour times. Roughly 20% of 4–year-olds, 50% of 5–year-olds, 75% of 6 year olds, and 100% of 8– and 10–year olds who have been tested have correctly stated the time for hour settings (Case, Sandieson, & Dennis, 1986; Friedman & Laycock, 1986; Springer, 1952).

With regard to 5–minute-times, Springer (1952) found that fewer than one-third of 5– and 6–year olds tested could correctly state the exact time for half– and quarter-hours. Friedman and Laycock (1986) reported that slightly more than one-third of 6–year-olds and more than 90% of 7–year-olds and older children could solve half hour times. Case et al. (1986) averaged across 5–minute-times and found that 0% of 4– and 6–year-olds, and more than two-thirds of 8–and 10–year-olds could correctly identify 5–minute-times.

Finally, on 1–minute-times, Case et al. reported that 0% of 4– and 6–year-olds, 33% of 8–year-olds, and 70% of 10–year-olds could identify such times correctly. Friedman and Laycock reported somewhat earlier understanding. Like Case, they found that almost none of the 6–year-olds could identify 1–minute-times, but they also found that by age 8, 70% of children could do so.

These observations together tell a fairly clear story about the ages at which middle and late 20th Century North American children can tell various times on analog clocks and the order in which the skills develop. The earliest signs of time telling ability emerge by 4 years, and the skills are still developing at 10 years. A majority of children appear able to identify hour times by age 6, 5 minute-times by age 7 or 8, and 1–minute-times by ages 8–10. It is possible that half hour and/or quarter hour times can be read earlier than other 5–minute-times. However, because none of the previous studies have systematically compared performance on all of the time settings, it is impossible to reach this precise a conclusion on the basis of the available data.

This limitation notwithstanding, we know a reasonable amount about *when* children can identify different times and the order in which they learn to do so. However, we know much less about *how* they decide what time it is and *how* they make the transition from unskilled to skilled time-telling.

From the perspective of the present model, these issues can be translated into the questions of what strategies children use while they are in the process of learning to tell time and how their choices among these strategies enable them to move from frequent use of backup strategies to consistent use of retrieval. Previous research has established several relevant facts. While children are learning to tell time, they appear to use a number of backup strategies. Four– to 10–year-olds report using such strategies as counting by 5's from the hour, counting by 5's from prominent reference points such as the half hour, counting backward from the hour, and counting from the nearest 5–minute time (Friedman & Laycock, 1986; Springer, 1952).

The previous research also has established that both adults and children have problem-specific associations between clock settings and verbally-statable times. Paivio (1978) asked adult subjects to determine which of two verbally-described clock settings would have the smallest angular separation between the minute and hour hands of a clock. For example, a subject might be asked "Where would the angle between the clock hands be greater: 1:35 or 12:05?"

The results suggested that subjects possessed specific associations between verbally-stated times and positions of clock hands. The main evidence was the appearance of symbolic distance effects dependent on the physical distance between the clock hands rather than the difference in times. The farther apart the clock hands, the faster the comparison. Thus 11:35 and 12:05 compared more rapidly than 11:35 and 12:35, even though the times were more discrepant in the latter comparison, In addition, subjects verbally reported having used imagery in making their judgements. In other words, adults had associated specific positions of clock hands with verbally described times and used these associations to perform Paivio's task.

Children also seem to associate particular positions of the clock hands with particular times. Both Springer (1952) and Friedman and Laycock (1986) found that when children were asked how they had known it was a given time, they sometimes said that they "just knew" or simply pointed to the hands of the clock. They tended to do this most often on hour-times, next most often on half hour times, and least often on 1–minute times.. Further attesting to the validity of the verbal reports, the frequency of such retrieval-based descriptions increased substantially with age.

The fact that children learning to tell time possess both backup strategies and problem-specific associations that allow them to retrieve answers suggests that the distribution of associations model may be useful for analyzing their performance. Siegler and Taraban (1986) hypothesized that only two prerequisites have to be met for the strategy choice model to apply to a given task: that the problem-solver have enough experience with the task to have associated specific answers with specific items, and that the problem solver possess one or more backup strategies to use when associative knowledge does not yield an answer on a problem. By this logic, the model should be applicable to time-telling. Further support for this expectation comes from the fact that time-telling has several features in common with the arithmetic domains where the model previously has been found to apply: knowledge of how to tell time is built up over an extended period; it involves both procedures and declarative facts stored in long-term memory; and the direction of change is from greater use of backup strategies to greater use of retrieval.

One feature of time-telling, however, clearly differentiates it from the arithmetic domains: time-telling is a highly perceptual task. None of the numerical domains require the kind of visual information processing that telling time does. One reason for conducting the experiment was to determine whether children's strategy choices in a domain with a large perceptual component would follow the same pattern as has been found in less perceptually-demanding domains.

AN EMPIRICAL STUDY OF CHILDREN'S TIME-TELLING

The main goals of the experiment were:

1. To systematically examine differences among clock times in percent errors, length of solution times, and percent use of backup strategies.
2. To specify the strategies that children learning to tell time use when identifying the time on an analog clock.
3. To assess the temporal and accuracy characteristics of each strategy, and the particular error patterns that each strategy generates.
4. To examine the ability of the distribution of associations model to account for when different strategies are used.

Method

PARTICIPANTS

Second and third graders were chosen for participation, because these were the grade levels at which the children's mathematics text book taught time-telling (and therefore the grades of which children would be in the transition to learning to tell time). The 33 children who participated (9 boys and 9 girls in Grade 2, 5 boys and 10 girls in Grade 3), were students at a middle-class suburban public grade school. The median CA for second graders was 96 mo. (SD=4.5 mo.), and that for third graders was 108 mo. (SD=4.75 mo.). The experimenters were a 31–year-old research assistant and a 21–year-old graduate student (the second author).

STIMULI

Each child was presented one of 3 equivalent sets of 28 clock settings. Each set consisted of all 12 of the 5–minute-times, and 16 of the 48 1–minute-times. Across the three sets, each of the 48 1–minute-times was used once. The 16 1–minute-times within each set consisted of 4 settings where the minute hand was 1 minute past a five mark (e.g. 4:41), 4 where it was 2 minutes past a five mark, 4 where it was 3 minutes past a five mark and 4 where it was 4 minutes past a five mark. For half of the times within each set, the minute hand pointed to a time before the half hour; for the other half, the minute hand pointed to a time after the half hour. The hour settings were chosen randomly, each hour appearing two or three times in each stimulus set. The three stimulus sets are listed in Table 5.1.

Table 5.1
STIMULUS ITEMS FOR THE TIME-TELLING EXPERIMENT

SET 1		SET 2		SET 3	
1:00	12:01	2:00	8:11	3:00	4:06
4:05	5:16	5:05	1:26	6:05	9:21
7:10	10:07	8:10	6:17	9:10	2:12
10:15	3:22	11:15	11:02	12:15	7:27
2:20	8:13	3:20	4:23	1:20	12:03
5:25	1:28	6:25	9:08	4:25	5:18
8:30	6:19	9:30	2:29	7:30	10:09
11:35	11:04	12:35	7:14	10:35	3:24
3:40	4:56	1:40	12:51	2:40	8:31
6:45	9:41	4:45	5:36	5:45	1:46
9:50	2:52	7:50	10:57	8:50	6:32
12:55	7:37	10:55	3:42	11:55	11:47
	12:48		8:38		4:43
	5:33		1:53		9:58
	10:44		6:49		2:54
	3:59		11:34		7:39

An InterDesign quartz kitchen clock was used to present the times. The clock had a bright yellow frame and a face 7" in diameter. The face was clearly numbered with 1" high numbers (1–12) around the inside circumference. It had dots at each minute mark (with bigger dots at the 5–minute-marks). It also had an opaque removeable cover, decorated with cartoon figures, that was used to cover the clock face between trials.

PROCEDURE

Children were presented the 28 times in their stimulus set on two occasions, separated by no more than 3 days. On each occasion, the child was brought individually to a vacant classroom. The experimenter told the child that she would be showing various times on a clock, and that the child's task was to say what the *exact* time was. Children were also told they could figure out the time in any way they wanted, and that the experimenter would be asking them to describe after each trial how they figured out the time on that trial. The 28 times were then presented in random order.

On each trial, the experimenter set the clock to a given time, placed the cover on the clock face, and then placed the clock in front of the child. The experimenter asked "Can you tell me what time it is now" and removed the cover. After the child answered, the experimenter asked "How did you figure that out?". If the child's answer was too vague (e.g., "I counted"), the experimenter would ask more specific questions such as "Where did you start counting from", or "Show me over again how you counted". After answering, the child was given non-specific reinforcement, and the experimenter proceeded to set the clock to the next time. The entire session was recorded on a videocassette recorder to allow careful analyses of children's strategies on each trial.

The procedure for the second testing occasion was identical except that a different random order of items was used. After completing both sessions, each child was given an explanation of the purpose of the experiment, and was given stickers as a reward for participating.

Results

An overview of the results may be useful for providing a sense of the 8– and 9–year-old's general level of performance. As expected, the children were in the transition between unskilled and skilled time-telling. They correctly identified 69% of the times. Their overall median solution time was 5.8 sec. In terms of both speed and accuracy, hour times were easiest, followed by half hour times, other 5–minute-times, and 1–minute-times. Third graders were slightly more accurate than second graders (70% versus 66% correct) and were considerably faster (mean solution time of 5.1 seconds vs 6.6 seconds). Finally, children generated their responses through use of at least 5 different strategies which produced quite different accuracy and solution time patterns. With these general features established, we can consider more specific analyses, first of children's performance on different times, and then of children's strategy use.

PERFORMANCE ON DIFFERENT TIMES

One factor likely to influence children's time-telling was the particular time that they needed to identify. The times can be divided into five groups: hours, half-hours, quarter-hours, other 5–minute-times, and 1–minute-times. One-way, within-subject ANOVAs were conducted to examine differences among these five types of times on three dependent measures: percent correct, median RT, and percent use of retrieval (percent of trials on which children showed no overt behavior between hearing the problem and stating the answer, and on which they said that they just knew the answer or that they remembered it).

PERCENT CORRECT. Percent correct on the five types of times differed significantly, $F(4,160)=23.10$, $p<.01$. Newman-Keuls post hoc analyses indicated that hour and half-hour times were identified more accurately than quarter-hour and other 5–minute-times, which in turn were identified more accurately then 1 minute-times. Means are shown in Table 5.2.

Table 5.2
PERFORMANCE ON DIFFERENT TYPES OF TIMES

	HOUR	½–HOUR	¼–HOUR	OTHER 5–MIN. TIMES	1–MIN. TIMES
PERCENT CORRECT	98	94	80	79	54
MEDIAN RT (SEC.)	3.5	4.1	5.1	5.2	7.4
PERCENT RETRIEVAL	98	96	80	73	28

SOLUTION TIMES. A parallel ANOVA for median solution time for each subject on each of the five types of times also showed a significant difference among the types of times, $F(4,160)=10.24$, $P<.01$. The post hoc analyses indicated that hour times were answered more quickly than quarter hour, other 5–minute times, and 1–minute-times, and that 1–minute-times were answered more slowly than any of the other types of times (Table 5.2).

PERCENT RETRIEVAL. As in the other two ANOVAs, the analysis of percent use of retrieval showed that the five types of times differed significantly $F(4,160)=70.63$, $p<.01$. The post hoc comparisons showed that hour and half hour times elicited a higher percent use of retrieval than did quarter hour times, which elicited a higher percent use of retrieval than did other 5–minute-times, which elicited a much higher percent of retrieval than did the 1–minute-times (Table 5.2).

ADDITIONAL SOURCES OF PROBLEM DIFFICULTY. The ANOVA's indicated that hour and half hour times were easier than other 5–minute-times, and that the other 5–minute-times were easier than the 1–minute-times. We wondered whether further specification of the sources of difficulty within the 5–minute and 1–minute groups were possible. To find out, we identified a number of factors that might predict problem difficulty within the group of 10 5–minute-times other than the hour and half hour and within the group of 48 1–minute-times. These factors were then used as predictors within separate multiple regression analyses of errors and solution times on the 5–minute and 1–minute-times. The predictors within all four regression analyses were number of minutes past the hour (0–59), absolute distance in minutes away from the hour (0–30), number of minutes past the previous quarter-hour mark (0–29), number of minutes before the next quarter-hour mark (0–29), number of minutes past the last 5–minute-mark (0–4), number of minutes before the next 5–minute-mark (0–4), whether the minute hand was before or after the half hour, and whether the time was a 5–minute or a 1–minute time.[1]

First consider the analyses of the 5–minute-times other than the hour and half hour. In the analysis of median solution time on these trials, three predictors accounted for the large majority of variance: whether the time was before the half hour accounted for 72% of the variance in solution times; number of minutes past the hour brought the total percent variance accounted for to 88%; whether the hour was a quarter hour brought the total variance accounted for to 94%. Times in the first half hour were easier than other times, as were times that were only a short distance past the hour, and times that were quarter hours.

In the analysis of percent errors on the 5–minute-times, whether the time was before the half hour accounted for 66% of the variance; including the time's absolute distance from the hour brought the variance accounted for to 80%. As with the analysis of solution times, whether the time was before the half hour was the best predictor in relative terms and a very good predictor in absolute terms. In this analysis, times that were close to the hour in absolute terms were easier than those that were farther from it.

The analysis of the 1–minute-times yielded less striking results. In the analysis of median solution times, minutes past the hour accounted for 21% of the variance; minutes past the previous 5–minute-mark brought the variance accounted for to 32%; and minutes away from the nearest quarter hour brought the variance accounted for to 39%. In the analysis of percent errors, absolute distance from the hour was the best predictor, accounting for 14% of the variance; number of minutes past the hour brought the variance accounted for to 26%; number of minutes past the previous 5–minute-mark brought the variance accounted for to 33%. The direction of the effects was the same as in the analysis of 5–minute times.

These analyses of differences in performance on different types of times replicate and extend the findings of Case et al., Friedman and Laycock, and Springer. In general, hour times are easier than half hour times, which are easier than quarter hour and other 5–minute-times, which are easier than 1–minute-times. Whether a time occurs before rather than after the half hour seems to be an additional contributor to the ease of identifying 5–minute-times. Overall, these analyses of performance on different types of times provide an intuitively reasonable description of sources of difficulty in learning to tell time.

On the other hand, examination of the different strategies that children used, and the varying pattern of speed and accuracy on different problems produced by these strategies, indicates that the differences among the types of times just scratch the surface of what is going on in children's time-telling. For example, across all trials, performance on 1–minute-times is much less accurate than performance on the other 4 types of times, 54% vs 82%. However, all of the difference comes in performance on the 50% of trials on which children used retrieval. On these retrieval trials, children were correct on 88% of 5–minute-times, versus only 29% on 1–minute-times. In contrast, on the 50% of trials where children used a backup strategy, they were actually a little more accurate on the 1–minute-times than on the 5–minute-times, 70% vs 63%. This interaction was not due to different amounts of use of retrieval by second and third graders. Children of both ages were correct much more often on 5–minute trials than on 1–minute trials when they retrieved, and were correct slightly *less* often on 5–minute trials when they used backup strategies. The point is that only by analyzing the patterns of performance produced by different strategies can the pattern of results be fully understood.

CHILDREN'S STRATEGIES

The children's overt behavior, together with their self-reports of what they had done, indicated that they used several strategies. Among the most common overt behaviors were sequentially pointing to different places on the clock face, naming aloud sequence of times, and moving lips. When children did not exhibit such overt behavior, or when the meaning of their overt behavior was unclear, we relied on the children's verbal reports to indicate what strategy they used.

For each of the strategies described below, children first appeared to locate the number that the hour hand had most recently passed, so that they could determine the correct hour. What differentiated the strategies was the children's subsequent behavior in trying to determine the minutes before or after the hour. More than 98% of trials were classified as involving one of five strategies, The strategies are listed below.

RETRIEVAL. On 50% of trials, children stated the time without any intervening overt behavior and said that they "could just tell" what time it was or that they "knew it just by looking". This approach was classified as retrieval.

COUNTING FORWARD BY 5'S OR BY 5'S AND 1'S FROM THE HOUR. On 14% of trials, children started at the hour and counted by 5's until they read the 5–minute-mark that the minute hand pointed to (if the time was a 5–minute time), or until they reached the 5–minute-mark immediately before the minute hand, from which point they incremented the count by 1's until they reached the minute hand.

COUNTING FORWARD BY 1'S FROM THE HOUR. On 2% of trials, children started counting from the hour (e.g. from 3:00), incremented the count by 1's until they reached the minute hand, and then stated the minutes past the hour.

COUNTING FORWARD FROM AN EARLIER 5–MINUTE-MARK. On 26% of trials, children counted forward from a 5 minute mark other than the hour. They would say the number of minutes past the hour indicated by their starting position and count-on by 1's, 5's, or a combination of the two until they reached the minute hand. This strategy involved a combination of retrieval (of the initial 5–minute-time) and counting. It was used on both 5 minute times (e.g.,10:25), where a subject might start counting by 5's from the 15– or 20–minute-mark, and 1–minute-times (e.g., 10:28), where a child might start from the 15– or 20–minute-mark, increment by 5's until the 25–minute-mark, and then increment by 1's.

COUNTING BACKWARD FROM A LATER 5–MINUTE-MARK. On

6% of trials, children started counting from a 5–minute-mark that was past the position of the minute hand and decremented by 1's (or, more rarely, by 5's or 5's and 1's) until the minute hand. For example, if presented 5:38, a child might decrement by 1's from 5:40.

As these descriptions suggest, children started counting from a variety of places around the clock. The two most prominent landmarks, the hour and half hour, constituted the starting points on 32% and 17% respectively of trials on which children counted. Put another way, children counted from these prominent landmarks on about half of trials on which they counted. On the other half of trials on which children counted, they started from a wide variety of 5–minute-marks. With one exception (the 55–minute-mark), each 5–minute-mark was the starting point on between 4% and 7% of counting trials. The finding indicated that models of time-telling must allow children who are learning to tell time to flexibly begin counting at a variety of 5–marks on the clock face, rather than always needing to start at the hour or half hour.

INDIVIDUAL STRATEGY USE

Variable strategy use was not just a group-level phenomenon. Individual children also used different strategies on different trials. All 33 children used at least three different strategies. Almost three-quarters of the children (73%) used at least three strategies on at least three trials each.

The extreme case of variability in strategy use is use of different strategies by a single child on a single problem presented on two occasions close in time. Even in this extreme case, there was considerable variability in strategy use. Individual children used different strategies on 34% of the pairs of presentations of particular items (the range for individual subjects was 11% to 57% use of different strategies on the two presentations of each time). Learning of the times between the two presentations was not a plausible explanation. First, the two testing sessions were separated by at most 3 days. Second, the direction of change in which strategy was used was inconsistent. In 39% of cases where different strategies were used on the two presentations of a time, the child first used a backup strategy and then retrieval; in 29% of such cases, the child first used retrieval and then a backup strategy; in 32%, the child switched from one backup strategy to another.

This variable strategy use is consistent with the distribution of associations model where, depending on the confidence criterion and the specific answer that is retrieved, any available strategy may be used on any item. It argues against less flexible models that depict children as always using the same strategy to solve a particular problem or class of problems. Further, it is consistent with our general hypothesis that when children have moderate amounts of experience with particular items on a task, they tend to use multiple strategies. Their use of multiple strategies in such situations contrasts sharply with their use of single rules or strategies on unfamiliar problems such as balance scale, projection of shadows, and liquid quantity conservation (Siegler, 1983). It appears that one of the skills that is acquired with experience on a problem is the ability to use multiple alternative strategies.

SOLUTION TIMES AND ACCURACY OF THE STRATEGIES

Table 5.3 indicates the speed and accuracy with which each strategy was executed, as well as how often it was used. To determine the relative speed of each pair of strategies, we compared the mean solution time on each time setting for those trials on which children used one strategy to the mean solution time on that time setting for the trials on which they used the other strategy. Solution times on retrieval trials were significantly faster than those produced by any other strategy, all t's>2.00, p's<.05. Solution times were also significantly faster on trials where children counted from an earlier 5–minute-mark or a later 5–minute-mark than on trials where they counted by 5's or by 5's and 1's from the hour.

A surprising feature of the solution times produced by different strategies was that counting by 1's from the hour was the second fastest strategy. This was largely attributable to the problems on which the strategy was used. The strategy was used almost exclusively on times between 1– and 4– minutes past the hour. Had the strategy been used equally often on different problems, it would probably have been the slowest strategy, since it would usually require the most counting steps. The unequal distribution of use of the strategy indicates the need to consider the problems on which each strategy is used as well as how often each strategy is used in analyzing solution time and accuracy data (Siegler, in press).

The point is equally important in comparing the accuracy of different strategies. Over all trials, the accuracy of retrieval was identical to that of other strategies (69% correct). However, this summary statistic masked great diversity on different problems in the accuracy of retrieval relative to that of other strategies. Retrieval was easily the most accurate strategy on 5–minute-times. However, it was the least accurate strategy on 1–minute-times. Its percent correct was three times as high on the 5–minute-times as on the 1–minute times (Table 5.3). Again, the performance generated by a strategy must be considered in the context of the problems on which the strategy was used.

Table 5.3
CHARACTERISTICS OF TIME-TELLING STRATEGIES

	STRATEGY	TRIALS ON WHICH STRATEGY USED (%)	MEDIAN SOLUTION TIME (SEC.)	CORRECT ANSWERS (%)
ALL TIMES	RETRIEVAL	50	4.0	69
	COUNT BY 1'S FROM THE HOUR	2	5.5	86
	COUNT BY 5'S FROM THE HOUR	14	11.1	61
	COUNT FROM EARLIER 5-MINUTE MARK	26	7.5	70
	COUNT FROM LATER 5-MINUTE MARK	6	6.8	77
	TOTAL		5.8	69
5-MINUTE TIMES	RETRIEVAL	77	3.8	88
	COUNT BY 1'S FROM THE HOUR	—	—	—
	COUNT BY 5'S FROM THE HOUR	12	9.0	70
	COUNT FROM EARLIER 5-MINUTE MARK	8	6.6	61
	COUNT FROM LATER 5-MINUTE MARK	2	6.0	31
	TOTAL		4.4	82
1-MINUTE TIMES	RETRIEVAL	29	4.6	29
	COUNT BY 1'S FROM THE HOUR	3	5.5	86
	COUNT BY 5'S FROM THE HOUR	15	12.0	55
	COUNT FROM EARLIER 5-MINUTE MARK	40	7.8	72
	COUNT FROM LATER 5-MINUTE MARK	10	7.0	83
	TOTAL		7.1	58

PATTERNS OF STRATEGY USE

Some of the strongest predictions of the distributions of associations model concern when different strategies will be used. Specifically, percentage of backup strategy use on a problem is expected to be a better predictor than any structural variable of solution times and errors on that problem, because backup strategy use, like errors and solution time, is a function of the underlying distribution of associations. An even more specific prediction is that the positive relation among percent backup strategy use, percent errors, and length of solution times is primarily a relation among percent backup strategy use, percent errors *on retrieval trials,* and solution times *on retrieval trials.* The reason is that errors and solution times on retrieval trials, like percent backup strategy use, are a function of the distribution of associations. In contrast, errors and solution times on backup strategy trials depend on other variables, such as the amount of counting to be done. Thus, percent backup strategy use was expected to correlate highly with percent errors on retrieval trials and solution time on retrieval trials, but not as highly with percent errors and solution times on backup strategy trials.

To test this prediction, several multiple regression analyses were performed. The predictor variables in each one were the same as in the previously-described analyses, except for the addition of one new predictor; percent use of backup strategies on the problem.

RELATIONS BETWEEN BACKUP STRATEGY USE AND SOLUTION TIMES. The distribution of associations model predicts that problems on which backup strategies were used often would also be ones where solution times were long. This proved to be the case. In a stepwise regression analysis of the median RT on each of the 60 times, percent backup strategy use on each problem correlated r=.76 with median solution time on each problem. Percent backup strategy use on a problem was the best predictor of solution time on that problem of all the predictors that were examined.

Separate regression analyses of solution times on the 5–minute-times and on the 1–minute-times revealed that the relation between percent backup strategy use and solution time was considerably stronger for the 5–minute than for the 1–minute-times. Specifically, across all 5–minute-times, the correlation between percent backup strategy use and solution time was r=.92. On the 1–minute-times, the correlation was r=.66. More important, however, for both subsets of items, percent backup strategy use was the best predictor of solution time of the 9 predictors in the regression equation.

This correlation arose at least in part because backup strategies require more time to execute; that is, use of backup strategies causes the longer times. A more specific prediction of the model not subject to this interpretation is that the correlation between percent backup strategy use and length of solution times is primarily a correlation between percent backup strategy use and length of solution times on retrieval trials. This correlation cannot be attributed to backup strategies requiring more time, because the times in the correlation are times on retrieval trials.

The data were consistent with this prediction. First consider the analysis involving median solution times on retrieval trials. The correlation between solution times on retrieval trials and percent backup strategy use was $r=.61$. In contrast, the correlation between percent backup strategy use and solution times on backup strategies was $r=.14$. Williams' (1959) modification of Hotelling's (1940) t statistic showed that the difference between these two correlations was significant, $Z=3.02$, $P<.01$. Thus, the predictions involving relations between use of backup strategies and lengths of solution times proved accurate.

RELATIONS BETWEEN BACKUP STRATEGIES USE AND PERCENTAGE OF ERRORS. The distribution of associations model also predicts that the problems on which backup strategies are used most often will have the highest error rates. Contrary to prediction, the correlation between percentage of errors on the 60 problems and percentage of backup strategy use on these problems was weak and nonsignificant, $r=.14$.

Separate analyses of 5–minute and 1–minute-times revealed that this small correlation masked the existence of two larger ones that ran in opposite directions. As expected, on the 5–minute-times, the correlation was fairly strong and positive ($r=.58$). Completely contrary to expectation, on the 1–minute-times, the correlation was fairly strong and negative ($r=-.54$).

As noted above, if percentage of errors, like percentage of backup strategy use, is a function of the distribution of associations, then the overall correlation between percentage of errors and percentage of backup strategy use should be primarily a function of the percent errors on retrieval trials. The correlation between percent backup strategy use and percentage of errors on retrieval trials was $r=.36$. The corresponding correlation for the backup strategy trials was $r=-.26$. The difference between these two correlations was significant, $Z=3.58$, $p<.01$. Again, however, the magnitude of the correlation was lower than expected and lower than correlations between these two variables in previous studies (Siegler, 1987b; 1988; Siegler & Shrager, 1984). A potential reason was suggested by the particular errors that children made.

ANALYSES OF PARTICULAR ERRORS

Analyses of children's errors revealed that they were of three primary types: misreading the hour, hour-hand/minute-hand reversals, and off-

-by–1–minute errors. Together, these three types of errors accounted for 78% of the total errors.

MISREADING-THE-HOUR ERRORS

Misreading-the-hour errors accounted for 33% of all errors. This included 28% of errors on retrieval trials and 38% of errors on backup strategy trials. Such misreading-the hour errors occurred when children identified as the hour the number that the hour hand was closer to, rather than the number preceding the hour hand. This procedure resulted in times such as 3:50 being read as 4:50. As would be expected from this description, such errors occurred exclusively (100%) on times where the minute hand was in the second half of the clock (and therefore where the hour hand was closer to the upcoming hour).

The second frequent error was *reversing the hour and minute hands.* This resulted in times such as 6:05 being read as 1:30. Such reversal errors accounted for 12% of all errors, 14% of errors on retrieval trials and 9% of errors on backup strategy trials.

OFF-BY–1–MINUTE ERRORS

Off-by–1–minute errors, the third frequent type of error, accounted for 33% of total errors. This included 39% of errors on retrieval trials and 25% on backup strategy trials. It is this type of error that seemed responsible for the surprising relation between the overall percent errors and the percent backup strategy use.

One clue to the pivotal role of this type of error is its different pattern on retrieval trials and backup strategy trials. On 94% of the retrieval trials on which this error occurred, the minute hand was set 1–minute past or 1–minute before a 5–minute-mark. This distribution deviated substantially from chance, *chi-square*(3)—100.79, $p<.01$. The error almost invariably (93% of instances) consisted of stating the nearest 5 minute-mark as the time.

In contrast, on backup strategy trials, off-by–1–minute errors were quite evenly distributed across the possible time-settings; 22% were on times that were 1–minute past a 5–mark, 23% were on times that were 2–minutes past, 36% were on times that were 3–minutes past, and 19% were on times that were 4–minutes past. This distribution did not deviate significantly from chance, *chi-square*(3)=4.11, $p>.10$.

These differing patterns suggest that off-by–1–minute errors are caused by different processes on retrieval trials than on backup strategy trials. On retrieval trials, but not on backup strategy trials, the errors seem due to a rounding process in which times within a minute of the nearest 5–minute-mark are rounded to that 5–minute-mark. On backup strategy trials, on the other hand, errors may reflect faulty execution of other processes, such as counting forward and backward.

This rounding interpretation of off-by–1–minute-errors on retrieval trials has several empirical implications. Two have already been noted: the preponderance of such errors should (and do) occur on times 1–minute from the nearest 5–minute-mark and the errors should generally be ones of stating the nearest 5–minute time.

Additional implications concern the opposite effects that the rounding process should exert on percent errors on retrieval trials and on percent use of retrieval. The rounding process increases use of retrieval on times 1–minute away from the nearest 5–minute-mark. The reason is that if such a time is interpreted as a 5–minute time, its associative strength will be higher than would otherwise be expected (due to the generally greater amount of experience children have with 5–minute-times). The fact that retrieval was used on 39% of 1–minute-times that were adjacent to a 5–minute-mark, versus 18% of 1–minute-times that were farther away from the nearest 5–minute-mark, supported this prediction.

The other half of the rounding interpretation was that percent errors on retrieval trials should be higher on times that were adjacent to a 5–minute-mark, where rounding would lead to incorrect answers, than on times not so close to the 5–minute-mark, where rounding would rarely be used. This also proved to be true. Percent errors on retrieval trials on times adjacent to a 5–minute-mark was higher than on times that were not adjacent to one, 73% versus 67%. In contrast, errors on backup strategy trials did not show this pattern, occurring on 29% of times adjacent to a 5–mark and 31% of times that were farther away.

Together, these results make understandable the initially puzzling weak correlation between percent errors and percent use of backup strategies. Recall that the weak overall correlation subsumed two stronger correlations that went in opposite directions. The correlation for 5–minute-times was in the expected (positive) direction, but the correlation for 1–minute-times was negative. The negative correlation on the 1–minute-times seems attributable to the opposite effects that the rounding process had on errors and strategy use on those 1–minute times that were adjacent to a 5–minute-mark. On such times, rounding would increase percentage of errors on retrieval trials (by leading children to answer with the nearest 5 minute-mark). However, it also would decrease percent use of backup strategies (by allowing greater use of retrieval than would otherwise be possible). Thus, both the weak overall correlation between percent errors and percent backup strategy use and the fairly strong negative correlation on 1–minute-times between percent errors and percent backup strategy use appeared to be due to the influence of the rounding process.

DISCUSSION

The results of this study allow a fairly detailed depiction of how children make the transition from unskilled to skilled time-telling. They also have implications for the relation of time-telling to other aspects of understanding of time. Below, we summarize our conclusions about children's time-telling, and then go on to speculate about related issues where the present findings are suggestive but not conclusive.

How Children Learn to Tell Time

Children's time-telling can be viewed either from the perspective of the times that they tell or from the perspective of the strategies that they use. Previous studies have in large part taken the first perspective, focusing on how children identify different times. Like previous investigators, we found that children learning to tell time were more effective in identifying hour times than other 5–minute-times, and in identifying both of these than in identifying 1–minute-times. The present study also made clear that children identify half hour times almost as effectively as hour times, and considerably more effectively than other 5–minute-times. Further, it showed that within the group of 5–minute-times, times in the first half of the hour are considerably easier than those in the second half. By directly comparing performance on all 60 times on three different measures—percentage of errors, median solution times, and percentage of retrieval—the study allowed more precise identification of differences among the times than previously available.

The main contribution of the study, however, is to illustrate the advantages of also taking the second perspective, and focusing on the strategies that children use to tell time. Clearly, children making the transition to skilled time-telling use a variety of strategies. This is true for individual children as well as across different children. Most individuals used at least three strategies. The children's variable strategy use was evident even within a single clock setting. On one-third of trials, the same child presented the same clock setting twice within a three day period used different strategies on the two occasions. Thus, strategy use varies within a single child and within a single time, as well as between children and between times.

The distribution of associations model provided a basis for predicting when children would use backup strategies. Basically, the prediction was that they would use backup strategies most often on the problems that elicited the highest percentage of errors and the longest solution times, and that their use of backup strategies would especially closely parallel percentages of errors and lengths of solution times on retrieval trials.

This prediction proved accurate for the relation between use of backup strategies and length of solution times. Across all clock settings, as well as within 5–minute and 1–minute-times, percent use of backup strategies was closely related to length of solution times. Also as predicted, the relation was primarily a relation between percent use of backup strategies on the problem and solution times on retrieval trials on it.

The predicted relation between frequency of backup strategies on each problem and frequency of errors on that problem was not found. However, the source of the incorrectness of the prediction was very informative. Examining children's particular errors suggested that a commonly-made error stemmed from a process that would push use of backup strategies and frequency of errors in opposite directions. Specifically, children seemed to round times that were within 1–minute of a 5–minute-mark to that 5–minute-mark. This rounding process increased number of errors on these problems, but also increased use of retrieval rather than a backup strategy. In making these errors, children seemed to be misencoding the 1–minute-time as the nearby 5–minute-time.

It seems, then, that one limiting condition on the generally strong, positive relation between problem difficulty and percent use of backup strategies involves the task's potential for misencoding. If items that have only weakly-associated responses are misencoded as being items with more strongly-associated responses, errors will increase but use of backup strategies will decrease. The opposite effects of such misencoding on errors and use of backup strategies will reduce or eliminate the usual positive correlation between the two variables.

Although the finding may at first seem to undermine the strategy choice model, it also can be seen as demonstrating its strength. Because the model generated clear predictions about the relations among backup strategy use, errors, and solution times, it helped us to detect the anomaly posed by the percentages of errors on different problems not paralleling the patterns of backup strategy use and solution times. Noting this anomaly led to our identifying the three major classes of errors, hypothesizing processes that would generate each type of error and predicting how the process hypothesized to underlie each type of error would affect the overall percentage of errors and percent use of retrieval on each problem. This analysis, in turn, led to our realizing that rounding errors would exert opposite effects on errors and use of backup strategies, and thereby work against the expected correlation. A major purpose of studying time-telling in the context of the strategy choice model was to examine whether the task's relatively strong perceptual recognition component would indicate limiting conditions on generalizations based on children's strategy choices in the previously-studied arithmetic tasks. Discovering how misencoding can differentially affect errors and strategy use was the payoff. We expect that the more precise we can make our models, the more often we will reap such payoffs.

RELATIONS BETWEEN TIME-TELLING AND OTHER ASPECTS OF TIME

Although the present investigation focused on strategy choices in time-telling, the theoretical approach is more generally applicable. Direct evidence for this view comes from a reanalysis of Friedman's (1986 and this volume) data (generously provided by Bill Friedman). These data involved a quite different aspect of children's understanding of time than the one studied here, their representation of the ordering of the days of the week and the months of the year. In the experiment of interest, Friedman asked fourth graders, seventh graders, tenth graders, and college students questions that required knowledge of how far one day of the week or one month of the year was from another. Fourth graders in the study often engaged in overt behaviors in solving these problems (41% of trials); older children and adults occasionally did so (about 4% of trials). More important than the absolute existence of such overt strategies, however, was when the children and adults used the strategies. Percent use of overt strategies was related to percent errors and mean solution times in the ways that the strategy choice model predicts. As shown in Table 5.4, 12 of the 16 correlations among these variables exceeded r=.60 and 6 of the 16 exceeded r=.80. All 12 of these relatively strong correlations were in the expected direction. The data are a little noisy, as would be expected given the small number of errors in the older groups and the fact that there were only 6 problems on the days-of-the-week task and 8 problems on the months-of-the-year task. Nonetheless, the overall pattern is clear. Frequency of use of overt strategies closely parallels problem difficulty in identifying the distance between days of the week and months of the year, as well as in time-telling. The parallel suggests that the way in which children choose strategies is similar across tasks involving quite different aspects of the time concept.

Table 5.4
CORRELATION OF OVERT STRATEGY USE WITH PROBLEM DIFFICULTY

DATA	VARIABLES CORRELATED	GRADE			
		4TH	7TH	10TH	UNDER-GRADUATES
A. WEEKS DATA	% OVERT STRATEGIES – RT	.89	.77	.88	.61
	% OVERT STRATEGIES – % ERRORS	.27	.65	.33	.88
B. MONTHS DATA	% OVERT STRATEGIES – RT	.74	.93	−.08	.80
	% OVERT STRATEGIES – % ERRORS	.62	.77	.57	.85

(Data from Friedman, 1986, Experiment 3)
NOTE: In the weeks task, each correlation is based on the 6 distances between days that were studied. In the months task, each correlation is based on the 8 distances between months that were studied. All correlations are Pearson Product Moment correlations.

What relation might time-telling have to the type of understanding usually viewed as being at the heart of the concept of time, understanding of temporal duration? Speculatively, learning to tell time may directly influence understanding of duration, as measured by performance on the classic Piagetian duration task. This task involves two vehicles moving in the same direction on parallel tracks; problems vary in the relative starting and stopping points, starting and stopping times, and total speed, distance, and time of travel. In trying to solve such problems, children progress through use of different incorrect rules. Five– and 6–year-olds usually use an end-point rule, in which they consistently say that the vehicle that stopped farther down the track traveled for more time (Levin, 1977; Piaget, 1946/1969; Richards, 1982; Siegler & Richards, 1979). In contrast, 8– to 12–year-olds' most common confusion on this problem is to confuse time with distance; they often claim that the vehicle that traveled the greater distance also traveled for the greater time, even when this is not the case (Richards, 1982; Siegler, 1983).

This change from an emphasis on stopping points to an emphasis on total distance improves the children's performance; considering the entire universe of such problems, time is more highly correlated with distance traveled than it is with the end point of travel (Siegler, 1983). However, this view leaves open the question of how children come to confuse time and distance and why the confusion continues for as many years as it does. It clearly is not the case that children of ages 5–12 years lack a concept of duration. The results of Berndt and Wood (1974) and Levin (1977) clearly indicate that they possess such a concept. Nor is it the case that ability to attend to only one dimension when spatial cues are present is the limiting factor. The fact that distance, rather than end points, interferes with their performance indicated that they are attending to both beginning and ending spatial cues.

A quite different interpretation is that learning to tell time on an analog clock contributes to the confusions of time with distance. In particular, learning to tell time may suggest to children that for moving objects, distance traveled and time of travel are related in a 1:1 fashion. Thus, children may rely on distance cues to judge temporal duration on the Piagetian task because they think the two dimensions are perfectly correlated and it is easier to estimate distance than elapsed time.

Several arguments favor this interpretation. Most children receive their first extensive instruction in time-telling at age 8 or 9 (second or third grade), the same age at which children start to confuse time with distance (Siegler & Richards, 1979). On an analog clock, the distance traversed around the circumference stands in a 1:1 relation to the amount of time that has passed; the minute hand's traveling a greater (linear) distance guarantees that a greater amount of time has passed. The relation between time and distance in the context of a clock may be viewed as specially informative, because it is virtually the only situation in which children can be sure of the exact amount of time that has elapsed. Thus, the 1:1 relation on the clock face may be interpreted as representative of a general 1:1 relation between time and distance for moving objects.

Discovering this 1:1 relationship may initially lead children to progress from judging time on the basis of spatial end points on the Piagetian temporal-duration task to the more-often-correct strategy of judging time on the basis of distance traveled. However, it may also be part of the reason that children continue to confuse time with distance for as long as they do. The fact that the object that traveled the longer distance usually is the one that traveled the longer time, together with the 1:1 relation between time and distance in the one situation where children can be sure of the amount of time that has passed, may conspire to make the confusion a difficult one to overcome.

Time-telling may seem like an isolated skill, just one of the thousand-and-one competencies that children acquire at different points in their lives. Closer analysis, however, reveals interesting relations to processes of considerably more generality. The basic strategy choice procedure that children use while they are in the transition to learning to tell time seems to be the same one that children use while in transitions to acquiring many other competencies. Within the context of the present strategy-choice model, studying time-telling proved to be specially informative, in that it indicated a limiting condition on the model's prediction of high correlations among accuracy, solution times, and strategy use. Specifically, the data on time-telling indicate that perceptual misencodings can push accuracy and strategy use in opposite directions, thus reducing or eliminating the usual correlations among the variables. Thinking about time-telling also has proved fruitful for understanding children's strategies for representing the cyclic structure of days of the week and months of the year and in suggesting an explanation for children's confusion errors on the classic Piagetian duration task. In short, there is more to be learned from studying time-telling than simply when children learn to identify different times.

Acknowledgment

Thanks are due to Miss Hawkins, Miss Perry, and the teachers and students of University Park Elementary School of Monroeville, PA, who made the research possible.

Notes

[1]The reason that the time to or past the quarter hour ranged from 0–29 minutes was that the only times in this analysis that were quarter hours were those that were 15 and 45 minutes past the hour.

References

Ashcraft, M. H. (1982). The development of mental arithmetic: A chronometric approach. *Developmental Review, 2,* 213–236.

Ashcraft, M. H. (1987). Children's knowledge of simple arithmetic: A developmental model and simulation. In J. Bisanz, C. J. Brainerd, & R. Kail (Eds.), *Formal methods in developmental psychology.* New York: Springer-Verlag.

Baroody, A. J., & Ginsburg, H. P. (1986). The relationship between initial meaningful and mechanical knowledge of arithmetic. In J. Hiebert (Ed.), *Conceptual and procedural knowledge: The case of mathematics,* 75–112. Hillsdale, NJ: Erlbaum.

Berndt, T. J., & Wood, D. J. (1974). The development of time concepts through conflict based on a primitive duration capacity. *Child Development, 45*, 825–828.

Brown, A. L., & Reeve, R. A. (1986). Reflections on the growth of reflection in children. *Cognitive Development, 1*, 405–416.

Carpenter, P. A., & Just, M. A. (1975). Sentence comprehension: A psycholinguistic processing model of verification. *Psychological Review, 82*, 45–73.

Case, R., Sandieson, R., & Dennis, S. (1986). Two cognitive-developmental approaches to the design of remedial instruction. *Cognitive Development, 1*, 293–333.

Cavanaugh, J. C., & Perlmutter, M. (1982). Metamemory: A critical examination. *Child Development, 53*, 11–28.

Chi, M. T., & Ceci, S. J. (1987). Content knowledge: Its roles representation and restructuring in memory development. To appear in H. W. Reese (Ed.), *Advances in Child Development and Behavior (Vol. 20)*, (pp. 91–142). Orlando, FL: Academic Press.

Clark, H. H. (1969). Linguistic processes in deductive reasoning. *Psychological Review, 76*, 387–404.

Clark, H. H., & Chase, W. G. (1972). On the process of comparing sentence against pictures. *Cognitive Psychology, 3*, 472–517.

Cooper, L. A., & Regan, D. (1982). Attention, perception, and intelligence. In R. Sternberg (Ed.), *Handbook of human intelligence*, 123–169. New York: Cambridge University Press.

Cooper, L. A., & Shepard, R. N. (1973). Chronometric studies of the rotation of mental images. In W. G. Chase (Ed.), *Visual information processing*, (pp. 75–176). New-York: Academic Press.

Egan, D. E. , & Grimes-Farrow, D. D. (1982). Differences in mental representations spontaneously adopted for reasoning, *Memory and Cognition, 10*, 297–307.

Friedman, W. J. (1982). Conventional time concepts and children's structuring of time. In W. J. Friedman (Ed.), *The developmental psychology of time*, (pp. 171–208). New York: Academic Press.

Friedman, W. J. (1983). Image and verbal processes in reasoning about the months of the year. *Journal of Experimental Psychology: Learning, Memory, and Cognition, 9*, 650–666.

Friedman, W. J. (1986). The development of children's knowledge of temporal structures. *Child Development, 57*, 1386 – 1400.

Friedman, W. J., & Laycock, F. (1986). *Children's analog and digital clock knowledge.* Unpublished manuscript.

Fuson, K. C. (1982). An analysis of the counting-on solution procedure in addition. In T. P. Carpenter, J. M. Moser, & T. A. Romberg (Eds.), *Addition and subtraction: A cognitive perspective*, (pp. 67–82). Hillsdale, NJ: Erlbaum.

Glushko, R. J., & Cooper, L. A. (1978). Spatial comprehension and comparison processes in verification tasks. *Cognitive Psychology, 10*, 391–421.

Groen, G., & Parkman, J. H. (1972). A chronometric analysis of simple addition. *Psychological Review, 79*, 329–343.

Hotelling, H. (1940). The selection of variates for use in prediction with some comments on the general problem of nuisance paramenters. *Annals of Mathematical Statistics, 11*, 271–283.

Huttenlocher, J. J., & Higgins, E. T. (1971). Adjectives, comparatives, and syllogisms. *Psychological Review, 78*, 487–504.

Levin, I. (1977) The development of time concepts in children. *Child Development, 48*, 435–444.

Levin, I. (1979). Interference of time-related and unrelated cues with duration comparisons of young children: Analysis of Piaget's formulation of the relation of time and speed. *Child Development, 50*, 469–477.

Levin, I, Wilkening, F., & Dembo, Y. (1984). Development of time quantification: Integration and nonintegration of beginnings and endings in comparing durations, *Child Development, 55*, 2160–2172.

MacLeod, C. M., Hunt, E. B., & Mathews, N. N. (1978). Individual differences in the verification of sentence-picture relationships. *Journal of Verbal Learning and Verbal Behavior, 17*, 493–507.

Mathews, N. N., Hunt, E. B., & MacLeod, C. M. (1980). Strategy choice and strategy training in sentence-picture verification. *Journal of Verbal Learning and Verbal Behavior, 19*, 531–548.

Paivio, A. (1978). Comparison of mental clocks. *Journal of Experimental Psychology: Human Perception and Performance, 4*, 61–71.

Piaget, J. (1946/1969). *The child's conception of time.* A. J. Pomerans, Trans. London: Routledge & Kegan Paul. (Originally published, 1946).

Richards, D. D. (1982). Children's time concepts: Going the distance. In W. J. Friedman (Ed.), *The developmental psychology of time*, (pp. 13–46). New York: Academic Press.

Shepard, R. N., & Metzler, J. (1971). Mental rotation of three-dimensional objects. *Science*, 171, 701–703.

Siegler, R. S. (1983). Five generalizations about cognitive development. *American Psychologist, 38*, 263–277.

Siegler, R. S. (1986). Unities across domains in children's strategy choices. In M. Perlmutter (Ed.), *Minnesota symposium on child development, Vol. 19*, 1–48. Hillsdale, NJ: Erlbaum.

Siegler, R. S. (1987a). The perils of averaging data over strategies. An example from children's addition. *Journal of Experimental Psychology: General, 116*, 250–264.

Siegler, R. S. (1987b). Strategy choices in subtraction. In J. A. Sloboda & D. Rogers (Ed.), *Cognitive processes in mathematics*, 81–106. Oxford: Clarendon Press.

Siegler, R. S. (1988). Strategy choice procedures and the development of multiplication skill. *Journal of Experimental Psychology: General, 117*, 254–273.

Siegler, R. S. (In Press). Individual differences in strategy choices: Good students, not-so-good students, and perfectionists. *Child Development.*

Siegler, R. S., & Richards, D. D. (1979). Development of time, speed, and distance concepts. *Developmental Psychology, 15*, 288–298.

Siegler, R. S., & Robinson, M. (1982). The development of numerical understandings. In H. Reese and L. P. Lipsett (Eds.), *Advances in child development and behavior, Vol. 16*, 241–312. New York: Academic Press.

Siegler, R. S., & Shrager, J. (1984). Strategy choices in addition and subtraction: How do children know what to do? In C. Sophian (Ed.), *Origins of cognitive skill*, (pp. 229–293). Hillsdale, N.J.: Erlbaum.

Siegler, R. S., & Taraban, R. M. (1986). Conditions of applicability of a strategy choice model. *Cognitive Development, 1*, 31–51.

Springer, D. (1952). Development in young children of an understanding of time and the clock. *Journal of Genetic Psychology, 42*, 615–629.

Sternberg, R. J. (1977). Intelligence, information processing, and analogical reasoning. Hillsdale, NJ: Erlbaum.

Sternberg, R. J., & Weil, E. M. (1980). An aptitude X strategy interaction in linear syllogistic reasoning. *Journal of Educational Psychology, 72*, 226–239.

Sternberg, R. J., & Powell, J. S. (1983). Comprehending verbal comprehension. *American Psychologist, 38*, 878–893.

Trabasso, T, Rollins, H., & Shaughnessy, E. (1971). Storage and verification stages in processing concepts. *Cognitive Psychology, 2*, 239–289.

Williams, E. J. (1959). The comparison of regression variables. *Journal of the Royal Statistical Society, Series B, 21*, 396–399.

TIME AND HUMAN COGNITION
A Life-Span Perspective
I. Levin and D. Zakay (Editors)

CHAPTER 6

CURT ACREDOLO

Assessing Children's Understanding of Time, Speed and Distance Interrelations

INTRODUCTION

Piaget (1969; 1970) set the stage for the investigation of children's understanding of time, speed and distance interrelations by insisting that a mature concept of time emerges during middle childhood and is built upon an understanding of the interrelations between the three dimensions. He was struck by the fact that young children's reconstruction of temporal events and their judgments of relative durations are not based on direct perception of start and stop times but rather on intuitive suppositions concerning the dependence of time on speed and on distance. These confusions eventually disappear, and Piaget argued that this comes about only when children replace their intuitive suppositions with an accurate representation of the interrelations between all three dimensions. Thus, from Piaget's point of view, the development of children's understanding of time, speed and distance interrelations was seen as the cornerstone of the development of the time concept.

Piaget's theory of the development of the time concept is remindful of his argument concerning the development of conservation, and the same criticisms may be applied to both. Piaget acknowledged that a rudimentary understanding of the conservation of quantity is present early in life, but throughout early childhood performance is poor on tasks that pit existing knowledge against strong illusions that play upon the child's empirical awareness of correlations between dimensions. In the case of liquid conservation, for example, young children are clearly aware that the absence of addition or subtraction of liquid means that the quantity of liquid is unchanged, but they readily fail to display that knowledge when confronted with a salient change in water levels, suggesting an increase in quantity. Young children are familiar with the empirical correlation of liquid height and amount but fail to understand that a change in height is neither sufficient nor necessary to support the conclusion that quantity has changed. Piaget therefore argued that before children can grasp that the absence of addition or subtraction of quantity is both necessary and sufficient information to conclude that quantity has been conserved, they must first build an accurate representation of the compensatory relations between liquid height, width and quantity so that all information present in the situation points to the same conclusion.

His arguments concerning the development of the time concept take the exact same form. Young children are clearly capable of perceiving equal and unequal time periods, but they readily fail to display that knowledge when confronted with two objects moving for the same amount of time but covering different linear distances, thereby suggesting different durations of travel. Young children are aware of the empirical correlation between the distance and duration of travel but fail to understand that a difference in distance is neither sufficient nor necessary information to support the conclusion that durations also differed. Piaget therefore argued that before children can grasp that relative start and stop times are both necessary and sufficient information by which to judge relative durations, they must first build an accurate representation of the interrelations between time, speed and distance so that all the information present in the situation points to the same conclusion.

Thus we see that for both concepts, conservation and time, Piaget felt that before children can come to trust and rely upon their nascent understanding, new knowledge must be added, and he argued strongly that no other explanation for the development of these concepts is possible. In several papers on conservation, however, I have pointed out that Piaget's contention that compensation must be added before conservation develops is actually an assumption requiring empirical proof, and evidence has accumulated suggesting that his assumption was incorrect (Acredolo, 1981; 1982; see also Silverman and Rose, 1981). Children can perform well in the standard conservation task and begin mastering number and other quantity concepts before understanding the compensatory relationships between the dimensions that had formerly led them astray. All that is required for conservation to develop is for children to recognize (1) the necessity and sufficiency of information concerning the absence of addition or subtraction of quantity and (2) the unreliability of all other cues when taken singly. The same challenge may be waged against Piaget's theory of the development of the time concept, and in fact, Levin (1982) has taken this very stand. Accumulated research now suggests that a grasp of the interrelations between time, speed and distance arrives relatively late in development, and children come to recognize that relative start and stop times are necessary and sufficient information for judging relative durations before they understand these interrelations.

If time, speed and distance interrelations may be dismissed as the cornerstone of the developing time concept, why then continue to study the development of their understanding? First, one must admit that a time concept accompanied by an understanding of time as it relates to speed and distance is certainly fuller than a time concept that lacks this knowledge, and it is certainly the case that the mature time concept toward which development proceeds includes an understanding of these interrelations. Thus the development of an understanding of time, speed and distance interrelations is still an important component of the developing time concept. Moreover, given the importance of time, speed and distance in physics, the continued study of an emerging understanding of their interrelations may eventually impact the development of science curricula in the early grades. And finally, it should be recognized that much of our cognitive development research and theory is primarily concerned with the emergence of an understanding of the interrelations between natural dimensions, and thus there is the possibility that a study of time, speed and distance interrelations will have implications for our understanding of cognitive development in general.

WHAT UNDERSTANDING ENTAILS

Time, speed and distance form a closed system in our universe. If one dimension is held constant, then a qualitative change in one of the remaining two dimensions necessitates a qualitative change in the other. Both speed and time bear direct (i.e., positive) relations to distance: if the duration of travel is held constant, greater speeds yield farther distances, while if speed is constant, greater durations of travel yield farther distances. But time bears an inverse (i.e., negative) relation to speed: if distance is held constant, greater durations require slower speeds. As a matter of convenience, we may use the term *bivariate* to refer to the necessary qualitative relations between pairs of dimensions when the third variable is held constant. What happens when all three dimensions are allowed to vary? Traveling a farther distance at a slower speed invariably leads to a longer duration but traveling a farther distance at a faster speed may lead to a longer, shorter or the same duration. In this latter case, there is no one necessary solution. Again, as a matter of convenience, we may use the term *trivariate* to refer to the necessary qualitative relations among dimensions when all three are allowed to vary. A complete understanding of the necessary interrelations between time, speed and distance implies mastery of both the bivariate and the trivariate relations.

It is possible, though not certain, that children may grasp the bivariate relations before the trivariate relations, rather than contemporaneously. That is, they may develop an understanding that greater distances always yield longer durations whenever speeds are held constant, and greater speeds always yield shorter durations whenever distances are held constant, but admit to uncertainty when all three variables are allowed to vary. We must be cautious, however, when assessing children's knowledge concerning the bivariate relations. As children become aware of the empirical fact that duration is positively correlated with distance and negatively correlated with speed, they may adopt these empirical correlations as convenient *rules* by which to judge and estimate durations. If, however, they overgeneralize these rules to situations in which the third variable is not held constant, then they are clearly not understanding either the bivariate or trivariate relations and they certainly should not be credited with an understanding of the necessary interrelations between dimensions. Thus, in the following review, I distinguish between a mere *awareness* of the correlations between pairs of dimensions and an *understanding* of these bivariate relations. Unfortunately, many researchers have credited children with an understanding of the bivariate relations when it is unclear whether or not their subjects appreciated the fact that the third variable was held constant. Some have done so even in cases where it is clear that their subjects did not appreciate this fact.

When do children become aware of the correlations between dimensions? Are even very young children aware that distance and duration are positively related while speed and duration are negatively related? Does the awareness of one relation precede the other? Do children ever change their belief as to the direction of these relations, assuming a negative correlation between distance and duration and a positive correlation between speed and duration? When is an awareness of these correlations replaced with an understanding of the natural necessities involved? At what age do children come to grips with the trivariate as well bivariate relations? These are the sorts of questions researchers have addressed and which I shall discuss in the following pages.

Methods of investigating children's understanding of time, speed and distance interrelations have fallen into four main groups. In one procedure, *Judging Relative Durations*, subjects observe two objects moving the same direction down parallel tracks and are asked to determine whether the two objects travelled for the same amount of time, and if not, which travelled for the longer amount of time. In a second procedure, *Estimating Relative Durations*, rather than directly confront subjects with moving objects, they are given information concerning relative values for the two objects on two of the three dimensions — for example relative speed and distance — from which they are to deduce the third — relative duration in this case. A third procedure, *Estimating Metric Duration*, has subjects consider a single moving object and requires that they estimate a value in one dimension given values for the other two. Finally, a fourth procedure, *Assessing the Possibility of Relative Time, Speed and Distance Combinations*, again asks subjects to consider two moving objects, but now they are presented information concerning relative values for the two objects on all three dimensions — their relative duration, speed and distance. Subjects must then determine whether the combination is possible or impossible. While no one method answers all the questions, and problems of validity exist with each, it will be shown that taken in total, a fairly clear picture of children's understanding of time, speed and distance interrelations results.

JUDGING DIRECTLY PERCEIVED RELATIVE DURATIONS

In most of the work investigating children's understanding of time, speed and distance concepts, researchers have adopted Piaget's technique of directly confronting children with physical displays of two objects moving down parallel tracks where it is the child's task to determine which of the objects has traveled the farther distance, the faster speed, and the longer period of time. Relative start and stop points, start and stop times, distances, speeds, and durations are systematically varied. Although this method is not specifically contrived as a means by which to study children's awareness or understanding of the necessary interrelations between dimensions, the data it yields suggest that children pass through a period in which they entertain incorrect notions concerning the correlations between pairs of dimensions. The data also suggest that all young children and many older children overgeneralize their interpretation of these correlations to situations where the third variable is not held constant, indicating that children do not fully understand the necessary interrelations between all three dimensions until at least middle childhood, and possibly not until much later.

In Piaget's original studies, it was observed that when children were asked to judge which of two objects traveled for the longest amount of time, the youngest (up through age 5–6) invariably confused time with distance traveled. This was labeled Stage 1. For the least mature children in this group, those still unsure about distance itself, Stage 1 is manifested in the equating of duration with stopping point. The object advancing farther in the direction of travel is thought to have traveled the longer amount of time regardless of meaningful differences in speed or actual start and stop times. Older Stage 1 children confuse duration with actual distance. The object covering the greater distance from start to stop point is thought to have traveled the longer amount of time regardless of differences in speed or duration. Thus, in both cases, duration is seen as having a positive correlation with distance, which is correct on the bivariate level, but since distance cannot be relied upon to dictate differences in duration unless speeds are equivalent, predictable errors are made when speeds are not held constant. Obviously, children at this stage understand neither the bivariate nor the trivariate relations. At most, it may be said that they are aware of the positive correlation between distance and duration.

Are the children in this group actually unaware of the negative correlation between speed and duration? We cannot tell for sure since this paradigm pits speed against distance. That is, young children may be aware of both correlations, but since they are forced to choose one or the other (or neither) as a basis for making a judgment, their awareness of the correlation between speed and duration may be hidden. As will be seen, other methods suggest that young children are indeed aware of the inverse relation between speed and duration. If this is so, why do they so reliably depend on relative distance instead of relative speed as the basis for judging relative durations? It may be that children regard relative distance as a more reliable clue to relative duration. Alternatively, they may regard speed and distance as equally reliable, but the displays typically used in this paradigm may make differences in distance more salient than differences in speed.

Beyond Stage 1 Piaget witnessed several other types of confusion.

Some children equated duration with the inverse of distance, while others confused duration with speed or with the inverse of speed. All such confusions were labeled Stage 2. While on face value, the data suggest that children actually become confused about the correlations between dimensions, entertaining the notion that duration is negatively correlated with distance and positively correlated with speed, Piaget (1969; 1970) and later Montangero (1979) provide evidence that children arrive at such incorrect judgments by juxtaposing two correctly interpreted relations. For example, when children repeatedly hold that the object traveling farther takes the shorter time, they appear to arrive at this conclusion by reasoning that greater distance implies greater speed and greater speed implies shorter duration. Subsequent studies (e.g., Acredolo & Schmid, 1981; Levin & Globerson, 1984; Siegler & Richards, 1979), however, show that many children in this period eschew consistent use of any simple rule. The bases of their judgments seem to change on every trial. Thus, children in this period appear to be in the process of recognizing that neither distance nor speed may be taken as a dependable clue to duration when taken in isolation, but they are still struggling to understand how the three dimensions interact. Obviously, these children do not yet understand the necessary interrelations among dimensions.

Stage 3, which according to Piaget is usually achieved around age 8 or 9, was reserved for children who no longer demonstrate confusions of time with distance or speed. Judgments are now an accurate reflection of differences between start and stop times, though the least mature Stage 3 subjects may attend only to end times, ignoring start times. As noted earlier, Piaget held that this accuracy comes about only when children completely understand the interrelations among dimensions. Thus, if we accept Piaget's thesis, the onset of Stage 3 behavior marks the point at which the necessary interrelations between dimensions are finally understood.

To various extents, Piaget's observations have been replicated by Fraisse and Vaultry (1952), Lovell and Slater (1960), Berndt and Wood (1974), Siegler and Richards (1979), Richards (1982) and Acredolo and Schmid (1981). Across studies, however, two primary disagreements with Piaget's findings emerge. First, most of the studies cited suggest that while some children may perform well at judging relative durations as early as 8 or 9 years of age, most children fail to demonstrate consistent accuracy before age 11–12. The accumulated research of Levin (1977, 1979, 1982; Levin, Israeli, & Darom, 1978; Levin, Gilat, & Zelniker, 1980; Levin & Simons, 1986) suggests that this difference between Piaget's observations and those from more recent studies is probably a function of the salience of the interfering distance and speed cues found in the newer studies. The concern here is the possibility that researchers may create such strong illusions and complex displays that errors are forced on children who actually understand the interrelations between dimensions and would otherwise have performed well. Thus, this method of assessing the point at which the necessary relations among dimensions are understood may yield false negative evaluations. Alternatively, if one accepts the argument presented in the introduction to this chapter that children can begin relying on start and stop times as cues to relative duration well ahead of the point at which they grasp the interrelations between dimensions, then false positive evaluations are also possible. Given the possibility of both false positive and false negative evaluations, application of this procedure leaves open the question of exactly when the bivariate and trivariate relations are actually understood — in middle childhood, late childhood, or later still.

The second disagreement with Piaget concerns the prevalence of Stage 2 behavior. Several of the cited studies suggest that the confusion of time with distance, Piaget's Stage 1, predominates and extends into late childhood, while responses characteristic of Piaget's Stage 2 are comparatively rare. These observations suggest that children first become aware of the correlation between distance and duration and are never really forced to reevaluate that relation. Rather, from that point on, development is primarily a matter of learning when and how speed moderates the relation between distance and duration. If these findings are accurate, it would suggest that children may develop an understanding of the bivariate distance $\longleftrightarrow$ time relation well before they develop an understanding of either the bivariate speed $\longleftrightarrow$ time relation or the trivariate relations. It can be noted, however, that the studies reporting an absence of Stage 2 behavior did not include a sufficient number of unique displays to insure the clear identification of such responses, should they occur. In a study with Jeannine Schmid (Acredolo and Schmid, 1981), we selected displays with the purposeful intent of testing Piaget's assertions concerning Stage 2 behavior, and in this case we observed a substantial proportion of 1st and 3rd grade children, 5–8 years of age, clearly confusing time with the inverse of distance, time with speed, and time with inverse speed, all Stage 2 responses. The confusion of time with end point or distance, Stage 1 behavior, was primarily observed among 1st grade children, 6–7 years of age, and did not appear at all among children beyond 3rd grade, 8–9 years of age. These results largely replicate Piaget's original observations and suggest that neither the bivariate nor the trivariate relations are understood until middle childhood, at the earliest. The fact that we can get differences between studies again demonstrates, however, that the choice of displays influences the results one obtains. Overall, it appears that we can not depend on this paradigm to reveal a clear picture of children's understanding of time, speed and distance interrelations. More direct approaches are needed.

Estimating Relative Durations

One very direct approach to the study of children's awareness of the relations between pairs of dimensions involves simply giving subjects information concerning the relative value on one dimension and asking them to deduce the relative value on a second given equality on the third. Thus subjects can be told which of two objects travels farther or which travels faster, and it is then left up to them to determine which travels for the longest amount of time. This approach has been used by Montangero (1977, 1979).

Montangero (1979) observed that 5– to 8–year-old children were surprisingly proficient at deducing qualitative relations on one dimension on the basis of information concerning a qualitative relation on a second. Thus a majority of young children appear aware of the correlations between distance and speed, between distance and duration, and between speed and duration. On the other hand, performance was not perfect, particularly on speed ⟷ time problems. Rather than accept that 5–8 year old children are actually still unclear about these correlations, however, Montangero adopted an argument first used by Piaget and suggested that the children's errors actually resulted from the application of accurate recall of the correlations between dimensions in conjunction with a fairly complicated line of reasoning involving forgetting to hold the assigned dimension constant. Thus, for example, when children argued that greater speeds imply longer durations, Montangero suggested that they got to this conclusion by recognizing that greater speed implies a farther distance, and a farther distance implies a longer duration. In support of this conjecture, Montangero demonstrated that when the children were asked to recall the problem, they indeed failed to hold the distance dimension constant.

Montangero's (and Piaget's) explanation of children's errors in this paradigm does not appear to be particularly parsimonious, and it may be challenged on several levels. If one wants to argue that children are incapable of remembering which dimension is held constant, one needs to consider how it is that they are capable of carrying out a line of reasoning involving asymmetries on all three dimensions. Further, if this line of argument can be used to explain children's incorrect judgments, one must wonder if their correct answers might be equally well explained by the application of an inaccurate recall of a bivariate relation in conjuction with the same sort of complicated reasoning. Thus, the child who correctly implies that duration is directly related to distance might have come to that conclusion by assuming that greater durations imply greater speeds and greater speeds imply greater distances. Note as well that Montangero's explanation of the speed ⟷ time error, presented above, does not actually suggest that the children who committed this error were aware of the inverse relation between speed and duration, only the direct relations between speed and distance and between distance and duration. Thus, we may still conclude that these children were not aware of the inverse relation between speed and duration. Finally, Montangero's conclusions may be called into question because they rely heavily on post hoc dialogs with children, and there is good reason to question whether the reasoning displayed by a child when asked to justify an answer mirrors the reasoning used when making the judgment. Similarly, there is good reason to question whether subsequent probing indicating that a child has forgotten that a dimension was held constant means that this same error was made when answering the initial question. In my opinion, whenever subsequent questioning implies that a child has forgotten or misconstrued a problem, the best procedure is to present the question again, insisting that the child maintain the given parameters during both judgment and explanation.

My purpose in developing such lengthy criticism of Montangero's analysis of errors is to emphasize that it is still unclear whether children in fact never reverse the relations between dimensions. However, even if we disregard Montangero's argument that judgment errors do not actually represent a misunderstanding of the correlations between dimensions, his results still support the conclusion that most young children are aware of both the positive correlation of duration with distance and the negative correlation of duration with speed. The reader should take note, however, that Montangero's findings do not provide evidence that young children *understand* the bivariate relations since there is no evidence that the children in his study appreciated the importance of having the third dimension held constant. Some modification of his procedure is needed before we can claim to have tapped children's understanding of the necessary interrelations among dimensions.

Estimating Metric Duration

Wilkening (1981, 1982) introduced an interesting and promising modification of Montangero's procedure, a modification based on Anderson's information integration approach (Anderson, 1980). Unlike Montangero's procedure, Wilkening's method attempts to assess both children's awareness of the correlations between dimensions and their understanding of the interrelations between dimensions. Rather than ask children to deal with nonmetric relations involving two moving objects, Wilkening asked subjects to estimate the duration, speed or distance of travel of single moving objects. Thus children were asked to estimate the precise distance traveled by one object on the basis of fairly precise speed and duration information, speed on the basis of distance and duration information, and duration on the basis of distance and speed information. It is this last condition that is of most interest here.

In the time portion of Wilkening's investigation, 5– and 10–year-old children were presented with a scenario in which they were to judge the amount of time an animal ran from a stationary barking dog on the basis of that animal's estimated speed and information provided about the precise distance it traveled. The children were shown models of three animals — a cat, a guinea pig, and a turtle — and asked to order these according to speed. Then, in separate trials, they were shown one animal and the distance it had run in that instance. Each animal was paired with each of three distances, yielding nine unique trials. On each trial the children had to estimate the time needed by the animal to cover the specified distance. They did so by activating a tape recording of a barking dog for that period of time. In analyzing the results there were three issues: (1) For the same animal shown traveling three different distances, would children demonstrate an awareness that longer distances necessitate longer durations?; (2) For equivalent distances, would children demonstrate an awareness that faster speeds necessitate shorter durations?; and (3) Would children demonstrate an awareness that the differences in duration between a slower and a faster animal must be less for shorter distances than for longer ones? Performance on this task was examined by submitting the data from each subject to a two-way repeated measures analysis of variance. The presence of a significant main effect for distance indicated that the child considered the differences in distance when estimating duration, while the presence of a significant main effect for speed indicated that the child considered the differences in speed. The presence of a significant distance-by-speed interaction indicated that the child understood the multiplicative relation between distance and speed when estimating duration.

An understanding of the bivariate and trivariate relations requires an awareness of how the relative value on one dimension influences the relation between the other two. Therefore, children who attended to speed or to distance or even to both of these dimensions when estimating durations may be said to have been aware of one or both of the correlations between dimensions, but unless they also showed an awareness of the interaction between distance and speed, they can not be said to have understood the bivariate and trivariate relations. Wilkening's data indicated that most of the 5–year-old children were aware of both the direct relation between distance and time and the inverse relation between speed and time, but only the 10–year-old children integrated these two relations in a multiplicative fashion. In terms of children's awareness of the bivariate relation, Wilkening's findings are largely in agreement with those of Montangero (1977; 1981). Young children appear to be aware of both correlations. In terms of children's understanding of the bivariate relations, his findings are in agreement with Piaget's. Children appear to understand the necessary interrelations between all three dimensions by middle childhood.

Unfortunately, Wilkening's conclusions may be called into question. As he notes, an eye movement strategy may explain his results. That is, his children may have simply visualized the animal running along the course as they activated the dog's bark. Given the grossly different speeds of the three animals involved, even a crude representation of their velocities would yield differences in durations as a function of both speeds and distances, and even an apparent multiplicative integration of speed and distance is not out of the question. Given this fact, the utility of Wilkening's procedure is uncertain.

Piaget held that an adequate testing of children's understanding of time requires that one confronts them with at least two simultaneous motions. The reason why this is the case can be seen in the fact that children may completely misconstrue a bivariate relation and yet still perform as if they understood that relation on Wilkening's procedure. For example, children may erroneously believe that greater speeds yield longer durations and display this belief when given Piaget's or Montangero's task, but when they imagine the fastest animal running down the track in Wilkening's procedure, they will not make that animal run slower than the others so that it will have the longer duration. They are bound by the empirical facts, and they will invariably appear to know that greater speeds yield shorter, not longer, durations. Since they are never asked to deal with two different velocities simultaneously, their error is never revealed, not even to themselves.

Some may choose to defend Wilkening's procedure by arguing that even adults solve all the problems discussed in this chapter by imagining the movements under consideration, and thus Wilkening's procedure has the advantage of directly addressing this capacity. However, if all that is required to solve problems involving simultaneous movements is to imagine these movements in accordance with the provided information, then we should expect no errors other than those that result from a forgetting of the premise information. There is obviously more to the matter. While there is no doubt that imagery is used by children and adults when solving reasoning problems concerning simultaneous movements, what is imagined probably varies more as a function of the anticipated outcomes than as a function of the provided parameters. That is, imagery works best (i.e., helps lead one to a correct judgment) when one first understands the relations correctly. It works poorly when the relations are themselves misconstrued. Wilkening's procedure unfortunately allows children to perform well even when the relations are poorly understood.

I suggest that Wilkening's procedure actually examines a skill akin to that which Piaget calls *covariation* in his discussions of the development of conservation. Covariation is the empirical knowledge of the quantitative relations involved when a quantity changes shape, such as the specific change in liquid height that must result from a specific metric change in cross-sectional area. Covariation is distinct from operational compensation in that the child does not appreciate the implications of this relation for the maintenance of quantity. Further, extensive covariation skills may develop well ahead of compensation, much later, or never at all. The two are relatively distinct. The ability to estimate the duration of travel on the basis of speed and distance information is undoubtedly also an empirical skill. It is conceivable that a child might become quite proficient at estimating the duration required by an object to cover a particular distance given a particular speed and yet not really understand the relations between dimensions in a more abstract and generalizable sense. Children may perform relatively well at this task long before they gain the capacity to evaluate the necessary relations between the three dimensions. It is also conceivable, however, that children could develop a thorough understanding of qualitative and metric relations between time, distance and speed, and yet never develop sufficient proficiency at estimating durations to show a clear multiplicative integration in Wilkening's procedure.

The questionable validity of Wilkening's procedure as a means of assessing children's knowledge of time, speed and distance interrelations is demonstrated in a study Karen Horobin and I conducted in which we pitted his *Estimating Metric Durations* paradigm against both Piaget's *Judging Relative Duration* and Montangero's *Estimating Relative Duration* procedures. If one accepts that Wilkening's method yields an accurate appraisal of individual children's awareness of the bivariate relations, then an assessment of the presence of this knowledge using his paradigm should usually be in agreement with the results of an assessment of the same knowledge based on the *Estimating Relative Duration* procedure. Similarly, if one accepts that Wilkening's method yields an accurate appraisal of individual children's understanding of the trivariate relationship, then an assessment of the presence of this knowledge using his paradigm should usually be in agreement with the results of an assessment of the same knowledge based on the *Judging Relative Durations* procedure. On the other hand, if one accepts the arguments that Wilkening's method measures an independent skill, then a very low level of concordance may be anticipated. A complete summary of the study follows.

STUDY 1: AN EXAMINATION OF THE CONCORDANCE BETWEEN METHODS CLAIMING TO MEASURE CHILDREN'S KNOWLEDGE OF TIME, SPEED AND DISTANCE INTERRELATIONS

In an effort to gain a better understanding of the differences between the three procedures described thus far, and in particular to evaluate the validity of Wilkening's *Estimating Metric Duration* procedure, we confronted a single group of 1st, 3rd and 5th grade children with three different assessments. In imitation of Piaget (1969; 1970), Siegler and Richards (1979) and Acredolo and Schmid (1981), we presented children 14 displays of two objects moving down parallel tracks and asked the children to determine which object had traveled, from start to stop, for the longest amount of time. We also confronted the children with four problems similar to those used by Montangero (1979) and with a replication of the time condition from Wilkening's (1981) study.

Subjects, Methods and Measures

The subjects were from a public school in a small agricultural community of Northern California. Each of 19 1st grade children (mean age: 7 years, 1 month) 18 3rd grade children (9 years, 0 months) and 20 5th grade children (11 years, 2 months) were exposed to all three assessments in a single sitting with the order of administration randomized for each subject. The *Judging Relative Duration* and *Estimating Metric Duration* procedures were administered on a portable computer using MBASIC programs written by the author. The *Estimating Relative Duration* procedure was administered verbally using two small porcelain rabbits, a porcelain dog, a cardboard doghouse and a long strip of matte board representing a road.

In the *Judging Relative Duration* procedure, the children were confronted with 14 displays of two "toads" hopping their way across the computer screen. Start and stop points, start and stop times, speeds, total durations and total distances of travel were all systematically varied. In each problem the children had to determine whether or not the toads traveled, from start to stop, for the same amount of time, and if not which traveled a greater amount of time. The 14 problems were selected to optimize the probability of identifying use of the end point, distance and end time rules. Children were encouraged to evaluate each problem carefully and to avoid responding impulsively. The computer enabled a replaying of each race as often as necessary until the children felt confident of their decision. Most children took advantage of this opportunity on virtually every trial.

Given the fact that in previous studies the end point remained in view following the movement of the two objects while no clue remained in view indicating speed or duration, we attempted to equalize the ease with which children could refer to all three dimensions when making their judgments of relative durations. This was done by having the toads leave "footprints" on each hop. Since they always hopped in unison, distances could be compared by looking at the relative lengths of lines of footprints, while relative speeds could be compared by looking at the relative distances between adjacent footprints, and relative durations could be compared by examining the total number of footprints. The children were, of course, not informed of these associations, but given that earlier studies had shown a preponderance of children attending to the one still visible cue, end point, it seemed reasonable to provide comparable cues for the speed and duration dimensions. Although differences between the number of hops, indicating relative duration, could have been quite salient if the number of hops had been in the subitizing range, the smallest number of hops on any trial was 12, and differences between the two runners in the number of hops were purposely kept small. Further, note that start and stop times were not represented, and given that the length of a line is the most salient cue supporting the nonconservation of number, the on-screen cues still encouraged the equating of time with distance.

In reducing the data from the *Judging Relative Duration* procedure, an initial effort was made to identify those children who were using simple end point, distance and end time rules as a guide in judging relative durations. Subjects were assumed to have used a rule only if their judgments matched at least 11 of the 14 answers that would be expected in using that rule. Only six children were identified as using the end point or distance rule and only two were identified as using the end time rule. As in the results of previous studies, a large proportion of children failed to demonstrate reliance on these simple rules and whatever mixture they were using could not be identified. On the other hand, 25 children (44%) answered 11 of the 14 questions correctly. This is a much higher percentage than would have been expected given the results of previous studies using this paradigm, but with the modifications in the procedure made possible by the use of the computer — primarily the ability to play any particular "race" over and over again — the higher frequency of accurate judgments was not unexpected. We suspect that the paradigm should always be presented in this fashion. For the purpose of analyzing the concordance between this procedure and Wilkening's procedure, subjects were assigned to one of two groups, those who answered at least 11 questions correct, and therefore supposedly understood the interrelations between dimensions, and those who did not.

In the *Estimating Relative Duration* procedure, based on the Montangero (1979) study, children were presented four problems concerning relative distances, speed and durations of travel of two rabbits running from a stationary barking dog. The rabbits always started running at the same place and at the same time, and they ran in the same direction. With one dimension held constant, children were presented information concerning the relative value on a second dimension and asked to judge the relative value on the third. Thus, children were asked to judge which rabbit, if either, had traveled for a longer amount of time when told that one had traveled faster though both had gone the same distance ($S \longrightarrow T$), and when told that one had traveled farther though both had gone the same speed ($D \longrightarrow T$). The children were also asked to determine which rabbit, if either, had traveled faster when told that one had traveled for a longer amount of time though both had gone the same distance ($T \longrightarrow S$), and to determine which animal, if either, had traveled farther when told that one had traveled for a longer amount of time though both had gone the same speed ($T \longrightarrow D$). Subjects were instructed to think each problem through carefully before answering. Premise information was repeated over and over again until the child made a judgment. In order to guard against the possibility that the children were forgetting the problem while generating their judgments, as soon as a judgment was made, the experimenter repeated the premise information and the child's judgment in the form of a syllogism, and the children were asked to confirm the validity of their conclusion. Children were allowed to withdraw their judgments at this point and reconsider the problem, and they did so frequently. No justifications were requested.

The data from the *Estimating Relative Duration* procedure were reduced to two variables, one indicating awareness of the correlation between distance and duration and the second indicating awareness of the correlation between speed and duration. The first was indicated by the passing of both $D \longrightarrow T$ and $T \longrightarrow D$, while the second was indicated by the passing of both $S \longrightarrow T$ and $T \longrightarrow S$.

Finally, in the *Estimating Metric Duration* procedure, based on Wilkening (1981), children were presented a graphic display of a trained horse running across the computer screen as the computer emitted a tone. It was explained that the horse was trained to run as fast as possible as long as a trainer blew a whistle (the tone). The children were shown that they could blow the whistle for any length of time by pressing and holding down one of the computer keys. Then, after establishing that a deer runs faster than a dog, and a dog runs faster than a skunk, the children were shown three different lengths of line each paired once with the information that either a trained deer, dog or skunk had run the indicated distance. In each of the nine resulting problems, the children were required to hold down a computer key that evoked the "whistle" for the period of time they felt would be necessary to get the animal to run that specific distance.

The data from the *Estimating Metric Duration* procedure were analyzed by submitting the responses from each subject to a hierarchical regression analysis with linear speed and linear distance factors loaded simultaneously in the first step and their interaction loaded in the second step. Nonlinear effects were added to error. The presence of a significant speed or distance effect indicated attention to that dimension when estimating duration, while a significant speed-by-distance interaction indicated a multiplicative integration of these two dimensions ($p<.05$). Subjects were assigned pass/fail scores on three variables. An awareness of the correlation between distance and duration was assumed if the child displayed a significant distance main effect or distance-by-speed interaction. An awareness of the correlation between speed and duration was assumed if the child displayed a significant speed effect or distance-by-speed interaction. An understanding of the interrelations between dimensions was assumed only if the child displayed a significant distance-by-speed interaction.

Results

Performance naturally improved across grade on all three assessments, though for this sample all statistical comparisons only approached significance. Nevertheless, if one accepts that each of these procedures provides a valid assessment of children's knowledge of time, speed and distance interrelations, then given that performance is related to age for each procedure, and a broad age span was sampled, one should indeed expect a comparatively high degree of concordance. In fact, however, and as predicted, a very poor concordance was observed.

First consider children's awareness of the correlation between distance and duration. Children aware of this correlation should have answered both the $D \longrightarrow T$ and $T \longrightarrow D$ problems correctly in the *Estimating Relative Duration* procedure and they should have shown a significant main effect for distance or a significant distance-by-speed interaction in the *Estimating Metric Duration* procedure. The degree of concordance between procedures could be assessed using the phi coefficient of correlation, while differences between procedures in the frequency with which they identified children as possessing an awareness of the relation could be assessed using the sign test. As anticipated, the correlation between the two procedures was not significant, r_{phi}=–.16. A pass on one was a poor predictor of whether or not the child would also pass the other. Further, the two procedures did not differ significantly in difficulty. Children were no more or less likely to obtain a pass on one than on the other.

Now consider children's awareness of the correlation between speed and duration. Children aware of this relation should have answered both the $S \longrightarrow T$ and $T \longrightarrow S$ problems correctly in the *Estimating Relative Duration* procedure, and they should have shown a significant main effect for speed or a significant distance-by-speed interaction in the *Estimating Metric Duration* procedure. The correlation between the two procedures was again nonsignificant, r_{phi}=.17, but this time children more frequently obtained a pass in the former than in the latter, p=.015. That is, more children displayed awareness of the correlation between speed and duration in the *Estimating Relative Duration* procedure and failed to demonstrate a similar awareness in the *Estimating Metric Duration* procedure than vice versa.

Finally consider children's understanding of the necessary interrelations between dimensions. Children in the present study who understood the bivariate and trivariate relations should have answered at least 11 of the 14 problems correctly in the *Judging Relative Duration* procedure and they should have displayed a significant distance-by-speed interaction in the *Estimating Metric Duration* procedure. The correlation was again non-significant, r_{phi}=.23, and children more frequently showed evidence of understanding the interrelations between dimensions in the *Judging Relative Duration* procedure than in the *Estimating Metric Duration* procedure, p<.001.

Discussion

This study supports the hypothesis that Wilkening's *Estimating Metric Duration* method is flawed both as a measure of children's awareness of the correlations between dimensions and as a means of assessing their understanding of the necessary interrelationships among dimensions. Not only does it fail to yield the same conclusions concerning the knowledge possessed by individual children, it appears to be more conservative than other methods. This is surprising given that Wilkening justified his procedure and criticized that of Montangero by arguing that asking children to estimate relative durations on the basis of information about relative speeds or relative distances puts too great a demand on their memory and processing capacity, and thus it is better to ask children to deal with only one moving body at a time. The implication of this argument is that his procedure can show the possession of knowledge that is missed with the other. The present data, however, suggest that this is not the case. Asking children to estimate relative durations on the basis of relative distances and speeds indicated the presence of an awareness of the correlation of duration with both distance and speed, while performance on Wilkening's paradigm showed evidence only of the former and not the latter. As noted in my criticism, performance on Wilkening's procedure requires a certain degree of skill rather than knowledge per se, and children may acquire knowledge without developing the associated skill.

It is obvious that to some extent the low level of concordance between Wilkening's procedure and the others must be attributed to the unreliability of assessments based on all three methods. But if unreliability were the only issue, then we certainly should have seen at least moderate levels of correlation. The almost total lack of concordance across procedures must be attributed primarily to problems of validity. While I have chosen to target Wilkening's procedure, it is possible that his procedure would fair somewhat better when compared to true values. That is, to some extent, the low concordance between methods may be attributed to the questionable validity of the *Judging Relative Duration* and *Estimating Relative Duration* methods as well.

CONCLUSIONS THUS FAR AND INTRODUCTION OF A FOURTH METHOD: ASSESSING THE POSSIBILITY OF RELATIVE TIME, SPEED AND DISTANCE COMBINATIONS

Regardless of whether we accept Wilkening's data or not, the conclusions drawn so far are the same. It appears that most young children are aware of both the positive correlation between distance and duration and the negative correlation between speed and duration. Although they appear to prefer relative distance as a clue to relative duration when confronted with displays of linear movement, this is probably a function of the relative salience of distance and speed clues present in those problems. The age at which children acquire an understanding of the bivariate and trivarite relations is still unclear. The results of studies using the Judging *Relative Durations* method suggest that understanding of the necessary interrelations among dimensions awaits middle or late childhood, but that procedure was not designed with an assessment of children's understanding of the interrelationships specifically in mind, and we need to confirm that conclusion with other methods. Wilkening was basically correct: What is needed is a very direct procedure, like Montangero's, but capable of revealing more than simply an awareness of the correlations between dimensions. The following method offers another variation on Montangero's approach. It attempts to assess children's understanding of the bivariate and trivariate relations by directly assessing their awareness of the natural necessities involved in the interrelations between dimensions.

In a series of exploratory studies, I observed that while children may correctly deduce, for example, that when the distance covered by two runners is equal, the one running faster covers the distance in the shorter duration, when then asked whether equal distance and faster speed might also result in an equal or longer duration, they sometimes agree that these outcomes are also possible. In this case it may be said that children do not yet understand that their original solution was also the only possible solution — a necessary solution. If we had taken the children's first response as evidence of an understanding of the speed ⟷ time relation, we would have credited them with more knowledge than they deserve. I suggest that if children possess only an awareness of the correlations between dimensions, or if they solve problems by imagining the described event and the outcome they "observe", they will do well on tasks that require that they provide a single solution to a problem, but they will generally display considerable difficulty evaluating the necessity of the solutions they report. In the following method children are asked to evaluate the possibility of every combination of relative speeds, distances and durations of travel for two moving objects, thereby providing an assessment of children's understanding of the necessary relations between dimensions, both bivariate and trivariate.

Two somewhat different applications of this method have been explored. The first is reported in Acredolo, Adams and Schmid (1984) and summarized below, while the second is reported here as Study 2. In the Acredolo, et al. study we obtained evidence suggesting that young children possess an understanding of both the distance $\longleftrightarrow$ time and speed $\longleftrightarrow$ time relations. It is demonstrated in Study 2, however, that this conclusion was incorrect, the result of a specific design flaw. Children do not fully understand the bivariate relations until late childhood at the earliest.

In the Acredolo, et al. study subjects were given problems similar to those used by Montangero (1979) in which they had to determine relative distance from information concerning relative time and relative speed, relative speed from information concerning relative distance and relative time, and relative time from information concerning relative distance and relative speed. But for each of these sets, in addition to problems where one of the two dimensions was held constant, subjects were given one problem in which both of the dimensions indicated an equality and two problems in which neither of the dimensions indicated an equality. The five problems in the time condition are of most interest here, and these are summarized in Table 6.1.

The reader should take time to study the notation used in Table 6.1 as it is also used in discussing the procedures and results for Study 2. The five problems are labeled *EQ*, *D*, *S*, *DS*, and *D/S* according to which dimensions, distance (*D*) and/or speed (*S*), differ between the two runners. The absence of either a *D* or *S* in the notation signifies that the runners were equal on that dimension. Thus, in problem *EQ* (equal), both runners traveled the same distance and the same speed. In problem *D*, runner *X* traveled farther than runner *Y* but at the same speed. In Problem *S*, runner *X* traveled faster than runner *Y* but the same distance. In Problem *DS*, runner *X* traveled farther and faster than runner *Y*, and in Problem *D/S*, runner *X* traveled farther but slower than runner *Y*. Note the use of the slash to indicate when one runner has a higher value on one dimension, but a lower value on a second. Outcomes (i.e., combinations of relative time, speed and distance) are similarly noted using all lower case letters. The presence of a *t* indicates a difference between runners *X* and *Y* in duration (time). Outcomes are always followed by a subscripted (p) or (i) indicating a possible versus an impossible combination of time, speed and distance, respectively. Thus $ds/t_{(p)}$ indicates the situation in which runner *X* travels farther, faster and for a shorter amount of time than runner *Y*, a possible combination, while $d/st_{(i)}$ indicates the situation in which runner *X* travels farther, slower and for a shorter amount of time than runner *Y*, an impossible combination. Note that there is only one possible outcome for Problems *EQ*, *D*, *S*, and *D/S*, but three possible outcomes for Problem *DS*.

Table 6.1.

THE FIVE PROBLEMS PRESENTED CHILDREN IN THE TIME CONDITION OF THE ACREDOLO, ADAMS AND SCHMID (1984) STUDY: POSSIBLE AND IMPOSSIBLE COMBINATIONS OF RELATIVE TIME, SPEED AND DISTANCE

SET	PROBLEMS AND POSSIBLE AND IMPOSSIBLE OUTCOMES	COMBINATION
EQ	"They ran the same distance, and they ran the same speed."	
	They ran the same amount of time.	$eq(p)$
	X or Y ran a longer amount of time.	$t_{(i)}$
D	"X ran for a farther distance, and they ran the same speed."	
	They ran the same amount of time.	$d_{(i)}$
	X ran a longer amount of time.	$dt_{(p)}$
	Y ran a longer amount of time.	$d/t_{(i)}$
S	"They ran the same distance, and X ran faster."	
	They ran the same amount of time.	$s_{(i)}$
	X ran a longer amount of time.	$st_{(i)}$
	Y ran a longer amount of time.	$s/t_{(p)}$
DS	"X ran for a farther distance, and X ran faster."	
	They ran the same amount of time.	$ds_{(p)}$
	X ran a longer amount of time.	$dst_{(p)}$
	Y ran a longer amount of time.	$ds/t_{(p)}$
D/S	"X ran for a farther distance, and Y ran faster."	
	They ran the same amount of time.	$d/s_{(i)}$
	X ran a longer amount of time.	$dt/s_{(p)}$
	Y ran a longer amount of time.	$d/st_{(i)}$

Note: the notation used in abbreviating the problems and outcomes are explained in the text. The 14 problems used in Study 2 are identical to the 14 combinations of relative time, speed and distance listed above.

After children gave their answer to each problem (i.e., selected one of three outcomes) they were asked to reconsider the possibility that either or both of the remaining alternatives might also result given the premise information. Thus they might be asked to determine which of two animals, a brown or white rabbit, had run the longer amount of time given that the rabbits traveled equal distances but the white ran faster. Did they take the same amount of time, or did the white take longer, or did the brown take longer? Following their initial selection from among the three provided alternatives, they were asked to reconsider the remaining two alternatives and to determine whether each of those outcomes was also possible. It is the total pattern with which children accepted combinations of relative time, speed, and distance that is of interest here.

The subjects were 1st through 5th grade children, 12 in each grade. The results are presented in the left-most columns of Tables 6.2 and 6.3. Table 6.2 shows the percentage of children in each grade displaying each of the possible patterns of response to each of the five problems, while Table 6.3 summarizes the percentage of children endorsing as possible each of the three outcomes to each problem — combinations of relative time, speed and distance.

The data suggested that most 2nd grade children, 7–8 years of age, understood both bivariate relations. That is, most children correctly endorsed the necessary solutions to these problems while rejecting all other alternatives as impossible. Performance on Problems *D* and *S* were well above chance for the 2nd through 5th graders, and while performance on Problem *D* was somewhat better than that on Problem *S*, it was not significantly so.

Although the 1st grade children also performed well on Problem *D*, it appeared most likely that they were using a "more-is-more" rule — a perceptually higher value on one dimension implies a higher value on all other dimensions. Levin (1979; 1982; Levin and Gilat, 1983) suggested that young children adopt such a rule when dealing with interrelations of time, speed, and distance, and given the 1st grader's excellent performance on Problem *D* and complete failure on Problem *S* where they opted for alternative $st_{(i)}$ over $s/t_{(p)}$, it appeared that they may indeed have been using such a rule. It was thus deemed inappropriate to credit them with an understanding of the bivariate distance ⟷ duration relation.

Performance was significantly poorer on problems *DS* and *D/S*. These problems have the potential of assessing children's understanding of the trivariate relationship. Given the indication that children understood the bivariate distance ⟷ time and speed ⟷ time relations by second grade, it was anticipated that older children might show evidence of understanding the trivariate relationship as well. Unfortunately, Problem *D/S* can be answered correctly by ignoring speed and treating the problem as if it were identical to Problem *D*. In both cases children should endorse the alternative that has *X* travelling the longer amount of time. Thus, we may not interpret accurate performance on Problem *D/S* as showing evidence that children understand the trivariate relation. Performance on Problem *DS*, on the other hand, in which children should endorse all alternatives, may still be defended as offering an insight into children's grasp of the complete trivariate relationship. Although six 4th grade children did comparatively well, only two 5th grade children did so (a frequency expected by chance). This fact and the observation that the children also did not perform well on Problem *D/S* led us to conclude that even the oldest children in the study were not yet integrating their understanding of the distance ⟷ time and speed ⟷ time relations.

The unexpected excellent performance of young children on Problems *D* and *S*, suggesting that these children actually understood the bivariate relations, and the particularly poor performance of fifth grade children on Problem *DS*, suggesting that these children still did not understand the trivariate relations, prompted the recognition of a potentially severe problem with this study. In order to perform well on Problem *DS* children must endorse a second and third alternative after identifying a first solution, but it is known that children have considerable difficulty with this sort of indeterminacy (Braine and Rumain, 1983). Karen Horobin and I (Acredolo and Horobin, 1987) have subsequently examined this phenomenon and we show that in paradigms such as this where three alternatives are offered, 1st through 5th grade children have great trouble acknowledging a second possible solution (partial indeterminacy), and even 6th grade children and adults are reluctant to endorse all available alternatives when all alternatives are possible (complete indeterminacy). Thus, the poor performance of the children on Problem *DS* may reflect this response bias rather than the inability to integrate distance and speed. Even more important, however, it was now recognized that children's performance on Problems *D* and *S* may have been spuriously high. These children may have refused to accept the other alternative as also possible only because of their unwillingness to accept indeterminacy and because they understood that those outcomes were in fact impossible. It was this recognition that led to the studies that follow.

Table 6.2.

PERCENTAGE OF SUBJECTS DISPLAYING EACH PATTERN OF JUDGMENTS FOR THE TWO OR THREE COMBINATIONS OF TIME, SPEED AND DISTANCE COMPRISING A SET: DATA ARRANGED BY STUDY AND BY GRADE

COMBINATIONS JUDGED POSSIBLE (P) OR IMPOSSIBLE (I)			ACREDOLO, ET AL. (1984) GRADES					STUDY 2A GRADES				STUDIES 2B&2C GRADES		
			1	2	3	4	5	2	3	4	5	4	5	ADULT
		n=	(12)	(12)	(12)	(12)	(12)	(13)	(15)	(13)	(13)	(18)	(18)	(30)
Set *EQ*														
$eq_{(p)}$	$t_{(i)}$													
I	I		—	—	—	—	—	8	0	0	15	3	0	2
P	*I*		*50*	*75*	*83*	*83*	*100*	*62*	*33*	*62*	*69*	*94*	*92*	*93*
I	P		17	8	8	17	0	15	13	0	0	0	0	0
P	P		33	17	8	0	0	15	53	38	15	3	8	4
Set *D*														
$d_{(i)}$	$dt_{(p)}$	$d/t_{(i)}$												
I	I	I	—	—	—	—	—	23	27	0	15	31	17	7
P	I	I	0	0	0	17	0	15	0	0	0	3	0	1
I	*P*	*I*	*83*	*67*	*58*	*58*	*75*	*15*	*13*	*15*	*46*	*31*	*67*	*72*
I	I	P	8	17	8	25	17	0	7	0	0	11	3	4
P	P	I	0	8	0	0	0	8	0	15	15	14	6	4
P	I	P	0	0	0	0	0	0	7	0	0	6	3	4
I	P	P	0	8	8	0	0	23	3	31	23	6	3	11
P	P	P	8	0	25	0	8	15	33	38	0	0	3	0
Set *S*														
$s_{(i)}$	$st_{(i)}$	$s/t_{(p)}$												
I	I	I	—	—	—	—	—	62	7	15	15	31	11	3
P	I	I	25	25	0	17	25	0	7	8	0	8	3	0
I	P	I	58	17	17	17	0	0	0	8	8	8	0	0
I	*I*	*P*	*0*	*50*	*83*	*67*	*75*	*23*	*33*	*23*	*77*	*36*	*67*	*78*
P	P	I	8	0	0	0	0	0	7	0	0	3	6	1
P	I	P	0	8	0	0	0	0	20	23	0	6	3	8
I	P	P	0	0	0	0	0	0	13	8	0	6	8	9
P	P	P	8	0	0	0	0	15	13	15	0	3	3	1

Table continued

Continuation of Table 6.2.

PERCENTAGE OF SUBJECTS DISPLAYING EACH PATTERN OF JUDGMENTS FOR THE TWO OR THREE COMBINATIONS OF TIME, SPEED AND DISTANCE COMPRISING A SET: DATA ARRANGED BY STUDY AND BY GRADE

COMBINATIONS JUDGED POSSIBLE (P) OR IMPOSSIBLE (I)			ACREDOLO, ET AL. (1984) GRADES					STUDY 2A GRADES				STUDIES 2B&2C GRADES		
			1	2	3	4	5	2	3	4	5	4	5	ADULT
		n=	(12)	(12)	(12)	(12)	(12)	(13)	(15)	(13)	(13)	(18)	(18)	(30)
							Set *DS*							
ds(p)	*dst(p)*	*ds/t(p)*												
I	I	I	—	—	—	—	—	8	13	0	0	3	0	0
P	I	I	0	8	0	0	0	0	7	8	8	0	0	0
I	P	I	58	25	8	8	42	31	7	0	8	19	19	2
I	I	P	0	17	17	33	25	8	13	8	8	6	3	4
P	P	I	25	8	0	8	0	15	7	23	15	17	19	4
P	I	P	0	0	8	0	8	8	7	8	0	0	3	8
I	P	P	8	33	33	0	8	15	7	0	8	33	3	2
P	*P*	*P*	*8*	*8*	*33*	*50*	*17*	*15*	*40*	*54*	*54*	*33*	*53*	*79*
							Set *D/S*							
d/s(i)	*dt/s(p)*	*d/st(i)*												
I	I	I	—	—	—	—	—	31	13	15	38	11	11	7
P	I	I	0	0	0	8	0	0	7	0	8	3	8	1
I	*P*	*I*	*50*	*33*	*58*	*17*	*58*	*46*	*33*	*31*	*54*	*50*	*42*	*58*
I	I	P	25	33	17	33	33	0	13	8	0	3	3	1
P	P	I	17	0	8	17	8	15	7	23	0	14	19	17
P	I	P	0	0	0	0	0	0	0	0	0	3	0	2
I	P	P	0	17	0	8	0	0	13	8	0	11	8	6
P	P	P	8	17	17	17	0	8	13	15	0	6	8	9

Note: Correct patterns are italicized. Since the nature of the procedure used by Acredolo, et al. (1984) made it impossible for subjects to reject all the combinations within a set, no entry is shown for those particular patterns.

Table 6.3

PERCENTAGE WITH WHICH SUBJECTS ENDORSED AS POSSIBLE EACH COMBINATION OF DISTANCE, SPEED AND TIME: DATA ARRANGED BY STUDY AND BY GRADE

COMBINATION	ACREDOLO, ET AL. (1984) GRADES					STUDY 2A GRADES				STUDIES 2B&2C GRADES		
	1	2	3	4	5	2	3	4	5	4	5	ADULT
n=	(12)	(12)	(12)	(12)	(12)	(13)	(15)	(13)	(13)	(18)	(18)	(30)
Set *EQ*												
$eq_{(p)}$	83	92	92	83	100	77	87	100	85	97	100	98
$t_{(i)}$	50	25	17	17	0	31	67	38	15	3	8	4
Set *D*												
$d_{(i)}$	8	8	25	17	8	38	40	54	15	22	11	6
$dt_{(p)}$	92	83	92	58	83	62	60	100	85	50	78	88
$d/t_{(i)}$	17	25	42	25	25	38	60	69	23	22	11	16
Set *S*												
$s_{(i)}$	42	33	0	17	25	15	47	46	0	19	14	10
$st_{(i)}$	75	17	17	17	0	15	33	31	8	19	17	11
$s/t_{(p)}$	8	58	83	67	75	38	80	69	77	50	81	96
Set *DS*												
$ds_{(p)}$	33	25	42	58	25	38	60	92	77	39	75	91
$dst_{(p)}$	100	75	75	67	67	77	60	77	85	92	94	88
$ds/t_{(p)}$	17	58	92	83	58	46	67	69	69	61	61	93
Set *D/S*												
$d/s_{(i)}$	25	17	25	42	8	23	27	38	8	25	36	29
$dt/s_{(p)}$	75	67	83	58	67	69	67	77	54	81	78	89
$d/st_{(i)}$	33	67	33	58	33	8	40	31	0	22	19	18

STUDIES 2A, B AND C: CHILDREN'S RECOGNITION OF THE NECESSARY INTERRELATIONS BETWEEN RELATIVE TIMES, SPEEDS AND DISTANCES

In this variation of the *Assessing Combinations* method, subjects were presented all 14 combinations of relative speed, distance and duration listed as outcomes in Table 6.1 — seven possible and seven impossible combinations. It was the subjects' task to evaluate each combination and determine on their own whether that combination was in fact possible. Whereas in the former study subjects were asked to consider the possibility of all three alternatives only after spontaneously endorsing one, in the present study the children were presented the same three combinations of relative speed, distance, and duration, but on separate trials, randomly ordered, so that each was considered independently from the others. In the former study subjects may have endorsed only one outcome for each problem because of a bias against answering a question by listing possible solutions. In the present procedure subjects were free to endorse more than one combination per set or none at all since each problem now required that the child answer by selecting only one of two alternatives, possible or impossible.

This basic procedure was actually used in three separate studies, grouped together here as Study 2a, 2b and 2c. Small differences in the application of the procedure prevent a direct comparison of one with another, but 2a is the primary study, while 2b and 2c may be considered follow-up studies. After more fully explaining the basic procedure shared by all three studies, I will fully detail Study 2a and then briefly summarize 2b and 2c.

General Procedure

Each of the 14 problems were presented to subjects in the context of evaluating the reported outcome of a long distance race between two people or animals. Subjects were instructed that the two runners always started at the same time and place, and although they followed the same course, they did not always run the same distance, the same speed, or for the same amount of time. Subjects were told the reported results of the race in terms of who ran farthest, who ran fastest, and who ran for the longest amount of time, from start to stop, and they then had to determine if this announced outcome was in fact possible.

The 14 problems were presented one at a time, and the order of administration was randomized for each subject. Problems were presented in both written and oral form, and subjects were free to review the problems as long as they wished. They were urged to think each problem through carefully before announcing their decision. No graphic displays of the races were presented, and subjects were not provided models by which they might attempt to duplicate the announced race.

It should be noted that the difficulty of problems involving inverse relationships may depend in part on whether one refers to both runners or to just one – "*X* traveled farther but *Y* traveled faster" versus "*X* traveled farther but slower". This variable was not systematically examined, but in all three of the studies reported here, the both runner method was always used.

In order to facilitate a comparison with the results of Acredolo, et al. the responses to the 14 questions from each of the studies in this section have been grouped into sets identical to those formed by the problems shown in Table 6.1. Further, the data have been analyzed in much the same fashion. Table 6.2. thus summarizes the percentage of children in each grade displaying each of the various response patterns for the problems in each of the five sets, while Table 6.3 summarizes the percentage who endorsed as possible each of the 14 combinations of time, speed and distance.

Study 2a

SAMPLE AND METHODS

In the first application of the procedure, 13 2nd grade, 15 3rd grade, 13 4th grade and 13 5th grade children from a rural Northern California public school were presented each of the 14 problems only once. The problems all concerned the outcome of the following event: Two rabbits feeding on a farmer's garden are surprised by a dog and together run as fast as possible down a road until they can run no farther. All problems were worded the same. The first sentence detailed which rabbit had gone farther, the second detailed which had run faster and the third detailed which had run longer. Each problem was presented in typewritten form on a 3" x 8.5" card. The experimenter first read the card then placed it before the child. The children were encouraged to think the problems through before giving their answers, and the experimenter reread the cards as often as needed.

RESULTS

The differences in performance across grade were slight on individual problems, but a one-way analysis of variance on the number of correct answers across all 14 problems revealed a significant grade effect, $F(3,50)=6.24$, $p<.001$. Subsequent comparisons indicated that performance did not differ significantly across the three youngest grades, but improved markedly between fourth and fifth grades, $F(1,50)=6.45$, $p<.025$. The 2nd through 4th grade children averaged 9.2 problems correct, while the 5th grade children averaged 11.6 problems correct.

Examination of Table 6.3 and 6.4 reveals that the differences in performance across grade occur primarily on the seven impossible combinations. Whereas the 5th grade children performed equally well on the seven possible and seven impossible combinations, the 3rd and 4th grade children performed significantly better on the seven possible combinations ($p<.05$, Wilcoxon test). Across the five sets of problems, the same basic pattern can be seen: There is little change across grades in the frequency with which a possible combination is correctly judged possible, but there was a sharp decline between 4th and 5th grades in the frequency with which an impossible combination is incorrectly judged possible. On Set *EQ*, there was little difference in the frequency with which children judged $eq_{(p)}$ as possible (particularly between 3rd and 5th grades), but there was a substantial decline by 5th grade in the frequency with which the children judged $t_{(i)}$ possible (Fisher's Exact $p=.044$ when contrasting 2nd–4th with 5th grades). On Set *D*, there was little difference across grades in the frequency with which children judged $dt_{(p)}$ possible, but a substantial decline by 5th grade in the frequency with which they judged $d_{(i)}$ and $d/t_{(i)}$ possible ($p=.048$ and $p=.006$, respectively, when contrasting 4th with 5th grades). On Set *S*, there was little difference across grades in the frequency with which children judged $s/t_{(p)}$ possible, but a substantial decline by 5th grade in the frequency with which they judged $s_{(i)}$ and $st_{(i)}$ possible ($p=.008$ and $p=.161$, respectively, when contrasting 4th and 5th grades). On Set *DS*, where all three combinations are possible, there was little developmental change at all. Finally, on Set *D/S*, there was little difference in the frequency with which children judged $dt/s_{(p)}$ possible, but a substantial decline in the frequency with which they judged $d/s_{(i)}$ and $d/st_{(i)}$ possible ($p=.080$ and $p=.048$, respectively, when contrasting 4th with 5th grade children).

Thus, younger children performed much worse in this procedure than they had in the Acredolo, et al. (1984) procedure. As anticipated, they had the ability to deduce a correct relative duration given information concerning relative distance and speed, but they could not recognize the natural necessities involved that make this solution the only solution possible. While the frequency with which children in the Acredolo, et al. study displayed the correct pattern of responses to Problems *D* and *S* clearly exceed chance, in the present study the frequency with which the 2nd through 4th grade children endorsed the correct pattern of responses to the problems in Sets *D* and *S* failed to exceed chance. Further, there were no significant differences in the frequency with which children answered correctly the problems in Sets *D* and *S* compared to the problems in Sets *DS* and *D/S*. These results suggest that the bivariate relations are not truly understood until much later than that suggested by Acredolo, et al. (1984), and they are probably mastered contemporaneously with the trivariate relations.

The 3rd and 4th grade children were clearly more discerning than the 2nd grade children. Almost all recognized that $cq_{(p)}$ is possible, and they continued to recognize that $dt_{(p)}$ is possible. But in addition, many now accepted $s/t_{(p)}$ and $ds/t_{(p)}$ as possible. On the other hand, many 3rd and 4th grade children were still judging possible many impossible combinations of time, speed and distance. That is, they still failed to display an awareness of the natural necessities involved in the interrelations of dimensions.

By 5th grade the responses are more orderly and accurate. A majority of these children correctly recognized possible combinations and rejected impossible combinations, and whereas the 3rd and 4th graders had greater difficulty with the impossible combinations than with the possible combinations, the 5th grade children had equal success at responding appropriately to both types of combinations. Even the problems in Sets *DS* and *D/S* were handled accurately by a majority of 5th grade children.

SUMMARY

These data contrast sharply with those from the Acredolo, et al. (1984) study, but in combination the two studies yield a clearer picture of children's capacity to reason about time, speed and distance interrelations. As suspected, the Acredolo, et al. paradigm yielded a spuriously high impression of children's understanding of the bivariate distance $\longleftrightarrow$ time and speed $\longleftrightarrow$ time relations. Although 2nd through 4th grade children do fairly well at deducing one possible relative duration on the basis of information concerning differing distances or speeds, they were quite deficient in recognizing impossible relative durations. These children do not yet understand the natural necessities involved in the interrelations between dimensions. Simply asking children to estimate durations on the basis of distance and speed information will not reveal this deficiency, and asking them to consider the possibility of other solutions after they have just endorsed one runs up against a strong response bias against endorsing more than one solution to a problem. It is only by asking children to consider combinations across independent trials that one sees the limits of the understanding. While the ability to accurately deduce relative durations on the basis of relative distance and speed information may appear as early as 2nd grade, at 6 to 7 years of age, the data from this study suggest that a complete understanding of the logical and natural necessities involved in distance ⟷ time and speed ⟷ time relations is not mastered before 5th grade, at 10 to 11 years of age, and possibly not until much later.

While the 5th grade children performed quite well in this study it was still unclear whether they were performing at a level equivalent to that displayed by adult subjects in the same procedure. Thus, in order to better evaluate the performance of the 5th grade children, we needed to assess adults' capacity to perform the same reasoning. The two studies that follow reexamine the observed differences in performance between 4th and 5th grade children and assess the capacities of adults on the same task.

Study 2b and 2c

SAMPLE AND METHOD

The next two applications of the paradigm were completed in collaboration with Anne Adams. Two major changes were made in the basic procedure. First, each subject was administered the 14 problems more than just once, and second, response times were recorded as well as judgments. In each administration of the 14 problems, the order in which time, speed and distance information appeared was systematically altered. Three of the six possible orders were selected, yielding three conditions. In one condition relative speeds were listed first, then relative times, and finally relative distances; in a second condition time was listed first, then distance, then speed; and in a third condition distance was listed first, then speed, and finally time. This last condition was identical to that used in Study 2a.

In Study 2b 18 4th grade and 18 5th grade children were each administered the 14 problems twice, each receiving two of the three possible conditions. The distribution of conditions and their order of administration was balanced within grade. Since these children were from a university community and attended a public school in which students had displayed outstanding performance on nationwide achievement tests, it was anticipated that their performance would exceed somewhat that of the same aged children in Study 2a. In study 2c, 30 undergraduate college students were each administered the 14 problems three times, each subject experiencing all three conditions with the order of administration balanced across subjects. In both studies, subjects received all 14 problems in one set before receiving problems in the next, and the order of problems within each set was randomized for each administration. Given that condition influenced performance only in complex interaction with the order in which conditions were administered, the condition variable will not be considered further in this report. Performance is thus averaged across all administrations of the same problem.

In both studies the problems were presented as representing the results of a race between two human runners. Male subjects were offered common male names for the two runners, while the females were offered common female names. Each problem was presented in typewritten form on a separate 4"x 6" card. The experimenter first read the card then placed it before the subject. In Study 2b, an assistant surreptitiously recorded the child's time-to-solution for each problem, while in Study 2c, the experimenter openly recorded time-to-solution after informing the undergraduates that this was being done to compare the difficulty of one problem with another and not to compare their performance with that of their age mates. Timing began the instant the card was placed in front of the subjects and ended the moment the subjects announced their judgment. Subjects were repeatedly encouraged to double-check themselves before announcing their solutions.

RESULTS

The resulting data can again be found in Tables 6.2 and 6.3, through it should be noted that in this case the numbers represent the percentage of responses rather than the percentage of subjects since each entry is averaged across two or three administrations of each problem. One-way repeated measures analyses of variance indicated that time-to-solution varied significantly across problems for both the 4th and 5th grade children, $F(13,455)=4.26$, $p<.001$, and for the adults, $F(13,377)=8.02$, $p<.001$. Post hoc comparison indicated, aside from the fact that Problem $eq_{(p)}$ was always solved very quickly, that times varied primarily as a function of whether or not the problem referred to one or both runners. For the children, Problem $d/s_{(i)}$ took significantly longer to solve than did Problem $ds_{(p)}$,

$F(1,35)=9.75$, $p<.005$, and Problems $ds/t_{(p)}$, $d/st_{(i)}$ and $dt/s_{(p)}$ took significantly longer to solve than did Problem $dst_{(p)}$, $F(1,35)=6.62$, $p<.025$. For the adults, Problem $d/t_{(i)}$ took significantly longer to solve than did Problem $dt_{(p)}$, $F(1,29)=5.43$, $p<.05$, Problem $d/s_{(i)}$ took significantly longer to solve than did Problem $ds_{(p)}$, $F(1,29)=15.05$, $p<.001$, and Problems $ds/t_{(p)}$, $dt/s_{(p)}$, and $d/st_{(i)}$ took significantly longer to solve than did Problem $dst_{(p)}$, $F(1,29)=4.438$, $p<.05$. For neither sample did time-to-solution vary systematically with the number of asymmetries involved in the problem (i.e. the number of dimensions on which the runners differed). Time-to-solution also bore no significant association with judgment (possible or impossible) or with accuracy.

Examination of Tables 6.2 and 6.3 shows that the 4th and 5th grade subjects in Study 2b were performing much as their age mates in Study 2a. In terms of total scores, the 5th grade children again outperformed the 4th grade children, $t(34)=2.07$, $p<.05$. The 4th graders averaged 10.4 problems correct, while the 5th graders averaged 11.5 problems correct. As in Study 2a, performance on Set *D* did not differ significantly from performance on Set *S*, and performance on Problem $dt_{(p)}$ did not differ significantly from performance on Problem $s/t_{(p)}$. Unlike the children in Study 2a, however, the 4th graders did exceed chance in displaying the correct pattern of response to the three combinations in Set *D* and to the three combinations in Set *S*, though only barely so, and they did not show significantly greater success on the seven possible combinations than on the seven impossible combinations. Thus, in this sample, the 4th grade children were at least approaching the standards set by the 5th grade children in Study 2a.

The adults in Study 2c, on the other hand, were clearly performing better than the 5th grade children in either Study 2a or Study 2b. Surprising, however, their performance was not flawless. This is probably attributable in part to the fact that they were being openly timed. In point of fact, six of the 30 adults (20%) did perform flawlessly across the 42 problems, and just three of the adults accounted for 40% of all the errors made. Disregarding the six who performed flawlessly and the three who performed poorly, the median number of errors was only 3.5 – slightly over one error in every set of 14 problems. Across all 30 subjects, the adults averaged 12.8 problems correct per set of 14.

While errors were infrequent among the adults, those errors that did occur can be explained easily if one accepts that they resulted when the adults, fatigued by having to evaluate 42 difficult problems, and feeling anxious and impulsive due to the open timing of their responses, fell back on intuitions. Note that the adults had the greatest difficulty with the problems in Set *D/S*. Their performance here was significantly worse than on the problems in each of the other sets (all $p<.05$, Wilcoxon test). The single most frequently missed problem was $d/s_{(i)}$ (i.e.,"*X* traveled farther, *Y* traveled faster, and *X* and *Y* travelled for the same amount of time"). This error should come as no surprise given the literature on false conservations (Lunzer, 1968; Pinard & Chase, 1977; Russel, 1976). Older children, adolescents and adults come to anticipate reciprocal relations between related variables, and they often assume the existence of conservations where there are none. In this case it may be conjectured that the subjects falsely anticipated a compensatory relationship between distance and speed relative to time (i.e., one can travel for the same amount of time by travelling a longer distance at a lower speed). This explanation also accounts for the occasional incorrect endorsement $d/t_{(i)}$ and the very low frequency of error on $s/t_{(p)}$. Time-to-solution for both $d/t_{(i)}$ and $d/s_{(i)}$ were among the longest seen, while that for $s/t_{(p)}$ was relatively short, suggesting that the adults recognized at some level the dubiousness of their logic for the former and the certainty of their logic for the latter. The errors on $d/st_{(i)}$ also require explanation. Time-to-solution was highest on this problem, and it may be supposed that the errors were in part a mere function of burdened memory. On the other hand, given the occasional acceptance of $d/s_{(i)}$ and $d/t_{(i)}$, it follows that subjects would also occasionally juxtapose these two intuitions and accept $d/st_{(i)}$ as possible. Again, however, it is important to recognize that all these errors were infrequent and never consistently offered by any one adult subject. It is reasonable, therefore, to accept that they represent only quickly offered intuitive solutions rather than systematic and stable misunderstandings.

SUMMARY

Study 2b replicated Study 2a in revealing a difference between 4th and 5th grade children in their ability to recognize possible and impossible combinations of distance, speed and time. Unlike the 4th grade children in Study 2a, however, the errors of the 4th graders in Study 2b were not primarily attributable to an inability to recognize impossible combinations.

Study 2c demonstrates that even adults make occasional errors when evaluating possible and impossible combinations of distance, speed and time, a fact that makes the performance of the 5th grade subjects in Studies 2a and 2b look all the more impressive. Nevertheless, it is clear that the average 5th grader was not yet performing at the average adult level.

Discussion

Before discussing the results of these studies and drawing final conclusions, it should be pointed out that there is one potential threat to the validity of this fourth method. The procedure presents subjects with particularly difficult reasoning problems, problems that clearly impose a load on working memory and processing capacity. The fact that most adults make at least occasional errors on these problems may be taken as evidence that the procedure assesses more than an understanding of time, speed and distance interrelations. It assesses general reasoning capacity as well. Thus it is unclear whether the observed differences in the performance of the 5th graders in Studies 2a and 2b and the performance of the adults in Study 2c represent differences in the proportion of subjects in the two age groups possessing a clear understanding of the interrelationships between the dimensions or merely differences in processing capacities of the two groups. I suspect that both factors combine to yield the observed differences. The degree to which age differences in processing capacity account for the observed differences in the performance of older versus younger children in Study 2a is similarly unclear. Thus, my conclusions concerning the exact age at which children gain an understanding of the necessary interrelations between time, speed and distance must remain conjecture, and further work will be required to clarify the matter. On the other hand, the findings from this method are in general agreement with investigations of the children's grasp of logical necessity. Piaget, for example (Inhelder and Piaget, 1958), suggested that the appreciation of logical necessity emerges late in childhood and is a prerequisite for hypothetico-deductive reasoning. In addition, several empirical studies (e.g., Bereiter, Hidi, & Dimitroff, 1979; Miscione, Marvin, O'Brien, & Greenberg; 1978; Somerville, Hadkinson, & Greenberg, 1979) suggest that notions of logical and natural necessity begin to emerge in middle childhood. Certainly a complete understanding of speed, time and distance interrelationships requires a grasp of the necessities involved, and it would be surprising to find children displaying this level of knowledge at a young age.

The above caution not withstanding, Study 2a and the follow-up studies 2b and 2c make one strong point. Although young children may be aware of the correlations between dimensions, and thus quite adept at using distance and speed information to deduce a possible outcome in terms of absolute or relative durations, they have considerable difficulty in recognizing when a particular combination of relative time, speed and distance is impossible. If we can trust the data obtained using the fourth method, then children do not understand the necessary interrelations of time, speed and distance until relatively late in the childhood period. Further, it appears that children begin to understand the natural necessities involved in the bivariate distance ⟷ time and speed ⟷ time relations at about the same time as they begin to grasp the complete trivariate relation.

SUMMARY AND CONCLUSIONS

Children's understanding of the interrelations between time, speed and distance has been investigated through the use of four different methods. All four suffer threats to their validity, but taken in concert, a fairly clear picture of the development of children's understanding of time, speed and distance interrelations emerges. It appears that by early childhood, most children are aware of the correlations between distance and duration and between speed and duration, and most have the capacity to imagine movements over specified distances at specified speeds, but they do not yet understand the necessary relations between dimensions. This is manifested in two ways. First, they overgeneralize their understanding of the relations between pairs of dimensions to situations in which the third variable is not held constant. Second, they accept as possible combinations of time, distance and speed that are in fact impossible. A complete understanding of the necessary interrelations between time, speed and distance appears to develop in middle or late childhood. The exact period is still uncertain given questions concerning the influence of performance factors on children's behavior in the various tasks described in this chapter. Further research will be needed to resolve the issue to greater satisfaction.

Young children's awareness of the correlations between pairs of dimensions gets them fairly far, and this knowledge may be sufficient for most day-to-day activities including academic pursuits. Their awareness of the correlations enables them do well on tasks that require that they determine exact or relative durations on the basis of speed or distance cues. On the other hand, as demonstrated by Piaget and Montangero, their incomplete understanding may still lead them to make occasional glaring errors such as arguing that duration is directly related to speed or inversely related to distance. Their lack of understanding concerning the necessary interrelations between dimensions also appears to lead them to relying on just distance or speed cues when asked to report which of two directly perceived moving objects travels for the longest amount of time.

Once children understand the necessary interrelations between dimensions, however, they may be expected to abandon any attempt to equate duration with distance and/or speed and turn instead to evaluating start and stop time cues.

Besides testing the above conclusions concerning the development of an understanding of the interrelations between time, speed and distance with still other methods, there are number of additional questions that deserve attention. For example, are other trivariate relations acquired at the same time? Does their acquisition mark a specific qualitative change in children's thinking? What level of understanding is necessary for children to benefit from specific curricula dealing with the interrelations between dimensions? The trainability of mature understanding is still unclear, but if training is possible, what broader benefits result in terms of general cognitive development and academic success?

References

Acredolo, C. (1981). The acquisition of conservation: A clarification of Piagetian terminology, some recent findings, and an alternative formulation. *Human Development*, **24**, 120–137.

Acredolo, C. (1982). Conservation-Nonconservation: Alternative explanations. In C.J. Brainerd (Ed.), *Children's logical and mathematical cognition: Progress in cognitive development research.* (pp.1–31). New York: Springer-Verlag.

Acredolo, C. & Schmid, J. (1981). The understanding of relative speeds, distances, and durations of movements. *Developmental Psychology*, **17**, 490–493.

Acredolo, C., Adams, A., & Schmid, J. (1984). On the understanding of the relationships between speed, duration, and distance. *Child Development*, **55**, 2151–2159.

Acredolo, A. & Horobin, K. (1987). Development of relational reasoning and avoidance of premature closure. *Developmental psychology*, **23**, 13–21.

Anderson, N. H. (1980). Information integration theory in developmental psychology. In F. Wilkening, J. Becker, & T. Trabasso (Eds.), *Information integration by children.* (pp. 1–45). Hillsdale, N.J.: Erlbaum.

Bereiter, C., Hidi, S., & Dimitroff, G. (1979). Qualitative changes in verbal reasoning during middle and late childhood. *Child Development, 50*, 141–151.

Berndt, T. J., & Wood. D. J. (1974). The development of time concepts through conflict based on primitive duration capacity. *Child Development*, **45**, 825–828.

Braine, M., & Rumain, B. (1983). Logical reasoning. In J. H. Flavell & E. M. Markman (Eds.), *Cognitive development. Carmichael's manual of child psychology (4th ed., pp. 263–340). New York: Wiley.*

Fraisse, P., & Vaultrey, P. (1952) La perception de l'espace, de la vitesse et du temps chez l'enfant de 5 ans. II: Le temp, *Enfance*, **1**, 102–119.

Inhelder, B., & Piaget, J. (1958). *The growth of logical thinking from childhood to adolescence.* New York: Basic Books.

Levin, I. (1977). The development of time concepts in young children: Reasoning about duration. *Child Development*, **48**, 435–444.

Levin, I. (1979). Interference of time-related and unrelated cues with duration comparisons of young children: Analysis of Piaget's formulation of the relation of time and speed. *Child Development*, **50**, 469–477.

Levin, I. (1982). The nature and development of time concepts in children: The effects of interfering cues. In W. J. Friedman (Ed.), *The developmental psychology of time.* (pp. 47–85). New York: Academic Press.

Levin, I., Israeli, E., & Darom, E. (1978). The development of time concepts in young children: The relations between duration and succession. *Child Development*, **49**, 755–764.

Levin, I. & Gilat, I. (1983). A developmental analysis of early time concepts: The equivalence and additivity of the effect of interfering cues on duration comparisons of young children. *Child Development*, **55**, 2151–2159.

Levin, I. & Gilat, I., & Zelniker, T. (1980). The role of cue salience in the development of time concepts: Duration comparisons in young children. *Developmental Psychology*, **16**, 661–671.

Levin, I. & Globerson, T. (1984). The development of time concepts among advantaged and disadvantaged Israeli children. *Journal of Genetic Psychology*, **145**, 117–125.

Levin, I. & Simons, H. (1986). The nature of children's and adults' concepts of time, speed, and distance and their sequence in development: Analysis via circular motion. In I. Levin (Ed.), *Stage and Structure: Reopening the debate.* (pp. 77–105). N.J.: Ablex.

Lovell, K., & Slater, N. (1960) The growth of the concept of time: a comparative study. *Child Psychology and Psychiatry*, **1**, 179–190.

Lunzer, E. A. (1968). Formal reasoning. In E.A. Lunzer & J. F. Morris (Eds.), *Development in human learning.* New York: American Elsevier.

Miscione, J. L. Marvin, R. S., O'Brien, R. G., & Greenberg, M. T. (1978). A developmental study of preschool children's understanding of the words "know" and "guess". *Child Development*, **49**, 1007–1113.

Montangero, J. (1977). *La notion de durée chez l'enfant de 5 à 9 ans.* Paris: Presses Universitaires de France.

Montangero, J. (1979). Les relations du temps, de la vitesse et de l'espace par course chez le jeune enfant. *L'Année Psychologie*, **79**, 23–42.

Piaget, J. (1969) *The child's conception of time.* London: Routledge & Kegan Paul.

Piaget, J. (1970) *The child's conception of movement and speed.* London: Routledge & Kegan Paul.

Pinard, A., & Chase, G. (1977). Pseudoconservation of volume and surface area of a solid object. *Child Development*, **48**, 1559–1566.

Richards, D. D. (1982) Children's time concepts: Going the distance. In W. J. Friedman, *The developmental psychology of time.* (pp. 13–45). New York: Academic Press.

Russel, J. (1976). Nonconservation of area: Do children succeed where adults fail. *Developmental Psychology*, **12**, 367–368.

Siegler, R. S., & Richards, D. D. (1979) The development of time, speed and distance concepts. *Developmental Psychology*, **15**, 288–298.

Silverman, I. W., & Rose, A. (1981) Compensation and conservation. *Psychological Bulletin*, **91**, 80–101.

Somerville, S. C., Hadkinson, B. A., & Greenberg, C. (1979). Two levels of inferential behavior in young children. *Child Development*, **50**, 119–130.

Wilkening, F. (1981) Integrating velocity, time, and distance information: A developmental study. *Cognitive psychology*, **13**, 231–247.

Wilkening, F. (1982) Children's knowledge about time, distance, and velocity interrelations. In W. J. Friedman, *The developmental psychology of time.* (pp. 87–112). New York: Academic Press.

TIME AND HUMAN COGNITION
A Life-Span Perspective
I. Levin and D. Zakay (Editors)

CHAPTER 7

WILLIAM J. FRIEDMAN

The Representation of Temporal Structure in Children, Adolescents and Adults

INTRODUCTION

One of the fundamental attributes of our environment is its patterning in time. We live in a world in which astronomical phenomena produce recurrent cycles of light and dark, phases of the moon, and seasonal changes in day length and temperature. Superimposed on our biological adaptation to these periodicities are cultural adaptations in the form of conventional time representations. Calendars, clocks and other schedules incorporate astronomical cycles, add to them series and cycles that are purely arbitrary, and these together provide frameworks for individual and collective action.

In this chapter I consider two temporal patterns on the long time scales of calendar time, days of the week and months. These patterns pose a substantial representational challenge because they include numerous elements, are experienced one element at a time, and are rich in structural features like order and recurrence. Yet adults are able to use this information flexibly to remember the time of past events,orient to the present and plan for the future. In the following discussion, I will try to characterize the representations and processes that underly this knowledge in adults and describe how they change from childhood to adulthood. We will begin by considering the nature of the information contained in the week and month systems and a number of ways in which this knowledge could be modeled. Next, I will present a particular model and describe a series of studies that apply it to adults' performance. The model is then used in several studies to examine the development of children's representations of the days of the week and months of the year. Finally, I will discuss the implication of these findings for our understanding of representational development.

MODELS OF THE REPRESENTATION OF TIME STRUCTURES

Properties of the Systems

What does it mean to say that someone understands the days of the week or months systems? At the most basic level is the knowledge that the elements belong to the sets—that Monday, Friday, etc. are days of the week or that March, September, etc. are months of the year. Other aspects might be knowing the conventional first element and perhaps knowing common associates of the elements. However, any real understanding of the systems must include the order in which they occur. Interestingly, this order can be construed in several different ways, and the way in which one characterizes it will influence the type of representational model one chooses. One sense of knowing the order of elements is knowing the day or month that follows any other one. A second is knowing what day or month is a particular "distance"—say three days or months—after or before another. Still a third is knowing that if it is Wednesday, then Saturday will occur before Monday does. We can easily construct a formal model, such as a repeating number cycle, that captures all of these aspects of order. But in order to choose a model that is psychologically accurate, it is essential to know what operations can be performed and how they are performed. By analogy, we cannot rely on mathematicians' formal descriptions of number but need to study the ability to count, to perform arithmetic operations, and so forth.

Before turning to studies of reasoning about the months and days of the week, it is useful to consider a number of possible models of knowledge of the order of elements in these systems. These models capture somewhat different aspects of order and lead to different predictions about performance on temporal problem solving tasks.

Possible Models

There are many ways in which the relationship between day and month elements could be encoded and processed. The following examples are by no means exhaustive, but serve to illustrate this variety. First, one could imagine that elements are linked by associations of various strengths in an associative network. Pairs of days or months that are contiguous would have stronger bonds than those that are farther apart in time. Second, the relationship between many or all pairs of elements could be stored in individual propositions. For example, one proposition in the week representation might encode the information that Thursday is three days after Monday. Semantic or categorical models offer a third way of representing order. In this kind of model, each element would be associated with one or more linguistic codes that correspond to part of the week or year. Monday might be linked to "early", Wednesday to "middle", and so forth. Fourth, one could construct an arithmetic model in which each element was associated with a number. Operations like addition and subtraction could be used to establish the relationship between different elements.

Two further models are discussed more fully in the next section, since they are the main models to be tested, One is a serial model, in which each element is linked to the next, such that elements can be sequentially activated. In the other, an image model, position-like information is directly encoded, allowing perception-like detection of the relative proximity of elements.

These six models make different predictions about how people judge the order of days or months. For example, a serial model implies that judging the separation of two months will take more time the greater the number of intervening months. A propositional model would not predict such an effect, assuming separations are directly coded. Another example is that numerical models would imply greater difficulty when elements from two cycles, say Friday of one week and Tuesday of the next, must be related. This is because the normal coding (e.g., 3 and 6) does not correctly capture their relative time of occurrence. Many of the models can be evaluated in the experiments to be described. However, I will emphasize the following particular model, because it has turned out to provide the best account of the available data.

The Image—Verbal-List Model

Much work in cognitive psychology seems to assume that a particular kind of representation underlies knowledge of a given domain. In my model I will propose that several representational-processing systems are involved in reasoning about the months and days of the week. Two of these, a verbal-list system and an image system, are assumed to be responsible for the ability to judge the order of days or months.

The verbal-list system codes links between each day or month and its successor, with reciprocal links being substantially weaker. Processing in this system involves the verbal-articulatory activation of individual elements either vocally or covertly. I assume that in the course of processing, one element is most active at any time, that there is a minimum activation time for an element, and that activating an element is a discrete event that can be counted.

These features have a number of implications for the behavior of people using the verbal-list system to solve order problems. First, the system should be especially difficult to use while counting, reciting the alphabet or performing other tasks presumed to involve verbal-list processing. Second, forward order judgments should be faster and more accurate than backward order judgments, because the elements are assumed to be more strongly linked to their successors than their predecessors. Third, processing time should increase monotonically with the number of elements to be activated. This follows from assuming a minimum time needed to activate each element. Finally, the verbal nature of the system would be consistent with overt reciting, lip movement or reports of covert reciting.

The verbal-list system would seem to be advantageous for "measuring" operations, such as determining what month is three after March. On the other hand, operations like comparing the order of nonadjacent months, particularly in a backward direction, should be relatively difficult to perform using this system.

The image system codes position-like information for each month or day, and is used to construct spatial-like mental models of the relative times of occurrence of different elements. These representations are assumed to be functionally analogous to overt schematizations of month or day positions in that information about multiple elements is simultaneously available, and this information is extracted by means of perception-like processes.

Use of the image system should lead to a number of specific effects. First, if spatial reasoning or spatial monitoring rely on image processes, as several authors assume (e.g., Brooks, 1968), we would expect selective interference between performing these types of tasks and using the image system to solve day or month problems. Second, the image system implies a number of "analog effects." Analog effects are similarities between the pattern of performance shown when subjects perform some mental task and the expected pattern when some overt perceptual task is performed. For example, one would expect that the difficulty of comparing the length of two intervals of months (e.g., February to May vs. July to November) would increase as the difference between their lengths becomes smaller. By analogy, comparison of the lengths of two line segments is more difficult the more similar their lengths (Woodworth & Schlosberg, 1965). Third, we might expect to find reports of the experience of imagery, such as descriptions of spatial forms of the months or days, when the image system is used.

Two predictions concern differences between properties of the image system and verbal-list system. Backward order judgments should be substantially more difficult than forward order judgments in the verbal-list system but this directional difference should be small or nonexistent for the image system. This is because the image system makes position information simultaneously available, and there is no reason to expect that the detection process will have strong directional properties. However, the verbal-list system does have a directional bias. Another difference between the two systems is in the time it takes to judge the relationship between two elements as a function of the number of elements between them. The verbal-list system requires more time to cover larger separations, because each intervening element must be activated. In contrast, position information is directly coded in the image system, so intervening elements need not be activated. Separation effects should occur in the image system only if some scanning-like operation is used, but we would still expect stronger "distance effects" in the verbal-list than image system.

In addition to image and verbal-list coding of order information, it seems likely that the elements are embedded in networks of semantic associations. These networks might link days and months with holidays, weather characteristics, personal events, and so forth. Seymour (1980a) has found some consensus in subjects' associations between months and colors, plant growth, and temperature. These sorts of associations probably play little role in judgments of the relative time of occurrence of different days or months, but they do seem to be important in recalling the time of past events (e.g., Baddeley, Lewis & Nimmo-Smith, 1978; Friedman & Wilkins, 1985).

A final assumption of the model described here is that the image and verbal-list systems will be spontaneously applied to different types of tasks, at least by adults who are presumed to have both systems available. The verbal-list system should be favored on "measuring" tasks, in which subjects are asked to identify the month or day that is *n* away from another or to compare the length of pairs of intervals that differ only slightly. This is because the sequential activation of elements lends itself to counting. The simultaneous availability of position-like information in the image system makes it suitable for judging the relative proximity of months, as long as most problems do not require fine discriminations. This system is likely to be used in such tasks as judging which of two nonadjacent days or months will come before the other when moving either forward or backward from a third day or month.

In this model I have assumed that the image and verbal-list systems differ in the way that temporal relational information is stored and processed. The format in which the information is stored is presumed to impose limits on how it can be manipulated. Of course one could devise a more elaborate model in which information from a common representation can be transformed into image-like or verbal-like temporary data structures. But it is not obvious how to empirically distinguish between a one-representation two-process model and a model with two representation-processing pairs. Thus it seems more productive to begin by evaluating the validity of the two-system distinction and to leave for future research the task of determining the ultimate representational format.

RESEARCH ON ADULTS' REPRESENTATIONS

In this section we will consider a number of different kinds of evidence that support the involvement of image and verbal-list processing in adults' reasoning about the months of the year and days of the week. The findings bear on the two-system distinction and help to characterize the nature of the underlying processes. Many of the findings also weigh against alternative models of performance on the tasks.

Selective Interference

STUDY 1

The first study that I will describe (Friedman, 1983, Experiment 1) used the method of selective interference to test the image—verbal-list distinction. The method is based on the assumption that two tasks that involve a common type of processing will be more difficult to perform concurrently than two that involve different types of processing. Perhaps the best known example of the selective interference paradigm is Brooks' (1968) study. Here subjects were asked to either imagine the sequence of left and right turns as one moves around the perimeter of a block letter or, in another condition, to decide whether each word in a memorized sentence is a noun or non-noun. The first task presumably involves spatial-image processing and the second verbal processing. Two response modes, pointing up or down and saying "yes" or "no", were assumed to involve these same two types of processing, respectively. Brooks found that the block letter task was more difficult when the response mode was pointing, whereas the word classification task was more difficult when the response mode was articulating.

In this experiment, two interference conditions were taken from an earlier study of spatial knowledge (Moar, 1981). The first, counting aloud by one's, seems to involve verbal-sequential processing. The second, pressing an unseen 5 x 5 matrix of buttons in a serpentine pattern, seems to involve spatial-image processing.

Two temporal tasks were designed to elicit image and verbal-list processing. In what we will call the "image" task, subjects were given pairs of months six months apart. One of the remaining 10 months was the stimulus on a given trial. Instructions were to say which of the two choice months would be encountered first if one went *backward* through the months from the stimulus month. For example, with the stimulus "October" and the choice pair "June-December", the correct answer would be June. In the "verbal-list" task, subjects were to say aloud the month that comes a specified number of months after the stimulus month. Separations of two, three and four months were used for the three trial blocks. For example, if the separation was three and the stimulus "June", subjects were to say "September". Each type of temporal task was paired with each interference condition.

At the start of each trial, subjects were either told to count or to press. When they said the number ten or pressed the tenth button, the stimulus month was given aloud. Counting or pressing continued until subjects gave their answer. Thus, problem solving took place while the interference activity was in progress.

Response time (RT), proportion correct and number of buttons pushed or numbers recited were each averaged for the four combinations of the two temporal tasks and the two interference conditions. I expected these measures to show that the image tasks were more difficult to perform while pressing than while counting, whereas the verbal-list tasks would be more difficult to perform while counting than while pressing. RT showed the predicted pattern (see Table 7.1). The ANOVA for RT showed that the verbal-list tasks took significantly longer to solve than the image tasks ($p<.001$) and, more importantly, that task type interacted with interference type ($p<.01$). The differences between the two interference types were significant by planned comparisons for each temporal task ($ps<.03$).

Table 7.1.
MEAN RESPONSE TIME (RT; IN SEC) AND PROPORTION CORRECT FOR EACH SET AND INTERFERENCE CONDITION IN STUDY 1

TASK	INTERFERENCE CONDITION	
	BUTTON PRESSING	COUNTING
IMAGE BACKWARD		
RT	1.84	1.64
SD	1.08	.82
PROPORTION CORRECT	.90	.89
SD	.11	.08
LIST FORWARD		
RT	2.31	2.60
SD	.64	.75
PROPORTION CORRECT	.85	.76
SD	.07	.13

From Friedman (1983). Copyright 1983 by the American Psychological Association. Reprinted by permission of the publisher.

Proportion correct showed significant effects for temporal task type ($p<.01$), interference type ($p<.01$), and their interaction ($p<.05$). As Table 7.1 shows, only the verbal-list task showed a difference between the two interference conditions. This difference was significant by planned comparison ($p<.001$). The analysis of button pressing and counting showed only that buttons were pressed faster than digits were counted. This shows that the interactions in RT and proportion correct can not be an artifact of a tradeoff between attention to the temporal tasks and attention to the interference tasks. However, these findings do not support a reciprocal selective interference effect of the temporal tasks on the interference activities.

Taken together, the results indicate that two distinct types of processing are involved in making judgments about the order of the months. One of these appears to share specific resources with spatial orientation or image processes. The other competes for specific verbal processing resources.

Analog Effects

In describing the image system, I claimed that image processing of order information is functionally similar in some respects to perceptual judgments of spatial positions. In this section we will consider a number of studies that show these analog effects when subjects are asked to make judgments about the proximity of months or days of the week. The findings will be related to the image model and to several alternative models.

Two other researchers have described effects related to the symbolic distance effect (SDE; Moyer, 1973) using the months as stimuli. The SDE is the tendency for subjects to take more time to compare two symbols (e.g., digits, animal names) as they become more similar on the dimension of comparison (e.g., magnitude, usual size of the animal; see Banks, 1977; Shepard & Podgorny,1978). Fairbanks (1969) asked his subjects to judge which of two stimulus months is closer to the end of the year. He found that RTs decreased as the separation between the two increased. Seymour (1980a, 1980b) conducted a number of studies in which subjects judged the position of months relative to locational categories, such as first half vs. second half of the year or "central months" (April-September) vs. "end months" (January-March and October-December). In each experiment the longest RTs occurred adjacent to the category boundaries.

The SDE is sometimes taken as evidence for the use of imagery (e.g., Paivio, 1978). According to an image model, some comparison operation functionally resembles the perceptual discrimination of the size of two objects or the proximity of a location to a reference point. However, some theorists (Banks, 1977; Banks, Fujii & Kayra-Stuart, 1976) believe the SDE is best explained by a semantic model similar to the one described in the section, "Possible Models". Semantic models assume that information about the magnitude of each symbol is stored in a linguistic code. Comparisons are made by activating the code linked to each symbol and determining which symbol's code better matches the criterion (e.g., "largest"). If the same code is activated for each symbol, the matching process is delayed until additional, discriminable codes are generated.

Seymour (1980a, 1980b) has proposed a semantic model to account for the findings of his month order experiments. In his model individual months are linked to "locative codes" such as "start, end, early, late, central, peripheral" (1980b, p. 392). When months fall near the category boundaries, the locative code is inadequate to specify on which side of the boundary the month falls. For example, the code "central" for June or July makes it inadequate for assigning these months to the first or second half of the year. Seymour assumes that in such cases a back-up code specifying relative positions of adjacent months must be used. A related explanation could be offered for Fairbanks' (1969) findings: the closer two months are to one another, the more likely they are to share location codes, thus necessitating some additional process to establish their order.

The Fairbanks and Seymour studies cannot be taken as support for the use of an image system in judging month order, because, as we have seen, their findings are also consistent with certain semantic models. However, the four studies that will be considered next demonstrate analog effects that are not easily explained by semantic models.

STUDY 2

In Study 2 (Friedman,1983, Experiment 2) undergraduates were asked to compare the length of two intervals of months, such as December to May vs. July to October. The analog prediction is that month pairs that are similar in interval length will be more difficult to compare. As we saw earlier, this interval comparison effect (ICE) would be expected from an analogous perceptual task, judging line lengths.

It is interesting to note that this sort of functional similarity seems to exist between perception and spatial representation. For example, in an unpublished study, I asked adults to judge which of two dots, projected on a screen, was closer to a third reference dot—the perceptual condition—and which of two named buildings was closer to a third reference building—the spatial memory condition. Unbeknown to the subjects, each perceptual stimulus corresponded to a spatial stimulus in that the dots were traced from a map of the spatial layout. I found that the mean response time of spatial problems was significantly correlated with the mean response time for matching perceptual problems (r=.33, r corrected for attenuation =.69; ps<.01). Furthermore, multiple regression showed that the ratio of shorter to longer distance in a problem accounted for most of the common variance (see also Baum & Jonides, 1979; Evans & Pezdek, 1980). This suggests a similar comparison operation which becomes more difficult as the intervals to be compared become closer in magnitude.

The ICE for months would be difficult for a semantic model, such as Seymour's, to explain. Semantic models assume that each month's position is coded but not that the lengths of intervals between pairs are coded. However, it is possible to advance associative and serial models for month interval problems. In an associative model, subjects might compare the associative strength of one pair of months to the other. In a serial model (such as one based on the verbal-list system), subjects might count the number of months in each interval.

To test associative and serial models, the problems were chosen to vary not only in the magnitude of the *difference* between interval lengths, but also to vary in the magnitude of the *sum* of two interval lengths. In a serial model, each month in the interval must be accessed in turn. This would lead to slower responses the greater the sum. Associative models would also seem to imply this sort of sum effect, because weaker associations should be more difficult to compare.

Subjects were read 80 problems which varied on both the difference and sum dimensions. Each problem included two pairs of months, and subjects were to judge whether the first or second interval was shorter. Table 7.2 shows RT as a function of each level of difference and sum. As the bottom row indicates, there was a strong effect of difference, with in-

Table 7.2.
MEAN RESPONSE TIME (RT; IN SEC) FOR EACH PROBLEM TYPE IN STUDY 2

SUM		DIFFERENCE				
		1	2	3	4	*M*
5						
	RT	2.81		1.34		2.08
	SD	2.14		.80		
6						
	RT		2.04		1.53	1.78
	SD		1.15		.88	
7						
	RT	2.91		1.79		2.35
	SD	1.80		1.35		
8						
	RT		2.30		1.68	1.99
	SD		1.49		.96	
	M	2.86	2.17	1.56	1.60	—

From Friedman (1983). Copyright 1983 by the American Psychological Association. Reprinted by permission of the publisher.

-terval differences of one month taking the most time and interval differences of three and four months the least. In contrast, the right-most column shows no consistent sum effect. Planned comparisons revealed a highly significant linear difference effect ($p<.001$) but a nonsignificant sum effect. Analyses of the accuracy data (Table 7.3) showed the same pattern of difficulty. Again, the difference effect was highly significant by planned comparison ($p<.001$), whereas the sum effect was nonsignificant.

TABLE 7.3.
MEAN PROPORTION CORRECT FOR EACH PROBLEM TYPE IN STUDY 2

SUM		DIFFERENCE 1	2	3	4	*M*
5						
	PROPORTION CORRECT	.84		.96		.90
	SD	.10		.06		
6						
	PROPORTION CORRECT		.91		.97	.94
	SD		.12		.04	
7						
	PROPORTION CORRECT	.81		.96		.89
	SD	.14		.05		
8						
	PROPORTION CORRECT		.90		.95	.93
	SD		.17		.08	
	M	.82	.91	.96	.96	

From Friedman (1983). Copyright 1983 by the American Psychological Association. Reprinted by permission of the publisher.

These findings not only show the ICE predicted by the analog model, but that the effects are asymptotic beyond interval length differences of three. Asymptotic difference effects would be expected given analogous findings on perceptual judgments of length (Woodworth & Schlosberg, 1965). The failure to show sum effects appears to rule out recite-and-count models and certain associative models.

STUDY 3

I applied the same paradigm to the days of the week in a second, unpublished study. The design and procedure were the same as in the month study, except that the two intervals were allowed to partially overlap. The results are shown in Tables 7.4 and 7.5.

Again, strong asymptotic difference effects are shown, whereas sum effects are inconsistent. Planned comparisons supported linear distance effects for both RT and accuracy ($p<.001$). A substantially weaker linear sum effect also reached significance for RT ($p<.03$), but the sum effect was not significant for proportion correct. As Table 7.4 shows, sum increases in RT are consistent only for interval length differences of one. This raises the possibility that subjects sometimes used a back-up sequential process, such as a verbal-list process, when they determined by some other method that the difference was small. In any case the results provide much stronger support for the analog model.

Table 7.4.
MEAN RESPONSE TIME IN SECONDS FOR EACH PROBLEM TYPE IN STUDY 3

SUM		DIFFERENCE			
		1	2	3	*M*
6					
	RT		1.19		1.19
	SD		.37		
7					
	RT	1.81		1.43	1.62
	SD	.98		1.03	
8					
	RT		1.65		1.65
	SD		.91		
9					
	RT	2.19		1.40	1.79
	SD	1.00		.55	
10					
	RT		1.55		1.55
	SD		.53		
	M	2.00	1.46	1.42	

Table 7.5.
MEAN PROPORTION CORRECT FOR EACH PROBLEM TYPE IN STUDY 3

SUM	DIFFERENCE 1	2	3	*M*
6				
PROPORTION CORRECT		.95		.95
SD		.05		
7				
PROPORTION CORRECT	.87		.95	.91
SD	.14		.07	
8				
PROPORTION CORRECT		.90		.90
SD		.09		
9				
PROPORTION CORRECT	.82		.98	.90
SD	.12		.04	
10				
PROPORTION CORRECT		.97		.97
SD		.09		
M	.84	.94	.97	

STUDY 4

Another technique produces analog effects that are particularly difficult for semantic models to explain. As we saw earlier, effects like Fairbanks' (1969) and Seymour's (1980a, 1980b) can be explained by either analog or semantic models. This is because their tasks treated the months as a linear continuum.

On a linear continuum, two symbols differ both in their absolute magnitude, as emphasized in the linguistic codes of the semantic models, and in their relative magnitude, as emphasized by the location-like codes of the analog models. However, the months are also a cyclic continuum, and this property offers ways of discriminating between the two types of models.

In this and the following experiment (Friedman, 1984, Experiments 1 & 2) I used a method that capitalizes on the cyclic nature of the months and days of the the week. The method is asking subjects to make "cyclic proximity judgments". On each trial subjects are given a pair of month or day names and asked to judge whether the second element is closer to the first going forward or backward in time. For example, for the pair October-June, the correct answer would be "backward", whereas for the pair November-March, the correct answer would be "forward".

In order to understand the analog prediction it is helpful to imagine a hypothetical perception study. In this study subjects would view a circular arrangement of lights, and on a given trial, two would be illuminated in sequence. The task would be to judge whether the second was closer to the first going in a clockwise or counter-clockwise direction. We would expect that this judgment would become progressively more difficult as the position of the second light approached 180° from the first. In the temporal tasks of Studies 4 and 5, I expected progressive increases in RTs and decreases in accuracy as the separation between the months increased from one to six months in either direction and the separation between the days increased from one to three days in either direction. This is based on the assumption that subjects would solve these tasks by imagining positions for the two elements and comparing the position of the second element to a boundary region farthest away form the first. I also expected that there should be no differences between forward and backward problems because of the simultaneous activation of location information in the image system.

It is difficult to see how a semantic process could allow subjects to solve this task. This is because the changing reference point from problem to problem renders absolute location codes inadequate. It is not clear how a code like "first", "early" or "central" could be matched to the response choices "forward" or "backward". Even if one accesses the location codes of each pair of stimulus months, one would need a complex set of decision rules, along with some back-up process for solving problems in which both elements fall in the same category or one or both fall near category boundaries.

Two other models can be tested in the cyclic proximity judgment tasks. Simple numerical methods will not work on these tasks, but coupling number with a set of four decision rules could (e.g., "If the first month is less than the second month and their difference is greater than 6, say "backwards"). This kind of model would not predict a boundary proximity effect. In addition, one would expect more rapid responses the smaller the absolute value of the difference between month numbers and the smaller the magnitude of the smaller number if subtraction is a component process (see Shoben, Cech & Schwanenflugel, 1983).

Serial models also make predictions that differ from those of the analog model. An optimal serial strategy for the months task would be to count through the months after the first stimulus month until encountering the second stimulus month or reaching five steps. If the second month is in this interval, the correct response would be forward; otherwise it would be backward. Use of this approach would lead to a linear increase in RT with each forward separation from one to five, and a flat curve with a still higher level for all months that are closer in the backward direction.

In Study 4 we presented all 120 pairs of month names excluding duplicates and pairs six months apart. The pairs appeared on a video monitor, and subjects were to press one of two keys indicating whether the second month is closer to the first going forward or backward in time. The same subjects also performed an analogous spatial task involving the names of pairs of 12 buildings spaced about equally around a campus square. Here one key signified that the second building was closer to the first in a clockwise direction and the other that it was closer in a counter-clockwise direction.

Figure 7.1 shows the mean RT for each number of months or buildings from the first stimulus to the second. The forward curves pertain to problems in which the second stimulus is closer to the first in the forward or clockwise direction, and the backward curves are for backward or counter-clockwise problems. Both the spatial and temporal curves provide a very good fit to the predictions of the analog model. The longest RTs occur adjacent to the direction boundary (six months or buildings), three out of the four curves show increasing RTs per month or building as the boundary is approached, and direction differences are fairly small. The forward temporal curve shows unexpectedly rapid responses at distances one and two, perhaps because the verbal-list process is automatically activated when the second month closely follows the first.

The ANOVA for RT showed a strong effect for Distance (1 to 5) ($p<.001$), and planned comparisons revealed significant linear and quadratic distance effects for both the temporal and spatial conditions ($ps<.01$). These linear and quadratic effects support the description of accelerating difficulty as the direction boundary is approached. Direction (forward/clockwise *vs.* backward/counter-clockwise) was a relatively weak effect ($p<.05$).

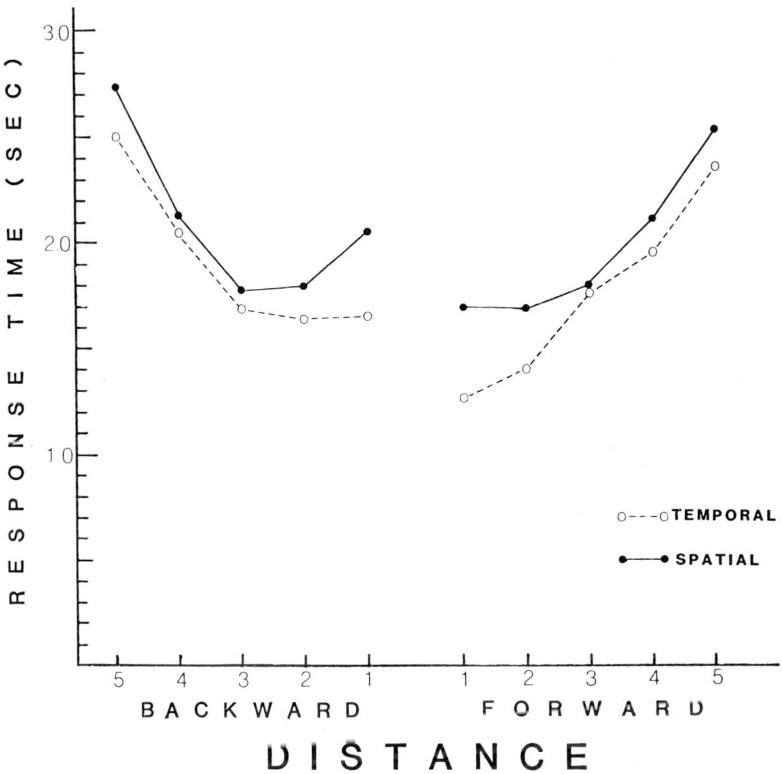

Figure 7.1. Mean response time in seconds for each distance and direction for the temporal and spatial tasks in Study 4. From Friedman (1984). Copyright 1984 by the Psychonomic Society. Reprinted by permission of the publisher.

The analog predictions were also supported by the results for accuracy. Figure 7.2 shows the number of errors out of a possible 12. Error rates were low for distances of one through three or four, with substantial increases thereafter. Distance was again a highly significant factor in the ANOVA ($p<.001$), but Direction was not significant. The planned comparisons supported linear and quadratic trends in the temporal condition ($ps<.01$). Only the linear trend was significant in the spatial condition ($p<.01$).

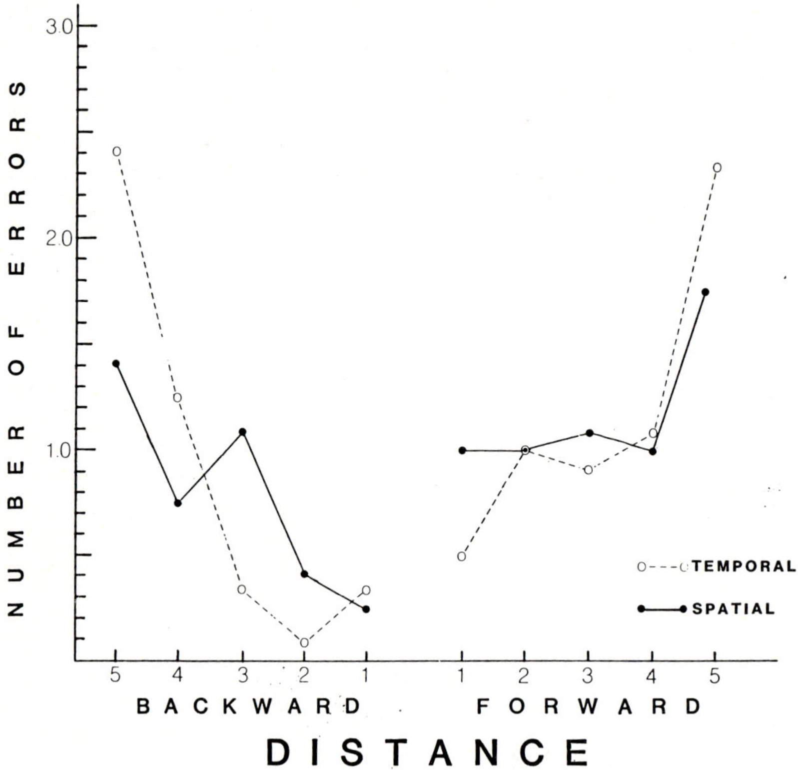

Figure 7.2. Mean number of errors out of a possible 12 for each distance and direction for the temporal and spatial tasks in Study 4. From Friedman (1984). Copyright 1984 by the Psychonomic Society. Reprinted by permission of the publisher.

The results are inconsistent with numerical and serial models. The strong boundary proximity effect was not predicted by the numerical model. Furthermore, regression analysis showed that two subtraction variables, difference between month numbers and magnitude of the smaller number, added trivial amounts of variance to the prediction of problem RTs beyond that contributed by distance from the direction boundary. Serial models cannot explain the approximate forward-backward symmetry or the quadratic distance effects.

STUDY 5

This experiment also used cyclic proximity judgments but with the days of the week as content. Subjects were read aloud each non-duplicating pair of days and judged whether the second day is closer "before" or "after" the first day. The pattern of RTs is shown in Figure 7.3. Again, we see a strong distance effect which seems to accelerate as the direction boundary is approached. The ANOVA showed a strong Distance effect ($p<.001$), and Direction was also significant ($P<.01$). Planned com-

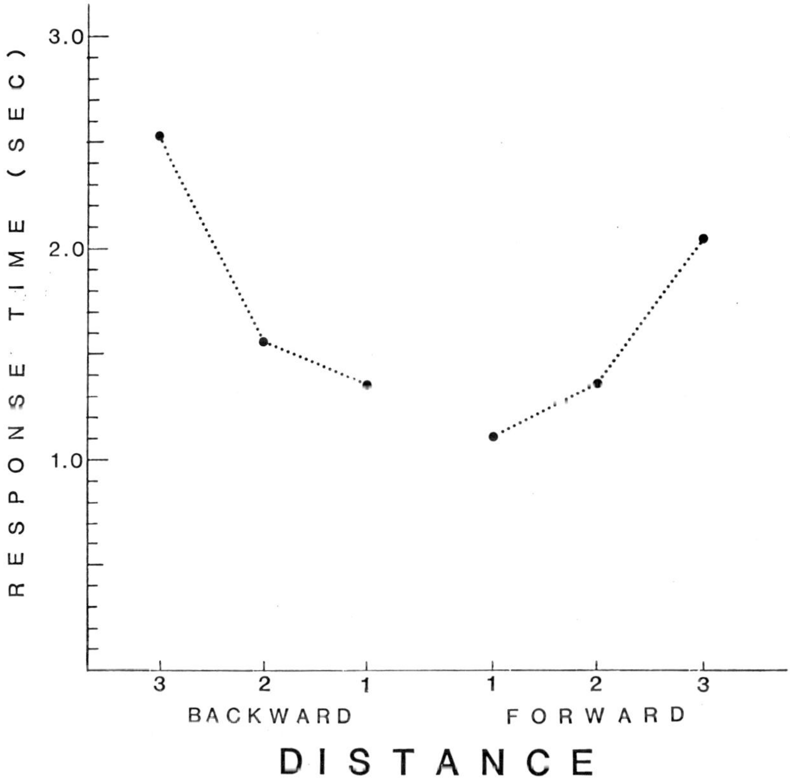

Figure 7.3. Mean response time in seconds for each forward and backward distance for the day-of-the-week task (Study 5). From Friedman (1984). Copyright 1984 by the Psychonomic Society. Reprinted by permission of the publisher.

parisons showed both a linear ($p<.01$) and a quadratic ($p<.05$) distance effect.

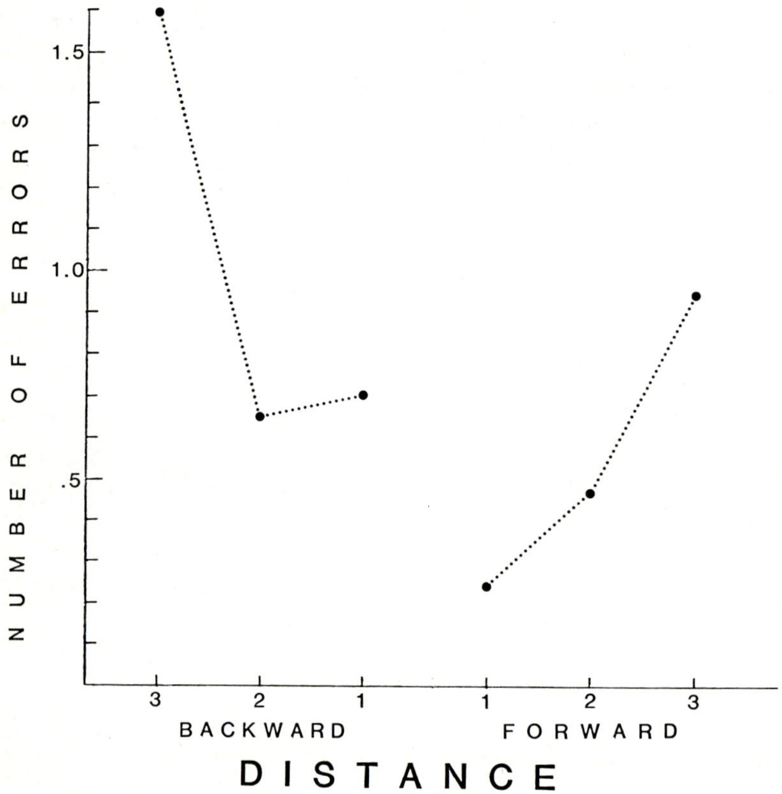

Figure 7.4. Mean number of errors out of a possible 12 for each forward and backward distance in the day-of-the-week task (Study 5). From Friedman (1984). Copyright by the Psychonomic Society. Reprinted by permission of the publisher.

The accuracy data (Figure 7.4) revealed a similar pattern. Again, the ANOVA produced a significant Distance effect ($p<.01$) and Direction effect ($p<.05$). Only the linear distance trend was significant by planned comparison ($p<.01$). The boundary proximity effects for RT and accuracy and the quadratic distance effect for RT support the analog model. However, the significant direction effects are not predicted. Direction effects have also appeared on other tasks which I predict invoke analog processes (see the next section). Perhaps in day-to-day thinking about the months and days of the week people use forward order operations more frequently. This might produce a bias like the left-to-right advantage for scanning shown by readers of English. In the present study I would need to assume that at some stage of processing, subjects must mentally scan from the first to the second day's location.

The results of this study, like those of the last, are inconsistent with numerical and serial models, and solution of the problems is difficult to explain using semantic models. The boundary proximity effect is not predicted by a numerical model. Serial models cannot explain the similarly shaped forward and backward curves nor the quadratic distance effect for RT.

Conclusion

The four studies described in this section have demonstrated effects related to the SDE, using tasks for which semantic models seem inappropriate. Serial, associative and numerical models were directly evaluated and found to make erroneous predictions on the interval comparison or cyclic proximity tasks. The ICE and direction boundary proximity effects were predicted by the analog model, and I take them as a support for the involvement of the image system in reasoning about the order of the months and days of the week.

Distance and Direction Effects

STUDY 6

The distinction between the verbal-list and image systems is tested in this section. In describing the verbal-list system, I claimed that processing consisted of sequential activation of elements and that forward links were stronger than backward links. In the image system, location-like information is simultaneously available for each activated element, and position comparisons need not involve attending to the location of intervening elements. These differences led to the predictions that backward order should be easier to judge in the image system than in the verbal-list system and that the temporal length of intervals should be a stronger determinant of processing time in the verbal-list system than in the image system.

The existence of strong distance and direction effects has been demonstrated by Seymour (1980a, Experiment III) using tasks that required judgments of exact separations of months and days of the week. These tasks should evoke verbal-list processing according to my model, so these effects are consistent with its predictions. Study 6 (Friedman, 1983, Experiment 4) was a stronger test of the model; it compared the magnitude of distance and direction effects in tasks designed to evoke image and verbal-list processing.

In this experiment adults were asked to solve two types of tasks. In what I will call the "measurement" (M) tasks, they judged which of two choice months was an exact distance from a third, reference month. The second type of task, "relative proximity" (RP), required subjects to judge the relative proximity of two non-adjacent months to a third reference month. As explained in the description of the model, the M tasks were expected to invoke verbal-list processing and the RP tasks to invoke image processing. In both task types, stimulus questions were of the same form, and the correct answers were the same set of forward and backward distances.

The RP and M tasks used the following three distances and directions to the correct answer: forward three months, forward six months, and backward three months. In the RP tasks, subjects judged which of the two choice months would come next going forward (or backward) from the reference month. The correct of the two choice months was always three months closer to the reference month. In the M tasks, subjects judged which of the two choice months comes three months after (or before) or six months after the reference month. The incorrect choice month was adjacent to the correct one, either two or four months away from the reference month in the forward three and backward three conditions and either five or seven months after the reference month in the forward six condition.

Table 7.6 shows mean RTs and proportions correct for the M and RP tasks as a function of distance and direction. The last two columns show the distance effects (forward 6 minus forward 3) and direction effects (backward 3 minus forward 3) for the two types of tasks. For both RT and proportion correct, the distance and direction effects are greater for the M tasks than the RP tasks. The RT differences for distance ($p<.03$) and direction ($p<.01$) were significant by planned comparisons. The comparisons for proportion correct were not significant, perhaps because performance on the RP tasks approached the upper limit of 100% correct.

Table 7.6.
MEAN RESPONSE TIME (RT IN SECONDS) AND PROPORTION CORRECT (PC) AS A FUNCTION OF TASK IN STUDY 6

TASK		FORWARD 3	FORWARD 6	BACKWARD 3	MEAN	DISTANCE EFFECT	DIRECTION EFFECT
RESPONSE TIME							
RP							
	RT	1.29	1.96	2.55	1.93	.67	1.26
	SD	.88	1.37	1.95	1.14	.93	1.75
M							
	RT	2.07	3.72	4.56	3.45	1.65	2.49
	SD	.95	2.04	3.12	1.68	1.79	2.90
PROPORTION CORRECT							
RP							
	PC	.97	.96	.95	.96	−.01	−.02
	SD	.06	.06	.12	.06	.08	.12
M							
	PC	.90	.83	.81	.85	−.06	−.09
	SD	.08	.20	.16	.09	.20	.18

These differential distance and direction effects are consistent with the image—verbal-list model. The verbal-list system seems to require approximately one half second for each additional intervening month in the forward direction and about .8 sec beyond that per month in the backward direction. The corresponding times for the image system are about half or less. It is not clear why the RP distance and direction effects are greater than zero. Perhaps subjects perform some image operation analogous to scanning, starting with the position of the reference month and ending with the position of the nearer choice month. Such a process might take more time to cover a greater distance. To explain the RP direction effect, one would have to further assume a forward scanning advantage (see also Study 5).

Individual Differences

A fourth kind of evidence for the image—verbal-list model comes from Study 6, partially described in the preceding section. In addition to the M and RP tasks, the same subjects were given a cognitive map task formally similar to the RP month task, an alphabet distance task, and two tests of spatial ability. The cognitive map task involved judging from memory the relative forward and backward order of buildings around the perimeter of a campus square. In the alphabet task, subjects were asked to write the letter of the alphabet that came three or six letters after a stimulus letter. The difference between the time required to identify the sixth versus the third letter was calculated for each subject. One of the spatial ability tests was Lansman and Hunt's Mental Rotations Test (adapted from Shepard & Metzler, 1971). This test requires subjects to judge whether two drawings of cube configurations are possible rotations of one another. The other was the Spatial Relations Test of Thurstone's Primary Mental Abilities Scale (Thurstone & Thurstone, 1965). Here the task is to determine which of several forms is a rotated version of a stimulus form.

If the verbal-list and image systems are distinct and if they are imaginal and verbal-sequential in nature, we might expect specific patterns of correlations between the month and other tasks. Performance on the M task should be specifically related to performance on the alphabet task, assuming the latter involves the sequential activation of letter names and that there are individual differences of some generality in speed of verbal-sequential processing. To the extent that the cognitive map and spatial ability tests involve general imagery abilities, they should correlate selectively with performance on the RP task.

These predictions were tested by correlating each subject's distance effect time on the M and RP tasks with his or her performance measures on each of the other tasks. Correlation coefficients were corrected for attenuation using reliability estimates for each task. As predicted, the magnitude of the distance effect on the M task was correlated with the alphabet measure (r=.58, p<.01) but not with the other measures. Also consistent with my expectations, shorter RP distance effects were strongly related to faster RTs on the cognitive map task (r=1.0, p<.01; uncorrected r=.71, p<.01) and not significantly related to the alphabet measure. However, RP distance effect was not significantly correlated with a composite score derived from the spatial abilities tests. This contradictory finding may be due to the fact that the RP task and the spatial abilities tests are each complex, and shared processes may be a small proportion of a larger set of processes on which individuals differ. It is notable that the cognitive map task, which was most similar to the RP task, was strongly correlated with it.

These results provide additional support for the image—verbal-list distinction. Like Study 1 they support the kinship of temporal image processing with certain spatial processes and of temporal verbal-list processing with other verbal-sequential processes. The selective pattern of correlations shown here is inconsistent with any model assuming a single underlying process. In addition, it is difficult to see how any of the alternative models we have considered would explain the pattern.

Introspections

Since Galton's (1883) early studies of "spatial forms", we have known that at least some people claim to have images of numbers, months, days of the week and other seemingly abstract continua. Later studies by Guilford (1926) and Oswald (1960) have also produced reports of imagery for temporal content. The best survey approach is probably Seymour's study of 100 undergraduate and secondary school students (1980a, Experiment I). He asked his subjects, "If you think of the months of the year, do they form any particular shape or pattern in your mind? Give a description or sketch" (p. 256). A similar question referred to days of the week. Seymour found that about 70–75% reported forms such as linear, circular or matrix arrangements of the months and days.

In most of my studies, I have asked participants to report their methods of solving the problems, using either rating scales or open-ended questions. The results show that the experience of imagery is common in tasks which are predicted to invoke imagery and that reports of covert reciting of days or months predominate in the intended verbal-list tasks (Study 6 and Friedman, 1983, Experiment 3). Following each task, subjects were asked to explain how they figured out their answers. Responses were assigned to categories including image (e.g., referring to continua, cycles, or calendars), reciting (e.g., saying the intervening months to oneself, counting, or reading through the months), both and other. Most responses fell in the image and reciting categories and these differed greatly by task type. Of responses assigned to one of these two categories, an average of 91% on the RP tasks were assigned to the image category and 89% on the M tasks were assigned to the reciting category. These results match the predictions of the image—verbal-list model.

In each of the experiments testing analog effects (Studies 2 through 5), I asked subjects to fill out method rating scales at the end of the procedure. These scales included "picturing the days/months in your mind", along with other methods like using numbers and saying intervening days/month to oneself. In all of the studies, planned comparisons showed that "picturing" was rated significantly more highly than other methods ($ps<.05$).

The content of the introspections is also interesting. One subject gave the following explanation for his performance on a month RP task, "I put the two you gave me on a line (gestures a line)... and put the month you gave me in relation to the other two". Other subjects reported moving, scanning, or "thinking" along the line or circle from the reference month to the first choice month in a given direction. On the month interval comparison task (Study 2), one subject responded, "I thought of them laid out on a rule with one month taking up one inch. Then I would think of the intervals and which would have a shorter line segment... ". These reports suggest several construction and transformation processes of the sort that would be expected under the image model.

Conclusions

The various lines of evidence described here offer good support for the importance of image and verbal-list systems in adults' reasoning about the order of months and days. It seems clear that no single representation or process can account for all of the patterns of performance shown in these experiments and even less for the task specificity of processes. Alternative models, such as semantic, associative and numerical models, seem ill suited to explaining how subjects solve the analog tasks, the selective interference effects and the specific pattern of correlation shown between the temporal tasks and spatial and verbal tasks.

Of course many questions still remain about the representation of temporal order in these domains. The image processes in particular can only be described in a rough way, by analogy to processes presumed to be involved in visual perception. Also, the means by which subjects match the image or verbal-list system to tasks with particular characteristics is unclear. Third, given the limited number of tasks that have been used so far, we cannot be confident that other representations would not be used to solve other order tasks. For example, it seems likely that if we asked subjects to determine the difference between the ordinal position of pairs of months in the year they would access month-number associations and subtract the smaller from the larger number. Finally, the studies reported in this section tell us nothing about the ages at which verbal-list and image systems can be used or the processes by which they are acquired. It is to these questions that we turn our attention next.

RESEARCH ON CHILDREN'S AND ADOLESCENT'S REPRESENTATIONS

The conventional time systems that structure the lives of adults are also important in the lives of children. From the preschool years onward, children attend to the time of birthdays, holidays and vacations on the annual scale and weekends, television shows and school events on the week scale. However, children only gradually come to be able to orient within these systems, initially relying on parents' knowledge of the structures. In most of the developmental research on knowledge of the days of the week and months, children are asked to say the elements in order or to give the present day or month (Friedman, 1978). It appears that these criteria are usually met at about five to eight years. Beyond these general age norms, there is little information in the research literature about the acquisition of this knowledge. We do not know what sorts of representations underly children's knowledge at different ages or how the representations change with development.

Since my model of adult representations seems to provide a useful account of the developmental "end point", it is tempting to apply it as a first approximation of representational development. For example, the earliest representations might be isolated associations encoding such information as the month of one's birthday or the day of a favorite television show. At this stage there is really no representation of the order of the elements; one simply knows what time name is associated with a given event. The first coding of order might take place at a later age in the form of verbal-list representations. The days and months are usually taught to children as lists to be recited, and this format seems to offer an efficient way of storing the order of a set of names, such as counting numbers or the letters of the alphabet. However, there may be pressures to supplement verbal-list with image representations at some later age, because, as we have seen, the verbal-list system is less efficient for extracting certain order relations.

While this three-stage model may have some intuitive appeal, it is difficult to predict the ages at which at least the last stage is reached. Preschool children have probably acquired many associations between time names and events, and six– to eight-year-olds may well recite the days or months using a verbal-list representation. Less clear is when image representations would be added to these other forms. Children use imagery on some tasks by the ages at which they learn the days of the week and months (e.g., Dean and Harvey, 1979; Marmor, 1975). But there is no evidence that shows when imagery is used to represent symbolic content.

In this section I will describe three experiments that were designed to test the notion that verbal-list representations of the days of the week and months are present at earlier ages than image representations of these systems. As in the adult studies, semantic-associative representations are assumed but not tested. The experiments also test the applicability of several of the alternative models presented in the section on possible models. Two methods are used to assess the representations and processes available in different age groups. In Studies 7 and 8, I compared the ability to judge backward and forward order of the elements. In Study 9 I examined the ability to judge the approximate "distance" of remote times from some reference point.

Direction Effects

According to the image—verbal-list model, verbal-list processing of backward order is substantially more difficult than forward order, whereas image processes can easily extract either forward or backward order relations. On tasks favoring the verbal-list system, where exact distances must be judged, strong direction effects are expected. On tasks involving relative order or proximity judgments, tasks suited to image processing, direction effects should be weak. These predictions were confirmed in Study 6, serving as one line of evidence that adults use both systems to judge the order of the months.

However, imagine that children of some age possess only verbal-list representations and that they are presented with forward and backward relative order problems (for example, if one goes forward/backward in time from Wednesday, will Saturday or Monday be encountered first?) It should not be difficult for them to solve the forward problems, as long as they can develop the strategy of activating each element after the reference element until one of the choices is encountered. But backward problems should be substantially more difficult, and we might expect many more errors. At some later age, when image representations are also available, the same tasks should show much weaker direction effects. Thus, decreases in the direction effect on relative order problems would indicate a developmental shift from a stage at which only verbal-list representations are available to one in which image representations are also present.

I used this approach in Studies 7 and 8 (Friedman, 1986) to see whether verbal-list representations precede image representations. In Study 7 children and adolescents from second grade through tenth grade and a group of undergraduates judged which of two days of the week would come next after a third, reference day going either forward or backward in time. In Study 8, nine– to twenty-year-olds made similar judgments about the order of the months of the year.

STUDY 7

In this study subjects were given relative order judgment problems of the form "Does Saturday or Monday come next after Thursday?" The problems were presented in two forward and two backward sets of seven problems each with the appropriate direction explained at the start of each set. As in the RP tasks of the adult direction studies, the choices were not adjacent to one another or next after the reference day. Also as in the earlier experiments, the problems assumed continuity between adjacent weeks. Seven problems in each direction had separations of two and four days between the reference and choice days, and seven had separations of four and six days. The participants in the study were fourteen children from each of grades 2, 4, 6, 8 and 10 and 16 undergraduates. Second grades only were asked if they knew the days of the week, and all successfully recited them.

The results were analyzed by finding the number of correct judgments for the forward and backward tasks and classifying subjects as passing a direction if they were correct on 12 or more of the 14 problems ($p<.02$ by the binomial test). Table 7.7 shows the number of subjects who met the criteria in each age group. The forward task was mastered by most children from the fourth grade onward, but it was not until grade 10 that most subjects in an age group met the same criterion for the backward task. Age improvement was significant in each task, as was the developmental priority of mastering the forward task ($ps<.001$).

These results indicate that for several years after children can extract forward order information, backward order relations remain difficult. This is compatible with the position that children develop verbal-list representations for those contents before they develop image representations. A possible alternative interpretation, that children simply do not understand the idea of going backward in time until about tenth grade, is inconsistent with the findings of two unpublished studies that show accurate backward order judgments of daily activities by third grade. Additional evidence for the two-stage interpretation comes from subjects' introspective

Table 7.7.
NUMBER OF SUBJECTS AT EACH AGE PASSING OR FAILING THE CRITERION FOR EACH TASK IN STUDY 7

	TASK			
	FORWARD		BACKWARD	
GRADE	PASS	FAIL	PASS	FAIL
SECOND	1	13	1	13
FOURTH	9	5	4	10
SIXTH	12	2	3	11
EIGHTH	8	6	4	10
TENTH	14	0	8	6
COLLEGE	16	0	16	0

From Friedman (1986). Copyright 1986 by The Society for Research in Child development. Reprinted by permission of the publisher.

reports. After one of the four problem sets, randomly determined, they were asked to explain how they solved the problems. Most subjects from grades 2 through 10 whose responses could be categorized reported saying the days to themselves. But from sixth through tenth grade about a third reported using some sort of spatial image of the days of the week. Adult subjects, who filled out Likert-type method scales, reported "picturing the days in your mind" far more frequently than "saying the intervening days to yourself".

Three of the alternative representational models presented earlier can be applied to these developmental data, but none is very successful. Semantic models run into the fundamental difficulty of not being able to explain accurate performance on the tasks. As we saw in the adult studies, semantic models rely on absolute position codes that are ill-suited to solving relational problems with a changing reference point. Serial models can explain performance on the forward task, and the verbal-list model is one such model that can account for the success of subjects from the fourth grade onward. But serial models cannot easily account for the high levels of performance eventually reached on the backward tasks. Finally, numerical models face a difficulty similar to that of semantic models, in that they rely on absolute position codes in the form of numbers. Numerical representations, coupled with simple arithmetic operations, work well when all of the days in a problem fall in the same conventional week (for example, does Wednesday [4] or Friday [6] come next after Monday [2]? but for cross-boundary problems (for example, does Sunday [1] or Tuesday [3] come next after Friday [6]?), additional operations are required to adjust post-boundary numbers, along with rules that specify when to do so. Even if such rules were applied by children as young as fourth graders, who can solve the forward problems, one would expect substantial differences between the accuracy of problems that cross and do not cross the boundary. But error analyses show quite small differences in the accuracy of the two kinds of problems. Numerical models are also inconsistent with the common reports of reciting and imagery.

STUDY 8

In this study the method was similar to that of Study 7 except that subjects were asked to make judgments of forward and backward relative orders of the months of the year. Eight starting months were selected for each direction, and choice months were six and eight months away in the appropriate direction. After the forward and backward sets, subjects were asked to explain their methods and then asked if they "said the month, or thought about a picture, or did it some other way". Responses were assigned to the categories "image" (referring to a continuum, cycle or calendar descriptively or by gesture), "reciting" (saying the intervening months to oneself, "counting" or "reading through the months"), or "other". Sixteen subjects from each of grades three, five, and ten and 16 undergraduates participated in the study. Third grade was the first grade in which, according to pilot testing, most children could recite the months in order.

Table 7.8.
NUMBER OF SUBJECTS AT EACH AGE PASSING OR FAILING THE CRITERION FOR EACH TASK IN STUDY 8

	TASK			
	FORWARD		BACKWARD	
GRADE	PASS	FAIL	PASS	FAIL
THIRD	3	13	1	15
FIFTH	9	7	2	14
TENTH	12	4	11	5
COLLEGE	16	0	15	1

Tablc 7.8 shows the number of subjects who met the criterion of 7 or 8 correct out of 8 problems on the forward and backward tasks. The criterion represents a minimum proportion correct of .87, similar to the .86 proportion used in Study 7 but somewhat less conservative against the null hypothesis of random responding ($p<.08$ by the binomial test). Most children could accurately judge forward order by fifth grade, but backward order judgments were inaccurate until the next age group, the tenth graders. The two older groups were about equally accurate on the forward and backward tasks. Age improvement was significant on both task types, as was the developmental priority of judging forward order ($p<.01$).

Table 7.9.
FREQUENCY OF REPORTED METHODS FOR EACH TASK IN STUDY 8

	TASK			
	FORWARD		BACKWARD	
GRADE	IMAGERY	RECITING	IMAGERY	RECITING
THIRD	2	11	3	11
FIFTH	2	12	2	9
TENTH	8	6	8	5
COLLEGE	13	2	16	0

Table 7.9 shows the number of method reports assigned to the image and reciting categories. At the third and fifth grades, most children reported reciting on both the forward and backward tasks. In contrast, imagery predominated on both tasks for the older groups. The age changes on both the forward and backward tasks were significant ($ps<.001$).

One final line of support for the transition from verbal-list to image processing on these tasks comes from observations of the children while they solved the problems. Third and fifth graders showed lip movement on about one quarter of the problems, whereas the undergraduates almost never did. (This information was not collected for the tenth graders).

Semantic and serial models face difficulties in accounting for these findings similar to those confronted in Experiment 7. Again, numerical models are awkward for these tasks, and a comparison of problems that did and did not cross the December-January boundary showed very small differences in accuracy.

Taken together, Studies 7 and 8 indicate that verbal-list processes are available a number of years before image processes. At about seven or eight years, most children can recite the days and months in order and within two years apply similar processes to relative order problems with changing reference points. But it is not until adolescence that backward order problems are solved, leading to the inference that image representations for these contents usually develop between childhood and adolescence. Of course failure to solve a particular type of task is not ideal evidence that some form of representation is missing. For this reason we will consider another line of evidence, using a task that is solved by fourth grade but on which pre-adolescents and adolescents appear to use different processes.

Categorical Distance Judgments

STUDY 9

One of the advantages of the image system, according to our earlier discussion, is that it can be used to determine the approximate relative times of occurrence of two elements without having to activate each intervening element. For example, we know that November is rather long after March, (say, more than four months) without having to attend to the times of occurrence of each intervening month. In contrast, if our only available representation of month order was a verbal-list representation, then it would be necessary to activate the months from March to November to extract this information. The direct vs. serial nature of the two processes suggests a way of testing the hypothesis that verbal-list representations precede image representations. This method involves what I will call "categorical distance judgments".

The categorical distance judgment tasks used in this study required judging the forward separation between one day or month and another. In the week task, subjects judged whether or not a given day of the week was one of the next three days after a reference day. In the month task, they judged whether or not a given month was one of the next four months after a reference month. In these tasks the time required to judge certain separations should be sensitive to the processes used to arrive at the answer. Subjects who have an image representation of the days or months should be able to rapidly determine that some "remote" element, beyond but not adjacent to the distance category boundary, is not in the near category. Subjects who have only verbal-list representations would have to activate at least the three days or four months after the reference element in order to determine that a remote day or month belonged in the post-boundary category.

If we plot RT as a function of the number of elements between the two stimulus days or months, we would expect different curves when image and verbal-list processes are used. The optimal verbal-list approach would lead to a substantial linear increase in RT up to the category boundary, with a flat curve thereafter. Judging from the results of Study 6, the slope to the third day or fourth month should be on the order of one-half second per element. These predictions are based on the assumptions that approximately equal amounts of time are needed to activate each additional element and that processing will end when either the second stimulus element or the pre-boundary element is encountered. If image processes are applied to these tasks, then remote distances should have RTs about equal to the next item or two after the reference element. The longest RTs should occur near the distance category boundary for the same reasons that they were predicted near the direction category boundaries in Studies 4 and 5: the second element's "location" may be difficult to discriminate from the boundary "location".

Because both processes are expected to lead to relatively long RTs near the distance category boundary, the clearest difference would occur when comparing remote items with items close to the reference element. This difference should be small for an image process, but a function of the roughly half second per element slope to the boundary distance for a verbal-list process.

Sixteen subjects from each of grades four, seven and ten and 16 undergraduates participated in this study. Categorical distance judgment tasks involving the days of the week and months were presented in the form of computer games. Problems were presented verbally on the computer screen, and subjects responded by pressing one key for the pre-boundary category and another key for the post-boundary category. The pretext for the week task was a game in which a space creature could remain invisible for the three days after he landed on earth but thereafter would be visible to his enemies. Stimuli on each trial were a pair of day names, with the second day following the reference day by distances of 1, 2, 3, 4, 5, or 6 steps. In the month task, subjects pretended to route messages to an astronaut who would be in orbit for the four months after the launch month but back at the home base thereafter. The second month displayed on the screen followed the reference month by distances of 1, 2, 3, 4, 6, 7, 8 or 9. The week task had 42 trials and the month task 48 trials. Participants were instructed to respond rapidly but accurately, and the computer program provided feedback on their accuracy on each trial. The experimenter observed subjects as they performed the task and made a trial-by-trial record of overt behaviors such as moving lips or tapping fingers periodically

Figure 7.5 shows the results for RT plotted as a function of distance in the week task. Overall RTs decreased with age, but more importantly the shape of the curves changed as well. At each age RT increased up to the boundary between distances three and four with no subsequent increases, but the slope from distance 1 to distances 5 and 6, the remote items, decreased substantially with age. Preliminary analyses showed significant effects of Group, Distance and their interaction (*p*s<.02). The main analysis of interest was conducted by finding the difference between the distance 1 mean and the distance 5 and 6 means for each subject and comparing the group means for this index. This analysis revealed a linear decrease from grade 4 through the college group in the difference between distance 1 and the remote items ($p<.001$).

The magnitude of these differences can be compared to our prediction for the verbal-list system: a one half second per step increase up to the boundary distance with no increase thereafter. This would mean that the remote items should differ from the distance items by about one second. Ninety-five percent confidence intervals placed around the mean differ-

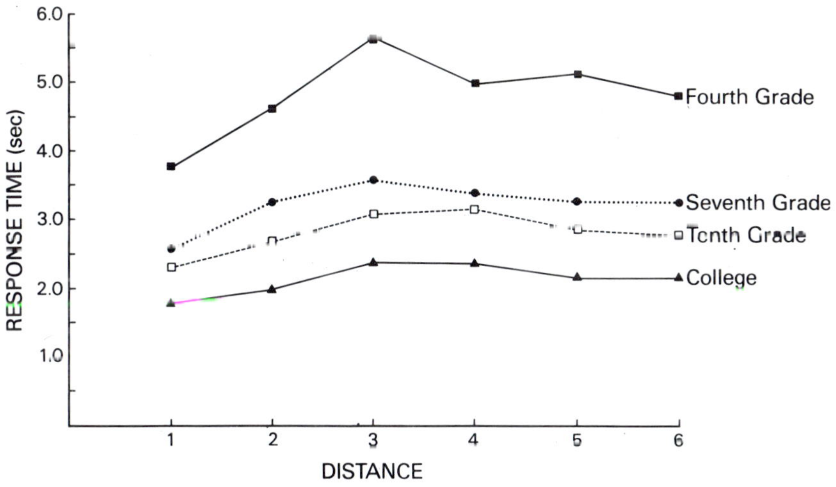

Figure 7.5. Mean response time in seconds for each distance in the week task of Study 9. From Friedman (1986). Copyright 1986 by The Society for Research in Child Development. Reprinted by permission of the publisher.

ence for each group showed that only the fourth graders' interval overlapped the one second value. The differences for the older groups appeared to be too small for a verbal-list process with these properties.

The analysis of accuracy on the week task showed no significant group differences. Distance 3 problems were the most difficult at each age. This resulted in a strong Distance effect ($p<.001$).

Overt behaviors were analyzed as a single category, since all appeared to reflect verbal-list or other serial processing. Overt behaviors were common for the fourth graders, occurring on a mean of .41 of trials, but rare at older ages (means of .04, .03 and .03). These findings further support the interpretation that verbal-list processes are used by fourth graders but some other process by older groups.

The results of the month task supported a similar developmental change. The RT pattern is shown in Figure 7.6. Again RT curves for each age group increase up to the boundary distance, with no subsequent increases. However, the slope from distance 1 to the remote distances (6,7,8, and 9) decreases substantially with age, with the greatest change taking place between grades 4 and 7. Group, Distance and their interaction were

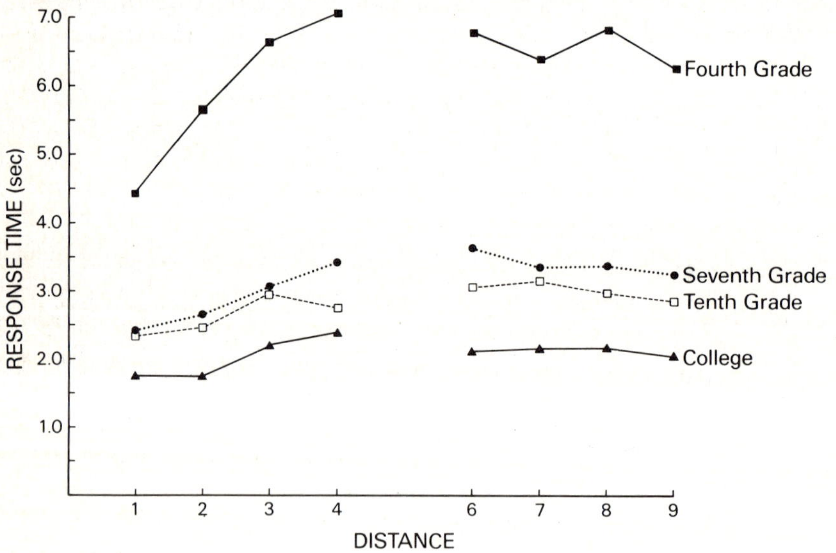

Figure 7.6. Mean response time in seconds for each distance in the month task of Study 9. From Friedman (1986). Copyright 1986 by the The Society for Research in Child Development. Reprinted by permission of the publisher.

all significant. The test for age changes in the difference between distance 1 and remote distances again showed a strong linear decrease with age ($p<.001$). Because there are three steps from distance 1 to the direction boundary, the expected value of the slope to the remote items under the verbal-list model is 1.5 sec. Both fourth and seventh graders' 95% confidence intervals overlapped this value, but older groups had significantly flatter slopes.

The accuracy data again showed the greatest difficulty just before the distance boundary, supported by a significant Distance effect ($p<.001$). The Group effect also reached significance ($p<.01$), apparently reflecting somewhat more accurate performance by the undergraduates than subjects at other ages. There were no consistent age trends among the school age subjects.

A tabulation of overt behaviors again revealed a sharp decrease after the fourth grade. The mean frequencies for the four groups are .37, .08, .05 and .04. This pattern suggests movement away from verbal-list processing, and, as for the RT difference slopes, the greatest change occurred between fourth and seventh grade.

The findings of both the week and month studies support a change from childhood to adolescence in the processes used to access information about the separation of two elements. Judging from the pattern of RTs as well as the observations of overt behaviors, fourth graders appeared to determine separations by activating each element after the reference day or month until either the second stimulus element or the boundary distance was reached. With increasing age there was a shift to processes allowing much more rapid access to information about the position of remote items. In light of the findings of Studies 1 through 8, it seems reasonable to suppose that the latter process involves the image system.

None of the alternative models provides a good account of the findings of this study. The semantic model cannot explain performance on these categorical distance judgment tasks because of the changing reference point and also fails to predict greater difficulty near the distance boundaries. These boundary effects are different from those explained by Seymour's (1980a, 1980b) model, because they cannot be attributed to precoded position categories. A purely serial model does not predict the developmental trends in distance 1–remote differences nor the rapid access to remote item position information in older groups. Numerical models cannot explain the distance category boundary effects, unless one assumes that problems become more difficult when the difference between the two numbers is close to the cutoff value of three or four. Even this explanation would only apply to problems that did not cross the boundary between one conventional cycle and another.

How the Representations Develop

Studies 7, 8 and 9 provide a number of lines of support for the position that representations of day and month order change from childhood to adolescence. For several years after the order of elements is first learned, children rely on the verbal-list system to extract order relations. In fact, a comparison of the ages of mastery of the forward tasks in Studies 7 and 8 with the ages at which children can recite the elements in conventional order suggests that even verbal-list representations develop. The delay of about two years is apparently not due to a failure to invoke verbal-list processing on the forward tasks — even the youngest subjects report and show overt behaviors compatible with reciting. Instead the difficulty seems to be in reciting accurately from an interior day or month, a problem similar to that of much younger children who are learning to count (Fuson and Hall. 1983).

Like most development research, the studies reported here describe the performance of children at different ages but do not show what processes lead to the changes. It would be particularly interesting to know whether the developmental changes that we found were due to general cognitive transitions, for example in the kinds of operations or processing capacity available, or whether the explanation lies instead in the history of operations performed on these particular contents. The first kind of explanation is tempting here because of the similar ages at which children apply verbal-list processes, and later image processes, to both the days of the week and months contents. But there are also several problems with such an explanation. The ages at which verbal-list processing is applied to these contents, about seven or eight years in these studies, are several years after apparently similar processes can be applied to the number series (e.g., Fuson and Hall, 1983; Siegler and Robinson, 1982) and the alphabet. Second, if we attribute the ability to solve backward order problems like those in Studies 7 and 8 to some general operation that subserves reversing temporal sequences, then it is clear that such an operation can be applied to several other contents by early or middle childhood. In two unpublished studies, I have found that children can make accurate judgments of the backward order of daily activities by six to nine years, the age depending on the particular task. The wider literature on the ability to reverse temporal sequences (e.g., Brown, 1976; Fivush and Mandler, 1985) also shows accurate judgments at early ages, usually by about six years.

A third comparison relevant to the generality of the change is between temporal and spatial representation. It is possible that the emergence of image representations during adolescence is the result of a broad shift in capacity or format that leads to new types of spatial representations as well. For example, Hardwick, McIntyre and Pick (1976) found that adults, but not fifth graders, could mentally rotate cognitive maps. In an earlier work (Friedman, 1982), I suggested that some common process appearing during adolescence may underly both this achievement and temporal imagery. The problem, it now seems to me, is knowing what level of spatial knowledge should be compared to the temporal image system. Certainly some configurational knowledge about space is present well before adolescence. For example, Hazen (1982) has shown that preschoolers can infer alternate routes to a goal, and, at a more advanced level, Anooshian and Young (1981) found that children from grades 1 to 5 had developed sufficiently general representations of their neighborhood that they could point to the location of landmarks that were out of view. The ability to manipulate spatial representations continues to develop into adolescence (Anooshian & Young, 1981; Hardwick et al., 1976), but it seems likely that the sorts of mental operations involved in my temporal image tasks can be applied to spatial images at earlier ages.

Given these difficulties for a general stage model, it seems useful to try to explain the ages and changes in terms specific to the day and month contents. To do so I think it is helpful to consider three kinds of influences on the development of representations for a particular domain, 1) the formal structure of the content, 2) natural representational and processing constraints, and 3) the history of operations that an individual performs on the content. The first factor determines what information must be captured in a representation. For the days of the week and months, relationships like forward order, recurrence, and the relative times of nonadjacent elements may be represented. For other contents different relationships are important. Alphabet representations need not encode recurrence, whereas number representations must capture additional information, such as decade structure or arithmetic relations.

The second constraint on representational development is that humans apparently can only process information in limited numbers of ways. For example, some theorists have suggested that verbal-articulatory and image systems are responsive for most operations that are performed in working memory (e.g., Baddeley and Lieberman, 1980; Paivio, 1971, 1978). In the image—verbal-list model, both systems are suitable for "on line" extraction of information about the order of days or months. But the cognitive system also allows other ways of extracting order information, such as the direct retrieval of associates to a problem (e.g., see Siegler and Shrager, 1984). The important point, from a developmental perspective, is that this set of processes offers potential ways of recovering structural information, but that the formal structure of a domain and the third factor, the history of operations performed on the content, determine which representations and processes are actually used at particular points in development.

By tracing the temporal tasks that children and adolescents typically face as they grow older, we can get some idea of why day and week representations might change when and in the way that they do. Children probably hear day and month names as early as they hear numbers. But direct teaching and rehearsal apparently begin earlier for the number series than the days of the week or months. By the early school years, number representations already include cyclic counting rules and many arithmetic problem-answer associations (Siegler and Robinson, 1982; Siegler and Shrager, 1984). Day and month order are usually just beginning to be taught at about this time. When parents and teachers do teach the days and months, they present them verbally as a series, and expect children to memorize that series. This is typically accomplished by about second or third grade. Interestingly, the development of number representations and day and month representations have diverged by this time, because children are not taught temporal operations analogous to addition and subtraction. If they were, adults would presumably be able to use retrieval rather than a lengthy search process to determine what day or month is *n* elements before or after another (see Study 6).

Probably in the years after the days and months are first learned, overt and covert recitation is the most frequent operation performed. Parents and teachers usually regard the ability to recite the elements in conventional order as the criterion for "knowing" the days or months. Most likely the verbal-list process is also used for day-to-day thinking about the order of days or months, such as how long it is until some time of interest (e.g., a weekend or birthday). As Studies 7, 8 and 9 indicated, verbal-list processes can be used to solve many such problems. The question is raised, then, why image representations eventually develop and why they do so around early to midadolescence.

Perhaps the answer relates to a decrease in late middle childhood in the frequency of prompted recitation and thus an increase in the proportion of operations devoted to real life problem solving. Whereas requests to say the days or months in order may strengthen verbal-list representations, day-to-day temporal problem solving may produce pressures for more flexible processing. For instance, in planning future activities, we often consider the relationship between two or more times. An example would be relating the present to the times when two assignments are due or the present to an upcoming holiday. The verbal-list system is not well suited to representing relative times of occurrence because of its sequential nature – only one element is easily available at a time. Possibly children begin extracting order information using the verbal-list system but convert it to spatial-like images in order to hold the relationship in working memory. If such working images are constructed frequently enough, information about the relative times of occurrence of more and more elements may be stored in a permanent image generating structure. This representation could then be used to construct images suitable to the demands of future problems.

The essential claim is that image representations of days of the week and month structure develop through a kind of "natural selection" process. Models of representation that are efficient in capturing important structural properties will develop through trial and error, subject to natural representational and processing constraints. The transition from the verbal-list stage to the stage at which image representations are also present takes place so late because of the heavy emphasis placed on recitation by parents and teachers, its utility in memorizing the order of verbal elements, and perhaps the relative infrequency of day-to-day temporal problem solving during the childhood years. It is also possible that exposure to time lines, perhaps around early adolescence, plays a role in the development of temporal imagery, but the very idiosyncratic nature of the images that adults report casts some doubt on the importance of conventional representations.

If the history of operations is the critical factor in determining timing and direction of change, it should be possible to design interventions that would induce imagery well before adolescence, just as one would expect that verbal-list representations could be induced in early childhood. Similarly, it seems likely that flexible representation of the temporal order of daily activities develop at substantially earlier ages than for days and months because of the frequency with which children think about the former relationships. I am currently conducting a series of studies designed to characterize representations of the times of daily events from early to middle childhood. The results so far indicate considerable flexibility in the operations that can be performed by six– and seven-year-olds.

This focus on the history of operations may also help us to understand the failures that even adults show in conceptualizing some temporal relations. For example, most adults seem to have difficulty understanding the effects of shifting to or from daylight saving time on the clock time at which natural events, such as the sun rising or feeling hungry for lunch, will occur. In an unpublished study, I have found that about 20 to 50 per cent of a sample of college students err on such questions. Examination of thinking-aloud protocols of students solving these sorts of problems indicates that they often have difficulty generating a representation of critical problem information. It seems that a particularly common error is thinking of the change being unidimensional (e.g., things are "later" or "earlier") rather than as a displacement between one reference system, clock times, and another, the sequence of natural events. Thus, for example, there is confusion over whether the clock time of eating lunch is "later" than before the shift to daylight saving time or eating lunch is "later" with respect to the natural sequence, the time at which one naturally becomes hungry. Presumably, attempts to solve these sorts of problems are so infrequent that adequate representations of the temporal relationships never develop.

SUMMARY

In this chapter I have considered the questions of how adults represent and process information about the order of the days of the week and months of the year and how these representations/processes change with development. A number of psychological models could be used to explain this knowledge, including associative, propositional and semantic models. However, several lines of evidence seem to favor the importance of image and verbal-list systems. The image system is assumed to code position-like information for each day or month and to allow simultaneous access to information about the "location" of multiple elements. The verbal-list system codes links between each element and its successor. Processing is assumed to involve sequential verbal-articulatory activation of elements. A number of properties were deduced from this characterization and tested in experiments using college students.

The first prediction was that concurrent verbal processing should interfere selectively with temporal tasks designed to engage the verbal-list system, whereas concurrent spatial monitoring should interfere selectively with temporal tasks designed to engage the image system. An experiment crossing the two task types with verbal and spatial interference conditions showed the expected pattern of results.

Another four experiments tested the prediction that processing in the image system is functionally similar to judging visible spatial positions. In two of these experiments, subjects compared the length of two intervals of months of the year or days of the week. Under the image model, one should expect that as the difference between the two intervals gets larger, problems become easier. Serial and associative models imply an independent prediction, that problems increase in difficulty as the total length of the two intervals becomes greater. The results for both week and month experiments supported the image model and were inconsistent with the other two models.

The next two experiments in this series required subjects to judge whether one day or month was closer to another reference day or month by going forward or backward in time from the reference element. The image model predicts increasing difficulty as separations approach one half of a cycle. Response times and accuracy showed the expected pattern in both experiments.

Another experiment tested two predicted differences between the image and verbal-list systems using tasks which, according to the model, would evoke the two types of processing. One prediction is that the disadvantage of judging backward relative to forward order would be greater for verbal-list than image processing tasks. The other is that the length of the interval covered would be a stronger determinant of problem difficulty for verbal-list than image tasks. Both of these predictions were confirmed.

Two additional types of evidence supported the distinction between verbal-list and image processing of the order of days of the week and months of the year. First, there were selective correlations between subjects' performance on a temporal image task and a spatial image task. Similarly, performance on a temporal verbal-list task was selectively related to performance on an alphabet judgment task. Second, introspections in several of the preceding experiments were consistent in content with the two-process model.

The remaining studies applied the image—verbal-list model to the development of children's and adolescents' knowledge of days of the week and months of the year. In two of these studies, subjects were asked to judge forward and backward relative order of days and months. I assumed that children who possess verbal-list, but not image, representations would be able to solve only the forward problems. Those who also possess image representation should be able to solve both sets. The results showed that forward problems were mastered by fourth or fifth grade, but it was not until about the tenth grade that most subjects could accurately solve the backward problems.

These age trends in the availability of image processing were supported by a final experiment. Subjects were asked to decide whether a given day or month was one of the next three days or four months after a reference element. I assumed that subjects who have only verbal-list processing available would need to search through each successive month or day after the reference element until they encounter either the other element or the third day (or fourth month). In contrast, subjects who also possess image representations should be able to rapidly access the information that a distant element was well beyond the decision boundary. The results showed a shift from the first to the second pattern between childhood and adolescence.

These findings indicate that image representations develop during early to mid adolescence, leading to more efficient ways of extracting certain order relationships. We cannot be sure what factors control the timing of this transition, but the developmental history of operations performed on these contents seems to offer a promising explanation. Whatever form the developmental account finally takes, it is clear that by adolescence representations are present that enable us to understand where, in our complexly structured temporal world, we are.

References

Anooshian, L. J. & Young, D. (1981). Developmental changes in cognitive maps of a familiar neighborhood. *Child Development, 52*, 341–348.

Baddleley, A. D., Lewis, V. & Nimmo-Smith, I. (1978). When did you last . . . ? In M. M. Gruneberg & R. N. Sykes (Eds.), *Practical aspects of memory.* London: Academic Press.

Baddleley, A. D., & Lieberman, K. (1980). Spatial working memory. In R. S. Nickerson (Ed.), *Attention and performance VII* (pp. 521–539). Hillsdale, NJ: Erlbaum.

Banks, W. P. (1977). Encoding and processing of symbolic information in comparative judgments. In G. H. Bower (Ed.), *The psychology of learning and motivation* (Vol.11). New York: Academic Press.

Banks, W. P., Fujii, M., & Kayra-Stuart, F. (1976). Semantic congruity effects in comparative judgements of magnitudes of digits. *Journal of Experimental Psychology: Human Perception and Performance, 2*, 435–447.

Baum, D. & Jonides, J. (1979). Cognitive maps: Analysis of comparative judgments of distance. *Memory & Cognition, 7* (6), 462–468.

Brooks, L. R. (1968). Spatial and verbal components of the act of recall. *Canadian Journal of Psychology, 22*, 349–368.

Brown, A. L. (1976). The construction of temporal succession by preoperational children. In A. D. Pick (Ed.), *Minnesota symposia on Child Psychology* (Vol.10) (pp. 28–83). Minneapolis: University of Minnesota Press.

Dean, A. L. & Harvey, W. O. (1979). An information-processing analysis of a Piagetian imagery task. *Developmental Psychology,* 15, 474–475.

Evans, G. W. & Pezdek, K. (1980). Cognitive mapping: Knowledge of real-world distance & location information. *Journal of Experimental Psychology: Human Learning & Memory, 6* (1), 13–24.

Fairbanks, B. A. (1969). Experiments on the temporal aspects of number perception (Doctoral dissertation, University of Arizona, 1969). *Dissertation Abstracts International. 30*, 403B. (University Microfilms No. 69–10, 052).

Fivush, R. & Mandler, J. M. (1985). Development changes in the understanding of temporal sequence. *Child Development, 56*, 1437–1446.

Friedman, W. J. (1978). Development of time concepts in children. In H. W. Reese and L. P. Lipsitt (Eds.), *Advances in child development and behavior* (Vol. 12) (pp. 267–298). New York: Academic Press.

Friedman, W. J. (1982). Conventional time concepts and children's structuring of time. (In W. J. Friedman (Ed.). *The developmental psychology of time* (pp. 171–208). New York: Academic Press.

Friedman, W. J. (1983). Image and verbal processes in reasoning about the months of the year. *Journal of Experimental Psychology: Learning, Memory, and Cognition, 9*, 650–666.

Friedman, W. J. (1984). Analog and semantic models of judgments about the months of the year. *Memory and Cognition, 12*, 306–313.

Friedman, W. J. (1986). The development of children's knowledge of temporal structure. *Child Development, 57*, 1386–1400.

Friedman, W. J. & Wilkins, A. (1985). Scale effects in memory for the time of events. *Memory & Cognition, 13* (2), 168–175.

Fuson, K. C. & Hall, J. W. (1983). The acquisition of early number word meanings: A conceptual analysis and review. In H. P. Ginsburg (Ed.), *The development of mathematical thinking* (pp. 49–107). New York: Academic press.

Galton, F. (1883). *Inquiries into human faculty and its development.* New York: Macmillan.

Guilford, J. P. (1926). Spatial symbols in the apprehension of time. *American Journal of Psychology, 37*, 420–423.

Hardwick, D. A., McIntire, C. W. & Pick, H. L. (1976). The content and manipulation of cognitive maps in children and adults. *Monographs of the Society for Research in Child Development, 41* (3, Serial No. 166).

Hazen, N. L. (1982). Spatial exploration and spatial knowledge: Individual and developmental differences in very young children. *Child Development, 53*, 826–833.

Marmor, G. (1975). Development of kinetic images: When does the child first represent movement in mental images? *Cognitive Psychology, 7*, 548–559.

Moyer, R. S. (1973). Comparing objects in memory: Evidence suggesting an internal psychophysics. *Perception & Psychophysics, 13*, 180–184.

Moar, I. *Spatial processing in the recall of directions.* Manuscript submitted for publication, 1981.

Oswald, I. (1960). Number-forms and kindred visual images. *Journal of General Psychology, 63*, 81–88.

Paivio, A. (1971). *Imagery and verbal processes.* New York: Holt, Rinehart & Winston.

Paivio, A. (1978). Dual coding: Theoretical issues and empirical evidence. In J. C. Scandura & C. J. Brainerd (Eds.), *Structural/process models of complex human behavior* (pp. 528–549). Alphen aan den Rijn, The Netherlands: Sitjhoff & Noordhoff.

Seymour, P. H. K. (1980a). Semantic and structural coding of the months. *British Journal of Psychology, 71*, 379–393.

Seymour, P. H. K. (1980b). Internal representation of the months, An experimental analysis of spatial forms. *Psychological Research, 42*, 255–273.

Shepard, R. N. & Metzler, J. (1971). Mental rotation of three-dimensional objects. *Science, 171*, 701–703

Shepard, R. N. & Podgorny, P. (1978). Cognitive processes that resemble perceptual processes In W. Estes (Ed.), *Handbook of learning and cognitive processes. Vol. 5. Human information processing* (pp. 189–237). Hillsdale, NJ: Erlbaum.

Shoben, E. J., Cech, C. G., & Schwaneflugel, P.J. (1983). The role of subtractions and comparisons in comparative judgments involving numerical reference points. *Journal of Experimental Psychology: Human Perception & Performance, 9*, 226–241.

Siegler, R. S. & Robinson, M. (1982). The development of numerical understandings. In H. W. Reese & L. P. Lipsitt (Eds.), *Advances in child development and behavior* (Vol. 16) (pp. 241–312). New York: Academic Press.

Siegler, R. S. & Shrager, J. (1984). Strategy choices in addition and subtraction: How do children know what to do? In C. Sophian (Ed.), *Origins of cognitive skills* (pp. 229–287). Hillsdale, NJ: Erlbaum.

Thurstone, L. L., & Thurstone, T. G. (1965). *The Primary Mental Abilities Tests.* Chicago, IL: Science Research Associates.

Woodworth, R. S., & Scholsberg, H. (1965). *Psychology* (Revised ed.). New York: Holt, Rinehart & Winston.

TIME AND HUMAN COGNITION
A Life-Span Perspective
I. Levin and D. Zakay (Editors)

CHAPTER 8

DOUGLAS POYNTER

Judging the Duration of Time Intervals: A Process of Remembering Segments of Experience

INFERRING TIME'S PASSAGE

It seems paradoxical to suggest that perception of time is actually the perception of something "nontemporal". Perhaps this is because other forms of perception are founded in the transduction of physical energy by a sensory organ, so that there is an obvious physical correlate to that which is perceived. The perceived brightness of a light source, for example, is a phenomenal correlate of the firing rate of cells in the retina, which in turn is a correlate of retinal illuminance. Here one can see a direct link between the physical dimension and the perceived dimension.

In contrast, the perception of time passage does not involve an obvious transduction of physical energy by a sensory organ. There are cell systems in the brain of many species of animals that are called "biological clocks", including the Suprachiasmatic Nuclei (see Moore-Ede et al., 1982), but these cell systems are not sensory organs. That is, they do not transduce amounts of physical time into amounts of biological time. They are called clocks because their biochemical functioning follows a cyclical pattern of change with a predictable period.

In fact, all clocks, biological or manmade, express time's passage by manifesting a cycle of change which is believed to be of constant (or at least predictable) duration. Of course one never knows for sure that a particular clock has a constant period. One can only gain evidence that it does by comparing the clock's output to the output of another clock believed to be more accurate. And to test the accuracy of the more accurate clock, its output is compared to yet another clock one has even more confidence in. Ultimately, the accuracy of our most trusted clock is inferred by comparing its timing of a natural phenomenon with independent calculations of the phenomenal duration; these calculations are made from measurements of nontemporal dimensions and trusted physical laws (e.g., the laws of Mechanics).

In all cases of interval timing that I can think of, it seems that the duration of an interval is inferred using one of two methods. One is to choose a process that is believed to output a regular pattern of observable change (e.g., the movement of a metronome), then monitor the number of cycles in that process that occur between the endpoints of the interval in question. The other is to measure the spatial distance traveled by a mass or particle-like energy (with a known velocity) through the course of the interval in question. The interval duration can then be inferred on the basis of the accepted relationship between time, distance, and velocity. The first type of interval timing provides the physical model for the change/segmentation hypothesis of duration judgment. The second type of interval timing seems a good model for explaining the Kappa effect, discussed near the end of the chapter.

In effect, both of these methods of duration judgment involve an accounting of change along a "nontemporal" dimension. In the first method, the changes attended to depend on the cyclic process involved. If sound is the nontemporal dimension, then changes in amplitude might be counted; if light intensity is the nontemporal dimension, then changes in candela/area might be counted. In the second method, where time is derived from the relationship between time, distance, and velocity, change in the spatial location of an object is measured.

So in the search for an explanation of how one perceives the passage of time, it seems reasonable to start with the assumption that we use the same strategy for measuring time without clocks that we do with clocks. Ernst Mach expressed this idea nicely in his book, *The Science of Mechanics* (cited in Bertotti, 1978):

> It is utterly beyond our power to measure the changes of things by time. Quite the contrary, time is an abstraction, at which we arrive by means of the change of things,

or as Gibson (1975) expressed it, "Events are perceivable, But time is not".

I believe Fraisse (1963) was the first to state a specific change hypothesis for time perception, and since then, several other researchers have proposed others (e.g., Block and Reed, 1978; Block, 1982; Poynter, 1983a; Poynter and Homa, 1983).

In the next section, I will discuss three models of duration judgment, including one based on the experience of *change*. Following that discussion, the models will be compared in terms of their ability to predict the results of experiments which have investigated the effects of interval content on duration judgment.

MODELS OF DURATION JUDGMENT

The three models discussed in this section each present somewhat different explanations of how humans estimate duration without the use of clocks. All three are cognitive (versus biological) explanations, because mechanisms of attention, memory, and information processing play an important role in their logic. None of the explanations are fully developed theories of time perception. In fact, they provide only qualitative predictions of some of the common findings which have emerged from the body of published studies. In addition, the experimental results presented as evidence for the validity of any one of the models can often be explained just as well by the other two. Yet each approach makes a unique and important contribution to the goal of understanding the way in which humans conceptualize time passage, and it is hoped that by the end of the chapter, each of these contributions will be clarified.

Duration Judgment Based on Storage-size

Ornstein (1969) suggested with his "storage-size" hypothesis that the perceived duration of an interval is based on the contents of memory associated with the judged interval. The idea is that the more information one stores during an interval of time, the greater will be its perceived duration. Ornstein proposed two specific factors that can influence the "size" of memory stores — the amount of information presented during an interval, and the complexity of that information.

In my reading of the literature, the storage-size model (SS) appears to be the most frequently cited explanation of duration judgment, and many studies have been performed to test its predictive utility. The model was originally applied to the estimation of relatively long durations (i.e., a minute or so). Fraisse (1984) referred to this as "retrospective duration estimation", to emphasize the fact that long-term memory mechanisms play an important role.

Duration Judgment Based on Processing Time

Several authors have proposed processing-time (PT) explanations of duration judgment, including Avant et al. (1975) and Thomas (Thomas and Brown, 1974; Thomas and Weaver, 1975). Thomas and Weaver's ideas in particular seem to have generated quite a bit of interest, and will be discussed in more depth here. While the model is focussed on the judgment of very short durations (<100 msec) presented in the visual modality, the basic concepts seem well suited to more general application.

One of the key assumptions of the model is that duration judgments are based on the output of two processors (a timer and a stimulus processor). Both processors influence duration judgment, but their individual contributions are determined by the share of attention allocated to each during the interval. When the amount of information in an interval is large, it is assumed that the share of attention allocated to the timer is small. As a result, the output of the timer is relatively low and unreliable, and its contribution to the duration judgment is subsequently small. Likewise, when the amount of stimulus information is small, the influence of the stimulus processor on the duration judgment is relatively small, because its output and reliability are low. In the case where a duration estimate is unexpectedly requested after the subject has experienced the interval, the estimate is assumed to be based almost entirely on the output of the stimulus processor. In the case where the subject is informed ahead of time that a duration estimate will be required, and the interval is devoid of stimuli, the duration judgment is assumed to be based almost entirely on the timer output.

Zakay, et al. (1983) has proposed another PT model which is similar to Thomas and Weaver's, in that it assumes a cognitive timer exists that requires attentional resources for its function. The model further assumes that as the amount of nontemporal information in an interval increases, attentional allocation switches from the timer to nontemporal processing; and this results in a reduction of temporal output. This is predicted to cause an inverse relationship between the level of stimulus processing required during an interval and perceived duration. The model differs from Thomas and Weaver's in that stimulus processing is not believed to directly affect duration judgment.

Duration Judgment Based on Change

Fraisse (1984) described the notion of time as embodying two primary concepts:

> The notion of time applies to two different concepts which may be clearly recognized from our personal experience of change: (a) The concept of succession, which corresponds to the fact that two or more events can be perceived as different and organized sequentially; it is based on our experience of the continuous changing through which the present becomes the past; (b) the concept of duration, which applies to the interval between two successive events. Duration has no existence in and of itself but is the intrinsic characteristic of that which endures.

Fraisse (1963), Block and Reed (1978), Block (1982), Poynter (1983a), and Poynter and Homa (1983) have all provided evidence for a change model of duration judgment. The approach emphasized in this chapter (see Poynter and Homa, 1983) shares several key assumptions with the two models previously described. First, it shares with the storage size model the assumption that the number and organization of memories associated with a time interval determines its perceived duration. Second, it shares with several of the processing time models the assumption that time perception is affected by the processing of interval events, and involves dynamic switching of attention between various types of information.

An important distinction between the change/segmentation approach (CS) and other models is that it does not rely on the notion of a single timing mechanism, or a single method for judging duration for all individuals and all contexts. Consonant with the ideas expressed by Fraisse in the quotation above, the change approach assumes that judgment of interval duration is based on the ability to remember the sequence of events experienced during an interval, and to infer inter-event duration on the basis of the "intrinsic characteristic of that which endures" in memory.

JUDGMENT OF "FILLED" TIME

Poynter and Homa (1983) have proposed that the number of sensory events "filling" a time interval should be an important factor in estimating duration, because the number of events determines the amount of "sensory" change experienced, and change is the psychological index of time passage. Not only the number of events in an interval, but also the degree of contextual change each event produces should affect perceived duration.

A small degree of change per event should produce a small effect on duration judgment, and a large degree of change per event should produce a large effect.

In addition to the number and magnitude of sensory changes occurring in the interval, the organization of these events should influence duration judgments. When events are presented in such a way that they can be easily remembered in an ordered sequence, then they make their maximum contribution to the size of the duration estimate.

JUDGMENT OF "EMPTY" TIME

The CS model assumes that judgments of empty duration can be based on several types of information, and that the particular type chosen depends upon a number of variables, including the duration of the interval to be judged, whether the judgment is "prospective" or "retrospective", and the temporal pattern of subintervals (regular vs. irregular).

If it is true that the perception of time is always the perception of change, then the perception of empty time must be assumed to follow from the monitoring of change which is not readily apparent. This seems a very strong assumption, given that our biological existence is defined by a myriad of cyclic biochemical changes that exist in homeostasis. We are all aware at some point or another of the rhythm of our hearts, and perhaps most frequently we are aware of it when our attention is not otherwise occupied with attention to stimulation through our primary senses (i.e., during "empty" time). I have previously called events like heart beats "organismic" change, to distinguish them from sensory changes that have a direct physical correlate in the external environment.

Aside from discrete organismic events like heart beats and respirations, human memory contains a wealth of learned routines which can be used as fillers, and therefore yardsticks, of empty time. These routines can be neuro-muscular "loops" (e.g., finger or foot tapping, tongue "clicking", counting "one-one thousand, two-one thousand, . . . " etc.), or the mental replaying of learned event sequences (e.g., melodies and musical rhythms). In some of my own research (Poynter and Homa, 1983) and in that of others (Schiffman and Bobko, 1974), subjects are sometimes asked to avoid using counting strategies, as if to imply that such methods of duration measurement are not part of the natural duration judgment mechanism. In retrospect, however, these strategies seem very much a part of the natural mechanism. In the developmental literature, researchers have observed that by the age of 7 years, most children spontaneously use counting strategies to measure the duration of events (Levin, Wilkening, and Dembo, 1984; Wilkening, Levin, and Druyan, 1987).

In the previous paragraphs, it was suggested that attending to organismic change is one method of tracking empty time. A second type of cue to the duration of so-called interstimulus intervals (ISIs) is the perceived discreteness of the stimuli that bound them. Consider the visual experience produced by each of the two event sequences in Figure 8.1. One can imagine that the perceived discreteness of pulses in Figure 8.1a would be less than in 8.1b, because the duration of empty time between pulses is greater in 8.1b.

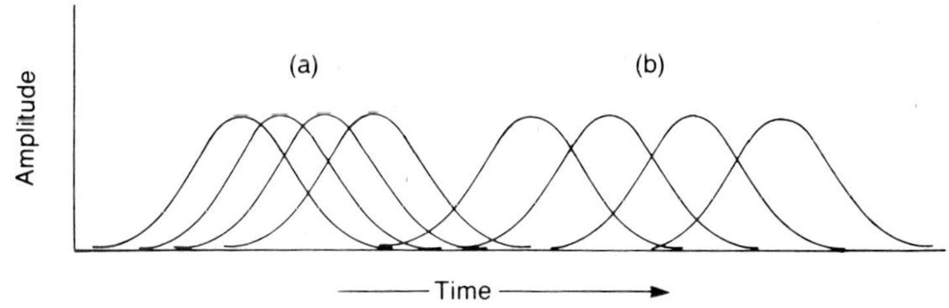

Figure 8.1. An example of how empty time might affect the perceptual quality of stimuli that bound an interval. The ISI in (a) results in a relatively low amplitude modulation compared to (b).

So in some cases, the length of the ISI can affect the quality of stimulus percepts. As a consequence, stimulus discreteness can be an indirect cue to the length of ISIs.

PROSPECTIVE VS. RETROSPECTIVE JUDGMENTS

The CS approach assumes that when a subject knows a duration estimate will be required, he will attempt to parcel experienced change into memorable segments of duration, following the same principles of "chunking" that seem to work so well for memorizing other types of information (e.g., telephone numbers). The markers he decides to use for time segmentation (and therefore the size of the segments) will depend on the clock duration of the interval. Naturally, then, he must generate an expectation about the interval length before he can be expected to select a proper segment size. If the interval is short, then articulating the utterances "one-one thousand, two-one thousand, etc." provides a memorable segmentation of the interval. If the interval is on the order of days or weeks, the circadian period provides a convenient timing segment. The logic here is that timing with man-made clocks and perceptual mechanisms follows the same simple rule — one does not use a millisecond stopwatch to time hours in duration, nor a sundial to time milliseconds in duration.

The passive observer, who does not seek regularly occurring events to help segment the interval into easily memorable units, is still automatically storing events that segment time. The difference is that the events are probably not organized in a way that is optimal for retrieval.

Whatever the coding strategy (or even if there isn't one), the CS model assumes that temporal segments, once remembered, can be mentally articulated as a method for reproducing duration, or compared to a second set of segments associated with a standard interval in categorical or magnitude estimation tasks.

When the time estimate is retrospective (i.e., the interval is experienced before the subject is informed about the time estimation task), the duration judgment will depend more on the task demands of the interval. If the interval is filled with sensory stimuli, then the estimate will be based primarily on the number and discreteness of the sensory changes remembered from the interval. If the interval is empty, then the estimate will depend on the number of discrete thoughts and other organismic events the subject can remember. If the interval is filled with a processing task (e.g., multiplying digits), then the estimate will probably depend on the number of processed items the subject can remember.

ESTIMATING TIME IN EVERYDAY LIFE

The change/segmentation approach begins with an assumption that to sense time passage is to sense change, and then describes duration judgment as a process of remembering segments of experience marked by sensory and organismic events. We are obviously inundated by events in everyday life, but only a few provide the milestones for partitioning the continuity of experience into sequential segments. The CS model assumes that the salience of events filling an interval, how discrete they are, and how they are organized in the interval are factors which affect the remembered duration of an everyday interval of time. Characteristics of the observer, including the motivation to attend to passing events, attentional demands, and attentional capacity, will also influence remembered duration.

Whether a given event turns out to be a useful marker of time passage depends on the length of time which is to be remembered. If the duration is on the scale of years (e.g., estimating how long a person has lived), then knowledge of lifespan changes in physical appearance are salient. If the scale is seconds, then heart beats are salient markers. If the scale is cosmic, then trusted physical laws are the only available clues to the passage of time, because durations of this scale are outside the realm of human experience. Learning temporal relations through observation of natural event sequences enhances the potential for inferring duration from non-temporal information. In fact, this type of duration inference is the most common explanation for the socalled Kappa effect, which refers to the influence of interstimulus distance on the perception of interstimulus duration. Here the temporal extent of an interval is being inferred from the relationship between time, distance, and velocity.

It would be a more difficult task to remember ordered sequences of change if they were bidirectional in time. In most cases, however, sequences of events occur in one direction, but not the other. From this observation comes the phrase "the arrow of time" (cf. Leggett, 1978). We know, for example, the proper time-ordered sequence of photographic frames imaging a gun, a bullet near the muzzle of the gun, and a hole in a target — the gun projects the bullet out of the muzzle, and the bullet makes a hole in the target. We are all firm in our belief the the actual sequence of events could never have occurred in the reverse direction. Through experience, then, we learn the proper relationship of events in time.

SUMMARY

The change/segmentation model proposes that duration judgments are a function of (1) the number of perceived events (both sensory and organismic) (2) the discreteness of the events, and (3) how memorable the events are — this in turn will depend on how easily the pattern of events can be "chunked" or reduced for efficient storage and retrieval. Here one can see that the change/segmentation approach, like the storage-size model, assumes storage and retrieval mechanisms play an important role in duration judgment. Finally, the model assumes, as do all the cognitive models of duration judgment, that attentional mechanisms play an important role in duration judgment.

A COMPARISON OF THE PREDICTIVE UTILITY OF THREE MODELS

Many of the duration judgment experiments I have read either directly or indirectly test the effects of processing "nontemporal" information during the judged interval. In this section, the *storage-size (SS), processing time (PT),* and *change/segmentation (CS)* models are compared in terms of their ability to predict the effects of the experimental manipulations listed below:

1) manipulations of the number of events, the organization of events, and event discreteness (e.g., Adams, 1977; Buffardi, 1971; Poynter, 1979; Poynter, 1983a; Poynter, 1983b; Poynter and Homa, 1983).
2) manipulations of the complexity of static stimulus patterns (e.g., Ornstein, 1969; Mulligan and Schiffman, 1979).
3) manipulations of the amount or type of nontemporal processing required of subjects (e.g., Burnside, 1971; Hicks et al., 1976; Zakay et al., 1983).

Number of Events, Event Organization, and Event Discreteness

NUMBER OF EVENTS

Two studies I have included in this section are actually manipulations of the number of stimuli remembered from the interval (with the actual number of stimuli held constant), while the other three studies are manipulations of actual number of stimuli, without regard for the number remembered.

Block (1974), for example, presented words in a 160 second interval either blocked by category membership or presented in a random format. The blocked condition produced significantly longer duration estimates and higher recall memory scores. In a similar experiment (Poynter, 1979), subjects judged the duration of a 195 second interval filled either with easy-to-remember words or hard-to-remember words. Half the subjects were given memory prompts just prior to the time estimation task. Consistent with the storage-size model, judged duration paralleled recall performance. That is, duration judgments were longest for the easy-to-remember intervals and for the group of subjects who were given memory prompts.

The effect of actual stimulus number on perceived duration has been studied by Adams (1977), Buffardi (1971), and Poynter and Homa (1983). In Buffardi's study, a paired comparison task was used to determine the effects of number and organization of stimulus events. Intervals were 1056 msec in duration, and were presented in the auditory (1200 Hz beeps), tactile (momentary vibrations on the index finger), and visual (light flashes) modalities. Results provided strong evidence for the effects of event number on perceived duration. Regardless of modality, duration judgments were a positive function of the number of events. Event number accounted for 69% of the response variability, and event organization accounted for 23%. Adams (1977) employed durations ranging from 800 to 1200 msec, filled with 0 to 5 auditory beeps. The magnitude of the FDI (i.e., the positive relationship between perceived duration and number of events) was found to depend on factors which presumably affected the degree of attention paid to the beeps filling the interval. Specifically, when the filler beeps were presented through a different earphone channel than the endpoint markers, the FDI decreased. Embedding the intervals in an ongoing sequence of background pulses also reduced the magnitude of the FDI. The effect of event organization found in this study will be discussed in the next section. Poynter and Homa presented subjects with intervals ranging from .8 to 16 secs in actual duration. Intervals were filled with a variable number of sensory events (0 to 8 light flashes), and the reproduction method of time estimation was employed. For short clock durations (<2.4 sec), the magnitude of reproductions was an increasing function of the number of light flashes. As the actual duration increased to 16 secs, however, the function relating number of flashes to duration estimates looked "U" shaped; intervals with less than two events were sometimes judged longer than more filled intervals. Figure 2 illustrates the hypothetical relationship between clock duration, event number, and perceived duration proposed by Poynter and Homa. The topography illustrates that the function relating number of sensory events to apparent duration is dependent upon the length of the judged interval. The function is positive when the clock duration is relatively short, negative when the clock duration is long, and "U" shaped when the clock duration is intermediate.

In one form or another, all of the models can predict the FDI in its most common form — increasing duration estimates with increasing number of interval fillers. The SS model predicts that with increasing number of events, storage-size increases and therefore duration judgments increase. A PT model that assumes a direct relationship between stimulus-processing time and duration judgment also predicts this finding — the more stimuli in an interval, the more time required to process them. For other versions of the PT model, predictions are less clear, however.

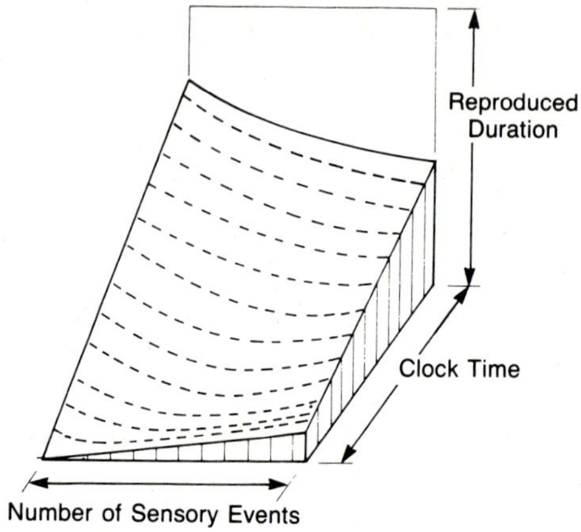

Figure 8.2. Hypothetical relationship between sensory-event number, clock duration, and reproduced duration based on data from Poynter and Homa (1983).

Can the theory that a single cognitive timer (requiring attentional resources for its operation) predict a positive relationship between number of sensory events and duration judgment? In the study by Burnside (1971), where the number of items processed was inversely related to task difficulty, one could assume that the cognitive timer was more active when many items were processed, because task difficulty was relatively low in this circumstance. This explanation for the FDI has been proposed by Zakay, et al. (1983). But when there is no reason to believe that the number of events filling an interval is confounded with task difficulty (Buffardi, 1971; Poynter and Homa, 1983), more events would always seem to result in less time allocated to the timer. And this should result in shorter time estimates, not longer.

The PT model of Thomas and Weaver explains the FDI for very short intervals with the following assumptions. First, it assumes that in estimating the duration of stimulus-filled intervals, the influence of the stimulus processor is large, because the ratio of filled to empty time is large. Second, it assumes that the output of the stimulus processor is a function of the processing time required to analyze the stimuli. For empty intervals, the duration judgment is thought to be based exclusively on the timer output, which should be equal to or less than the actual duration (depending on the attention allocated to the timer during the interval).

Other researchers have claimed that retinal persistence can account for the FDI in studies using very brief visual intervals (Long and Beaton,

1980; Long and Beaton, 1981). For longer intervals filled with a number of sequential stimuli, it could be argued that the FDI results from the cumulative effect of "neural" or "informational" persistence — that is, the persistence of the representation of a sensory event after its offset (Coltheart, 1980). A testable hypothesis follows from this explanation. An interval filled with stimuli of brief duration (that persist long after physical offset) should be judged longer than an equivalent interval filled with fewer stimuli of longer physical duration. This prediction is based on the idea that duration judgments are a function of the total amount of time required to process interval events. When the interval is filled with very brief stimuli, total processing time will exceed the sum of stimulus durations, so the interval should be judged longer than when longer-lasting stimuli fill the interval.

The CS model assumes that duration judgments are based on change, and in the absence of other differences, the more sensory events in an interval, the more change. Beyond just being another source of change, however, sensory events can serve to segment time into more easily encodable chunks of temporal experience. The presence of sensory events may therefore expand perceived duration by breaking the interval into segments that are easily stored and retrieved. On this basis, it follows that the presence of sensory events in an interval will sometimes produce longer estimates (the traditional FDI), and other times, shorter estimates. The latter will occur when interval events produce relatively small amounts of observable change (i.e., lack discreteness) or have little value as temporal markers because they are poorly organized, yet have priority access to attentional capacity. Events that are hard-to-remember, or dispersed in a way that does not lead to efficient storage of temporal segments, have little value as temporal markers. This idea helps to explain the type of interaction seen in Figure 8.2 between number of sensory events and clock duration. With short durations, lots of sensory events produce long duration estimates because their number is relatively large compared to organismic changes which could have been attended to had the sensory ones not been there. With longer intervals, however, the presence of occasional sensory events may only serve to interrupt the subject's focus of attention on mentally-generated segmenters (whether they be clicks of the tongue, taps of the foot, mental articulations like "one-one-thousand, two-one thousand", etc.), thereby degrading the structure of the memorial representation. In other words, vigilance to the occurrence of sparse sensory events can have a negative effect on duration judgments by taking attention away from more efficient strategies of temporal encoding involving organismic processes (e.g., mental counting, etc.)

To explain the interaction between clock duration and number of sensory events, the dual-processor PT model would have to assume that the weight given the timer increases with the ratio of (clock duration)/(number of events). The SS model would have to assume that storage-size is larger for filled intervals when clock duration is short, and larger for empty intervals when clock duration is long. This assumption would imply that storage and retrieval of covert events is taking place. With this assumption, the SS model and CS model say about the same thing.

As previously stated, the CS model assumes that subjects often segment time intervals with either mentally-generated events or experimenter-generated events that allow efficient chunking of temporal information. One of the implications of this assumption is that a subject's expectations of both interval content and duration will guide his choice of mental-timing routines or segmenters that are best for the interval at hand. Because these expectations will develop over the course of trials, it stands to reason that duration judgments on any one trial will be affected by experience in previous trials; in other words, response biases should be expected in duration judgment. Such biases do seem to occur, at least for duration reproduction. In Poynter and Homa's experiment, one group of subjects reproduced the duration of intervals containing 0–4 visual flashes, and a second group reproduced the same physical durations containing 4–8 flashes. Comparison of the duration estimates from each of these groups indicated that subjects observing the set of trials with 0–4 flashes estimated the 4–flash interval to be shorter than did the subjects who observed the 4–8 flash set. In other words, subjects who experienced more sensory markers in general tended to give longer estimates in general, suggesting a central tendency bias for reproduction estimates. This has also been demonstrated by Bobko et al. (1977).

In my own work, I have typically compared absolute duration judgments between experimental conditions, rather than the relative accuracy of judgments. But in estimation techniques where an accuracy score has a straightforward interpretation (e.g., reproduction), the latter analysis can provide additional insight. In Poynter and Homa's (1983) study, for example, the most accurate duration judgments were those associated with empty intervals. Whether these empty-interval judgments were short or long relative to judgments of filled, but otherwise comparable intervals, depended upon how many fillers were present and the clock duration of the interval. Perhaps this accuracy of empty-time estimates resulted from uninterrupted attention to the timer (Thomas and Weaver, 1975; Zakay et al. 1983), or in CS terms, from freedom to mentally generate individual– and duration-specific markers for efficient storage and retrieval of temporal information.

The general observation that degree of under– or overestimation depends on the interaction between number of sensory events and clock time seems to be consistent with models that believe both a timer (or equivalently, organismic change) and a stimulus processor (or equivalently, sensory change) contribute to the duration estimate.

EVENT ORGANIZATION

Several studies indicate that duration judgments are affected by the way in which events are arranged in the interval. Poynter (1983a), for example, presented subjects with relatively long intervals (3–4 minutes) that contained a set of unrelated nouns intermixed with a number of U.S. presidents' last names. In one condition the presidents' names were grouped at the beginning and end of the interval, and in another they were dispersed evenly throughout the interval. Subjects were told to try to remember all words in the list, but pay special attention to the presidents' names. While no differences in word recognition, recall, or perceived-number-of-events were found between conditions, duration judgments were much longer for the condition where presidents' names were interspersed between the other words in the list. Poynter suggested that the presidents' names were markers that served to segment temporal experience for subsequent retrieval. Given there were no memory differences for list items between the two conditions, the SS model can not predict these results, unless the claim is made that storage-size was not adequately measured. The PT models can not explain this finding either, unless one does not accept the assumption that the same amount of processing was required for both segmented and nonsegmented arrangements. An argument based on the number of switches back and forth between a timer and a nontemporal processor would not help explain the results, since both intervals contained the same number of events, and events were dispersed evenly throughout the interval.

Previously it was suggested that empty intervals can sometimes be reproduced more accurately than filled intervals (as was the case in Poynter and Homa's experiment) because subjects are free to internally generate their own regular pattern of fillers, at a rate which is individual and clock-duration specific. The claim was that a regular sequence of subject-generated events might help segment the interval for more efficient storage and retrieval. If the pattern of sensory events provided by the experimenter is regular, then storage and retrieval should also be facilitated, leading to relatively accurate judgments. In fact, evidence for this effect can be found in Schiffman and Bobko's (1974) study, in which medium-complexity intervals (filled with regularly occurring flashes of light) were estimated most accurately. In another study (Adams, 1977), categorization of stimulus durations was most accurate when interval fillers were regularly placed, so that repetition of a given subinterval occurred.

Buffardi (1971) found in his experiment that duration estimates were longer when interval fillers were placed at the beginning versus the end of the interval. This could be explained with the assumption that events occurring at the beginning defined the segment size for marking empty time through the rest of the interval. Because the entire interval was segmented into equal subintervals, storage of segments proceeded efficiently, resulting in full retrieval of temporal information. When the fillers were placed at the end, however, the subject's own strategy for encoding subintervals was interrupted by the onset of sensory events, resulting in unequal subintervals, less efficient storage, and fragmented retrieval of temporal information. This type of explanation could also be made with a PT model. A storage size explanation would have to rely on the assumption that when events are placed at the end of the interval, smaller storage-size results. This again requires the assumption that storage and retrieval of nonsensory information took place. As previously stated, the SS model looses distinction from the CS model with this added assumption.

EVENT DISCRETENESS

The individual distinctiveness of events filling an interval (i.e., event discreteness) can also influence duration judgments. The manipulations of experiments 3–5 in Poynter and Homa (1983) can be thought of manipulations of event discreteness, in that the amount of change between interval events was varied with each manipulation. In all three experiments, paired comparison judgments of duration were directly related to event discreteness.

The discreteness of sensory events filling an interval can also be an important determinant of duration judgments when a reproduction task is employed. In one experiment (Poynter, 1983b) subjects were required to reproduce intervals filled with a sequentially-presented set of 42 squares. Each square was placed at a different spatial location, so that by the end of the interval, the zig-zag pattern shown in Figure 8.3 was filled. The 42 locations in the pattern were filled in one of three sequences. In the first sequence (Figure 8.3a), locations were filled from top left to bottom right. The second sequence (Figure 8.3b) was more fragmented — each segment of the pattern developed in a sequence from left to right or top to bottom, but the order of segment development was random. In the third sequence (Figure 8.3c), the event order was entirely fragmentary — that is, there was no spatio-temporal correlation.

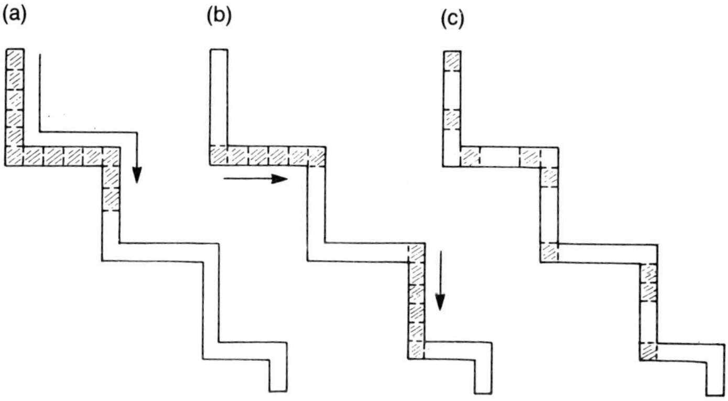

Figure 8.3. Illustration of the sequence of events observed by subjects in Poynter (1983b). (a) the 42 squares were presented from top left to bottom right, (b) each segment developed from top to bottom or left to right, but segments did not develop in a systematic order. (c) the pattern of development was entirely random.

Each pattern was bounded with 2000 Hz beeps to signal the beginning and end of time intervals. The end beep was followed by a two second empty interval, followed by another beep, which was the beginning of the reproduction. Subjects pressed a button when they believed that the duration of the preceding visual display had been reproduced. Each of twelve subjects reproduced the three patterns of Figure 3 four times. In two of the replications, the squares flashed on, then immediately off, and in the other two the squares persisted once they appeared. One of two replications in each of these conditions was 6.2 sec in duration, and the other 8.2 sec. This gave a presentation rate of 6.7 and 5.1 squares/sec, respectively. When the squares flashed on then off, each square was present for approximately .12 sec.

There were two significant results of this study. Mean reproductions were longer (and less accurate) when events disappeared than when they persisted. ($F(1,11)=25.0$, $p<.001$). On average, reproductions were 2% underestimates of clock duration when events persisted, and 14% overestimates when events disappeared.

Second, the magnitude of this event-discreteness effect depended on the pattern of events filling the interval ($F(2,22)=10.0$, $p<.001$). Differences between persistent and disappearing trials were 30%, 11%, and 8%, for patterns a, b, and c, respectively. In other words, the more complicated the order of events in the interval, the smaller the effect of event discreteness. Further research is needed to clarify exactly why this occurred; one explanation is that subjects were not able to remember the events in the interval as well when they disappeared, and this was especially true for the more complicated patterns (b and c). As a result, the effect of event discreteness was to some degree offset by difficulty in remembering temporal markers for these patterns. In other words, the discrete changes experienced in an interval can only affect duration reproductions to the extent that they can be remembered in the estimation task. The importance of event retrieval in duration judgment has been demonstrated in several previous experiments (e.g., Ornstein, 1969; Poynter, 1979).

The CS model has a simple explanation for the main effect of event discreteness on duration judgment. An event's discreteness is a correlate of the amount of change it produces. So intervals filled with discrete events are also filled with many changes, and are therefore perceived as relatively long.

A PT model might explain the effect by assuming that discrete stimuli take longer to process than more uniform or continuous stimulation, and perceived duration is directly related to stimulus processing time. The SS model would have to claim that storage size is directly related to event discreteness.

Complexity of Stimulus Information

Several studies have examined the relationship between the complexity of information filling an interval and the length of duration estimates (Ornstein, 1969; Mulligan and Schiffman, 1979). Ornstein proposed that stimulus complexity affects the amount of storage space required to encode stimulus information; and as a result, stimulus complexity affects perceived duration. Mulligan and Schiffman (1979) and Ornstein (1969) tested the effects of stimulus complexity on judged duration. Both of their experiments used 60 second intervals, similar strategies for manipulating complexity, and a retrospective duration judgment task. In Mulligan and Schiffman's study, a code for interpreting the stimulus pattern was provided either before the stimulus interval, after the stimulus interval (but before the duration judgment), or not at all. Duration estimates were in line with what the storage-size model predicts. Subjects presented with a complex stimulus (along with a code to help simplify its interpretation) reported shorter stimulus durations than subjects who saw the same stimulus without the simplifying code. The stimuli for these experiments were ambiguous line drawings or verbal passages.

The storage-size explanation for this finding is that the simplifying code allowed the subjects to store the stimulus information in a more efficient and organized manner than when no code was available. And presumably, the more efficient the storage, the smaller the storage size.

The CS model requires a similar assumption about the contents of memory, except that the emphasise is on the number of discrete elements representing the stimulus pattern, rather than the storage space required. In other words, complex stimulus patterns are sometimes perceived to be longer than simple patterns because the representation of the information is less unified, and broken into more segments. Supplying a simplifying code allows for more holistic encoding, which reduces the number of temporal segments to refer to estimating the duration of the interval.

If one assumes that complex stimuli require more processing time than simple stimuli, then PT models emphasizing attention to a timer predict that complex stimulus intervals should be estimated as shorter than simple stimulus intervals, not longer. For dual-processor models, an assumption seems to be required that the output of the nontemporal processor is weighted very highly in such retrospective judgments. As will be discussed in the next section, however, the PT models must assume that attention to the nontemporal processor is what causes a *reduction* in the estimation for other experiments.

Amount of Information Processing

Most of the studies discussed in this section could be considered to employ manipulations of stimulus number, complexity, or organization, as well as the amount of stimulus processing required. In each experiment of this category, one or more stimuli are presented within an interval, and subjects are asked to analyze the stimuli in some way beyond just observing them (e.g., reading digits, multiplying digits, analyzing semantic content of words, etc.).

For the most part, these experiments show that with increasing processing effort (assumed to correlate with "task difficulty", "response uncertainty", "processing time"), duration judgments decrease (Michon, 1965; Vroon, 1970; Hicks, et al., 1976; Burnside, 1971; Zakay et al., 1983; Brown,

1985). It should be noted that in most studies showing this relationship, subjects have known beforehand that a time estimate will be required. In studies where this is not the case, the relationship seems to depend upon the nature and extent of the processing task (Underwood and Swain, 1973; Hicks et al., 1976; Brown, 1985).

In order for the SS model to explain this result, it must be assumed that the higher the level of stimulus processing, the smaller the storage size. Perhaps SS proponents could appeal to the notion that stimuli which are processed in depth are represented in a more efficient manner, and therefore occupy less storage space than stimuli processed superficially. As a result, active processing of stimuli could result in shorter duration estimates because interval contents are stored more efficiently in memory.

The PT model of Zakay et al. (1983) seems well suited to explain the inverse relationship between amount of stimulus processing and duration judgment, because it relies on the idea of a cognitive timer which requires attention for its function. As the amount of stimulus processing increases, less attention can be allocated to the timer, resulting in shorter time estimates. Similarly, the dual-processor PT model can assume that attention is divided between the processing task and the timing of duration; therefore, more processing results in lower estimates because less time is dedicated to the timer. However this explanation requires the assumption that the output of the stimulus processor was not large enough to compensate for the reduced output from the timer.

Because the number of items which can be processed during an interval depends on the amount of processing required per item, most of the studies referred to in this section can be explained in terms of either processing time or the number of stimulus events/changes processed or remembered. For example, the studies of Block (1974), Burnside (1971), Hicks, et al. (1976), Poynter (1979), and McClain (1983) can each be interpreted as demonstrating the positive relationship between number of processed or remembered items and duration judgment, or the negative relationship between stimulus-processing time and duration judgment. The disadvantage of relying on processing time as the explanatory variable is that it requires arbitrary assumptions regarding the processing requirements of certain tasks. For example, does reading 15 one-digit numbers require more or less processing effort than multiplying 7 pairs of one-digit numbers? In comparison, determining the number of items processed seems less arbitrary.

It is not always the case that the level of stimulus processing and the magnitude of duration estimates are inversely related. Thomas and Weaver (1975) found that when subjects were asked to memorize the visual content of very brief intervals (<100 msec), the perceived duration of empty intervals was shortened, and that of filled intervals was lengthened. The authors used their dual-processor PT model to explain this result. They assumed that the memory task increased attentional allocation to the visual processor. For empty intervals, then, shifting attention to the visual processor (and away from the timer) resulted in shortened time estimates, because timer output was reduced without any counterbalancing output from the visual processor. For filled intervals, however, shifting more attention to the visual processor resulted in an increase in its output, which lengthened duration estimates in comparison to the no-memory condition. Burnside (1971) found that duration estimates of intervals during which subjects read digits were about equal to (actually somewhat longer than) estimates of empty intervals. The CS model explains this finding by assuming that the number of temporal segments marked off by reading digits was about equal to the number marked off by generating internal events in the empty interval. The dual processor PT model would probably explain the finding by suggesting that the sum of the outputs from the timer and the stimulus processor happened to come out about equal in the "reading" versus "empty" conditions. Because it would be difficult to disprove either one of these explanations, neither is very desirable from a theoretical standpoint. Poynter and Homa (1983) asked some subjects to memorize the spatial pattern of light flashes that occurred during time intervals they would subsequently reproduce. We found that the difference between duration estimates made under the memory versus no-memory condition varied with the clock duration of the interval. With long durations the no-memory produced substantially longer estimates than the memory condition: for shorter durations (<4 sec.), the memory condition produced longer estimates. Again, both the dual processor and CS models must rely on convenient assumptions to explain this finding. According to the CS model, the presence of stimulus information can elicit either long or short estimates depending on whether the information facilitates the segmentation of time into chunks which are easily stored and retrieved. Following Long and Beaton's (1980, 1981) ideas regarding retinal persistence, it could be that attending to very brief flashes in a relative short interval extended perceived duration because the persistence of the stimuli extended beyond their actual duration. For short durations, this expansion had a much larger relative effect on the overall duration judgment than for long durations, because the flashes occupied a much greater proportion of the interval. For longer intervals, vigilance to the occurrence of a few sensory events may have preoccupied attention, thereby preventing subjects from generating mental events that would have facilitated the encoding of temporal segments. Essentially the same explanation could be developed from Thomas and Weaver's dual-processor model. Attending to a timer could be attending to organismic events and attending to a visual processor could be attending to sensory events.

THE RELATIONSHIP BETWEEN PERCEIVED TIME AND DISTANCE

The tau and kappa effects are illusions in which the perceived distance between two stimuli is distorted by the time between them (tau), or the perceived duration between two stimuli is distorted by the distance between them (kappa). As the distance between two stimuli increases, so does the perceived duration of the interval between them (e.g., Newman and Lee, 1972; Price-Williams, 1954). Similarly, as the duration between two stimuli increases, so does the perceived distance between them (Helson and King, 1931; Cohen, et al. 1953).

These effects have been explained with the "imputed velocity hypothesis" (see Jones and Huang, 1982). The idea is that subjects impute motion to a display of sequential stimuli, and are therefore prone to make distance and duration judgments in line with the relationship between time or distance travelled given constant velocity. In other words, subjects make the perceptual mistake of thinking that the time between two sequential events must be great if the distance between them is, or the converse. Underlying this idea is the assumption that subjects are prone to rely on nontemporal, or nonspatial dimensions in judging duration and distance, respectively; almost as if uncertainty related to the sensation of the judged dimension is reduced by incorporating related sensory experiences into the final judgment. I have previously described the importance of change in "nontemporal" dimensions in the judgment of time, and I believe that the kappa effect is one more piece of evidence in support of this idea — the perceived duration between two sequential events is determined by the amount of change experienced, and one salient type of change is a change in spatial location. The observation that the tau effect also occurs may indicate that the change hypothesis could be applied to distance as well as time. In fact, several studies indicate that distance judgments are affected by several factors in the same way that these factors affect duration judgments, suggesting that a common principle might explain both sets of findings. For both time (e.g., Poynter and Homa, 1983) and distance judgments (e.g., Luria, et al., 1967), filled intervals are frequently judged longer than empty intervals. For both time and distance, intervals containing more segments are perceived to be longer (Poynter, 1983; Sadalla and Magel, 1980). Finally, time/distance intervals containing complex stimuli tend to be judged longer than intervals containing simpler stimuli (Ornstein, 1969; Rogers and Gogel, 1975).

Geldard and Sherrick (1986) have studied a very interesting phenomenon they call "saltation". The basic effect is an illusory displacement of one touch of the skin toward a second touch that occurs within about 250 msec or less. One of its very interesting aspects is that the distance across which this perceptual time-space dependency can be elicited is different for different parts of the body. Secondly, the illusion can not be elicited across the midline of the body. The saltatory phenomenon therefore reflects two general characteristics of the cortical representation of touch — left/right side dichotomy, and a correlation between illusory field sizes and receptive field sizes within these body halves. As the authors point out, these observations could indicate that "saltation" is related to the interaction of spatially contiguous neural events in the cortex. In other words, it seems as if the illusory displacement of an event at point A toward an event at point B is caused by a neural interaction of the codes for A and B. The fact that point A is seen to move toward B rather than the reverse could result from the fact that the neural signal for B is stronger given it is the last stimulus, and therefore unmodified by subsequent events. Geldard and Sherrick also point out that the experience of the event's "sharpness, and perhaps some of its size and intensity" is also lost (Geldard and Sherrick, p. 05). In other words, the time-space relationships between two stimuli may affect other perceptual dimensions besides distance. Perhaps the perceived temporal relationship between events could also be a function of the degree of interaction between the neural signals which represent the events.

Kossyln, et al. (1978) demonstrated in a number of experiments that as the subjective distance between two sensory events increases, so does the amount of time required to subsequently scan the mental image of that distance. The same effect was found with subjective size, such that the larger the subjective size of an object, the longer it took to scan the image of the object.

These findings suggest a reasonable explanation for the kappa effect, at least when a duration reproduction task is employed. Subjects in duration reproduction experiments that I have conducted frequently claim that they mentally replay (or scan) the visual events filling an interval as a strategy for reproducing the interval duration. The fact that the kappa effect indicates a positive relationship between perceived time and interevent distance seems entirely consistent with the relationship between scan (i.e., replay) time and interstimulus distance discussed above.

SUMMARY

Disregarding the presence of stimulus information, a power function with an exponent slightly less than one seems to describe the relationship between judged duration and clock duration (see Eisler, 1976). Judgments of relatively short durations are frequently overestimates, while those of relatively long durations are almost always underestimates. The presence of discrete interval fillers (e.g., light flashes, auditory clicks, etc.) usually increases the judgment of interval duration, but this effect is dependent upon clock duration. When clock duration is short (say less than 10 seconds), filled intervals are judged longer than empty intervals; for long durations, empty intervals are judged longer. Requiring subjects to actively process information filling an interval usually reduces its perceived duration, especially when the subject knows that a duration judgment will be required. When the duration judgment is unexpected, the relationship between information processing and duration judgment is less clear, perhaps because it depends on the type of processing done as well as the amount. Finally, the perceived duration of an interval bounded by spatially-separated markers is a positive function of the distance between them.

Three models of duration judgment were compared in terms of their ability to explain these common findings. One emphasized the role of memory content, another the role of processing time, and the third the role of change. While I have spent a large share of this chapter supporting the change/segmentation approach, it is in fact based to a large degree on ideas proposed in the other two models. It seems clear, for example, that retrieval of information contained in an interval is a prerequisite to that information's effect on duration judgment. Also consistent with the storage-size model, the type of information is considered to be important in the change/segmentation approach; complex, hard-to-reduce stimuli tend to produce longer estimates than stimuli which can be represented with the aid of a simplifying code. And finally, the idea that duration judgments are constructed from temporal segments marked off by sensory and organismic change follows the theoretical framework supplied by Thomas and Weaver's dual-processor model.

Perhaps the main advantage to the change/segmentation approach is parsimony. It explains that we perceive duration without the aid of man-made clocks in the same way that we measure time's passage with them — by accounting for the "nontemporal" change between delimiting events.

References

Adams, R. D. (1977). Intervening stimulus effects on category judgments of duration. *Perception and Psychophysics 21(6)*, 527–534.

Avant, L. L., Lyman, P. J., & Antes, J. R. (1975). Effects of stimulus familiarity on judged visual duration. *Perception and Psychophysics, 17*, 253–262.

Bertotti, B. (1978). The riddles of gravitation. In R. Duncan & M. Weston-Smith (Eds.), *The Encyclopedia of Ignorance* (pp. 91–98). New York: Wallaby Books.

Block, R. A. (1974). Memory and the experience of duration in retrospect. *Memory and Cognition, 2*, 153–160.

Block, R. A. & Reed, M. A. (1978). Remembered duration: Evidence for a contextual change hypothesis. *J. of Experimental Psychology: Human Learning and Memory, 4*, 656–665.

Block, R. A. (1982). Temporal judgments and contextual change, *J. of Experimental Psychology: Learning, Memory, and Cognition, 8(6)*, 530–544.

Bobko, D. J., Thompson, J. G., & Schiffman, H. R. (1977). The perception of brief temporal intervals: Power functions for auditory and visual stimulus intervals. *Perception, 6*, 703–709.

Brown, S. W. (1985). Time perception and attention: The effects of prospective versus retrospective paradigms and task demands on perceived duration. *Perception and Psychophysics, 38*, 115–124.

Buffardi, L. (1971). Factors affecting the filled-duration illusion in the auditory, tactual, and visual modalities. *Perception and Psychophysics, 10*, 292–294.

Burnside, W. (1971). Judgment of short time intervals while performing mathematical tasks. *Perception and Psychophysics, 9*, 404–406.

Cohen, J., Hansel, C. E. M. & Sylvester, J. D. (1953). A new phenomenon in time judgment. *Nature, 172*, 901.

Coltheart, M. (1980). Iconic memory and visible persistence, *Perception and Psychophysics, 27*, 183–228.

Eisler, H. (1976). Experiments on subjective duration 1868–1975: a collection of power function exponents. *Psychological Bulletin, 83(6)*, 1154–1171.

Fraisse, P. (1963). *Psychology of Time.* New York: Harper & Row.

Fraisse, P. (1984). Perception and estimation of time. *Annual Review of Psychology, 35*, 1–36.

Geldard, F. A. & Sherrick C. E. (1986). Space, Time, and Touch. *Scientific American, 255*, 90–95.

Gibson J. J. (1975) Events are perceivable but time is not. In J. T. Fraser & N. Lawrence (Eds.), *The Study of Time, Vol. 2.* Berlin: Springer.

Helson, H. & King, S. M. (1931). The tau effect: an example of psychological relativity. *Journal of Experimental of Psychology, 14*, 202–217.

Hicks, R. E., Miller, G. W., & Kinsbourne, M. (1976). Prospective and retrospective judgments of time as a function of amount of information processed. *American Journal of Psychology, 89*, 719–730.

Jones, B. & Huang, Y. L. (1982). Space-time dependencies in psychological judgment of extent and duration: Algebraic models of the Tau and Kappa effects. *Psychological Bulletin, 91(1)*, 128–142.

Kossyln, S. M., Reiser, B. J., & Ball, T. M. (1978). Visual images preserve metric spatial information: Evidence from studies of image scanning. *J. Experimental Psychology: Human Perception and Performance, 4*, 47–60.

Leggett, A.J. (1978). The arrow of time and quantum mechanics, In R. Duncan & M. Weston-Smith (Eds.), *The Encyclopedia of Ignorance* (pp. 101–110). New York: Wallaby Books.

Levin, I., Wilkening, F., & Dembo, Y. (1984). Development of time quantification: integration and nonintegration of beginnings and endings in comparing duration. *Child Development, 55*, 2160–2172.

Long, G. M. & Beaton, R. J. (1980). The contribution of visual persistence to the perceived duration of brief targets. *Perception and Psychophysics, 28(5)*, 422–430.

Long, G. M. & Beaton, R. J. (1981). The effects of stimulus numerosity, retinal location, and rod contrast on perceived duration of brief visual stimuli. *Perception and Psychophysics, 29(4)*, 389–394.

Luria, S. M., Kinney, J. S., & Weissman, S. (1967). Distance estimates with 'filled' versus 'unfilled' space. *Perceptual and Motor Skills, 24*, 1007–1010.

McClain, L. (1983). Interval estimation: Effects of processing demands on prospective and retrospective reports. *Perception and Psychophysics, 34*, 185–189.

Michon, J. A. (1965). Studies on subjective duration II. subjective time measurements during tasks with different information content. *Acta Psychologica, 24*, 205–219.

Moore-Ede, M. C., Sulzman, F. M., & Fuller C.A. (1982). *The clocks that time us.* Cambridge: Harvard University Press.

Mulligan, R. M. & Schiffman, H. R. (1979). Temporal experience as a function of organization in memory. *Bulletin of the Psychonomic Society, 14*, 417–420.

Newman, C. V. & Lee, S. G. (1972). The effect of real and imputed distance on judgments of time: Some experiments on the kappa effect. *Psychonomic Science, 29*, 207–211.

Ornstein, R. E. (1969). *On the experience of time.* Middlesex, England: Penguin Books.

Poynter, W. D. (1979). *Human time perception and memory processes: the role of retrieval in duration estimates.* Unpublished master's thesis, Arizona State University, Tempe, Az.

Poynter, W. D. (1983a). Duration judgment and the segmentation of experience. *Memory & Cognition, 11*, 77–82.

Poynter, W. D. (1983b). *Temporal segmentation of intervals filled with visual events.* Unpublished manuscript.

Poynter, W. D. & Homa, D. (1983), Duration judgment and the experience of change. *Perception and Psychophysics, 33*, 548–560.

Price-Williams, D. R. (1954). The kappa effect. *Nature, 173*, 363–364.

Rogers, S. P. & Gogel, W. C. (1975). Relation between judged and physical distance in multicue conditions as a function of instructions and tasks. *Perceptual and Motor Skills, 41*, 171–178.

Sadalla, E. K. & Magel, S. (1980). The perception of traversed distance, *Environment and Behaviour, 12*, 64–78.

Schiffman, H. R. & Bobko, D. J. (1974). Effects of stimulus complexity on the perception of brief time intervals, *J. of Experimental Psychology, 103*, 156–159.

Thomas, E. A. C. & Brown, I., Jr. (1974). Time perception and the filled duration illusion. *Perception and Psychophysics, 16*, 449–458.

Thomas, E. A. C. & Weaver, W. B. (1975). Cognitive processing and time perception. *Perception and Psychophysics, 17*, 363–367.

Underwood, G. & Swain, R. A. (1973). Selectivity of attention and the perception of duration. *Perception, 2,* 101–105.

Vroon, P. A. (1970). Effects of presented and processed information on duration experience. Acta Psychologica, 34, 115–121.

Wilkening, F., Levin, I., and Druyan, S. (1987). Counting strategies for time quantification and integration: A developmental study. *Developmental Psychology, 23,* 823–831.

Zakay, D., Nitzan, D. & Glicksohn, J. (1983). The influence of task difficulty and external tempo on subjective time estimation. *Perception and Psychophysics, 34,* 451–456.

TIME AND HUMAN COGNITION
A Life-Span Perspective
I. Levin and D. Zakay (Editors)

CHAPTER 9

RICHARD A. BLOCK

Experiencing and Remembering Time: Affordances, Context, and Cognition

1. INTRODUCTION

Experimental psychology originated in the late 1800s, and ever since then psychologists have investigated the nature of time-related experiences and behavior. The many empirical studies that researchers have conducted reveal that the psychology of time is extremely complex. No simple theory can adequately handle the variety of temporal behaviors and experiences that have received attention. Recently, I have been exploring the heuristic value of a contextualistic model of temporal experiences, and this chapter uses it as an organizing tool to view some of the diverse experimental findings and theories, focusing especially on duration experiences.

Several previous articles (Block, 1985a, 1985b, in press) have explained the origins and development of this general contextualistic model. I begin by summarizing the model.

2. A CONTEXTUALISTIC MODEL OF TEMPORAL EXPERIENCE

The general contextualistic model holds that four kinds of factors interact to influence temporal experiences. The model may, therefore, be diagrammed as a tetrahedron (Block, 1985a, in press). The model adapts one that Jenkins (1979) used in his summary of research on levels of processing. Bransford (1979) used a similar model to describe processes involved in learning, understanding, and remembering. Each of the four factors is a cluster of variables which interact with each of the other factors to influence temporal experiences. Variables grouped within the same factor for the sake of simplicity also interact in various ways.

The model helps in classifying experiments on the psychology of time, most of which manipulate only one or two of these factors. It also reveals differences among theories, as well as the limitations of any theoretical formulation (Block, in press). I first summarize this classification of factors. Then I consider in detail some of the more specific variables and processes involved in temporal experiences.

One factor is the kind of temporal behavior under consideration. Experiments investigate this factor by requesting different kinds of temporal judgment, or estimation—judgment of simultaneity, successiveness, rhythm, order, spacing, duration, and so on. Further, researchers use a range of different methods to study each of these kinds of temporal judgment. Another factor is the characteristics of the time period which a person experiences and, perhaps, also evaluates and judges. This includes the absolute duration of the time period, as well as various contents—events, whether external or purely cognitive, that occur during it. Characteristics of events include their number, their complexity, their modality, and so on. Another factor is the characteristics of the experiencer. Within an individual, the variables included here range from fixed and unchanging (such as species and sex) to somewhat changeable (such as personality and interests) to relatively transient and changeable (such as previous experiences in an experimental setting). The final factor is activities during the time period. A person may engage in various activities, ranging from relatively effortless nonattending through relatively effortful information-processing strategies. Kinds of activities are primarily influenced by the events occurring during a duration, instructions provided by an experimenter, and previous learning of strategies.

A complete understanding of any kind of temporal experience is possible only if we consider complex interactions among all of these factors. The contexture of psychological time, according to this model, is a complex, multifaceted pattern. None of the factors ever operates in isolation from the others. When one factor changes, the precise nature of the interactions of the other factors also changes. In practice, however, most experiments on the psychology of time manipulate only one or two of these factors. If we consider lower-order interactions we get a somewhat limited, but nevertheless useful, understanding of a particular kind of temporal experience.

With this in mind, I now review evidence showing some ways in which each of the factors influences temporal experiences.

3. TEMPORAL JUDGMENT METHODS

3.1 Judgment of Simultaneity and Successiveness

Awareness of the successiveness of events is a fundamental aspect of temporal experiences. Early observations suggested that humans may experience successiveness, rather than simultaneity, if the interval between two brief auditory events is at least 2 ms (see James, 1890; Hirsh, 1959). However, relatively accurate temporal-order judgments apparently require that an interval between two events be at least 20 ms, and this is the case regardless of the modality of the events (Hirsh & Sherrick, 1961).

3.2 The Psychological Present

A rather compelling experience of a psychological present occurs whenever a person perceives a sequence of events lasting a few seconds. James (1890) asserted that people are "constantly conscious of a certain duration—the specious present—varying in length from a few seconds to probably not more than a minute" (p. 642). More recent theorists put the upper limit of this experience at about 5–10 s, with the clear implication that it is a phenomenon attributable to the dynamics of activated, or short-term, memory. Fraisse (1963) commented that this psychological present enables us to "perceive units of change which ... are elements from which we construct the unity of our whole psychological life" (p. 98). There is no single method that enables a precise measurement of the psychological present; however, experiences of rhythm critically depend on the tempo of the sequence of events—if the rate is too slow, a person will not apprehend a rhythmic grouping. Thus, experiences of rhythm seem to involve an awareness of durations of events and of intervals between events in the psychological present.

3.3 Spacing, Order, and Position Judgments

Research using longer intervals shows that people are able to judge fairly accurately the temporal positions of occurrences of a repeated event (Hintzman & Block, 1971). A relatively automatic retrieval of previous occurrences by a subsequent repetition might mediate these judgments (Hintzman & Block, 1973). The automatically retrieved information about a previous occurrence of an event includes contextual information, such as the person's feelings or thoughts at that time, as well as the modality, approximate recency, and other features of the occurrence. A person may then judge the spacing of a repeated event by relying on this contextual information.

The same kind of contextual information may also allow a person to judge the order, or temporal position, and the spacing of unrelated events (e.g., Hintzman, Block, & Summers, 1973; Hintzman, Summers, & Block, 1975). These judgments are considerably less accurate, however, and they are heavily influenced by a person's activities during the time period—that is, by controlled strategies of information processing. Jackson (1985, 1986) found that individual differences in the accuracy of subsequent position judgment of words in a temporal series are related to the mnemonic strategies which different subjects had used. Elaborative kinds of rehearsal, such as combining words to form a connected story, are related to fairly accurate temporal-position judgment; whereas simple kinds of rehearsal, such as repeating single words, are related to less accurate position judgment. In addition, temporal-order judgment is more accurate following semantic-feature processing of events than following mere physical-structure processing. Jackson and Michon (1984) also found that position judgments are more accurate for concrete than for abstract wordlists, and cuing subjects to forget words impairs subsequent temporal-order judgments involving those words. Jackson (1986) concluded that "relative order judgments may indeed reflect some automatic encoding of intrinsic order, but ... such coding is not sufficient to enable subjects to perform more complex temporal judgment tasks adequately" (pp. 81–82).

3.4 Duration Judgment

Outside of the laboratory, there are several major ways by which a person typically expresses duration judgments. Perhaps the most common type of report is simply that an expected event seems like it is taking "forever" to occur, or that a past time period seemed to be long. It is less common to hear that a past time period seemed relatively short. It is rare to hear someone say that a future event is approaching more rapidly that expected. In other words, people more often become aware of a duration if various factors influence it in such a way that it seems lengthened, but much less frequently if factors influence it in such a way that it seems shortened (cf. Fraisse, 1963, pp. 201–210). Instances in which a person gives a numerical estimate of a duration show the same sort of psychological influences.

Laboratory experiments typically use one of four major types of duration-judgment methods—production, verbal estimation, reproduction, and comparison (Bindra & Waksberg, 1956). Production and verbal estimation methods use a "translation" of duration into conventional time units (i.e., minutes, seconds, and so on), whereas the latter two methods do not require this translation (although a subject may covertly use such a translation in making a judgment). Apparently because production and verbal estimation methods require such a translation, these methods usually show considerable intersubject variability (Fraisse, 1963).

In the method of production, the experimenter asks the subject operatively to delimit a verbally-stated duration. For example, the subject must press a key at the start and at the end of what he or she judges to be a one-minute period. In the method of verbal estimation, the experimenter operatively delimits a duration, and the subject must estimate it in conventional time units. In the method of reproduction, the experimenter first operatively delimits a duration, such as in the method of verbal estimation. Then the subject must operatively reproduce it, perhaps in the same sort of way as in the method of production. In this case, however, no verbal coding of time is required. In the method of comparison, the experimenter delimits two durations, and the subject estimates them by using some procedure involving a comparison of the two.

Seemingly opposite results may be obtained by using the method of production as compared with the methods of verbal estimation or reproduction, and confusion is possible unless one uses terminology carefully. For example, a subject might be said to "underestimate" a 60–s duration by producing a 50–s duration or to "overestimate" a 60–s duration by verbally judging it to be 68 s long. However, in both cases, the person's experience of duration is lengthened relative to clock time. It is for this reason that the terms "underestimation" and "overestimation" are meaningless unless they are used in the context of a specific judgment method. To avoid any confusion, I usually prefer to speak of duration experience as being lengthened or shortened.

When this distinction is made, duration experience is occasionally found to depend on the particular judgment method used, which may also interact with other contextual factors (see section 9). Because experiments on the psychology of time have tended to use various kinds of duration-judgment methods more often than other kinds of temporal-judgment methods (e.g., successiveness, spacing, order), the remainder of this chapter mainly focuses on processes involved in duration judgment.

4. CHARACTERISTICS OF THE TIME PERIOD

4.1 Duration of the Time Period

If an event persists for a very brief time, such as for only a few milliseconds, people do not experience duration per se—the event seems instantaneous. However, people can experience and judge duration in a fairly veridical way if an event lasts more than a few hundred milliseconds. That is, as duration increases, judgments follow an approximately linear relationship in the range from about one-half second to a few minutes, as well as in the range from a few hours to a few days (see Block, 1979; Michon, 1975).

Relatively few experiments have studied the range from a few minutes to a few hours. However, the results of a recent study by Aschoff (1985; see also Aschoff, 1984) suggest that "long and short time estimates are based on different mechanisms" (p. 41). Aschoff's subjects lived in isolation, with no external time cues, for periods of 7 days to more than a month. Each of 30 subjects gave two kinds of duration judgment. One kind, a long-duration estimate, required the subject repeatedly to produce 1–hr durations (by signaling every subjective hour, as long as the subject was awake). These productions were, on the average, longer than an hour. The mean production of each subject was positively correlated with the subject's duration of wakefulness as well as with the length of his or her circadian (i.e., sleep-wake) cycle. The other kind, a short-duration judgment, was experimenter-initiated: The experimenter asked the subject to press a button in order to produce a verbally stated duration, which could range from

10 to 120 s. Although there was considerable individual variation, the average production tended to be fairly accurate (e.g., the mean production of a 10–s duration was 11.7 s and that of a 120–s duration was 116.8 s) These judgments were not correlated with the 1–hr productions. In contrast to those long-duration judgments, these short productions were not correlated with either the duration of wakefulness or the length of the sleep-wake cycle.

The conclusion that the processes involved in making short-duration (10–120 s) judgments differ from those involved in making long-duration (1 hr) judgments should be regarded as tentative. It could be that the short productions differed qualitatively from the long productions because of the difference in methods used to obtain them. As Aschoff noted, his findings need to be replicated in an experiment that uses the same method to assess both short and long duration experiences.

4.2 Affordances and Changes

Since its inception, the experimental study of time has been widely referred to as that of the "perception of time". But in an important (yet widely ignored) paper, Gibson (1975) claimed that the perception of time is an insoluble problem. He said that "there is no such thing as the perception of time, but only the perception of events and locomotions" (p. 295). It is relatively easy for us to agree with Gibson that the perception of space is based, at least in part, on the processes by which an observer picks up information about environmental surfaces, such as that involving texture gradients. Alternatively, it seems that each observer is, as a result of biological evolution and individual learning, "at any given moment, tuned to resonate to the incoming patterns that correspond to the invariants that are significant for it" (Shepard, 1984, p. 433). But what are the ecologically significant incoming patterns, or invariants—what Gibson called *affordances*—to which an observer tunes when he or she experiences time, rather than space? According to Gibson (1975), "a sequence of external stimuli or, at the very least, the rhythms of the observer's body, provide a flow of *change*, and it is this we perceive rather than a flow of time as such" (p. 299). Gibson also emphasized that "the observer perceives *both what is altered and what remains unaltered in the environment*" (p. 298). I contend that what is altered or changed is most critical for temporal experiences. Along related lines of thinking, the physicist Mach (1883/1942) observed:

We must not forget that all things in the world are connected with

> one another and depend on one another, and that we ourselves and all our thoughts are also a part of nature. It is utterly beyond our power to *measure* the changes of things by *time*. Quite the contrary, time is an abstraction, at which we arrive by means of the changes of things ... (p. 273).

An ancient Chinese document, *The I Ching, or Book of Changes*, made perhaps the first distinction between different kinds of change (see Block, in press). To "translate" the distinction made in the *Book of Changes* into more contemporary language, nonchange is what remains unaltered in the environment. It is the automatically processed background upon which all cognition of change occurs. The *Book of Changes* also discussed two kinds of change, cyclic and successive. Cyclic changes are events that recur on a periodic basis; an organism's cognitive system usually processes these events in a relatively automatic (i.e, nonconscious) way. Successive changes are relatively unique, nonrecurrent events which the cognitive system typically processes in a relatively controlled (i.e., conscious) way, depending on familiarity with the event, the focus of attention, and many other factors.

An ecological description illustrates the ways in which cyclic and successive changes are superimposed on a background of relative nonchange. The typical external environment of a person is fairly stable, or nonchanging, from one moment to the next. Most of the objects in a room—walls, desks, carpeting, and so on—remain largely unaltered for relatively long periods. Against this background of stability, some changes occur: a telephone rings, a bird flies by the window, a neighbor interrupts with a request. These changes, or events, take place in an ordered sequence.

Modern physicists, who have very little need for noetic conceptions of time, acknowledge the possibility of a local ordering of events—event *a* may be said to precede event *b*, at least from one particular spatial frame of reference. As one wry definition says, "Time is nature's way of keeping everything from happening at once" (source unknown). This inevitable ordering of events seems to be a fundamental property of the universe, even one in which no sentient beings speculate about time. This successive ordering also affords us a major source for our common geometrical representation of time's passage, that of a straight line. The fundamental psychological basis for the detection of order relationships is the person's cognitive system. At the time that a person perceives a present event, he or she may remember an event that precedes it and may anticipate an event that might follow it. It is the relatively simultaneous and automatic operation of the totality of remembering-perceiving-anticipating processes that give us an awareness of the fundamental ordering of events.

Another basic temporal affordance concerns relationships between intervals. According to Allen and Kautz (1985), thirteen primitive relationships form the basis for all knowledge about the relationship between any two or more events. These relations are *equals, before/after, meets/met by, overlaps/overlapped by, starts/started by, during/contains,* and *finishes/finished by.* For example, if we say that event X overlapped event Y, then we are asserting that: (a) The interval in which X occurred began before the interval in which Y occurred; (b) The interval in which Y occurred began before the conclusion of event X; and (c) The interval in which Y occurred ended after the conclusion of event X. Information about some of these relationships, such as before/after, may by picked up and stored in memory as a by-product of the apparently automatic encoding of contextual information along with the memory representation of an event (cf. Hintzman & Block, 1971, 1973; Hintzman et al., 1973, 1975). The cognitive system probably does not automatically encode all of these relationships, however, and a person frequently must draw inferences about relationships among events. Consider, for example, the temporal ambiguities in the sentence: "Before the dinner party began, John felt apprehensive, but Mary's comment relaxed him". In the context of this chapter, two important concepts of Allen and Kautz's theory are that "our perception of time is intimately connected (or identical to) our perception of events" and that "time (or events) appears to be hierarchically organized" (p. 253).

Allen and Kautz (1985) also discussed "a logic for reasoning about durations, which is separate from, but integrates nicely with, the basic interval logic" (p. 259). From a psychological—rather than a purely logical— viewpoint, I previously argued that if one considers a cohesive sequence of events, distinctive events mark the beginning and end of the interval. Most importantly, a distinctive cognitive context persists throughout such a time period, and it is "what unifies long durations, so that even long time periods can be properly called durations" (Block, 1979, p. 187).

In addition to relatively unpredictable events, there are other, somewhat more predictable ones, changes that are cyclic. Rhythms of light and darkness, relative cold and warmth, regular activities such as work schedules, and other cyclic events form a somewhat more slowly changing background to our lives than the more abrupt, transient, successive changes. The cyclic changes which we experience also include internal, biological rhythms—heart beats, wakefulness and sleep, hunger, and so on. Even if there are few or no external changes—such as when a person is in a condition of isolation—internal rhythms may be salient enough to enable the person to construct a near-veridical frame of reference in time.

Campbell (1986) studied the "estimation of empty time" by subjects who spent 60 hr confined to bed in an isolation unit affording only minimal temporal cues. He prohibited them from engaging in activities like reading, exercise, listening to music, and so on. At various relatively long intervals (ranging from 5.2 to 23.5 hr) during the isolation period, he asked them to estimate the time of day. Campbell found that subjects verbally underestimated the intervals—"the mean subjective hour [continued] for 1.12 h in real time" (p. 205). However, as Campbell noted, Lavie and Webb (1975) had found that subjects verbally underestimate long intervals by about the same amount in experiments in which they are not strictly isolated—that is, those in which subjects may fill the time period by engaging in various kinds of activity.

What cues might a person use to judge duration in an isolated environment? For that matter, what cues might a person use to judge duration in a more normal environment? In a discussion of memory, Bower (1972) mentioned several different kinds of internal contextual elements: interoceptive stimulation (such as posture, temperature, nausea, boredom) and the "psychological context"—"what the subject is thinking about", or "the internal monologue" (p. 93). Over longer periods, a person might remember the number of sleep epochs, menstrual cycles, and so on.

Hewitt (1979) distinguished between two kinds of contextual elements. There are some characteristics of a stimulus that a person must encode in order to perform a task. Hewitt called these the *intrinsic context.* There are also background attributes or features that a subject need not necessarily encode. Hewitt called these the *extrinsic context.* In this regard, Hewitt adopted the traditional, narrow view that context is a property of the external environment. Baddeley (1982) thought that Hewitt's distinction was too passive and stimulus-determined; he preferred to emphasize the processing in which the person engages rather than the characteristics of the stimulus material. As an alternative, then, Baddeley distinguished between what he called *interactive context* and what he called *independent context.* Contextual information is interactive if it "determines the way an item [i.e., some focal information] is encoded" (Baddeley, 1982, p. 710). On the other hand, if a person may encode contextual information and focal information separately, the contextual cue is independent.

Hewitt's and Baddeley's distinctions are both useful, although they differ only slightly in emphasis. It is important to remember that context is always an internal, cognitive construction, just as time is a construction based on change. This implies a recognition of a broader meaning of the term *context*, in which it refers to cognitive structures, or knowledge, supplied by a person as he or she interacts with the environment. Although Baddeley's shift in emphasis is a step in this direction, both the background characteristics of a person and individual differences in activities or strategies of information processing receive too little emphasis in Hewitt's and Baddeley's accounts.

4.3 Number of Events

Several studies have found that the number of events which occur during a time period influences duration judgment. The nature of the influence, however, depends on whether the judgments are made prospectively or retrospectively (see section 5.3), and it may also depend on the duration of the time period (see Poynter & Homa, 1983).

Under prospective conditions, subjects experience a brief (e.g., a few seconds or less) duration that is filled by external events, such as a series of tones, as being longer than an equal duration that is "empty", or unfilled by external events (e.g., Thomas & Brown, 1974). Subjects also experience a brief stimulus that contains a greater number of elements as being longer in duration than one that contains fewer elements (Mo, 1971). For longer durations, however, such as those measured in minutes, hours, or days, a commonly reported experience is that time seems to pass more quickly if more events are occurring. When there is less than the desired amount of contextual change, such as when one is waiting for a steady Pacific Northwest U. S. drizzle to end, time in passing may seem endless (see section 9).

Under retrospective conditions, though, a person may use an availability heuristic to reconstruct the duration: To the extent that a greater number of events is available in memory, a person remembers the duration of a time period as being longer (Ornstein, 1969; Vroon, 1970). However, it is clear that people do not base this judgment on the degree of recallability of events from the time period (Block, 1974). Other processes, such a person's implicit assessment the amount of contextual change during the duration, appear to be involved (see sections 4.4 and 6.3).

4.4 Complexity of Events and Sequences of Events

In one of Ornstein's (1969) experiments, subjects viewed a single geometric figure during a 30s time period. Ornstein found that the remembered duration of the time period lengthened if subjects had viewed a more complex figure, although increased figural complexity only influenced duration judgments up to a limit. Two subsequent experiments on complexity clarify the way in which it influences such retrospective judgments of duration (Block, 1978). The first experiment reveals that if a duration contains a sequence of events, the average complexity of each event does not necessarily influence remembered duration. This finding seems to contradict that of Ornstein. However, the second experiment shows that subjects remember a more complex sequence of events as being longer in duration than a less complex sequence. In Ornstein's study on complexity, the sequence of interpretations of a stimulus is probably more complex if the person is viewing a complex figure than if the person is viewing a simple figure. Thus, the amount of contextual change during a sequence of mental events is apparently the critical factor, not the inherent complexity of the individual stimuli per se.

In another experiment, Ornstein (1969) also found that information provided after an information-processing task may influence the remembered duration of the task. Subjects studied a line drawing for 60 s. Then the experimenter gave some of them a simple interpretation of the drawing. These subjects remembered the duration of the time period as being relatively shorter than did subjects who had received no such simple interpretation. Ornstein explained this finding in terms of the organization of memory. An alternative explanation is that subjects who received the simple interpretation did not retrieve all of their previous interpretations of the figure (i.e., contextual changes) at the time they made the duration judgment.

This latter explanation is also consistent with Poynter and Homa's (1983) finding that if there is less "regularity" of events during a time period, subjects experience the duration of the time period as being longer. There is, in other words, a rough equivalence between the complexity of a sequence, the degree of segmentation of events in a sequence, and changes in cognitive context. If high-priority events periodically segment other events, the high-priority events apparently serve as marker events, or subjective referents of time's passage, and a person remembers a segmented duration as being longer than an unsegmented one (Poynter, 1983).

Predebon (1984) also investigated the complexity of coding of information. He studied how the ability to organize and interpret a prose passage might influence remembered duration. Some subjects received thematic information before the passage, while others received no thematic information. This manipulation influenced memory for the information in the passage in the expected way: Subjects who received thematic information before the passage recalled and comprehended more of it than did the control subjects. However, the manipulation did not influence the remembered duration of the passage. Predebon interpreted his findings in terms of a contextual-change hypothesis on remembered duration (Block, 1978, 1979). Remembered duration is apparently not based on the size of the storage space occupied by memories of stimulus events per se, as Ornstein (1969) suggested, but rather on the overall amount of change in cognitive context during the time period (see sections 6.3 and 7).

5. CHARACTERISTICS OF THE EXPERIENCER

5.1 Biological Rhythms

Endogenous biological rhythms apparently control some time-related behaviors, such as those involved in circadian cycles of activity level (see, for example, Groos & Daan, 1985). Chronobiological research on species such as ground squirrels and honeybees reveals that these biological rhythms, which are genetically programmed characteristics of a species, control behavioral rhythms. Neural pacemakers, such as that located in the suprachiasmatic nucleus of some species, apparently underlie the biological rhythms. Under certain conditions, events during a time period—zeitgebers such as the onset of bright light and other exogenous factors—may entrain, synchronize, and reset these brain mechanisms.

Chronobiologcal models attempt to explain many diverse cyclical behaviors by seeking the physiological basis of a single mechanism, a master pacemaker in the brain of the organism. These models relegate external events to only a minor role, largely because chronobiologists have discovered that many cyclical behaviors continue on an approximately 24-hr (i.e., circadian) cycle even if an organism is isolated from all exogenous changes (see, for example, Aschoff, 1984). This chronobiological account seems necessary, as well as relatively sufficient, to explain the regulation of cyclical behaviors. If it also emphasized influences of various strategies of the organism—such as a person strategically choosing when to sleep and when not to sleep following time-zone shifts that result in "jet lag" experiences—the account might become completely sufficient as an explanation for circadian periodicities in behavior. It might be fruitful to investigate potential interactions between different contextual factors even if the account considers only a single category of time-related behavior, cyclical activity.

In the early part of this century, various "internal clock" theories were popular. One example is Hoagland's (1933) attempt to explain all duration experiences solely in terms of biochemical processes in the brain. Early theorists like Hoagland extended a biological model beyond its rather limited domain of explanation. Further, he and others ignored the role of activities of the individual. It is now apparent that many temporal experiences and behaviors involve much more than the relatively simple processes proposed in these models.

5.2 History of Reinforcement and "The Internal Clock"

Behavioral psychologists typically study how the contents of short time periods (those measured in seconds and minutes) influence overt responding. Their research on schedules of reinforcement, usually studying animals such as pigeons and rats, shows that animals are sensitive to different interval schedules. On these schedules, the presentation of a reinforcer such as food is contingent upon the organism emitting a specific response, but only after a certain interval has elapsed.

Behavioral psychologists have studied interval schedules in order to try to answer a basic question: In addition to timing durations by relying on intrinsic changes in external stimuli, can animals also use an event-independent timer, or internal clock? The answer is apparently *yes*. One model (see, for example, Church, 1984; Roitblat, 1987) postulates an internal clock which consists of a pacemaker, a switch, and an accumulator. The pacemaker generates pulses at more or less regularly spaced intervals. This implies that there is a linear relationship between subjective duration and actual duration. Experiments, in fact, reliably find such a relationship. At the start of an external timing signal, the switch engages, and pulses begin to be counted in the accumulator. The switch is needed in order to handle the finding that changes in stimuli (e.g., an interrupted timing signal) may stop the clock (i.e., the accumulation of pulses from the pacemaker). In this regard, the internal clock functions like a stopwatch. A working memory briefly maintains a total pulse count, and a reference memory records the approximate number of pulses that elapsed prior to some past reinforcement. On interval schedules, responding increases in probability as a comparison (by a comparator mechanism) of working memory and reference memory shows a similar number of pulse counts.

The proposed timing system is flexible in the sense that it can time various kinds of signals. However, the general contextualistic model suggests that this behavioral model is limited: It does not consider all of the potentially important contextual aspects, such as other activities of an organism during an interval. For example, organisms may time a duration by engaging in various progressive or repetitive movements that take an appropriate amount of time (see Pouthas, 1985; Richelle & Lejeune, 1980, pp. 188–189). More fundamentally, it remains to be demonstrated that we can generalize this animal model to studies of human temporal experience and behavior.

5.3 Prospective versus Retrospective Outlook

It is critical to distinguish between prospective and retrospective judgment of duration. Fortunately, the failure to consider this distinction in interpreting experimental findings is much less common than it has been in the past. Although the distinction may be viewed as involving a difference in method, interpretations of findings become clearer if this variable is considered to involve a relatively temporary alteration in temporal outlook, a characteristic of the experiencer.

In a prospective paradigm, the experimenter informs a subject beforehand that the experimenter will subsequently ask the subject to make a duration judgment. Usually each subject makes many such judgments for different time periods. Hicks, Miller, Gaes, and Bierman (1977) called the temporal experience involved under prospective conditions "the experience of time-in-passing" (p. 443). I call it *experienced duration* (Block, 1979). In a retrospective paradigm, on the other hand, a subject receives only general orienting instructions beforehand, and only after the time period does the experimenter reveal that the task involves making a duration judgment. I call this *remembered duration.*

This distinction is closely related to the different methods of duration judgment (see section 3.4). When an experiment uses the method of production, a prospective paradigm must be used: The subject must be informed of the task before he or she produces the required duration. When the methods of verbal estimation or comparison are used, either a prospective or a retrospective paradigm may be used. The method of reproduction is a hybrid: The subject may or may not be informed before the duration that is to be reproduced, but the actual reproduction must be made prospectively.

Several theorists have noted that prospective and retrospective paradigms may produce different, even opposite, sorts of duration experiences. James (1890) proposed that experienced duration lengthens when "we grow attentive to the passage of time itself" (p. 626), whereas remembered duration lengthens as a function of "the multitudinousness of the memories which the time affords" (p. 624). Fraisse (1963) suggested that "direct time judgments [are] founded immediately on the changes we experience and later on the changes we remember" (p. 234). In more recent literature, internal-clock or interval-timer models, which usually focus on experienced duration and ignore the role of controlled strategies of information processing, differ considerably from cognitive-process models, which often focus on remembered duration and emphasize controlled strategies.

The usual conclusion is that a prospective outlook lengthens experienced duration, presumably because a person is "attending to the passage of time itself" (for reviews, see Block, 1979; Hicks et al., 1977). S.W. Brown (1985) found that prospective judgments (verbal estimates and reproductions) tend to be somewhat longer and more accurate than retrospective judgments. He did not find any interaction of paradigm (i.e., prospective vs. retrospective outlook) and "nontemporal task demands" (i.e., difficulty of the information-processing task). However, some researchers (e.g., Hicks, Miller, & Kinsbourne, 1976) have reported interactions of paradigm and other factors, such as the amount of information processed. Such interactions are common, and I describe research revealing interactions between paradigm and other contextual factors later (see sections 7.2 and 9).

5.4 Previous Experience and Changes in Environmental Context

Block (1982) conducted three experiments investigating environmental context as a potential source of contextual changes. In the first two of them, subjects processed the same number of words in the same way during each of two durations. Thus, both the number of events and the complexity of coding of the events were constant. The experiments manipulated the environmental context (i.e., the room, the experimenter, the form of the materials, and so on) in which the two durations occurred. For some other subjects, the environmental context was both disrupted and changed between the two durations—that is, they experienced the second time period in an environment which was different from that in which they spent the first time period. These subjects remembered the duration of the second time period as being relatively longer than did subjects in a control condition in which the environmental context had been neither disrupted nor changed. For some other subjects, the environmental context was simply disrupted between the two durations—that is, subjects left and then returned to the same room in between the two time periods. These subjects remembered the duration of the second time period as being slightly longer than did subjects in the control condition. Thus, to the extent that the encoding of the environmental context during the second time period was changed in some way, subjects remembered the duration of the second time period as being relatively longer. These experiments reveal clearly that characteristics of the experiencer—specifically, the person's previous experiences in a particular environment—influence remembered duration.

5.5 Previous Experience and the Time-Order Effect

Research on remembered duration also reveals another major finding: With all other factors equal or controlled by counter-balancing, subjects remember the first of two equally long time periods as being longer in duration than the second time period. This so-called *positive time-order effect* is so robust and ubiquitous that it plays an important theoretical role in the present contextualistic view, as well as in exploring influences of different contextual factors. A theoretically important question concerns whether or not the effect can be eliminated. Changing the environmental context that prevails during the second of two durations does, in fact, eliminate it (Block, 1982). It is also eliminated if changes in emotional context that might ordinarily have occurred during the first duration occur instead during a preceding experimental task (Block, 1986). These changes in emotional context are the feelings, moods, and concerns that accompany a new task, such as being a participant in an experiment. Thus, we can attribute the typical finding of a positive time-order effect in remembered duration to the greater contextual changes that ordinarily occur during the first of two durations. The encoded cognitive context apparently changes much more rapidly as a person initially experiences a particular situation than it does later.

6. ACTIVITIES DURING THE TIME PERIOD

6.1 Information-Processing Strategies

Recent cognitive research in general, and cognitive research on time in particular, has tended more and more to emphasize controlled strategies of information processing (see, for example, Michon, in press). The selection and use of particular strategies, such as kinds of attentional deployment and mnemonic involvement, depend on the ways in which each individual, with a certain past history of learning, interacts with an information-processing task. As I noted earlier, Jackson (1985, 1986; Michon & Jackson, 1984) has obtained considerable evidence that individual differences in controlled strategies influence temporal information processing, such as that which provides the basis for judgment of temporal order or serial position.

Other evidence that a person's information-processing activities might be important comes from Underwood's studies of remembered duration (G. Underwood, 1975; Underwood & Swain, 1973). Underwood and Swain found that subjects remembered a prose passage which required greater selectivity of attention for its analysis as being longer in duration than one which required less attention. Other studies, however, have not found the expected influence of attentional manipulations on remembered duration (S. W. Brown, 1985; Gray, 1982). The ways in which attentional selectivity might influence remembered duration are still unclear, but it seems likely that attentional selectivity interacts with task demands and information-processing strategies. In the present contextualistic model, attentional selectivity, which Underwood regarded to be the principal determinant of duration experience, is merely one of several factors. Like the others, it influences duration experiences through interactions with other factors.

6.2 Levels of Processing

Block and Reed (1978) conducted two experiments that reveal one way in which information-processing strategies influence remembered duration. In their first experiment, subjects processed words at either a shallow, structural level or at a deep, semantic level. Then they performed the other kind of processing during a second time period of equal length. Subjects remembered the duration of the deep-processing task as being about as long as that of the shallow-processing task. (As expected, subjects recognized the words that they had processed in a deep way much more accurately than those that they had only processed in a shallow way.) Level of processing, by itself, apparently has little or no influence on remembered duration.

6.3 Changes in Processing

In a second experiment, Block and Reed (1978) required subjects either to perform structural or semantic processing (as in the first experiment)—unmixed processing—or to alternate between the two kinds of processing—mixed processing. During the first of two durations, some subjects engaged in unmixed processing, whereas others engaged in mixed processing. During the second time period, subjects performed the other kind of task. Subjects remembered the duration during which they performed mixed processing as being longer than the duration during which they performed unmixed processing, regardless of whether the unmixed processing was structural or semantic. Thus, the remembered duration of a time period lengthens if there are changes in the kinds of activities, or strategies, that a person uses to encode events occurring during the time period.

Based on these findings, Block and Reed (1978; see also Block, 1979) proposed that remembered duration involves an implicit assessment of memory for the overall change in cognitive context during a time period. In their experiments, variations in what they called *process context*—the context accompanying the performance of different kinds of tasks—apparently produced a major kind of contextual change, a change in certain aspects of the internal context. Because the mixed-processing task required different kinds of cognitive processes, the cognitive context changed. The quality of the mental events that occurred during the time period apparently influenced remembered duration in a fairly direct way. Remembered duration apparently involves a cognitive construction based on this quality, what Block and Reed called the amount of contextual change—rather than one based on memory for stimulus events per se.

7. TWO-FACTOR INTERACTIONS

There are six different two-factor interactions between the four general factors I have discussed. In this section I mention only two of the more widely investigated two-factor interactions.

7.1 Characteristics of the Time Period and Activities during the Time Period

Vroon (1970) conducted two experiments on remembered duration that reveal interactions between the contents of a time period and a person's activities during the time period. In the first one, the task required subjects merely to pay attention to some presented information; across subjects, a different number of tones occurred during the time period. The remembered duration of the time period lengthened if there had been a greater number of tones. Thus, the more numerous were the changes, the longer was the remembered duration of the task. In contrast, Vroon's second experiment required subjects to make one of two overt responses to each tone, depending upon its pitch. In this situation, the subjects remembered the duration of the time period as being shorter if they had processed a greater amount of information; this is the opposite sort of finding from that of the first experiment.

One possible interpretation for these findings is that active processing requires substantial attention, so that for each item which a subject must actively process, correspondingly less attention is available for a subject to encode changes in events occurring during the time period. In other words, subjects who actively make decisions about information encode and remember fewer changes during the time period if there are more decisions that they must make, and as a result they judge the remembered duration as being shorter. The specific cognitive processes involved when a person remembers the amount of information presented or the amount of information processed are not obvious, and neither are the processes involved when a person remembers the overall amount of change during a time period. Future research must attempt to investigate this critical issue.

7.2 Characteristics of the Experiencer and Activities during the Time Period

Several studies have explored possible interactions between characteristics of the experiencer and activities during the time period. Hicks et al. (1976) varied the temporal outlook of subjects by telling half of them that they would later be asked to make a duration judgment (prospective condition); the experimenter did not mention this to the other half of the subjects (retrospective condition). In addition, the experiment varied the amount of information that subjects processed during a time period. Subjects either dealt standard playing cards into a single pile (0–bit condition), sorted them by color (1–bit condition), or sorted them by suit (2–bits condition). Then all subjects verbally estimated the duration of the task. In the prospective condition, the experienced duration of the task was shorter if the subjects had processed more information. This is what we expect if the more difficult tasks competed with the implicit request that subjects attend to temporal cues, such as contextual changes. In the retrospective condition, on the other hand, the remembered duration of the task was not influenced by the amount of information processed, a finding which contrasts with that of Vroon (1970).

Miller, Hicks, and Willette (1978) required subjects to study a 30–word list for a differing number of trials prior to a critical trial. This varied the person's familiarity with the materials, a characteristic of the experiencer. Before the critical trial, the experimenter told half of the subjects that they would later be asked to make a duration judgment (prospective condition) but did not tell the other half about the subsequent judgment (retrospective condition). This varied another characteristic of the experiencer—the person's temporal outlook. On the critical trial—either the first, third, or ninth trial—half the subjects were told to rehearse the words, whereas the other half were told to rest. This varied the person's activity during the time period. Then all subjects verbally estimated the duration of the critical trial. Verbal estimates were greater in the prospective condition than they were in the retrospective condition. Prior experience (i.e., previous trials) did not influence the duration judgment of subjects who did not actively rehearse; there was only a main effect of temporal outlook (prospective vs. retrospective). For subjects who rehearsed, on the other hand, the experienced duration of the time period lengthened as the number of previous study trials increased, whereas the remembered duration of the time period shortened as trials increased.

Thus, just as James (1890) originally claimed, the experience of duration in passing may differ from the experience of duration in retrospect. In Miller et al.'s study, the two kinds of temporal outlook interacted with other contextual factors to influence duration judgment. Miller et al. interpreted their finding that experienced duration lengthened as the number of previous trials increased by referring to decreased information-processing demands. In other words, the rehearsal task was less attention-demanding for subjects who had more experience with the events occurring during the time period, so they were able to allocate more attention to temporal information processing. In the retrospective condition, on the other hand, Miller et al. concluded that "duration judgments are based on memory for the amount of processing done" (p. 178). An alternative interpretation is that contextual changes are greater when a person is encountering relatively novel information, just as in situations which show a positive time-order effect (see section 5.5).

The third experiment in a series that I described earlier (Block, 1982; see section 5.4) also explored possible interacting influences of characteristics of the experiencer and activities during the time period. Specifically, the first variable was whether or not subjects spent the second duration in a room that was different from the one in which they spent the first duration. The other variable was whether subjects engaged in mixed semantic and structural processing or engaged in only a single type of processing (cf., Block & Reed, 1978, Experiment 2, which I discussed in section 6.3). Duration judgments showed a main effect of processing type which replicated that found in the earlier experiment. More importantly, the two kinds of contextual factors interacted: If there had been no change in environmental context between the two durations, there was a substantial influence of type of processing; but if the environmental context had been changed, there was no influence of type of processing. A possible explanation for the interaction is that changes in environmental context were more salient than changes in type of processing. In other words, different kinds of contextual factors may not simply add to lengthen remembered duration. A person's subjective reaction to the quality, or total meaning, of the situation is critically important.

Several other experiments also reveal interactions between characteristics of the experiencer and activities during the time period. Block (1986) conducted four experiments in which subjects saw the same number of words during each of two equal time periods. During each time period, they performed one of two different kinds of imagery tasks involving the words. One task, the environmental-imagery task, required the deliberate encoding of environmental stimuli. Subjects imagined the referent of each presented word interacting with a unique object or location in the experimental room. The other task, the internal-imagery task, restricted the deliberate encoding of environmental stimuli. Subjects imagined the referent of each word either in a single location or interacting in an internal image with the referent of the preceding word. The results in either case were the same: Subjects remembered the internal-imagery task as being longer in duration than the environmental-imagery task. Two additional experiments suggest a possible explanation for the influence of imagery task. Before performing the imagery tasks, subjects wrote either a description of the experimental room, relying on ordinary perceptual processes, or a description of another room, relying on imagery processes. The preceding description condition interacted with the subsequent imagery task: If subjects performed a certain kind of cognitive processing during the preceding description task, they remembered the duration of the imagery task that required a different kind of cognitive processing as being relatively longer.

These findings rule out a contextual explanation in terms of the encoding of varied environmental associations, because subjects remembered the environmental-imagery task as being shorter, rather than longer, than the internal-imagery task. In addition, the findings suggest another kind of contextual explanation: The factor that is critical in determining remembered duration in this situation involves the more holistic changes in context attributable to the type of processing involved in the performance of an imagery task. In other words, an overall change in context from the preceding period to the judged duration, operating during the judged duration, is apparently responsible.

8. THREE-FACTOR INTERACTIONS

The chronobiological and behavioral models which I discussed earlier (see section 5.1 and 5.2) are actually three-factor models, although the emphasis that they place on some of the factors is very minimal (Block, in press). In addition, these models typically do not acknowledge possible complex interactions between factors, only relatively simple cause-and-effect relationships, which are bound to be a misleading oversimplification of the reality of any complex process.

Some cognitive models, such as Ornstein's (1969) storage-size model, are also fundamentally three-factor models. But cognitive models typically discuss how activities during the time period, such as strategies, interact with other contextual factors to influence temporal experiences. However, some of these models also do not include all of the potentially important interactions of factors, and usually the models focus only on one kind of temporal judgment, such as duration judgment. Thus, many cognitive models also tend to be somewhat limited in scope.

9. FOUR-FACTOR INTERACTIONS

To my knowledge, no one has systematically explored the complex, four-factor interactions predicted by the general contextualistic model. However, one set of experiments comes rather close.

My colleagues and I (Block, George, & Reed, 1980) varied all four kinds of factors in a series of experiments on the watched-pot phenomenon (as in the aphorism, "A watched pot never boils"). We asked people to observe a beaker of water on an electric burner. We varied one characteristic of the experiencer by giving some of the observers a prospective outlook: We told them that we would later ask them to judge duration. We gave other observers a retrospective outlook: We told them that the experiment concerned perception, and we included no forewarning about the subsequent duration judgment. We varied changes in the focal contents of the duration by arranging for the water to boil for some of the observers, whereas for the others it did nothing at all. We varied the observers' activities during the duration by distracting some of them with questions unrelated to the task. These three factors interacted, and the nature of the interaction depended on whether the duration-judgment task involved reproduction or verbal estimation of the duration.

By exploring interactions among all four contextual factors, we arrived at a better understanding of the watched-pot phenomenon. Previous theories have focused on variables such as attention to the passage of time, waiting, vigilance, and selectivity of attention. Our study confirms that the degree to which a person is attending to the passage of time is an important factor. We can assume that observers in the prospective condition were highly aware of the duration while it was in progress, and they reproduced it as longer than did those in the retrospective condition. One of the interactions also supports this explanation: If there were no changes in events occurring during the time period (i.e., no boiling), observers in the prospective condition reproduced the duration as longer if they were not distracted than if they were distracted. Thus, "attention to the passage of time" seems to be characteristic of a person adopting a prospective outlook on the ongoing situation.

On the other hand, circumstances which are thought to produce the watched-pot phenomenon did not have the expected influence on reproductions made under retrospective conditions. Observers remembered the duration of the time period as being longer if there were either changes in the contents of the time period (i.e., boiling), changes in the observer's activities (i.e., a distraction), or both. These findings support the contextual-change hypothesis on remembered duration which I described earlier (see section 6.2).

10. DEVELOPMENT OF TEMPORAL EXPERIENCES AND CONCEPTS

A general contextualistic model can also help clarify the processes involved in the development of temporal experiences and concepts. During the earliest stages of human development, a child apparently cannot separate relatively stable objects in space from relatively transient events in time. Presumably, simultaneity and successiveness are more fundamental than other kinds of time-related concepts, such as duration. Some of the processes involved in experiences of simultaneity of two (or more) interacting event sequences probably occur fairly automatically. These processes may provide the basis for subsequent acts of temporal measurement and judgment. In spite of this automaticity of some processes, judgment of simultaneity is actually rather complex, in the sense that several physiological and cognitive factors, such as stimulus modality and attentional focus, influence the underlying processes (for a review, see Block, 1979). Preoperational children tend to make errors in judging velocity and duration which can be traced, in part, to their inability to coordinate the simultaneities of different events (Piaget, 1946).

As remembering and anticipating abilities develop in the young child, so too does the notion of an extended present—the "saddle-back, with a certain breadth of its own on which we sit perched, and from which we look in two directions into time" (James, 1890, p. 609). The changes from which a child constructs the notion of a present are the interweavings of events occurring in different progressions, or movements—activations of different, yet now related, schemata forming the contents of consciousness. The experiencing of rhythm, such as in music or speech, is apparently also based on such contextual relationships between events forming part of the psychological present.

Fairly young children (as young as age 7, and perhaps younger) can often remember the relative order or recency of two events that occurred in the same strand, or progression of events. From ages 7 through 18, there is also little or no developmental trend in the accuracy of recency judgments (A. L. Brown, 1973). These findings suggest that contextual encoding of events occurs relatively automatically and that under some circumstances the stored contextual information is sufficiently distinct to support some temporal judgments. Yet even adults have difficulty remembering the temporal order of events that did not occur in a natural order, or of unrelated events that were encoded in a similar context (Hintzman & Block, 1973).

During the concrete- and formal-operational periods of development, remembering temporal-order relationships may require particular encoding strategies as well as relatively effortful processes involving the reconstruction of relationships between landmark events—easily remembered activities, seasons of the year, and so on (Friedman & Wilkins, 1985; B. J. Underwood, 1977). A child is then able to form "the notion of different event sequences crisscrossing each other but converging upon the momentary state of the reflecting observer" (Riegel, 1977, p. 8).

The experienced duration of an event or interval between events must necessarily depend on an ability to remember the initial onset of an event, an ability which appears very early in human development (see Pouthas, 1985). However, as other cognitive abilities also develop, many other factors begin to influence experienced duration, such as anticipation. Older children and adults realize that the remembered duration of a time period is a personal reconstruction that may be influenced by a wide variety of contextual factors (see section 11). In addition, a typical concrete-operational child is probably aware that a time period which contains many personally important marker events might seem relatively long, as compared to the experience of another observer, such as a parent.

During the formal-operational period of development, most adolescents are able to form relatively abstract, scientific-like conceptions of time (see section 11). As a result, they are able to view time in a more absolute way, rather than in a way which is entirely relative to their personal experiences. It is then that adolescents attain a broad temporal perspective—a way of relating to past, present, and future events, which may be remembered, experienced, and anticipated. Of course, adults construct a temporal perspective not only from relatively automatic, species-wide temporal experiences, but also from relatively controlled, culturally specific temporal conceptions and beliefs. Consider now adults' temporal conceptions and beliefs.

11. ADULT BELIEFS ABOUT TIME AND TEMPORAL EXPERIENCES

My colleagues and I designed and conducted a reasonably comprehensive survey of beliefs about time and temporal experiences (Block, Saggau, & Nickol, 1983–84). The respondents were college students in the U.S. Subsequently, we surveyed college students in Japan and Malawi as well (Block, Buggie, & Saggau, 1987). We asked all of them to respond to a questionnaire—the Temporal Inventory on Meaning and Experience (TIME)—concerning physical time, personal time, experienced duration, and remembered duration. For example, in a part on experienced duration the respondents indicated whether a time period that a person is experiencing seems to pass more quickly or more slowly if the person is performing a pleasant versus an unpleasant activity, or a single kind of task versus several kinds of tasks. In a similar part of the TIME concerning remembered duration, respondents rated whether the same kinds of factors would make a time period that a person is remembering seem shorter or longer.

What is especially striking about these data is that the respondents' beliefs about experienced and remembered duration were remarkably similar. Regardless of the country, the respondents reported that many different kinds of factors influence the experiencing and remembering of duration.

It seems that people are "naive contextualists": They agree that a wide variety of factors influence the quality of human temporal experiences. Perhaps people from around the world develop these similar beliefs as a result of experiencing certain common phenomena of psychological time. This personal awareness of various contextual influences on duration experiences is apparently somewhat limited, however. When we asked how various factors, such as feeling strong emotions, influence how quickly or slowly time seems to pass, respondents' beliefs usually were in accord with evidence obtained in studies using prospective duration judgments. But when we asked how the same factors might influence whether a person remembers a time period as being relatively short or long, the reported beliefs often conflicted with evidence obtained in studies using retrospective duration judgments. In general, reported beliefs did not reflect the typical conclusion that a time period which seems to pass quickly (for whatever reason) might later be remembered as being relatively long, rather than relatively short. The naive contextualism displayed by the respondents is not necessarily the same as the scientific contextualism revealed by empirical studies of duration judgment.

Responses to statements concerning physical time are also of interest. On these, reported beliefs varied considerably from one country to the next. For example, Japanese respondents agreed more frequently than American or Malawian respondents that time is cyclical. Japanese respondents also agreed more frequently with statements expressing a relativistic, Einsteinian view of physical time, as opposed to an absolute, Newtonian view. These relatively large differences in beliefs concerning more abstract, scientific-like views on physical time may occur because people do not have any first-hand experiences relevant to scientific conceptions of time. Education and scientific training might be heavily involved in the formation of beliefs about physical time.

12. CONCLUSIONS

A general contextualistic model is a useful heuristic for viewing the results of experiments. It forces us to consider and to appreciate the complex interactions of contextual factors involved when people construct and represent time. In addition to this heuristic value, a contextualistic model facilitates the interpretation of recent findings. Many experiments on the psychology of time (only a few of which I have mentioned in this chapter) reveal how interactions among four major kinds of contextual factors influence psychological time. A contextualistic framework can easily accommodate other kinds of evidence, such as from reported beliefs of nonscientists about temporal experiences.

We need to continually question the models we implicitly or explicitly adopt. Given our present understanding of the psychology of time, though, a contextualistic model has been and will continue to be a fruitful one.

References

Allen, J. F., & Kautz, H. A. (1985). A model of naive temporal reasoning. In J. R. Hobbs & R. C. Moore (Eds.), *Formal theories of the commonsense world* (pp. 251–268). Norwood, NJ: Ablex.

Aschoff, J. (1984). Circadian timing. In J. Gibbon & L. Allan (Eds.), *Timing and time perception* (pp. 442–468). New York: New York Academy of Sciences.

Aschoff, J. (1985). On the perception of time during prolonged temporal isolation. *Human Neurobiology, 4*, 41–52.

Baddeley, A. D. (1982). Domains of recollection. *Psychological Review, 89*, 708–729.

Bindra, D., & Waksberg, H. (1956). Methods and terminology in studies of time estimation. *Psychological Bulletin, 53*, 55–59.

Block, R. A. (1974). Memory and the experience of duration in retrospect. *Memory & Cognition, 2*, 153–160.

Block, R. A. (1978). Remembered duration: Effects of event and sequence complexity. *Memory & Cognition, 6*, 320–326.

Block, R. A. (1979). Time and consciousness. In G. Underwood & R. Stevens (Eds.), *Aspects of consciousness: Vol. 1. Psychological issues* (pp. 179–217). London: Academic Press.

Block, R. A. (1982). Temporal judgments and contextual change. *Journal of Experimental Psychology: Learning, Memory, and Cognition, 8*, 530–544.

Block, R. A. (1985a). Contextual coding in memory: Studies of remembered duration. In J. A. Michon & J. L. Jackson (Eds.), *Time, mind, and behavior* (pp. 169–178). Berlin: Springer-Verlag.

Block, R. A. (1985b). World models for the psychology of time. *Teorie & Modelli, 2* (Suppl. 1), 89–111.

Block, R. A. (1986). Remembered duration: Imagery processes and contextual encoding. *Acta Psychologica, 62*, 103–122.

Block, R. A. (in press). A contextualistic view of time and mind. In J. T. Fraser (Ed.), *Time and mind: The study of time VI*. Madison, CT: International Universities Press.

Block, R. A., Buggie, S. E., & Saggau, J. L. (1987). *Beliefs about time in Japan, Malawi, and the United States.* Manuscript in preparation.

Block, R. A., George, E. J., & Reed, M. A. (1980). A watched pot sometimes boils: A study of duration experience. *Acta Psychologica, 46,* 81–94.

Block, R. A., & Reed, M. A. (1978). Remembered duration: Evidence for a contextual-change hypothesis. *Journal of Experimental Psychology: Human Learning and Memory, 4,* 656–665.

Block, R. A., Saggau, J. L., & Nickol, L. H. (1983–84). Temporal Inventory on Meaning and Experience: A structure of time. *Imagination, Cognition and Personality, 3,* 203–225.

Bower, G. H. (1972). Stimulus-sampling theory of encoding variability. In A. W. Melton & E. Martin (Eds.), *Coding processes in human memory* (pp. 85–123). Washington, DC: Winston.

Bransford, J. D. (1979). *Human cognition: Learning, understanding, and remembering.* Belmont, CA: Wadsworth.

Brown, A. L. (1973). Judgment of recency for long sequences of pictures: The absence of a developmental trend. *Journal of Experimental Child Psychology, 15,* 473–480.

Brown, S. W. (1985). Time perception and attention: The effects of prospective versus retrospective paradigms and task demands on perceived duration. *Perception & Psychophysics, 38,* 115–124.

Campbell, S. S. (1986). Estimation of empty time. *Human Neurobiology, 5,* 205–207.

Church, R. M. (1984). Properties of the internal clock. In J. Gibbon & L. Allan (Eds.), *Timing and time perception* (pp. 566–582). New York: New York Academy of Sciences.

Fraisse, P. (1963). *The psychology of time.* New York: Harper & Row.

Friedman, W. J., & Wilkins, A. J. (1985). Scale effects in memory for time of events. *Memory & Cognition, 13,* 168–175.

Gibson, J. J. (1975). Events are perceivable but time is not. In J. T. Fraser & N. Lawrence (Eds.), *The study of time II* (pp. 295–301). New York: Springer-Verlag.

Gray, C. (1982). Duration differences: Attentional demand or time error? *Perception, 11.* 97–102.

Groos, G., & Daan, S. (1985). The use of biological clocks in time perception. In J. A. Michon & J. L. Jackson (Eds.), *Time, mind, and behavior* (pp. 65–74). Berlin: Springer-Verlag.

Hewitt, K. (1979). *Contextual aspects of memory in normal and pathological states.* Unpublished master's thesis, Cambridge University.

Hicks, R. E., Miller, G. W., Gaes, G., & Bierman, K. (1977). Concurrent processing demands and the experience of time-in-passing. *American Journal of Psychology, 90,* 431–446.

Hicks, R. E., Miller, G. W., & Kinsbourne, M. (1976). Prospective and retrospective judgments of time as a function of amount of information processed. *American Journal of Psychology, 89,* 719–730.

Hintzman, D. L., & Block, R. A. (1971). Repetition and memory: Evidence for a multiple-trace hypothesis. *Journal of Experimental Psychology, 88,* 297–306.

Hintzman, D. L., & Block, R. A. (1973). Memory for the spacing of repetitions. *Journal of Experimental Psychology, 99,* 70–74.

Hintzman, D. L., Block, R. A., & Summers, J. J. (1973). Contextual associations and memory for serial position. *Journal of Experimental Psychology, 97,* 220–229.

Hintzman, D. L., Summers, J. J., & Block, R. A. (1975). Spacing judgments as an index of study-phase retrieval. *Journal of Experimental Psychology: Human Learning and Memory, 105,* 31–40.

Hirsh, I. J. (1959). Auditory perception of temporal order. *Journal of the Acoustical Society of America, 31,* 759–767.

Hirsh, I. J. & Sherrick, C. E., Jr. (1961). Perceived order in different sense modalities. *Journal of Experimental Psychology, 62*, 423–432.

Hoagland, H. (1933). The physiologic control of judgments of duration: Evidence for a chemical clock. *Journal of General Psychology, 9*, 267–287.

Jackson, J. L. (1985). Is the processing of temporal information automatic or controlled? In J. A. Michon & J. L. Jackson (Eds.), *Time, mind, and behavior* (pp. 179–190). Berlin: Springer-Verlag.

Jackson, J. L. (1986). *The processing of temporal information.* Doctoral dissertation, Rijksuniversiteit te Groningen.

Jackson, J. L., & Michon, J. A. (1984). Effect of item concreteness on temporal coding. *Acta Psychologica, 57*, 83–95.

James, W. (1890). *The principles of psychology, Vol. 1.* New York: Henry Holt.

Jenkins, J. J. (1979). Four points to remember: A tetrahedral model of memory experiments. In L. S. Cermak & F. I. M. Craik (Eds.), *Levels of processing and human memory* (pp. 429–446). Hillsdale, NJ: Erlbaum.

Lavie, P., & Webb, W. B. (1975). Time estimates in a long-term time-free environment. *American Journal of Psychology, 88*, 177–186.

Mach, E. (1942). *The science of mechanics* (5th ed., T. J. McCormack, Trans.). LaSalle, IL: Open Court. (Original work published 1883.)

Michon, J. A. (1975). Time experience and memory processes. In J. T. Fraser & N. Lawrence (Eds.), *The study of time II* (pp. 302–313). New York: Springer-Verlag.

Michon, J. A. (in press). Timing your mind and minding your time. In J. T. Fraser (Ed.), *Time and mind: The study of time VI.* Madison, CT: International Universities Press.

Michon, J. A., & Jackson, J. L. (1984). Attentional effort and cognitive strategies in the processing of temporal information. *Annals of the New York Academy of Sciences, 423*, 298–321.

Miller, G. W., Hicks, R. E., & Willette, M. (1978). Effects of concurrent verbal rehearsal and temporal set upon judgments of temporal duration. *Acta Psychologica, 42*, 173–179.

Mo, S. S. (1971). Judgment of temporal duration as a function of numerosity. *Psychonomic Science, 24*, 71–72.

Ornstein, R. E. (1969). *On the experience of time.* Harmondsworth, England: Penguin.

Piaget, J. (1946). *Le developpement de la notion de temps chez l'enfant.* Paris: Presses Universitaires de France.

Pouthas, V. (1985). Timing behavior in young children: A developmental approach to conditioned spaced responding. In J. A. Michon & J. L. Jackson (Eds.), *Time, mind and behavior* (pp. 100–109). Berlin: Springer-Verlag.

Poynter, W. D. (1983). Duration judgment and the segmentation of experience. *Memory & Cognition, 11*, 77–82.

Poynter, W. D., & Homa, D. (1983). Duration judgment and the experience of change. *Perception & Psychophysics, 33*, 548–560.

Predebon, J. (1984). Organization of stimulus events and remembered apparent duration. *Australian Journal of Psychology, 36*, 161–169.

Richelle, M., & Lejeune, H. (1980). *Time in animal behavior.* Oxford: Pergamon.

Riegel, K. F. (1977). The dialectics of time. In N. Datan & H. W. Reese (Eds.), *Life-span developmental psychology: Dialectical perspectives on experimental research* (pp. 3–45). New York: Academic Press.

Roitblat, H. L. (1987). *Introduction to comparative cognition.* New York: Freeman.

Shepard, R. N. (1984). Ecological constraints on internal representation: Resonant kinematics of perceiving, imagining, thinking, and dreaming. *Psychological Review, 91*, 417–447.

Thomas, E. A. C., & Brown, I., Jr. (1974). Time perception and the filled-duration illusion. *Perception & Psychophysics, 16*, 449–458.

Underwood, B. J. (1977). *Temporal codes for memories: Issues and problems.* Hillsdale, NJ: Erlbaum.

Underwood, G. (1975). Attention and the perception of duration during encoding and retrieval. *Perception, 4*, 291–296.

Underwood, G., & Swain, R. A. (1973). Selectivity of attention and the perception of duration. *Perception, 2*, 101–105.

Vroon, P. A. (1970). Effects of presented and processed information on duration experience. *Acta Psychologica, 34*, 115–121.

TIME AND HUMAN COGNITION
A Life-Span Perspective
I. Levin and D. Zakay (Editors)

CHAPTER 10

DAN ZAKAY

Subjective Time and Attentional Resource Allocation: An Integrated Model of Time Estimation*

INTRODUCTION

Time is a highly complex notion (Fraisse, 1984). Virtually no other concept is so central to human life and yet so poorly understood as psychological time. One reason for this is the lack of an obvious physical correlate to time perception, or as Gibson (1975) puts it, "events are perceivable, but time is not".

Both Piaget (1969) and Fraisse (1984) distinguished between two concepts basic to psychological time: succession, "which corresponds to the fact that two or more events can be perceived as different and organized sequentially"; and duration, "which applies to the interval between two successive events" (Fraisse, 1984, p. 2). These two concepts do not exist independently of each other; duration is meaningless without succession. The experience of the flow of time from one moment to another at an ever-changing tempo is central to our life. We experience moments which seem

*The research reported in this chapter was supported by research grants from the Israeli Academy of Science and the Basic Research Fund of Tel-Aviv University. The author wishes to thank Iris Levin and Yehoshua Tsal for their helpful comments on the manuscript.

to last forever and others which appear to fly by almost unnoticed. Research in time psychology is mainly concerned with the experience of duration (Vroon, 1976). This chapter focuses on understanding the cognitive processes of short duration estimation.

Fraisse (1984) differentiates between time estimation and perception. This difference has to do with the fact that no specialized sensory receptors in our perceptual system are devoted to the perception of time. Hence, perception of time is used to describe the ongoing feeling of the "psychological present" which is bounded by durations of no more than 4 seconds. On the other hand, "estimation of duration takes place when memory is used either to associate a moment in the past with a moment in the present or to link two past events" (Fraisse, 1984, p. 9). Thus intervals of up to 4 seconds are considered to be "preceived" as a "psychological present", whereas longer intervals span the present and the past. Duration is therefore commonly categorized into ranges of less than 1 second, between 1 and 4 seconds, from 4 seconds to a few minutes, from minutes to hours, days, months and years, historical time, and geological time. While the exact boundaries are hard to define, it is logical to assume that different cognitive processes are used for estimating durations in the various categories (e.g., Aschoff, 1984; 1985). Conceivably, sensory memory is employed in perceiving the psychological present, while short-term memory is needed to estimate intervals from seconds to a few minutes. Long-term memory is probably called into action for estimating hours, days, and years, and it is likely that knowledge, past experience, and attitutes are involved in this process as well. Because of this, the range from 4 seconds to 1–2 minutes is the most relevant for the study of duration estimation processes. Indeed, most of the research in this field has dealt with this range.

THEORIES OF SHORT INTERVAL DURATION ESTIMATION

A convenient paradigm widely used to study time estimation processes involves manipulating the level of information processing load during an interval and measuring the resulting changes in the length of its duration estimation. The filled interval illusion, whereby intervals filled by some activity are estimated as longer than comparable "empty" intervals, is commonly accepted in the literature (e.g., Coren, Porac & Ward, 1984). Theories of time estimation must provide an explanation for this phenomenon. A useful review of time estimation theories is provided by Poynter (this volume), and there is no point in repeating it. I would, however, like to suggest categorizing the various theories into two types: 1) those based on memory processes, such as the storage-size model (Ornstein, 1969); and 2) those based on attentional processes, such as Frankenhauser's (1959) cognitive timer model.

Memory-Based Models

Ornstein (1969) introduced the storage-size metaphor to explain the time estimation process. According to this model, the higher the complexity of a stimulus, the higher the subjective estimate of the duration of its exposure. This follows from the assumption that storage size, on which time estimation is based, is larger for a complex stimulus than for a simple one. Empirical support for the storage-size model has been found in several studies (e.g., Gray, 1982; Michon, 1965; Underwood, 1975). Another model based on long-term memory as the main cognitive mechanism of time estimation was proposed by Block (1978) and Block and Reed (1978). According to this "change" model, duration estimates are correlated with the amount of change in cognitive context or in the type of information processing performed during an interval. Poynter (1983, 1988, this volume) elaborated on this idea, suggesting that judged durations are a positive function of the degree to which an interval is segmented. Thus, task complexity is interpreted differently by "change" models than by Ornstein. However, the predicted pattern of the relationship between task complexity or information processing load and judged duration is identical in all memory-based models, namely a positive one.

Attentional Models

Although memory-based models gained impressive empirical support, many contradictory findings in which the relationship between judged duration and task complexity proved to be negative, were obtained as well (e.g., Devane, 1974; Fraisse, 1963; Hicks, Miller & Kinsbourne, 1976; Hicks, Miller, Gaes & Bierman, 1977; Vroon, 1970). These findings are explained by attentional models (e.g., Frankenhauser, 1959, Hicks, Miller, Gaes & Bierman, 1977; Priestly, 1968), which hold that judged duration is a direct function of the amount of attention allocated to the passage of time. It is assumed that a cognitive unit (which might be called a timer or counter), exists, whose purpose it is to process and encode temporal information.

This counter, however, demands attentional resources for its operation. As nontemporal information load is reduced, more attentional resources may be allocated to the cognitive timer, whose storage of temporal information is thereby increased, resulting in longer judged durations. Hence, as task complexity increases, and thus also information processing load, less attention can be devoted to the cognitive counter, resulting in fewer subjective time units accumulated in it. In this case, judged duration length is an inverse function of task complexity.

Subjective Time as a Double-Faceted Phenomenon

How can we account for the fact that both memory-based and attentional models gain empirical support from opposite and contradictory results? One possible solution is to look for another model able to explain these seemingly incongruous findings. Thomas and Weaver (1975) proposed a model which partially combines the two contradictory views. They suggest that each stimulus is analyzed by two processors: 1) a timer P(t) which processes temporal information and whose output is a temporal encoding which is directly related to the stimlus duration; and 2) a nontemporal information processor P(i) whose output contains encodings of the nontemporal stimulus features along with an encoding or memory of the time spent processing these features. Attention is divided between P(t) and P(i) according to the nature of the task. The values and reliability of the two outputs are a function of the amount of attention allocated to each processor. Perceived duration is a weighted average of the P(t) output and the encoding of the time spent processing nontemporal information. Thomas and Weaver's model was originally proposed for the perception of intervals shorter than 1 sec., and its application has been restricted to durations of less than 100 msec. (Allan, 1979). However, this model does not seem to account for empirical findings obtained for both prospective and retrospective estimates of durations longer than 1 sec. In both cases, since the longer the P(i) the fewer the subjective time units accumulated in P(t) and vice versa, the output of P(t) and the encoded time spent by P(i) should complement each other, and the results should be equal duration estimations for both complex and simple tasks, which is not the case.

I would like to propose an elaboration of Thomas and Weaver's model for the estimation of short durations which are longer than 1 sec. Accordingly, only the output of the most reliable processor is used as the origin of duration estimation, while the nonreliable processor's output is eliminated. What is needed is the defintion of the conditions which determine when

P(t) alone or P(i) alone will serve as the basis for time estimation. Given such conditions, one can assume that memory-based models apply to the cases where P(i) dominates the estimation process because it is linearly and positively correlated with information processing load, whereas attentional models apply to the cases where P(t) dominates the scene because it is linearly but negatively correlated with information processing load. These definitions can be supplied by the contextualistic approach.

The Contextualistic Approach

Block (1985, this volume) presents a contextualistic model of temporal experience and defines several contextualistic factors which influence it. Block's factors include the kind of temporal behavior involved, the characteristics of the time period which a person experiences, and the characteristics of the experiencer and his/her activity during the time period. Other investigators have also noted the dependency of subjective time on factors affecting its measurement (e.g., Allan, 1979; Clausen, 1950; Fraisse, 1984; Wallace and Rabin, 1960). Hicks, Miller & Kinsbourne (1976) listed the following factors as influencing subjective estimates: 1) method of time estimation; 2) duration of estimated interval; 3) the nature of processing required of the subject during the estimated interval; 4) the nature of the measurement paradigm – e.g., a prospective paradigm in which the subject knows in advance that he or she will be required to estimate the elapsed time, or a retrospective paradigm in which the subject is told to do so only after the target interval is over. It appears likely that the factor which determines the selection of either P(t) or P(i) as the sole source for time estimation might be found among these factors. Indeed, Block (1988, this volume) argues that "a complete understanding of any kind of temporal experience is possible only if we consider complex interactions among all of these factors."

Prospective vs. Retrospective Estimations

The time estimation paradigm used seems to play a major role in determining the attentional focus during time estimation. Hicks et al. (1976) suggested that time judgments in a retrospective paradigm are proportional to the amount of content retrieved from an interval, rather than to the amount of processing performed during it. Hicks et al. (1977) found support for the attentional model only with a prospective paradigm, while no clear cut pattern of results was obtained with a retrospective paradigm. These findings indicate the possibility that different temporal processes are responsible for prospective and retrospective time estimation. Zakay & Meran (1988) analyzed the features of prospective and retrospective estimation and arrived at the following dissimilarities: 1) retrospective estimations rest heavily on long-term memory processes, while prospective estimations rely mostly on short-term memory processes; 2) subjects can actively engage in temporal related processes under prospective conditions.

The outcome of these two procedural dissimilarities is that in a retrospective situation time estimation must rely on nontemporal information stored in long-term memory because short-term memory is already occupied during the estimation phase. One strong argument in favor of this claim is that in a retrospective paradigm the instructions for time estimation are necessarily given to the subject only after the termination of the target interval. These instructions, which are significant to the subject, separate in time the retrospective estimation from the target interval and occupy STM.

Under prospective conditions, on the contrary, subjects can actively accumulate and store relevant temporal information, and if the estimation is done immediately upon termination of the target interval without any interruption, this temporal information can be used.

I would propose the following model, which is a combination of Thomas and Weaver's (1975) two processor model and Block's (this volume) contextualistic one: in a prospective paradigm, the occupation with time makes P(t) the basis for time estimation. In a retrospective paradigm, however, P(t)'s output is not available at the estimation phase and hence P(i) will be the basis for time estimation. The predictions of this paradigm-dependent model encompass those of both memory-based and attentional models. Support for it was found by a meta-analysis (Zakay and Meran, 1988) of the time estimation literature, which revealed that, indeed, in most of the studies where the realtionship between estimated duration length and task complexity was found to be positive, a retrospective paradigm was employed, whereas in most studies where a negative relationship was found, the paradigm employed was a prospective one.

The Role of Attention in Prospective and Retrospective Estimation

It has been established (Curton & Lordahl, 1974; Fraisse, 1963) that expectations and attention play an important role in the estimation of durations. It would be wrong, however, to assume that this is the case only in regard to prospective estimations and to ignore the role of attention in retrospective estimations. Brown (1985) found support for an attentional allocation model in both prospective and retrospective situations. It should be remembered that nontemporal information processes consume attentional resources, and that the more complex a stimulus is, the more attentional resources are needed for its processing. Hence, a distraction of attention should impair the processing, resulting in a lesser depth of processing and a "smaller" storage size manifested in shortened retrospective estimations.

RESOURCE ALLOCATION MODEL OF TIME ESTIMATION (RAM)

In light of the above considerations, I propose the following resource allocation model of time estimation, an elaboration of the paradigm-based model. Here, attentional resources are at all times divided among all tasks which the organism must perform (Kahneman, 1973). More resources are allocated to tasks of higher internal priority. In the case of time estimation, this estimation is an attention consuming task competing with nontemporal information processing. Prospective instructions assign high priority to the time estimation task and hence more resources are allocated for P(t) which then becomes the sole source of time estimation. At the same time, nontemporal information processing demands its own share of resources, and hence the more complex a task, the fewer resources allocated to P(t), resulting in the negative function between length of time estimate and task complexity. Any contextualistic element, such as expectations as in the case of the "watched pot" paradigm (e.g., Block, George and Reed, 1980), will increase the priority of P(t) and result in longer prospective subjective durations. On the other hand, any distraction of attention away from P(t) will result in shortened prospective subjective durations (e.g., Smith, 1969).

In a retrospective estimation, priority is given to P(i), and the more resources allocated to it because of instructions or task demands, etc., the deeper the processing, and the higher the level of perceived changes. Since the information produced by P(i) and stored in memory is the basis for retrospective estimations, the more resources allocated to P(i), the longer the retrospective estimations. Any distraction of attention from P(i), however, should result in shortened retrospective estimations.

The following sections present four studies aimed at finding support for the hypothesized dissimilarity between prospective and retrospective estimates and validating the resource allocation model in both paradigms by manipulating and shifting the focus of subjects' attention.

STUDY 1 – IMMEDIATE AND REMOTE TIME ESTIMATION(1)

The purpose of this study was to demonstrate the different nature of the cognitive mechanisms responsible for time estimation in prospective and retrospective paradigms. A new factor was introduced here, namely the estimation delay which is the time lapse between the termination of an interval and its actual estimation. We defined Immediate Estimation (IE) as an estimation performed immediately upon the termination of the target interval, and Remote Estimation (RE) as an estimation performed only after a given period of time had elapsed after the interval's termination. It was held that the accessibility of the temporal information accumulated in the cognitive timer P(t) during an interval decreases as a function of the time elapsing after the termination of the target interval, as does the relevancy of that information for the estimation of the interval's duration. This assumption reflects the nature of the cognitive timer (Frankenhauser, 1959; Thomas and Brown, 1974; Thomas and Weaver, 1975; Zakay, Nitzan and Glicksohn, 1983). This timer is assumed to be single channeled, and consequently can, at any given time, store temporal information for only one duration marked by some start and stop signs. P(t) is activated nonintentionally by any signal which is interpreted as the commencement of a specific interval, and the subjective "counting" of time units reflecting the duration of that interval is continued until a signal interpreted as termination of the interval is received. P(t) is then "reset" unintentionally upon receipt of a new starting signal. The information accumulated in P(t) is probably stored in short-term memory, and as such is subject to decay processes (Allan and Rousseau, 1976). It is not logical to assume that such information, which has a very low significance, is stored and accessible later on from long-term memory. Hence, in an IE paradigm regarding short intervals, the temporal information is still accessible from short-term memory and can be utilized by the cognitive system. This is not the case, however, in an RE paradigm. First, it should be noted that upon termination of the target interval, P(t) is reset and the elapsing time is probably considered a new interval whose duration is now being measured. Hence, when an RE is made, the relevant temporal information is not necessarily accessible and the probability of a retrieval error is greater. It is therefore suggested that in IE, time estimation is most likely based on the temporal information originating in the cognitive timer, while in RE the estimation mechanism is most probably based on long-term storage size accumulated during the target interval. As described earlier, duration estimation based on the cognitive timer yields a negative relationship between subjective duration and information load during the estimated interval, while duration estimation based on storage size yields a positive relationship between these two factors. It is important to note that both IE and RE are possible within the framework of a prospective paradigm, but retrospective estimations are always RE because of the delayed instructions. However, in this study an estimation performed immediately after the instructions were given was still considered immediate retrospective estimation.

The following predictions ensued: 1) in a prospective immediate estimation paradigm (PIE) the relationship between subjective duration and information processing load will be negative, while in a prospective remote estimation paradigm (PRE) it will be positive; 2) in both a retrospective immediate estimation (RIE) and a retrospective remote estimation (RRE) the same trend will be found, most probably a positive one.

Method

SUBJECTS

Eighty subjects, all of whom were first year social science students at Tel-Aviv University ranging in age between 19 and 30 years, participated in the experiment in partial fulfillment of course requirements.

INSTRUMENTS

In order to test these predictions, the W and the CW tasks of the Stroop color-word test (Stroop 1935) were utilized. In the W task the name of a color is to be read, while in the CW task color names written in incongruent colored inks are presented and subjects are required to name the color of the ink while ignoring the color name. The difference in information processing load in the W and CW tasks has been well established, where the CW task is more demanding as reflected by longer reaction times and higher number of errors as compared with the W task (Dyer, 1973). In addition, the CW task involves naming a stimulus, which is a more complex process than reading the name of this stimulus (Fraisse, 1979) as required in the W task. In attentional terms, Logan and Zbrodoff (1979) and Logan (1980) claim that in the Stroop CW task much attention is required for the analysis of each stimulus as there is a need to divide attention between reported and nonreported dimesions, which is not the case in the W task. In order to test the validity of the tasks' complexity level, subjects evaluated each task's difficulty level on a 7 point scale, where 1 stood for "very easy" and 7 for "very difficult". The average difficulty rating was 1.40 for the W task and 3.72 for the CW task, thus validating the difference between the two tasks in terms of complexity level.

PROCEDURE

The subjects were randomly assigned to one of eight experimental groups: 1) Retrospective, IE, W task (RIW); 2) Retrospective, IE, CW task (RICW); 3) Retrospective, RE, W task (RRW); 4) Retrospective, RE, CW task (RRCW); 5) Prospective, IE, W task (PIW); 6) Prospective, IE, CW task (PICW); 7) Prospective, RE, W task (PRW); 8) Prospective, RE, CW task (PRCW). The time elapsing between the termination of the target interval and the remote estimation was 60 sec. The objective time of all target intervals was 10 sec. Each subject was tested individually, with the time interval measured by an electronic timer and delimited for the subject by the experimenter saying "start" and "stop". Subjects were asked to perform either the W or the CW task during that interval. In the prospective paradigm they were told in advance that they would later be asked to estimate the duration of the target interval, whereas in the retrospective paradigm they were told this only immediately before the actual estimation. In all groups, subjects were asked to perform the task as quickly and accurately as possible. The estimation was done by having the subject press a button for the same duration which she/he felt corresponded to the duration of the task. Pressing the button activated a hidden electronic timer, and the time recorded was taken as the time estimate.

Results

The time estimates (TE) obtained were subjected to a 3–way ANOVA of paradigm (prospective versus retrospective) x estimation delay (IE versus RE) x task (W versus CW). Significant main effect was obtained for estimation delay [$F(1,72) = 4.17$; $p < 0.05$], while the main effect of paradigm was close to significance [$F(1,72) = 3.34$; $p < 0.07$]. Specific comparison between complexity levels within each paradigm revealed significant differences between PRCW and PRW and PICW and PIW only (Schéffé tests $p < 0.01$). The trends obtained are presented in Table 10.1.

Table 10.1.
TE MEANS (IN SEC. – N=10 IN EACH CELL)

PARADIGM	ESTIMATION DELAY	TASK COMPLEXITY	
		LOW (W)	HIGH (CW)
PROSPECTIVE	IE	9.69	5.98
	RE	8.64	10.45
RETROSPECTIVE	IE	6.93	5.58
	RE	8.91	7.49

Discussion of Study 1

The results obtained in Study 1 indicate that IE and RE affect time estimation differently in prospective vs. retrospective paradigms. In the prospective paradigm the predictions were fully validated, i.e., a negative trend reflecting an attentional-based process was found with IE, while a positive trend reflecting a storage size-based process was found with RE. As for the retrospective paradigm, a similar type of trend in both IE and RE was indeed found, as predicted, but the trend was closer to a negative one than to the predicted positive one. In statistical terms, however, the significant differences obtained between complexity levels in RIE or RRE were contrary to the respective significant differences in both PIE and PRE. These findings clearly indicate the use of different time estimation strategies in prospective and retrospective paradigms. The retrospective condition seems to evoke an unsystematic time estimation process which might reflect storage size, memory traces of the temporal information stored in the cognitive timer, memory of high priority events (Poynter, 1983), memory of the content processed during the target interval, or any combination of these elements. Similarly to the results reported here, Hicks et al. (1976) failed to find any significant well-defined function between judged time and response uncertainty using the retrospective paradigm. On the other hand, time processes with the prospective paradigm seem to be clear-cut because of subjects' awareness of the need to process temporal information.

Study 2 was designed to further validate the attentional model in prospective time estimation.

STUDY 2 – THE INFLUENCE OF TASK DIFFICULTY AND EXTERNAL TEMPO ON PROSPECTIVE TIME ESTIMATION(2)

The objective of Study 2 was to demonstrate the validity of the attentional model within the framework of a prospective paradigm. Two variables were manipulated: task difficulty and external tempo rate non-relevant to the task to be performed during the estimated interval. The rationale for manipulating task complexity is clear, as the relationship between complexity level and time estimation length is a crucial test for the attentional model. As for environmental rhythmic stimulation, this was manipulated in order to test several hypothesized properties of the cognitive counter. Both Frankehauser (1959) and Ornstein (1969) found that subjective time estimations (STE) were longer the faster the beat of a metronome. Denner, Wapner, McFarland and Werner (1963) reported that STEs were longer with fast rhythmic physical activity. These findings might be interpreted as supporting either the storage-size model or the attentional model. On the one hand, it might be claimed that the higher the rate of environmental stimulation the higher the overall information processes per unit of objective time, resulting in increased storage size. On the other hand, one might surmise that the nonrelevant environmental information is not processed as part of the relevant information, but rather acts directly on the cognitive counter, which might be considered "a psychobiological clock that can speed up or slow down, depending on external as well as internal conditions" (Zakay et al., 1983, p. 452). This study proposed that the cognitive counter is activated by the focusing of attention on temporal information and, in addition, operates in accordance with some internal rate. The higher that rate, the shorter the subjective time unit and the more time units registered whenever the timer is activated. When nonrelevant external rhythmic stimulation is presented, more attention will be paid to temporal information the faster the rate of the stimulation because of the associations that it arouses with a clock. In addition, the cognitive counter will "speed" up and the number of subjective time units which are registered, will increase. The opposite will be the case in regard to slower external rhythmic stimulation. Hence, a positive relationship between rate of external tempo and STE length was predicted. To sum up, the following predictions were made here on the basis of the two competing models. According to the storage-size model, one would expect: 1) a positive relationship between task difficulty and length of STE; 2) a shorter STE for "empty" intervals than for "filled" ones; 3) a positive relationship between number of responses and length of STE; and 4) a positive relationship between rate of nonrelevant external tempo and length of STE.

According to the attentional model, one would expect: 1) a negative relationship between task difficulty and length of STE; 2) a longer STE for "empty" intervals than for "filled" ones; and 3) a positive relationship between rate of nonrelevant external tempo and length of STE. No specific relationship was predicted between number of responses and STE, but, for the sake of consistency, a negative relationship between number of responses and task difficulty was expected.

It should be stressed that since the predictions concerning the relationship between external tempo and STE were identical for both models, the real test was in the internal consistency of all the predictions. A set of results inconsistent with either of the two models would fail to support both.

Method

SUBJECTS

Ninety-six students with an average age of 25, participated in the experiment in partial fulfillment of the requirements of a first-year introductory psychology course at Tel-Aviv University.

APPARATUS AND STIMULI

The concurrent task was a verbal one with three levels of difficulty: 1) easy level, reading words (W); 2) intermediate level, naming task (N); and 3) difficult level, providing synonyms for given words (S). This ranking of task difficulty was based on Fraisse (1963) The stimuli were presented on white 6 x 9 cm. cards. For each task, 25 stimuli were presented. For the first task, the stimuli were Hebrew words. For the second, they were pictures of various objects whose names appear with the same frequency in Hebrew as the words in the first task. For the third task, the stimuli were Hebrew words whose frequency of occurrence was lower than that of the words in the other two tasks.

MANIPULATION OF EXTERNAL TEMPO

External tempo was manipulated in the foloowing manner: 1) Visual "tempo" – a white light bulb was positioned 1 m. away from the subject. This bulb could be either totally inactive or flickering at one of two frequencies: 0.5 sec. (fast) or 2 sec. (slow); 2) Auditory "tempo" – an electronic buzzer provided tones at the same two frequencies as above or not at all. In both visual and auditory "tempo", the stimulation was present during the entire target interval to be estimated.

METHOD OF TIME ESTIMATION

The method used was one of reproduction in a prospective paradigm. The subjects were required to press a switch for a period of time subjectively equal to the length of time used to carry out the task. Pressing the switch activated a hidden electronic timer from which the subjective time estimates (STE) could be recorded.

PROCEDURE

The subjects were divided randomly into five groups: fast visual, fast auditory, slow visual, and slow auditory, with 16 subjects in each, and a control group of 32 subjects. Each subject was tested individually and provided four STEs for each of the four tasks. Order of presentation of tasks was counterbalanced. The objective time interval, which was 14 sec. for all tasks, was delineated by the experimenter saying "start" and "stop" with reference to an electronic timer. In each task, a pile of 25 cards was placed before the subject, who turned over each card in succession. The subjects were asked to perform each task as quickly and as accurately as possible. In the condition of "empty" interval, the objective time interval was demarcated in the same manner by the experimenter. However, the subject was not required to perform any task. The experimenter did not draw the attention of the subject to the external tempo, which was activated or not according to the experimental group to which the subject belonged. The subject was not required to do anything with regard to this external stimulation so that it would not appear to be relevant information. For each subject, both the STEs and the number of responses (e.g., cards) completed for each task were recorded.

Results

In order to test whether external tempo was modality specific, the obtained subjective time estimates (STE) were subjected to an ANOVA with three factors (task x tempo rate x modality (visual vs. auditory)), with repeated measures for task. Significant main effects for tempo rate [$F(1,60) = 13{,}81$, $p < 0.01$] and task [$F(3,180) = 139.85$, $p < 0.01$] were found. No effect for modality [$F(1,60) = 0.28$] and no interactions were found. Hence, a two-way ANOVA (external tempo rate x task), collapsed over modality and with the control group as a level in tempo rate and repeated measures for the task factor, was conducted. Significant main effects for external tempo rate [$F(2,93) = 7.01$, $p < 0.01$] and task [$F(3,279) = 197.58$, $p < 0.01$] but no interactions, were found. The trend of results is presented in Figure 10.1.

The number of responses was subjected to an ANOVA in the former design, but without task E, revealing only a significant main effect for task [$F(2,186) = 270.71$ $p < 0.01$]. In all experimental groups and under all conditions, number of responses decreased as task difficulty increased. It should

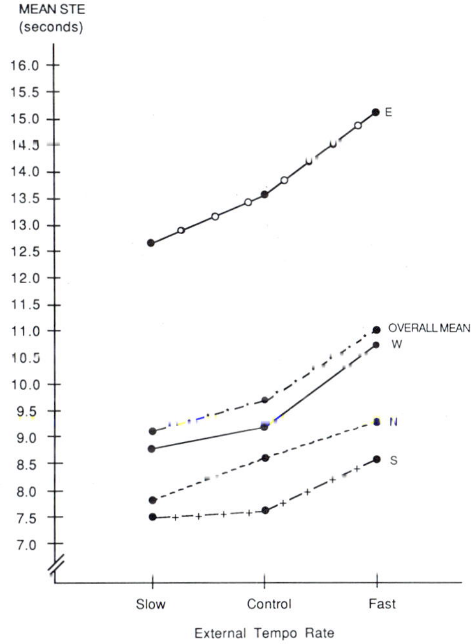

Figure 10.1. Mean STEs by experimental conditions (collapsed over modality) (From Zakay, Nitzan & Glicksohn, 1983).

be noted that almost no errors were made and task difficulty was manifested through the number of responses only.

The relationship between number of responses and STE was further analyzed by means of Pearson correlations. Most of the correlations found were low and not significant, and the overall pattern revealed an inconsistent and nonsystematic relationship. The same pattern was obtained for each modality alone. Trend analysis was performed on STE. A significant linear trend [$F\ 1{,}93) = 6.75$, $p < 0.05$] was found for STEs in the E task, with the STEs in the order of slow external tempo, control, and fast external tempo. The same was true for the W task [$F\ (1{,}93) = 4.22$, $p < 0.05$]. The quadratic trends were nonsignificant in both cases.

Discussion of Study 2

The findings obtained in this study clearly indicate that STE is a negative function of task difficulty in all experimental groups and tasks. "Empty" intervals were consistently estimated to be of significantly longer duration than "filled" intervals, again, in all experimental groups and tasks. It can be concluded that in the case of prospective time estimation the results support the attentional model and refute the storage-size model. External tempo was found in all experimental conditions to monotonically increase STE as the tempo rate was increased, which both models predict. However, according to the explanation provided by the storage-size model, one would expect even slow external stimulation to add to the amount of information stored and therefore the STE to be longer than for the control group with no external stimulation. Nevertheless, STEs were consistently found to be shorter with slow-rate external tempo than in the control group. This is especially evident in the E task. Hence, it would seem that even the finding of a positive relationship between length of STE and external tempo rate is not consistent with the storage-size model. On the other hand, the trend revealed might be explained by the counter model, since it is plausible to assume that the slow external tempo was slower than the natural internal tempo of the timer, causing the cognitive timer to slow down.

A further result of interest is the lack of influence of external tempo rate on number of responses. If it were true that external stimulation was processed and added to storage, then, since it was found that responses decreased significantly as task difficulty increased, one would predict the number of responses to similarly decrease as external tempo rate increased. Hence, it might be concluded that nonrelevant external stimulation did not increase information-processing load. It should also be noted that no systematic relationship was found between the number of responses and STE. This relationship was dependent on experimental conditions, and even when it reached significance it explained, at most, only 16% of the variance. This indicates that the relationship between number of responses and STE is not a direct one but is mediated through task difficulty. Thus, on the basis of the total findings, it can be said that all the predictions stemming from the counter model were consistently supported, while the opposite was the case in regard to the storage-size model.

In summary, Studies 1 and 2 demonstrate that: 1) retrospective and prospective estimations are based on different processes; and 2) the attentional model is valid for prospective estimations.

The following two studies sought to demonstrate the validity of the RAM model by manipulating resource allocation by methods which are more direct than the manipulation of task complexity. These methods are effective only within the framework of a prospective paradigm, and hence both Studies 4 and 5 deal with prospective estimations.

STUDY 3 – A COMPARISON OF TIME ESTIMATION AS A PRIMARY OR SECONDARY TASK(3)

The objective of this study was to further confirm the validity of the resource allocation model in a prospective paradigm by directly manipulating the resource allocation policy utilized by subjects during the target interval. One of the best experimental methods by which to achieve such a goal is the secondary task technique in which residual resources are absorbed by introduction of the secondary task. Differences in task resource demands are thus reflected by secondary task performance (Wickens, 1984). The established relationship between information processing load and subjective time led mental load investigators to propose the use of time estimation for the measurement of mental load, but it generally served as a secondary task only. Hart (1975) assumed that if subjects were asked to produce constant intervals of time simultaneously with a primary task, an internal mental counter would be employed to produce these intervals and, as a consequence, as the primary task load increased, the counter would slow down. Typically, when using the secondary task technique it is the primary task which is actually of interest and whose priority is emphasized. The present research, however, sought to investigate time estimation processes, and the idea was to treat them as either a primary or a secondary task. It was assumed that if subjects were instructed to treat temporal processing as a primary task, subjective durations would be longer than if time estimation were treated as a secondary task, because of the effect of the instructions on subjects' resource allocation policy. If time estimation were the primary task, more resources would be allocated for temporal processes and P(t) would be accelerated, the opposite being the case if time estimation were treated as a secondary task.

Another technique which can be used to induce temporary changes in subjects' resource allocation policy, is the exposure of subjects to distracting stimuli. A strong distracting stimulus presented during a target interval should therefore reduce the overall amount of resources devoted to P(t) during the estimated period, and thus we would expect the estimated duration to be shortened.

A third experimental manipulation, which was already utilized in the research reported on above, is that of task complexity. What is predicted here, of course, is a negative linear relationship between duration estimate length and task complexity. The interaction expected among the three manipulations was additive, namely, a lack of significant interactions in ANOVA. This assumption derived from the fact that all three manipulations influence P(t) similarly. The more complex a task, the more a presented stimulus distracts attention, and as time estimation is treated as a secondary task, the less P(t) is energized and the shorter subjective estimations should be.

Method

SUBJECTS

Eighty undergraduate students at Tel-Aviv University, with ages ranging between 22 and 30 years, participated in the experiment in partial fulfillment of course requirements.

INSTRUMENTS

Two tasks of the Stroop color word test (Stroop, 1935) were used. The W task was used as a simple task, and the CW task as a complex one. The rationale for this, as well as empirical data supporting its validity were outlined earlier in this chapter (see Study 1). The Stroop tasks were presented following the procedure described in Study 1 above. Time was allotted and measured by an electronic timer. In order to obtain the distraction manipulation, subjects were connected by electrodes to an E.E.G. instrument which was never really operated, but was set so that noises were heard giving the impression that something was awry.

EXPERIMENTAL DESIGN

A 2x2x2 complete factorial design was used. The independent variables were task complexity with two levels (low and high, represented by the W and CW tasks respectively), distractions with two levels (with and without distraction), and resource allocation with two levels (time estimation as a primary or secondary task). Three different manipulations of attentional focusing were utilized in order to ensure the desired outcome. The estimation paradigm was prospective.

PROCEDURE

Subjects were randomly assigned to each of the 8 experimental groups, although this was done independently for males and females so that 5 males and 5 females were tested under each condition. Each subject was tested individually. The objective duration of the intervals to be estimated was 10 seconds in all groups. Subjects were given the following instructions: "You are participating in an experiment designed to test the relationship between task performance and time estimation. Please start the task upon receipt of a 'start' signal, and terminate its performance upon receipt of a 'stop' signal. Then press a button for a length of time which you feel is identical with the duration of the task you performed." The primary task groups were then told that "the most important task in this experiment is the time estimation and we are interested in testing your time estimation ability", whereas the secondary task group was told that "it is important that you perform your reading task as accurately as you can". The appropriate Stroop task was then explained (see Study 1). In the distraction groups, subjects were told that their E.E.G. activity during the experiment would be recorded, after which the electrodes were attached to their heads. Time estimation was obtained by reproduction. Subjects pressed a button, which activated a hidden electronic timer, for the same duration which they felt corresponded to the duration of the task.

Results

The means and standard deviations of the time estimates obtained in the various groups are presented in Table 10.2

Table 10.2.
MEANS AND STANDARD DEVIATIONS (IN PARENTHESIS) OF TIME ESTIMATES (IN SEC. N=10 IN EACH GROUP)

RESOURCE ALLOCATION	TASK COMPLEXITY			
	LOW (W TASK)		HIGH (CW TASK)	
	DISTRACTION		DISTRACTION	
	–	+	–	+
PRIMARY TASK	(1) 9.69 (2.42)	(2) 8.89 (2.66)	(5) 6.30 (1.51)	(6) 5.12 (1.53)
SECONDARY TASK	(3) 8.12 (2.19)	(4) 7.86 (2.27)	(7) 5.90 (1.58)	(8) 4.91 (1.27)

Three way ANOVA revealed significant main effects for task complexity [$F(1,72) = 4.34$, $p < 0.05$], for primary vs. secondary task [$F(1,72) = 3.31$, $p < 0.05$] and for distraction [$F(1,72) = 5.17$, $p < 0.05$]. No significant interactions were obtained, as predicted.

Specific contrasts were tested via Schéffé tests. The significant contrasts obtained are presented in Table 10.3.

Table 10.3.
SIGNIFICANT CONTRASTS (SCHÉFFÉ TESTS)

CONTRAST*	SIGNIFICANCE
8–1	0.01
8–2	0.01
8–3	0.01
8–4	0.01
8–5	0.05
5–1	0.01
6–2	0.01
7–3	0.01
6–5	0.05
1–3	0.05

* Contrasts are defined in terms of cell numbers as indicated in Table 10.2.

Discussion of Study 3

The results obtained in this study confirmed the tested hypotheses and supported the resource allocation model of time estimation in a prospective paradigm. When time estimation was treated as a primary task, all estimates were longer than when it was treated as a secondary task under identical conditions. The distraction manipulation was found to be effective, and since resources were attracted away from the counter, estimations were shorter in the presence of a distraction than when no distraction was employed. Under all conditions task complexity was negatively correlated with estimate length and the contrast between low and high complexity estimates was always statistically significant. Again, it is logical to assume that task demands were the dominating factor in determining a subject's internal resource allocation policy.

The three factors influenced the time estimation task in quite a similar fashion, as was to be expected since all three were assumed to manipulate resource allocation in the same direction. Their effect can thus be considered additive. The shortest estimate was obtained when all three factors pulled resources away from the counter, i.e., when the task was difficult, a distraction was presented, and time estimation was treated as a secondary task. The longest estimate, on the other hand, was obtained where all three factors directed resources to the operation of the counter, namely, when the task was simple, no distraction was present, and time estimation was treated as the primary task.

The present study might have some practical implications for the methodology of utilizing time estimation as a secondary task in mental load measurement. Hart (1975) found that both retrospective and produced estimates were longer as the difficulty of the primary task increased. This seeming discrepancy is a methodological illusion reflecting the failure to consider the estimation paradigm. Under a retrospective paradigm, storage-size or the number of perceived changes are the relevant mechanisms on which time estimation rests, and hence the more difficult a task the longer the estimate of its duration should be. Under a prospective paradigm, the more complex a task, the fewer resources devoted to $P(t)$, and as a result its duration estimates will be shorter and the produced interval longer. The lesson to be learned from this is that it is meaningless to measure mental load by retrospective time estimates, since these are neither a direct nor a reliable reflection of resource allocation. Only prospective estimates can serve this purpose.

STUDY 4 – LATENT INHIBITION AND TIME ESTIMATION(4)

Study 4 was designed to directly manipulate the resource allocation policy in order to test its influence on the prospective estimation of short intervals. When task complexity or even the primary and secondary task techniques are used, subjects can still perceive or interpret given instructions or complexity levels in unpredictable idiosyncratic ways. In the present study a method was sought which would influence the subjects' resource allocation policy without their being able to control it intentionally. Additional sources of experimental "noise" are variables such as motivational level and task or stimulus' familiarity which could interfere with and influence the time estimation process. Indeed, Avant, Lyman and Antes (1975) and Lyman and Avant (1975) manipulated stimulus familiarity and found that it modified perceived duration in prerecognition visual processing. However, in those studies the durations estimated were of tachistoscopic flashes of 30 msec. Hence, the affected underlying process was preattentional.

In the present study, a cognitive process which is assumed to directly affect the attentional mechanism and resource allocation policy without subject's awareness was used. This method, called latent inhibition (LI), is defined as "the decremental effect of nonreinforced preexposure of the to-be-conditioned stimulus on subsequent learning" (Ginton, Urca & Lubow, 1975, p. 5). For example, if an infant is exposed to a stimulus several times, its efficiency as a conditioning stimulus later on decreases significantly. LI is a robust phenomenon (Lubow, 1973) found across a variety of species and learning tasks (e.g., Kaniel & Lubow, 1986; Lubow, Alek & Arzi, 1975; Lubow, Caspy & Schnur, 1982) in animals as well as human children and adults. Lubow (1973) reviewed the various explanations suggested for LI and concluded that a model of LI should include both attentional and learning constructs. Conditioned Attention Theory (CAT) (Lubow, Weiner & Schnur, 1981) is such a model. CAT states that "nonreinforced preexposure to a stimulus retards subsequent conditoning to that stimulus because during such preexposure the animal learns not to attend to it" (Ibid, p. 3). One of the basic assumptions of CAT is that with repeated stimulus presentation, the attentional response inevitably declines. Empirical support for CAT has been found in a large number of studies (for a review see Lubow, Weiner & Schnur, 1981).

It was suggested in this study, on the basis of both CAT and the resource allocation model of time estimation, that in a prospective paradigm the estimated duration of a stimulus exposure after an LI manipulation will be longer than the estimate of an identical duration of the same stimulus but without its preexposure in an LI inducing situation. The rationale behind this hypothesis is that as a result of an LI manipulation, an inattentional response to the stimulus is conditioned. Hence, when this stimulus is subsequently presented in a prospective paradigm, the level of attention devoted to P(i) will be lower and more attention will be allocated to P(t) than if the same stimulus is presented without first inducing conditioned inattention. In the latter case, it will be treated as a novel stimulus and P(i) will attract more attentional resources.

Method

SUBJECTS

Sixty first year students at Tel-Aviv University, whose ages ranged between 20 and 32 years, participated in the experiment in partial fulfillment of course requirements.

LI-INDUCING MANIPULATION

While LI is induced quite easily in young children by means of a simple preexposure manipulation of the target stimulus, it does not normally occur under the same conditions in adults, as indicated by Kaniel and Lubow (1986) in a developmental study. In particular, it would appear that a distracting task which serves to draw the subject's attention away from the preexposed to-be conditioned stimulus, is required to produce LI in adults (e.g., Ginton, Urca and Lubow, 1975; Lubow, Caspy and Schnur, 1982). In the distracting condition, the subject is required to perform some information processing task simultaneously with preexposure of the target stimulus. The role of the distracting task is to attract attention away from the target stimulus during the preexposure phase in order to enhance the creation of conditioned inattention. The expectation that distraction would allow the LI effect to become manifest in adults is based on Spence's (1966) theoretical account of the role of distraction in retarding extinction in human classical conditioning studies. Spence's notion is that humans have more cognitive control and are not bound by the explicit stimulus properties of the conditioning situation. The human adult can use mediational responses, mostly verbal, that reduce the differences in responses to stimuli when those stimuli differ on a dimension that is irrelevant for action. Kaniel and Lubow (1986) noted that in the LI paradigm, number of preexposures is an irrelevant dimension for action for adults. As soon as the shift to acquisition is made, the human adult is immediately cognizant of the change and responds only to the new situation. It should be mentioned that in some specific cases (e.g., Cannon, Best, Batson and Feldman, 1983; Feldman, 1982) LI was formed in adults without a distracting task. However, according to Brandeis (1974), at least 30 preexposures are required in adults for LI to occur. On the other hand, experiments using distraction clearly demonstrate a very powerful LI in human adults. Hence, for this study a distracting manipulation which was similar to (but more difficult than) the one used by Lubow, Caspy and Schnur (1982) was chosen. Subjects had to concentrate on three six-digit numbers in order to determine which of the six digits were common to all three numbers.

APPARATUS

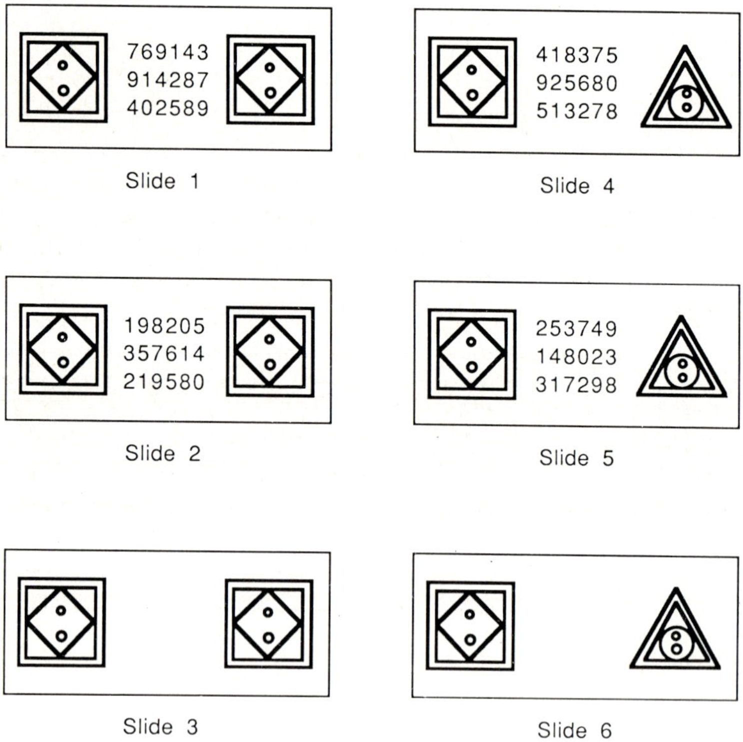

Figure 10.2. The six experimental slides.

Two stimuli, equivalent in level of complexity according to the criteria of Attneave (1959) and Orenstein (1969), were constructed. The two stimuli consisted of the same number of geometrical forms and differed only in regard to color (red, green, or blue) and shape (diamond, triangle, or circle). The two stimuli were utilized in the construction of six slides. The first slide was composed of one of the stimuli (A) which appeared on both the right and left sides. In the middle, between the two stimuli, three six-digit numbers were printed, one below the other. Two digits were common to all three numbers. The second slide was identical to the first, but with numbers composed of other digits. The third slide consisted of stimulus A on both sides, but an empty space in the middle. The other three slides were similar to the first three, except that stimulus B was used instead of stimulus A. The slides appear in Figure 10.2. They were presented by a Ralph Gerbrands tachistocope, Model T2B-C.

EXPERIMENTAL MANIPULATIONS AND EXPERIMENTAL DESIGN

Three experimental manipulations were utilized: 1) No Preexposure (NPE), in which subjects estimated the duration of a target stimulus upon its first presentation; 2) Preexposure (PE) in which the target stimulus was preexposed twice before being presented for time estimation; and 3) Preexposure with Distraction (PED), in which the target stimulus was preexposed twice with the distracting task before being presented for time estimation.

By comparing the estimates given by subjects for the durations of the stimuli after the PED, PE, and NPE manipulations, it was possible to test the hypothesis. However, in order to make sure that any effect found was not due to the influence of a specific stimulus, each manipulation and the control (NPE) situation were conducted twice, once with stimulus A and once with B. In addition, in order to test the specificity of each manipulation in regard to the manipulated stimulus, two duration estimates were made after each manipulation, one for the manipulated stimulus and a second for the other nonmanipulated stimulus. This last estimate was always second, in order not to interfere with the effect of the experimental manipulation. As this might have confounded with order of testing, we tested for order effect by obtaining a second time estimate from the control (NPE) groups as well. Thus, the experimental design (see Table 10.4) enabled testing of both the hypothesis and specificity of each manipulation, as well as determination of a possible order effect.

Table 10.4.
EXPERIMENTAL DESIGN

GROUP	PREEXPOSURE PHASES		TEST PHASES	
	1	2	3	4
1. NPE – STIMULUS A	–	–	Stimulus A (Slide 3)	Stimulus B (Slide 6)
2. NPE – STIMULUS B	–	–	Stimulus B (Slide 6)	Stimulus A (Slide 3)
3. PE – STIMULUS A	Slide 3	Slide 3	Stimulus A (Slide 3)	Stimúlus B (Slide 6)
4. PE – STIMULUS B	Slide 6	Slide 6	Stimulus B (Slide 6)	Stimulus B (Slide 3)
5. PED – STIMULUS A	Slide 1	Slide 2	Stimulus A (Slide 3)	Stimulus B (Slide 6)
6. PED – STIMULUS B	Slide 4	Slide 5	Stimulus B (Slide 6)	Stimulus A (Slide 3)

PROCEDURE

Subjects were randomly assigned to six groups of 10, and each group was randomly assigned to one of the experimental or control conditions. Each subject was tested individually. In the preexposure phases of the PE manipulation, subjects were instructed to study the stimuli. In the preexposure phases of the PED manipulation, subjects were instructed to respond to the distracting task, as explained above. Exposure time of each slide was 6 seconds in all phases, including the testing phases. In order to create a prospective paradigm, prior to testing subjects were asked to study the stimuli as they would later be asked several questions about them and their exposure times. However, no emphasis was placed on either the stimuli or the time, and thus subjects were not directed as to how to allocate attentional resources. Durations were estimated by a reproduction method. Immediately after each presentation, subjects were asked to press a button for an interval equivalent in duration to that of the slide presentation. Pressing the button activated a hidden electronic timer, and the recorded time was taken as the time estimate.

RESULTS

In order to test for differential effects of the two stimuli (A and B), the exposure time estimates (ETE) obtained in the first testing phase (column 3 in Table 10.2) were subjected to a 3 (experimental manipulations: NPE, PE and PED) x 2 (stimulus A or B) ANOVA. The only significant effect found was that of the experimental manipulation [$F(2,54) = 3.28$, $p < 0.05$]. Duncan multiple range tests revealed significant effects between conditions PED and NPE for both stimulus A and B ($p < 0.05$). The ETE means are presented in Table 10.5. Since no significant difference was found between ETEs for the two stimuli, data from these conditions were combined in all other analyses.

A second 3x2 ANOVA with repeated measures was performed with one factor being the experimental manipulation, as before, and the second one the testing phase (first or second). The respective ETE means are presented in Table 10.6.

A sigificant interaction between testing phase and experimental manipulation was found [$F(2,57) = 15.21$, $p < 0.01$]. This interaction appears in Figure 10.3. Schéffé tests were performed in order to compare each specific experimental manipulation to the control situations. The only significant difference found was between ETEs after PED manipulation and after NPE [$F(5,54) = 3.92$, $p < 0.01$].

Table 10.5.
ETE MEANS (IN SEC.) BY EXPERIMENTAL GROUP AND STIMULUS TYPE

EXPERIMENTAL GROUP	ETE MEANS		
	STIMULUS A	STIMULUS B	
CONTROL (NPE)	3.16 (n=10)	3.78 (n=10)	3.47
PE	4.80 (n=10)	5.01 (n=10)	4.05
LATENT INHIBITION (PED)	5.55 (n=10)	5.37 (n=10)	5.46
	4.53	4.72	

Table 10.6.
ETE MEANS (IN SEC.) BY EXPERIMENTAL MANIPULATION AND TESTING PHASE

EXPERIMENTAL MANIPULATION	TESTING PHASE	
	FIRST	SECOND
CONTROL (NPE)	3.47 + (n=20)	4.94 ++ (n=20)
PE	4.95 * (n=20)	4.44 ** (n=20)
LI (PED)	5.46 * (n=20)	4.55 ** (n=20)
	4.63	4.64

+ The control situation for testing the effect of the experimental manipulations; ++ The control situation for testing order effect; * Target stimuli manipulated; ** Target stimuli not manipulated.

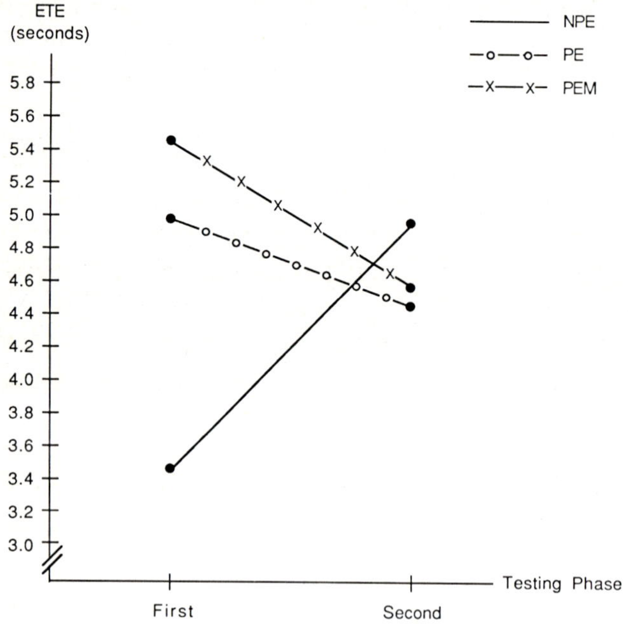

Figure 10.3. Interaction between experimental manipulation and testing phase.

Discussion of Study 4

The hypothesis tested was confirmed. It was found that stimulus duration estimates were influenced by LI procedures; the durations were estimated to be significantly longer after the PED manipulation as compared to the control situation. The effect of LI induced by means of the distracting task was stronger than that of mere preexposure which, in itself, was not found to differ significantly from the control situation. However, it is of interest to note that preexposure did have some effect, although not a significant one, in lengthening time estimates, as can be seen in the PE group, first phase. The results of the second phase show that in the NPE condition time estimates tended to be longer than in the first phase. This might be explained by a slight familiarity effect which resulted from the similarity of the stimuli. This effect dissipated in other conditions because of the stronger effects of preexposure and, of course, of latent inhibition. As for preexposure, a significant effect might have been obtained if the number of preexposures was larger. In a pilot experiment, even 4 and 5 preexposures were not enough to cause a significant effect. This is in line with the conclusion cited earlier that at least 30 preexposures are needed. Nevertheless, the distracting task seems to successfully cause LI, in accordance with the findings of Ginton, Urca and Lubow (1975), Kaniel and Lubow (1986), Lubow, Caspy and Schnur (1982), and others cited above.

A claim can be made that the lengthening of time estimates in the PED condition should not be attributed to LI, but rather to the fact that the stimuli used for time estimation in the PED condition (slides 3 or 6) differed from the stimuli used to create LI (slides 1, 2 or 4, 5). This does not seem logical however, since such a difference can only increase the novelty level of slides 3 or 6 resulting in a higher level of attention paid to it and thus in shorter time estimates. The pattern of results obtained contradicts such an explanation and supports the attentional model of resource allocation in a prospective paradigm.

SUMMARY AND GENERAL CONCLUSIONS

I have proposed here a resource allocation model to explain time estimations of short durations longer than 1 sec., presenting several studies in which the model was empirically tested.

The RAM model is based on the following assumptions:

1) Each stimulus is analyzed by two processors: a cognitive timer P(t)

which accumulates subjective time units (STU) during an interval, and a nontemporal information processor P(i).

2) The output of the timer P(t) is the number of STUs stored in working memory and available for retrieval only for a short period equal to the decay time of elements in STM.

3) P(t) is reset every time a stimulus which is interpreted as the start of a new meaningful interval is perceived.

4) P(t) needs attentional resources for its operation. The more resources allocated to it, the more STUs accumulated in it.

5) The output of P(i) is stored encoded information which reflects the amount of information processed, the depth of its processing, and the number of meaningful changes which occurred during an interval. This output is stored first in STM, and part of it is then transferred to LTM, making it available for a long period.

6) The more attention devoted to P(i) the larger the storage-size transferred to LTM.

7) Attention is shared by P(t) and P(i). The resource allocation policy is determined by subjects' expectation, instructions given, task difficulty, subjective meaning of the situation, etc.

8) Under prospective conditions, P(t) is preferred as the origin of duration estimation, and the estimation is a positive linear function of the number of STUs accumulated. Hence, the more resources allocated to P(i), the fewer STUs accumulated in P(t) and the shorter the duration estimation will be. Prospective estimates of an empty interval should be longer than that of an equal filled interval.

9) Under retrospective conditions, P(t)'s output is not available because it is already erased from STM, as a result of the instructions given and of other stimuli perceived during the estimation delay period. Because of this, the product of P(i), which is the storage still available in LTM, is used as the origin of duration estimation, so that retrospective estimations are a positive linear function of storage-size. The more resources allocated to P(i), the higher the storage-size and the longer retrospective duration estimations will be. A filled interval should be retrospectively estimated as longer than an equivalent empty interval.

The empirical findings reported in this chapter are promising but, nevertheless, cannot be said to provide unconditional support for the model. The picture is particularly ambiguous regarding retrospective estimations. This might derive from the uncontrolled influences of contextualistic elements of which the experimenter is unaware, and which might affect subjects' allocation of resources between P(i) and P(t). The prospective situation, on the other hand, is much clearer. It is possible that retrospective experiments are more situation specific than prospective experiments.

The resource allocation model is clearly well-suited to limited capacity models of attention (e.g., Kahneman, 1973), but, I would further argue that multiple resource models (e.g., Navon & Gopher, 1979) should not refute it. Temporal processes of short durations are assumed to affect short-term memory, which is the storage in which P(t) is assumed to function. Since the flow of incoming information should pass through STM, then even if STM is a resource by itself, there is direct competition between P(t) and P(i) for STM resources.

Time estimations of short durations is a cognitive process contingent on the context within which it takes place. This is equally true of other cognitive processes such as decision making (Payne, 1982). Perhaps this similarity alludes to a general principle governing the operation of the cognitive system.

Notes

(1) The author wishes to thank Elsevier Science Publishers for granting permission to quote Zakay and Fallach (1964).

(2) The author wishes to thank the Psychonomic Society Publications for granting permission to quote Zakay, Nitzan and Glicksohn (1983).

(3) Acknowledgement is due to D. Fallach and I. Karp for their help in conducting this research.

(4) The author would like to express his thanks to Prof. R.E. Lubow for his valuable advice and suggestions, and to Devora Nitzan for her help in conducting the experiment.

References

Allan, L.G. (1979). The perception of time. *Perception & Psychophysics, 26*(5), 340–354.

Allan, L.G., & Rousseau, R. (1976). Backward masking in judgments of duration. *Perception & Psychophysics, 21*, 482–486.

Aschoff, J. (1984). Circadian timing. In: J. Gibbon & L. Allan (Eds.), *Timing and time perception* (442–468). New York: New York Academy of Science.

Aschoff, J. (1985). On the perception of time during prolonged temporal isolation. *Human Neurobiology, 4*, 41–52.

Avant, L.L., Lyman, P.J., & Antes, J. (1975). Effect of stimulus familiarity upon judged visual duration. *Perception and Psychophysics, 17*, 253–262.

Attneave, F. (1959). *Applications of Information theory to Psychology*. New York: Holt, Rinehart & Winston.

Block, R.A. (1974). Memory and the experience of duration in retrospect. *Memory and Cognition, 2*, 153–160.

Block, R.A. (1978). Remembered duration: effects of event and sequence complexity.

Memory & Cognition, 6, 320–326.

Block, R. A. (1985). Contextual coding in memory: Studies of remembered duration. In J. A. Michon & J. L. Jackson (Eds.). *Time, mind, and behavior* (pp. 169–178). Berlin: Springer-Verlag.

Block, R.A., George, E.J., & Reed, M.A. (1980). A watched pot sometimes boils. A study of duration experience. *Acta Psychologica, 46*, 81–94.

Block, R.A., & Reed, M.A. (1978). Remembered duration: Evidence for a contextual change hypothesis. *Journal of Experimental Psychology: Human Learning and Memory, 4*, 656–665.

Brandeis, R. (1974). *The influence of number of preexposures to one stimulus and to two stimuli on the latent inhibition effect in human conditioning.* Unpublished Master's Thesis: Bar Ilan University. Israel.

Brown, S.W. (1985). Time perception and attention. *Perception & Psychophysics, 38*(2), 115–124.

Cannon, D.S., Best, M.R., Batson, J.D., & Feldman, M. (1983). Taste familiarity and apomorphine-induced taste aversion in humans. *Behavior Research and Therapy, 21*, 669–673.

Clausen, J. (1950). An evaluation of experimental methods of time judgment. *Journal of Experimental Psychology, 40*, 756–761.

Coren, S., Porac, C., & Ward, L.M. (1984). *Sensation and perception* (2nd edition). New York: Academic Press.

Curton, E.D., & Lordahl, D.S. (1974). Attentional focus and arousal in time estimation. *Journal of Experimental Psychology, 103*, 861–867.

Denner, B., Wapner, S., McFarland, J., & Werner, H. (1963). Rhythmic activity and the perception of time. *American Journal of Psychology, 76*, 287–292.

Devane, J.R. (1974). Word characteristics and judged duration for two response sequences. *Perceptual & Motor Skills*, 38, 525–526.

Dyer, K.N. (1973). The Stroop phenomenon and its use in the study of perceptual cognitive and response processes. *Memory and Cognition, 1*, 106–120.

Feldman, M.A. (1982). The effect of command preexposure on instruction following behavior in severely retarded adolescents. *The Psychological Records, 32*, 529–535.

Fraisse, P. (1963). *The Psychology of time.* New York: Harper & Row.

Fraisse, P. (1984). Perception and estimation of time. *Annual Review of Psychology, 35*, 1–36.

Frankenhauser, M. (1959). *Estimation of time.* Stockholm: Almquist & Wiksell.

Gibson, J.J. (1975). Events are perceivable but time is not. In: J.T. Fraser, N. Lawrence (Eds.), *The study of time, vol 2.* Berlin: Springer.

Ginton, A., Urca, G., & Lubow, R.E. (1975). The effects of preexposure to a nonattended stimulus on subsequent learning: Latent inhibition in adults. *Bulletin of the Psychonomic Society, 5*, 5–8.

Gray, C. (1982). Duration differences: Attentional demand. *Perception, 11*, 97–102.

Hart, S.G. (1975). Time estimation as a secondary task to measure workload. *Proceedings, 11th annual conference on manual control. NASA, TMX–62.* pp.64–77. Washington: U.S. Government Printing.

Hicks, R.E., Miller, G.W., & Kinsbourne, M. (1976). Prospective and retrospective judgments of time as a function of amount of information processed. *American Journal of Psychology, 89*(4), 719–730.

Hicks, R.E., Miller, G.W., Gaes, G., & Bierman, K. (1977). Concurrent processing demands and the experience of time-in-passing. *American Journal of Psychology, 90*(3), 431–446.

Kahneman, D. (1973). *Attention and effort.* New York: Prentice Hall.

Kaniel, S., & Lubow, R.E. (1986). Latent inhibition: A developmental study. *British Journal of Developmental Psychology.*

Logan, C.D. (1980). Attention and automaticity in Stroop and priming tasks: Theory and data. *Cognitive Psychology, 12*, 523–553.

Logan, G.D., & Zbrodoff, J. (1979). When it helps to be misled: Facilitative effects of increasing the frequency of conflicting stimuli in a Stroop-like task. *Memory and Cognition, 7*, 166–174.

Lubow, R.E. (1973). Latent inhibition. *Psyhological Bulletin, 79*, 398–407.

Lubow, R.E., Alek, M., & Arzy, J. (1975). Behavioral decrement following stimulus preexposure: The effects of number of preexposure, presence of a record stimulus and interstimuli interval in children and adults. *Journal of Experimental Psychology: Animal Behavior Processes, 1* 178–188.

Lubow, R.E., Caspy, T., & Schnur, P. (1982). Latent inhibition and learned helplessness in children: Similarities and differences. *Journal of Experimental Child Psychology, 34*, 231–256.

Lubow, R.E., Weiner, I., & Schnur, P. (1981). Conditioned Attention Theory. In G. Bower (Ed.), *The psychology of learning and motivation, Vol. 15.* New York: Academic Press.

Lyman, P.J., & Avant, L.L. (1975). Stimulus familiarity modifies perceived duration in precognition visual processing. *Journal of Experimental Psychology, 104*, 205–213.

Michon, J.A. (1965). Studies on subjective duration: Subjective time measurement during tasks with different information content. *Acta Psychologica, 24*, 205–219.

Navon, D., Gopfer, D. (1979). On a conceptual hierarchy of time, space and other dimensions. *Cognition, 6*, 223–228.

Ornstein, R.E. (1969). *On the experience of time.* Middlesex, England: Penguin.

Payne, J.W. (1982). Contingent decision behavior. *Psychological Bulletin, 93*, 382–402.

Piaget, J. (1969). *The child's conception of time.* London: Routledge & Kegan Paul.

Poynter, W.D. (1983). Duration judgment and the segmentation of experience. *Memory & Cognition, 11*, 77–82.

Priestley, J.B. (1968). *Man and time.* New York: Dell.

Smith, N.C. (1969). The effect on time estimation of increasing the complexity of a cognitive task. *Journal of General Psychology, 81*, 231–235.

Spence, K.W. (1966). Cognitive and drive factors in the extinction of the conditioned eyeblink in human subjects. *Psychological Review, 73*, 445–458.

Stroop, J.R. (1935). Studies of interference in serial verbal reactions. *Journal of Experimental Psychology, 18*, 643–662.

Thomas, A.C., & Brown, L. (1974). Time perception and the filled duration illusion. *Perception & Psychophysics, 16*, 449–458.

Thomas, E.A.C., & Weaver, W.B. (1975). Cognitive processing and time perception. *Perception & Psychophysics, 17*, 363–367.

Underwood, G. (1975). Attention and the perception of duration during encoding and retrieval. *Perception, 4*, 191–198.

Vroon, P.A. (1976). Effects of presented and processed information on duration experience. *Acta Psychologica, 34*, 115–121.

Wallace, M., & Rabin, A. (1960). Temporal experience. *Psychological Bulletin, 57*(3), 213–233.

Wickens, C.D. (1984). *Engineering Psychology and Human Performance.* Columbus: Charles E. Merrill.

Zakay, D., Nitzan, D., & Glicksohn, J. (1983). The influence of task difficulty and external tempo on subjective time estimation. *Perception & Psychophysics, 34*(5), 451–456.

Zakay, D., & Fallach, E. (1984). Immediate and remote time estimation – A comparison. *Acta Psychologica, 57*, 69–81.

Zakay, D. & Meran, V. (1988). *A meta analysis of time estimation research.* Unpublished manuscript: Tel-Aviv University. Israel.

Author Index

C

D

H

I

J

K

T

U

V

W

XY

Z

Subject Index

C

D

U

V

W